8TH EDITION

D0081906

Comparative Economic Systems

MARTIN C. SCHNITZER
Virginia Polytechnic Institute and State University

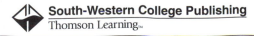

South-Western College Publishing
Thomson Learning™

Australia • Canada • Denmark • Japan • Mexico • New Zealand • Philippines
Puerto Rico • Singapore • South Africa • Spain • United Kingdom • United States

Comparative Economic Systems, 8th edition, by Martin Schnitzer
Vice President / Publisher: Jack W. Calhoun
Acquisitions Editor: Keri L. Witman
Senior Developmental Editor: Susanna C. Smart
Marketing Manager: Lisa L. Lysne
Production Editor: Peggy K. Buskey
Manufacturing Coordinator: Charlene Taylor
Cover Design: Ann Small, A Small Design Studio
Cover Images: PhotoDisc©1999
Production House: Lachina Publishing Services, Inc.
Printer: R.R. Donnelley & Sons Company, Crawfordsville Manufacturing Division

Printed in the United States of America
1 2 3 4 5 02 01 00 99

For more information contact South-Western College Publishing, 5101 Madison Road, Cincinnati, Ohio, 45227 or find us on the Internet at http://www.swcollege.com

For permission to use material from this text or product, contact us by
• telephone: 1-800-730-2214
• fax: 1-800-730-2215
• web: http://www.thomsonrights.com

Library of Congress Cataloging-in-Publication Data

Schnitzer, Martin.
      Comparative economic systems / Martin C. Schnitzer—8th ed.
          p. cm.
      Includes bibliographical references and index.
      ISBN 0-324-00428-1
      1. Comparative economics. I. Title.

   HB90.S35 1999
   330—dc21

This book is printed on acid-free paper.

Contents

CHAPTER 8
The Russian Federation

CHAPTER 9
Poland, the Czech Republic, and Hungary

PART IV
Market and Nonmarket Mechanisms in Developing Economies

CHAPTER 10
Problems of the Less Developed Countries

CHAPTER 11
China

CHAPTER 12
India

CHAPTER 13
Latin America: Argentina, Brazil, and Mexico

CHAPTER 16
The Twenty-First Century

361

Index

383

Preface

INTRODUCTION

The twentieth century has come to an end. In 1900 approximately 60 countries existed in the world; now there are more than 200. Two world wars altered the map of the globe. The Cold War divided the world into two parts, one dominated by the Soviet Union and the other by the United States. The Depression of the 1930s marked the advent of the welfare state. Two alternatives to capitalism—communism and fascism—were tried and found wanting. Communism did not deliver on its promise to create a classless society in which resources would be allocated from those according to their abilities to those according to their needs. Eventually fascism died with the defeat of Nazi Germany in 1945.

The 1990s made up one of the more eventful decades of the century. The Cold War ended, the Soviet Union—having been fragmented into a number of smaller countries—became a thing of the past, and the United States entered the twenty-first century as the world's only superpower. The former Soviet satellite countries of Poland, Czechoslovakia, Hungary, Romania, and Bulgaria moved into various stages of capitalism, with Poland having led the way, and Yugoslavia became the trouble spot of Europe. The European Union is a fait accompli, and the euro is now the monetary unit of commerce there. Japan—predicted by many experts to be the dominant economic power of the twentieth century—developed serious economic and social problems that will affect that country well into the twenty-first century. Europe was expected to become the dominant economic power of the twenty-first century, but it too has problems—of unemployment and an aging population—leaving the United States to dominate what has been termed "The Second American Century."

PURPOSE OF THE TEXT

An important purpose of the eighth edition of this book is to update world economic events since the seventh edition was published. Much has happened in the interim, including three major financial crises in East Asia, Russia, and Brazil that have affected financial centers around the globe and introduced an element of financial instability into the world.

As with the previous editions, this book introduces the reader to the economics of socialism and capitalism, and compares the three variants of capitalism as used by the United States, Germany, and Japan. Though all three countries embrace capitalism, differences among their views and systems are based on culture, history, politics, and past economic factors.

In addition, the text compares some of the major world trading blocs that will become more important in the future, particularly the European Union and NAFTA. Technology and the exchange of information have increased the integration of production, as the globe becomes smaller and national boundaries less important to economies. The result of such integration is the expansion of financial and trade ties among nations. While the close relationships of global economies are intended for good, the effects of interdependence are evidenced by the global financial crisis of the late 1990s.

Finally, the text looks at the problems of countries that are developing and in transition and those that are less developed. Several chapters are devoted to the less-developed and developing countries of the world: China, India, and Latin American and African countries. Mass poverty persists worldwide, with basic consumption needs remaining unfulfilled, and environmental degradation continues to be at the forefront of problems of developing and less-developed countries.

As with previous editions, the eight edition provides the most current information on international economic issues from U.S. and international sources such as publications from the OECD, the World Bank, and the International Monetary Fund; the United Nations Development Report; monthly bulletins of the European Central Bank; publications of the Inter-American Development Bank; and the monthly report of the Deutsche Bundesbank.

Each chapter ends with a summary, several discussion questions, and a list of recommended readings providing the most current bibliography available on the subjects discussed in each chapter.

New to the text are Internet margin addresses, which direct readers to sites containing data and information that expand upon the text material.

SUPPLEMENTS

An *Instructor's Manual/Test Bank* is available to instructors. Each chapter contains a brief outline and answers to the discussion questions. The Test Bank portion, expanded by Steven C. Hackett of Humboldt University, consists of true/false and multiple-choice questions.

A text *Web site* contains links and updates to the Internet addresses throughout the text and in the instructor materials. In addition, the South-Western Economics Resource Center Web site offers other valuable features:

- *EconDebate Online* keeps you informed on today's most crucial economics policy debates. Each EconDebate provides a primer on the issues, links to background information, and current, in-depth commentaries from experts around the world. The EconDebates consist of a statement of the policy question under debate, a summary of the issues and the background, an annotated list of primary resources with which to better understand the debate, and a carefully chosen annotated list of position papers highlighting different perspectives in the debate.
- *EconNews Online* provides summaries of the latest economics news stories, indexed by topic for convenience. Each EconNews summary contains a headline, topic category, key words, three- to five-paragraph summary of a news article, article source line, and questions to spur further thought.

ACKNOWLEDGMENTS

Many people have contributed to the writing of this book. I would like to thank my wife, Joan, and my secretary, Melissa, for their invaluable help in putting together the book. I would also like to thank my friend, Larry Thompson, who has traveled extensively, including to Ethiopia and Rwanda for Refugees International, and who knows intimately the Seychelles, Botswana, and many other countries. I wish to thank my editors at South-Western College Publishing: Keri Witman and Susanna Smart, for their editorial contribution to the substance and format of the text; Peggy Buskey, for her patient attendance to the details of producing the book; and Diane Colwyn of Colwyn Editorial Services, for her help throughout the process.

In addition, the following reviewers have helped to shape the contents of this and previous editions:

Robert J. Jensen, Pacific Lutheran University; Robert T. Jerome, James Madison University; Kehar S. Sangha, Old Dominion University; William C. Schaniel, West Georgia College; Scot A. Stradley, University of North Dakota; Irvin Weintraub, Towson State University; Irvin Weintraub, Towson University; John A. Sondey South Dakota State; John E. Charalambakis, Asbury College; Edward F. Stuart, Northeastern Illinois University; Robert Welch, Midwestern State University; Scott A. Stradley, University of North Dakota; Edward T. Merkel, Troy State University.

About the Author

Martin C. Schnitzer received his Ph.D. in Economics from the University of Florida. He teaches graduate and undergraduate courses in International Management at Virginia Tech. Professor Schnitzer is an author of ten books, including *Comparative Economic Systems*, as well as numerous monographs. Mr. Schnitzer has lectured in Hungary and Poland and has served on the U.S. East-West Trade Commission, the Virginia Export Council, and the Advisory Board of Economists to Governor John H. Dalton. He has also served as an economics consultant to the U.S. Joint Economic Committee and the U.S. House Ways and Means Committee on European economic policy.

PART I

The World of the Twentieth Century

CHAPTER 1
The American Century

CHAPTER 1

The American Century

At the beginning of the twentieth century the British empire was the largest empire in history, on which it was said that "the sun never set." Queen Victoria celebrated her diamond jubilee in 1900. She had been queen for sixty-three years, and representatives from every colony in the empire came to pay her homage. Kings, including her cousin Kaiser Wilhelm of Germany, were also in attendance. Never at any time in history had so much pomp and ceremony been bestowed on a monarch. The parade in her honor was six miles long and took seven hours to complete. Britain was the world's leading sea power, and the pound sterling was the world's strongest currency and the foundation for the gold standard.[1] A year later she was dead, and in 1914 World War I began, marking the beginning of the decline of the British empire.

The United States will enter the twenty-first century in the same position that England had at the beginning of the twentieth century. Its economy is the largest and strongest in the world; it is the leading military power; and the dollar has replaced the pound as the leading world currency. Its culture, is, for better or worse, well on its way to becoming the dominant world culture, and there are those who loudly trumpet its praise. Alan Greenspan, chairman of the Federal Reserve, concluded that "only free-market systems"—that is, the American model— "exhibit the flexibility and robustness to accommodate human nature and harness

http://

Check the U.S.
News archives for
articles on the
21st Century at
www.usnews.com/
home.htm. A book
excerpt from *The
American Century*
by Harold Evans is
at www.usnews
.com/usnews/
issue/981005/
5exce.htm.

technology to ever higher living standards."[2] Mortimer Zuckerman, editor-in-chief of *U.S. News and World Report*, wrote an essay called "A Second American Century."[3] It begins by proclaiming "Why We Will Remain Number One" and ends by suggesting that the 21st century will belong to America.[4]

So how did the United States get to this happy state of events? The answer is part location and part luck. Location spared the United States the devastation that occurred in Europe and Japan during the two major wars of the twentieth century. Luck enabled the United States to develop new technologies that were put to use once the wars were over. The development of computers during World War II led to the creation of a new industry. Improvements in aircraft during the war led to the development of larger and more efficient planes that revolutionized air transportation. But other factors were also at work. Immigration provided new waves of citizens who contributed to the economic development of the United States. The country is endowed with a good climate and natural resources and seems to have an abundance of entrepreneurial talent.

A REVIEW OF THE TWENTIETH CENTURY

In 1900 the population of the world was around 1.6 billion, one third of which lived in China and India. The leading world powers were the United States, England, France, Italy, the Austro-Hungarian Empire, Russia, and Japan. With the exception of the United States and France, all were ruled by monarchs. The total GDP of the world was around $1.6 trillion. Around sixty countries existed, and international currency exchange was governed by the gold standard. Most of the world was part of the British, Dutch, French, and German colonial empires. The leading export nations were the United States, England, and Germany. Foreign direct investment by the major world powers amounted to $108 billion and was most heavily concentrated in the mineral resources of Latin America. Three fourths of all investment was made by England, the United States, Germany, and France. The average per capita income difference between the Western and Asian countries was 5 to 1, and for the Western and Latin American countries 3 to 1.[5]

Table 1-1 presents the nine major countries of the world in terms of population, real per capita GDP, and real GDP in 1900. Japan had just started the process of economic development that eventually made it a world power. In 1900 it ranked twenty-third among all nations; by the end of the century, it ranked among the three most important exporting nations in the world. The population of the United States has tripled since 1900, while the population of France has increased by only 16 million, the United Kingdom by 17 million, and Germany by 24 million. The greatest gains in population were made by China and India; today, they account for around 35 percent of the world's population.

The prevailing economic system at the beginning of the twentieth century was free-market, laissez-faire capitalism as practiced in the United States and England. In the United States, for example, the period from the end of the Civil War to 1900 can be called the golden age of laissez-faire capitalism. Business had just

TABLE 1-1 *Population, Real per Capita GDP and Total Real GDP for Major Countries in 1900*

Country	Real GDP ($ billions in 1990 prices)	Real per Capita GDP ($ thousands in 1990 prices)	Population (millions)
United States	312,866	4,096	76,391
China	260,800	652	400,000
United Kingdom	190,862	4,593	41,185
India*	177,750	625	284,400
Germany	170,884	3,049	56,046
Russia	127,469	1,218	128,687
France	115,645	2,849	38,940
Italy	53,908	1,663	32,416
Japan	50,057	1,135	44,103

*India was a part of the British empire.

Source: Angus Maddison, *Monitoring the World Economy, 1820–1992* (Paris: Organization for Economic Cooperation and Development, 1995), pp. 105, 107, 111, 115, 181, 183, 187, 191, 195, 197, 201, 205.

about anything its own way. The government, particularly the federal government, did nothing to intervene until business abuses of the market system became so prevalent that regulation became necessary. The growing concentration of economic power in the hands of a few persons also created a problem—extremes of wealth and poverty. There were no federal income taxes on individuals, so vast fortunes were free from any form of taxation.

The Industrial Revolution began in England. When a country started to industrialize, there was a serious shortage of manufactured products at prices sufficiently low to be bought by any but the wealthy. However, the development of new machinery and the Napoleonic wars increased the quantity of goods turned out by British industry at lower prices than elsewhere. Interest rates were low, and there was one way in which money could be put to use—the development of manufactured goods that were sold both at home and in foreign markets. The colonial possessions of England furnished the raw materials to England and served as a repository for British exports of textiles. The Bessemer process facilitated the development of the British steel and shipbuilding industries. However, by the end of the century the United States and Germany had begun to challenge England's industrial supremacy.

THE YEARS 1900 TO 1950

The years before World War I were years of high prosperity. Among the developed countries of the world, economic growth was the highest in the United States and Canada and the lowest in England. The United States had recently become the world economic leader, a position held by England during most of the nineteenth century. This leadership was based in part on its natural resources and in part on high rates of investment and an ever-expanding labor force. European countries had lower rates of investment, but the growth of exports increased economic growth because it facilitated specialization and economies of scale. However, Latin America achieved a faster rate of economic growth than either North America or Europe during the pre–World War I years. For example, Argentina's huge natural resource base, coupled with high rates of investment and increased immigration from Europe, created the fastest rate of economic growth in North and South America.[6]

The world changed dramatically from 1900 to 1950. Two world wars and the Depression of the 1930s were responsible for most of the change. Two alternative economic and political systems were created as an alternative to capitalism and democracy. They were communism and fascism, but neither survived the century. Capitalism was altered to conform to a changing set of political and economic circumstances that were a product of the Depression of the 1930s. The writings of the economist John Maynard Keynes started to influence government economic policy more than that of Adam Smith, and increased government intervention in the capitalist countries became an accepted fact of life.

World War I, 1914–1918

World War I destroyed the old political order. The Austro-Hungarian empire disappeared, and with it the Hapsburg monarchy. In Germany the monarchy collapsed when Kaiser Wilhelm fled to the Netherlands. In Russia the Bolshevik Revolution of 1917 deposed the czar and ushered in a communist regime. The Treaty of Versailles terminated World War I and imposed harsh measures on Germany, including the loss of much of its territory and the payment of damages to the victors.[7] These measures led to the rise of fascism and to World War II. The United States was the main winner. It began the war as the world's leading debtor nation, and through loans and sales of munitions, ended up as the world's leading creditor nation.[8]

The Bolshevik Revolution of 1917.　The Bolshevik Revolution was one of the seminal events of the twentieth century.[9] It grew out of the general economic and social developments of Russia. Several factors contributed to the revolution. The first was the condition of factory labor in Russia. Wages were low and paid irregularly, hours were long, and working conditions deplorable. The position of the peasants was no better. Although serfdom had been abolished, most peasants did not own land. Russia had also met an embarrassing defeat by Japan in the Russo-Japanese war of 1904. Public discontent led to the Russian Revolution of 1905. Although modest reforms were introduced by Tsar Nicholas, social unrest continued to exist.

World War I was the catalyst that led to the Bolshevik Revolution of 1917. Russia entered the war and suffered a humiliating defeat by Germany. Urban workers had to work long hours to keep the industrial system going, food was scarce, and inflation increased the cost of living. A series of bread riots caused by an acute shortage of food fueled strikes throughout Russia. On March 15, 1917, Nicholas resigned and a provisional government was created. Conflicts within the provisional government paved the way for the November 1917 revolution in which the Bolsheviks took over the government. Land was declared the property of the state and industry was nationalized.[10] Beginning in 1929, a countrywide system of economic planning was introduced to foster industrial development.

The Depression

The Depression of the 1930s was the prelude to World War II. Mass unemployment created serious economic problems and threatened the survival of the capitalist countries. In Germany Adolf Hitler and the National Socialist Party gained control of the government, and the democratic Weimar Republic was no more. In Japan the military gained government control. Fascism became the new economic and political order, joining communism as an alternative to capitalism, which many people began to see as incapable of dealing with the problems created by the Depression. The gold standard, which had been in existence for some 110 years, went out during the Depression, and each country imposed its own form of international currency exchange control. In England, the writings of John Maynard Keynes led to the creation of a new school of economic theory called Keynesian economics. This theory, which purported to explain the causes of unemployment and its cure, became a standard part of economic policy in Europe after World War II.

Fascism.   Fascism was an economic and political system that existed in Italy, Germany, Spain, and some of the Latin American countries.[11] It can be defined as a political system represented by a centralized autocratic government headed by a dictator. It involved economic and social repression and the elimination of opposition parties. Hitler and the Nazi party epitomized fascism as it was practiced in Germany. Although private property and free enterprise were permitted, the end goal was the enhancement of the power of the Reich. Economic planning was used by placing a number of controls on private industry, which was organized into cartels under the direction of a national ministry. However, under this control, private individuals and firms owned wealth, ran the businesses, and made profits.[12]

http://

For a historical description of Fascism, go to www.fordham.edu/halsall/mod/mussolini-fascism.html.

World War II, 1939–1945

World War II brought about four important changes:

1. It reshaped Europe and destroyed fascism as an economic and political system. Western Europe, helped in part by the Marshall Plan aid from the United States, was able to recover from the devastation caused by the war.
2. It created two world superpowers that dominated the world for most of the remainder of the century, the United States and the Soviet Union. The world

was divided into two spheres of influence, one dominated by the United States and the other dominated by the Soviet Union.

3. It ended colonialism. The various empires of the world collapsed as former colonies declared their independence. India declared its independence from England in 1947 and then split into three separate countries based on religion, India, Pakistan, and Bangladesh. Singapore also became independent from British rule and Indonesia broke away from Dutch rule. A number of African countries were created out of the former colonial enclaves of England, France, Spain, and Portugal. The number of countries in the world more than doubled.

4. It created a new currency and trading system meant to eliminate many of the trade problems that had contributed to prolonging the Depression. One problem involved tariff retaliation, where one country would raise its tariffs against other countries to reduce imports and the other countries would retaliate by raising their tariffs, which reduce trade and increased unemployment. Currency devaluation was a second problem. One country would devalue its currency to increase its exports by making them cheaper. Other countries would retaliate by devaluing their currencies. A new world monetary and trading system was created by the Bretton Woods Agreement and the General Agreement on Tariffs and Trade (GATT).

The Bretton Woods Agreement (1944).   Representatives of the United States and of other countries met at Bretton Woods, New Hampshire, in July 1944 to reorganize the world monetary system, which previously had been based on gold. The dollar, which was the world's most important currency, was made convertible at $35 an ounce of gold. Each nation fixed an exchange rate for its currency in relation to the dollar. For example, the West German DM exchanged at the rate of 4.1 DM = $1.00 and 1 DM = $.24.[13] This new currency system, which was to last to 1973, was a modified gold standard. Deficits in a country's balance of payments did not have to be covered by gold but in dollars. The whole rationale for the new monetary system was to prevent a repetition of what had happened during the Depression. By using trade restrictions, export subsidies, and currency devaluation to make their goods cheaper, nations tried to export their unemployment problems by exporting more and importing less.

Bretton Woods also laid the foundation for two very important international financial institutions, the International Monetary Fund (IMF) and the World Bank. The IMF was created to oversee the functioning of the new monetary system by promoting international monetary cooperation and a stable monetary system.[14] The World Bank was created to refinance the reconstruction of Europe after World War II. Its mission has been expanded over time to help the economies of the less developed countries by providing loans and loan guarantees to finance projects to improve the infrastructure, such as engineering and agricultural projects or the construction of a dam to provide hydroelectric power. Service and educational loans are also granted.

The General Agreement on Tariffs and Trade (GATT).   The GATT was created in 1947 by thirty-three countries, including the United States, which met in

http://

Do a site search for Bretton Woods Agreement at the IMF Web site at www.imf.org.

http://

Information on the GATT can be found at www.wto.org.

Havana, Cuba, to reduce trade barriers that had contributed to prolonging the Depression.[15] It is dedicated to four basic principles:

1. Nondiscrimination in trade through adherence to most favored nation (MFN) treatment, meaning that any preferential treatment granted to one country must be granted to all countries.
2. Reduction of tariffs through negotiations with member countries.
3. Reduction of import quotas that impose numerical limitations on imports.
4. Resolution of disputes among countries through consultation.

THE YEARS 1950 TO 2000

In 1950 the United States was the dominant world economic power. Its real per capita GDP of $9,573 was almost 50 percent higher than that of the United Kingdom, and its real GDP was almost three times higher than that of the Soviet Union. Table 1-2 presents a comparison of the nine most important countries in 1950 as measured by population, real per capita GDP, and the size of real GDP. In terms of real GDP in 1950, as in 1900, Japan still was in last place, and its real per capita GDP was about one fifth that for the United States.[16] However, its performance during most of the second half of the century was superior to that of the other nations, and it came to rival the United States as a major economic power.

The Marxist claim that depression and wars would destroy the capitalist system did not materialize, as governments adopted Keynesian economic policies

TABLE 1-2 *Population, Real per Capita GDP, and Total Real GDP for Major Countries in 1950*

Country	Real GDP ($ billions in 1990 prices)	Real per Capita GDP ($ thousands in 1990 prices)	Population (millions)
United States	1,457,624	9,573	152,271
USSR[1]	510,143	2,834	180,050
United Kingdom	344,859	6,843	50,363
China[2]	335,530	614	546,815
France	218,409	5,221	41,836
India[3]	214,288	597	359,000
Germany[4]	213,796	4,281	49,983
Italy	161,351	3,425	47,105
Japan	156,546	1,873	83,563

[1]*Russia became the Soviet Union in the late 1920s.*
[2]*China became a communist country in 1949.*
[3]*India achieved independence and became a country in 1947.*
[4]*Germany had been split into two separate countries, the Federal Republic or West Germany, and the German Democratic Republic on East Germany. The data are for West Germany.*

Source: Angus Maddison, *Monitoring the World Economy, 1820–1992* (Paris: Organization for Economic Cooperation and Development, 1995), pp. 105, 107, 111, 115, 181, 183, 187, 191, 195, 197, 201, 205.

TABLE 1-3
Government Expenditures as a Percent of GDP for Selected Periods

Country	1920	1937	1960	1980
Canada	13.3	18.6	28.6	38.8
France	27.6	29.0	34.6	46.1
Germany	25.0	42.4	32.4	47.9
Japan	14.8	25.4	17.5	32.0
Netherlands	13.5	19.0	33.7	55.2
Norway	13.7	15.4	29.9	37.5
Sweden	8.1	10.4	31.0	60.1
United Kingdom	26.2	30.0	32.2	43.0
United States	7.0	8.6	27.0	31.8

Source: "The Future of the State," *The Economist*, December 30, 1997, p. 8.

aimed at attaining full employment.[17] Laissez-faire economics was pretty much abandoned in favor of government-led economic measures designed to stimulate aggregate demand. The role of government increased significantly through the development of a wide variety of social welfare programs. Table 1-3 presents a comparison of the relationship between government spending and GDP for selected time periods. The year 1937 was the heart of the Depression, and Germany and Japan were armed for war. The period 1960 to 1980 showed the greatest increase in government intervention, as European countries developed what can be called a system of social welfare capitalism.[18]

Several major events happened in the last half of the twentieth century. The first was the end of colonialism and the concomitant creation of a number of new countries that did not exist at the beginning of the twentieth century. Most of these countries were in Africa and in East and Southern Asia. The second is technological change, which has substituted ideas, skills, and knowledge for natural resources. The third was the collapse of communism, which was one of the two most important economic and political ideologies of this century. In 1991 the former Soviet Union was dissolved into fifteen countries. The Cold War was over, and gone with it were ideological debates over the roles of the state and the market. The fourth is the creation of the European Union and other trading blocs in the 1980s and 1990s.

The End of Colonialism

The race to acquire colonies, particularly in Africa, began in the nineteenth century. At the Treaty of Berlin in 1885, five European countries decided to divide Africa into economic enclaves. Belgium got that area known as the Congo, which became one of the largest copper-producing areas in the world. England, which was already established in Egypt and the Cape of Africa, acquired the Sudan, southern Africa, and a part of southwest Africa. France, which already had Algeria, was given West Africa. Germany was given parts of east Africa and southwest

Africa, and Portugal was given what was left, including the areas that are now the countries of Angola and Mozambique. Two world wars changed all of this, and in the 1950s and 1960s most of these colonies became independent nations. Some fifty new countries were created.

Colonialism also ended in Asia. Laos, Cambodia, and Viet Nam, once former French colonies, became independent countries. Singapore, Malaysia, Burma, and India, which split into Pakistan, India, and Bangladesh, became independent from England. The countries of North Korea and South Korea were once Japanese possessions. The United States lost the Philippines, and the Dutch lost Indonesia. China, which had been dominated by foreign powers for more than one hundred years, became a communist nation in 1949. The East Asian countries, which includes Japan, South Korea, Singapore, and Taiwan, developed as one of the most important trading nations in the world. As Table 1-4 indicates, the East Asian countries outperformed Latin America from 1950 to 1990. East Asia relied on an export-driven policy to promote economic development, while Latin America relied on import substitution for economic development. Tariffs were kept high on imports of manufactured goods to protect home industries from foreign competition.

Technological Change

At the beginning of the twentieth century, manufacturing companies dominated the American economy. Most were based where natural resources were available. For example, U.S. Steel was located near sources of coal and iron; Standard Oil

Asian Countries	
Korea	7.3
Hong Kong*	5.6
Indonesia	4.6
Malaysia	4.1
Singapore	6.3
Thailand	5.0
Latin American Countries	
Argentina	−0.3
Brazil	2.4
Chile	1.6
Mexico	1.5
Peru	−0.4
Venezuela	−0.8

TABLE 1-4

Average Annual Growth Rates in Real per Capita GDP for Asian and Latin American Countries, 1965–1966 (percent)

Hong Kong is now a part of China.

Source: The World Bank, *World Development Indicators, 1998* (Washington, D.C.: The World Bank, 1998), pp. 24–27.

located its production facilities near sources of oil in Mexico and the United States; Armour and Swift were located in Chicago, where their meatpacking plants were near supplies of beef and pork; American tobacco was located in North Carolina, where tobacco was produced; and Anaconda Copper based its operations in Chile, where copper was abundant. Countries that had natural resources were better off than those that did not. Thus, the resource-rich countries of Argentina, Brazil, and Mexico had much higher real per capita incomes at the beginning of the century than Japan, which had no natural resources. Comparative advantage favored countries that had natural resources over those that did not.[19]

But times have changed. Skill and knowledge stand alone as the only sources of comparative advantage. High-value brainpower industries are now important, and investments are now made in knowledge and skills instead of in natural resources. A global economy exists and corporations can base their operations any place in the world. Success or failure depends on whether or not a country can make a transition to the human-made brainpower industries of the future. The international transfer of technology means that anything can be produced anywhere and sold everywhere. Transportation and communication costs have fallen dramatically and their speed has risen exponentially. Research and design can be coordinated in different parts of the world, and components can be made wherever it is cheapest to do so and shipped to assembly points that minimize total cost. Technology has created world capital markets, where firms can borrow in New York, Frankfurt, Paris, or Tokyo.

The Collapse of Communism

Another major event of the end of the twentieth century was the collapse of communism as a political and economic system. There were many inefficiencies in the Soviet-type of command economy called socialism.[20] The quality of consumer goods was poor, the distribution system was inefficient, and waste and corruption were endemic. Work incentives were poor, alcoholism was widespread, and life expectancy had declined, in part because little attention was paid to maintaining a safe environment.[21] An ever-increasing flow of resources was committed to the military and to the support of client countries such as Cuba and Viet Nam. Foreign trade was controlled by the Council for Mutual Economic Assistance (CMEA) and was uncompetitive by world standards.[22] Direct action to reform the Soviet economy was insufficient and came too late. At the time of its demise, the Soviet Union was not competitive even with developing countries such as South Korea.

Table 1-5 presents a comparison of real per capita GDP for Western and Eastern European countries for three time periods, 1937, 1950, and 1990. The first period is before World War II, when the Eastern European countries were not communist. The second period marks the time when the division between Western and Eastern Europe based on ideologies had been established, but the economies of each country were not yet in place. The economies of Eastern Europe adopted the system of the Soviet Union and relied on central economic planning to allocate resources. The plans emphasized the heavy industry and resource sector of each economy at the expense of the consumer goods sector. The

Country	1937	1950	1990
Western Europe			
Austria	3,177	3,731	16,792
Denmark	5,453	6,683	17,953
France	4,444	5,221	17,777
Italy	3,247	3,425	16,112
United Kingdom	5,947	6,847	16,302
Eastern Europe			
Czechoslovakia	2,882	3,501	8,464
Hungary	2,543	2,480	6,338
Poland	1,915	2,497	5,113
Romania	1,130	1,182	3,460
USSR	2,156	2,834	6,871

TABLE 1-5
Comparisons of Western and Eastern European Countries for 1937, 1950, and 1990 ($ real per capita GDP in 1990 prices)

Source: Angus Maddison, *Monitoring the World Economy, 1820–1992* (Paris: Organization for Economic Cooperation and Development, 1995), pp. 194, 195, 197, 200, 201.

Western countries emphasized market mechanisms to allocate resources. As the table indicates, differences in living standards widened between Western and Eastern Europe.

Regional Trading Blocs

Regional trading blocs have multiplied in past decades. Their purpose is to liberalize international trade among their members. There are several types of regional trading blocs. The first is a free-trade area designed to encourage trade among members by eliminating trade barriers. An example is the North American Free Trade Agreement (NAFTA), which reduces trade barriers between the United States and Canada. Then there are customs unions, which combine features of a free-trade area with common trade policies toward nonmember countries. An example is MERCOSUR, composed of Argentina, Brazil, Paraguay, and Uruguay.[23] Finally, there is the European Union (EU), which represents a complete economic and political integration of its member countries. It will have one currency, the euro, a central bank that will coordinate monetary policy for its member countries, and a common tax system.[24] The political integration will create a Council of Ministers, a European Parliament, and a European Court of Justice.

THE END OF THE TWENTIETH CENTURY

The United States began the century as the world's leading economic power and will finish in the same position. However, Japan is the success story of the century. With few natural resources to support it, it transformed itself into a major world

TABLE 1-6   *Estimated Population, Real per Capita GDP, and Total Real GDP for Major Countries in 2000**

Country	Real GDP ($ billions in 1990 prices)	Real per Capita GDP ($ thousands in 1990 prices)	Population (millions)
United States	6,559,280	23,800	275,600
China	4,420,000	3,400	1,300,000
Japan	2,808,190	22,100	127,100
Germany**	1,761,510	21,300	82,700
India	1,526,400	1,600	954,000
France	1,176,120	19,800	59,400
United Kingdom	1,148,480	19,400	59,200
Italy	1,123,060	17,700	57,800
Russian Federation	572,130	3,300	146,700

*Estimates for each country are based on a fifteen-year moving average.
**Germany after reunification

Source: Angus Maddison, *Monitoring the World Economy, 1820–1992* (Paris: Organization for Economic Cooperation and Development, 1995), pp. 105, 107, 115, 181, 183, 195, 197, 205.

power.[25] It began the twentieth century with a real per capita GDP less than half that of Argentina, a country far better endowed with natural resources, and ended the century with a real per capita GDP three times that of Argentina.[26] At the beginning of the century it was not ranked among the top ten countries; at the end of the century in terms of real GDP, it ranks third in the world. Table 1-6 presents a comparison of the position of the nine major countries at the beginning and at the end of the century. Some of the countries are not in their original forms. Germany is a good example. In 1900 a part of France, much of Poland, and the western part of the Czech Republic were formerly a part of Germany.

WHY SOME NATIONS ARE RICH AND OTHERS ARE POOR

Professor David Landes of Harvard has written a book called *The Wealth and Poverty of Nations* in which he attempts to explain why some nations are rich and others are poor.[27] It begins with a discussion of geography, which he believes determines a nation's destiny. His premise is that a nation's natural endowments, including a temperate climate, have given certain areas of the world, such as Europe and the United States, an advantage over other areas. The Industrial Revolution occurred in Europe because its mild summers permitted intensive economic activity impossible in the tropics, whose heat and humidity limited economic activity. The agricultural revolution of the nineteenth and twentieth centuries also occurred in nations with favorable climates and rainfall and raised their living standards. This may be contrasted to a tropical climate, where jungles and rainforests have inhibited the growth of agriculture.

us can change behaviors about which we remain unaware. For example, an adult who stutters and has experienced repeated speech attempts and failures might internalize feelings of negativity, worthlessness, and pessimism. It is not hard to visualize how such feelings could affect all aspects of one's life. In contrast, imagine the potential for positive change when a clinician discusses with a person who stutters realistic options through sensitive and strategic intervention planning. When adults who stutter become explicitly aware of their personal constructs, they (and their clinicians) can use this awareness to effect positive changes in the way they view themselves as communicators and in the control they exercise over their own speech fluency. A central tenet here is that when adults who stutter become aware that their interpretation of past events and thereby anticipation of future events was incorrect or undesirable, they may revise their construct system to achieve outcomes that were not or did not seem possible (e.g., speaking with greater fluency, using self-corrections more often, using fluency facilitating controls outside settings, etc.) (Shapiro, 1999). This is the role of the clinician: to make what seems impossible, possible; to help people imagine and realize their own communication dreams.

Family Systems Theory

Because stuttering and people who stutter exist within a family context, both must be addressed within this context to be understood. Furthermore, experiences and change of a person who stutters trigger compensatory changes in family members and significant others (Shapiro, 1999). One part of the family cannot be understood in isolation from the other members of the system (Epstein & Bishop, 1981; Luterman, 1996). Efforts to involve family members in the intervention process often inadvertently continue to center on the person who stutters, an individual, as the center of the treatment. While family members might be directed to participate in activities outside of the clinical setting, they still are not valued and involved as active and equal members of the treatment team. Under this arrangement, the most significant changes are viewed as occurring in the treatment session, which might be enhanced by family cooperation and understanding. In contrast, treating a person who stutters within the context of a family system requires the entire family to be involved in all aspects of assessment and treatment. Such involvement requires understanding by the clinician of the nature and dynamics of the individual family. Within this context, counseling becomes the medium for discussing aspects of family interactive patterns that facilitate or inhibit the goals and procedures that are jointly determined. What this means is that clinicians must assess and understand the strengths, needs, and level of functioning not only of the adult who stutters, but of the family as factors in the intervention process.

Stuttering Modification/Fluency Shaping Considerations

Stuttering modification and fluency shaping are bipolar theoretical endpoints along a clinical continuum. Understanding these two elements and the continuum that lies between them is useful for intervention planning (Guitar & Peters, 1980; Peters & Guitar, 1991; Shapiro, 1999). Stuttering modification therapy assumes that stuttering results from avoiding or struggling with disfluency, avoiding feared words and/or feared situations, and from negative attitudes toward speaking. The intervention seeks to reduce these behaviors, fears, and negative attitudes while modifying the form of stuttering. This is accomplished by reducing the struggle behavior, smoothing out the stuttering into a more gentle form, and reducing the tension and rate of stuttering. On the other hand, fluency shaping assumes that stuttering is learned, and treatment is based upon the principles of behavior modification (i.e., operant conditioning and programming). Fluency is first established in a controlled stimulus environment, and fluent responses are then reinforced and stuttered responses are punished. Both approaches first attempt to achieve spontaneous fluency, with controlled fluency as an acceptable but less preferred goal. If these cannot be achieved, stuttering modification seeks to achieve a level of acceptable stuttering. Any noticeable stuttering, however, would be seen as evidence of program failure to a fluency shaping clinician. Stuttering modification emphasizes the importance of studying and understanding feelings and attitudes and thereby reducing speech-related fears and negative emotions. This is done within a counseling framework where the clinician and client actively discuss and participate in all aspects of the treatment process. In contrast, fluency shaping does not attempt to reduce communication-related fears and avoidances. Rather, fluency shaping is conducted within a structured context where stimuli, responses, and subsequent events are preprogrammed. In reality, most treatment falls somewhere along the continuum. Typically, an intervention oriented more toward stuttering modification is indicated when the person who stutters hides the stuttering, avoids speaking, feels penalized by stuttering, and feels poorly as a communicator. Fluency shaping is indicated when the person who stutters does so openly, does not avoid speaking, does not feel penalized by stuttering, and feels positive as a communicator. The way these and other factors combine guides the clinician toward stuttering modification or fluency shaping in intervention planning.

Summary of Procedural Principles Derived from the Various Theoretic Perspectives

Having reviewed maintaining factors from different theoretical perspectives, I identify a set of procedural principles. These principles may be used to develop a procedural approach for specific clients. Box 10.1 lists these principles, their derivation source, and their applications to procedure planning.

Case Example: Initial Clinical Portrait

Mr. Frederick (Fred) Johnson was a man of 55 years when he was referred by his family physician for a communication assessment because of his severe stuttering. Both Fred and his wife, Mary, attended the scheduled evaluation. Fred's stuttering reportedly began early in childhood and has remained constant in degree and type as long as both Fred and Mary can recall. While Fred has not had treatment in the last 30 years, he did experience two brief periods of treatment before that time involving oral elocution and neuropharmacology (i.e., medication by prescription). Fred reported that he is typically disfluent but that

B O X **10.1**

**Selected Procedural Principles, Their Derivation Source,
and Their Application to Intervention Planning[a]**

Principles Fluency is facilitated by:	Theoretic Derivation	Maintaining Factors Addressed	Implications for Procedures
1. The client's experience of fluency	Personal construct Fluency shaping	Psychosocial Sensorimotor	Design treatment activities as to ensure fluency
2. The client's heightened awareness of fluency	Personal construct	Cognitive	Help client identify behaviors, thoughts, and feelings that characterize fluency Shift responsibility for identifying fluency from self to client
3. The use of fluency facilitating techniques during instances of stuttering	Personal construct Fluency shaping	Cognitive Sensorimotor	Help the client decide on one or two behaviors or techniques that can facilitate fluency (e.g., slow and gentle, cancellation)
4. Addressing thoughts, feelings, and attitudes directly	Personal construct Family systems	Psychosocial	Involve clients in direct discussions of positive and negative feelings (e.g., "What do you feel when you discipline your children and you find yourself stuttering?" Or "What was it like when you ordered for your wife in a restaurant for the first time in your 35-year marriage?")
5. Transferring fluency facilitating techniques to extra clinical settings.	Fluency shaping	Cognitive Psychosocial	Extend clinical assignments beyond the treatment room
6. Preparing for relapse	Personal construct Family systems	Cognitive Psychosocial	Help the clients and families understand the nature of relapse and prepare them for the likelihood of its occurrence (i.e., "Relapse Happens!")
7. Becoming one's own clinician	Personal construct Family systems	Cognitive Psychosocial	Resist the temptation to enable the client to become dependent on the clinician Discuss the changing roles and responsibilities of each participant Jointly establish goals and design procedures

(continued)

Principles Fluency is facilitated by:	Theoretic Derivation	Maintaining Factors Addressed	Implications for Procedures
8. Deliberately revisiting the past	Personal construct	Cognitive Psychosocial	Review with the client video tapes of pretreatment communication
			Celebrate the client's achievements
			While viewing the video tapes, encourage the client to discuss previous thoughts and feelings of himself as a communicator and how these have evolved
9. Reexamining one's personal construct	Personal construct	Cognitive Psychosocial	Help client understand the nature of fluency possessed
			Involve the client and family actively in the treatment process and related decisions
			Help the client to think of himself in ways other than a person who stutters
10. Integrating treatment changes within the communication system	Family systems Fluency shaping	Psychosocial Cognitive	Encourage conversational partners (family, friends, coworkers, teachers, employers) to adjust and thereby support the changes that have taken place

[a]For complete treatment of these issues see Shapiro (1999).

he does not let his communication skills hold him back. He indicated that he could only predict fluency when he speaks alone and when talking to the family's dog. Fred is a long-time factory employee and has no other family history of communication disorders.

An analysis of Fred's conversational speech indicated a rate of 41 words per minute, significantly below the average of 160, reflecting the severity of Fred's disfluency. Disfluencies included rapid initial and medial syllable repetitions for periods of 1 to 16 seconds; part-word, whole-word, and phrase repetition varying from 1 to 9 units of repetition; and syllable, word, and phrase interjections of 1 to 10 units of interjection/repetition. A randomly selected sentence of 13 words lasted 55 seconds and contained 50 distinct units of disfluency. Associated characteristics included facial tension, pitch increase indicative of laryngeal tension, and rapid and vertical jaw movements during syllable repetitions. Islands of complete fluency lasted up to 16 words. Reading proved to be a more disfluent context. When reading "My Grandfather," Fred's rate of speech was 12 words per minute. Types of disfluency were similar to those noted in conversation; however, the severity and intensity were more pronounced. For example, syllable repetition (e.g., guhguhguh . . . grandfather) was extremely rapid and lasted up to 90 seconds in duration. Word interjection lasted up to 20 seconds in duration. All other parameters of articulation, language, and voice (i.e., during fluent, nonstuttered speech) were within normal limits. Trial management combining

PART II

Market Mechanisms and Capitalism

CHAPTER 2

Capitalism as an Economic System

A fundamental dilemma of any economic system is a scarcity of resources relative
to wants. Decisions are necessary to determine how a given volume of resources is
to be allocated to production and how the income derived from production is to be
distributed among the various factors—capital, labor, and land—that are responsible for it. Human wants, if not unlimited, are at least indefinitely expansible. But
the commodities and services that can satisfy these wants are not, and neither are
the factors of production that can produce the desired goods and services. These
productive factors usually have alternative uses; that is, they can be used in the
production of a number of different goods and services. The system must allocate
limited productive resources, which have alternative uses, to the satisfaction of
greater and growing human wants.

Large amounts of capital will not be available for use in production unless
there is a process of saving and capital formation. This process is fundamentally
the same in all types of economic systems. It cannot operate unless the available
productive resources are more than adequate to provide a bare living for the people of the system. When it *is* able to operate, the process involves spending part of
the money income of an economy, directly or indirectly, for capital goods rather
than for consumer goods. In a nonmonetary sense, saving and capital formation
require the allocation of a part of the productive resources of a country to produc-

21

ing capital goods rather than consumer goods. The cost of obtaining capital goods is the same in all economic systems: It means going for the present without the quantities of consumer goods and services that could have been produced by the factors of production.

In general societies have endless ways of organizing and performing their production and distribution functions. In economic and political terms, the possible range is from laissez-faire capitalism through totalitarian communism. The economy of the United States today by no means represents a pure laissez-faire capitalist system. It is, rather, a mixed economic system. There are public enterprises, considerable government regulation and control, and various other elements that hinder the unrestrained functioning of market forces. However, to understand how a capitalist system works, it is necessary to know something about its institutional arrangements. For practical purposes, an *institutional arrangement* is a practice, convention, or custom that is a material and persistent element in the life or culture of an organized group. *Economic institutions* are ways of reacting to certain economic and social phenomena in certain economic situations. Some economic institutions rest on custom, while others are formally recognized through legislative enactment.

INSTITUTIONS OF CAPITALISM

http://

See Ed Yardeni's site on capitalism at www.yardeni .com/capitalism .html.

A number of institutional arrangements characterize a capitalist economic system. These arrangements reflect a set of basic beliefs that define how a society should be organized, how goods and services should be produced, and how income should be distributed. In the United States these beliefs are incorporated into the institutional arrangements that typify a capitalist system—private property, the profit motive, the price system, freedom of enterprise, competition, individualism, consumer sovereignty, the Protestant work ethic, and limited government. Each of these institutions will be discussed in some detail.

Private Property

Under capitalism there is private ownership of the factors of production—land, labor, and capital. There are also certain rights concerning property. An individual has the right to acquire property, to consume or control it, to buy or sell it, to give it away as a gift, and to bequeath it at death. Private property ownership is supposed to encourage thrift and wealth accumulation and to serve as a stimulus to individual initiative and industry, both of which are considered essential to economic progress.

However, private ownership of property is subject to certain limitations. In practice, even under capitalism, property rights are often restricted by the actions of social groups or government units. Also, a good deal of the private wealth of capitalist systems, such as that of the United States, is owned not by individuals, but rather by business firms. There is actually a good deal of publicly owned property within a capitalistic system. Where public property exists, the exclusive control of wealth is exercised by a group of individuals through some political process.

The Profit Motive

The kinds of goods produced in an economy that relies on market arrangements are determined in the first instance by managers of business firms or by individual entrepreneurs. They are directly responsible for converting resources into products and determining what these products will be, guided by the actions of consumers in the marketplace. The profit motive is the lodestar that draws managers to produce goods that can be sold at prices that are higher than the costs of production. In private enterprise, profit is necessary for survival; it is the payment to owners of capital. Anybody who produces things that do not, directly or indirectly, yield a profit will sooner or later go bankrupt, lose the ownership of the means of production, and so cease to be an independent producer. There can be no other way. Capitalism, in other words, uses profitability as the test of whether any given item should or should not be produced, and if it should, how much of it should be produced.

The Price System

Individuals and businesses under capitalism are supposed to make most types of economic decisions on the basis of prices, price relationships, and price changes. The function of prices is to provide a coordinating mechanism for millions of decentralized private production and distribution units. The prices that prevail in the marketplace determine the kinds and quantities of goods and services that will be produced and how they will be distributed. Price changes are supposed to adjust the quantities of these goods and services available for the market.

The Price Mechanism. It is through the mechanism of prices that scarce resources [*short in supply*] are allocated to various uses. The interaction between the price system and the pursuit of profits is supposed to keep economic mistakes down to a reasonable level. Profit, which depends on the selling price of goods and the cost of making them, indicates to businesses what people are buying. An industry with a product that commands high prices relative to costs draws businesses, whereas low prices relative to costs check production by causing businesses to drop out.

Price Determination. In a free-market economy, demand and supply determine the price at which a purchase or sale of a good is made. Demand originates with the consumer. It involves a desire for a good or service expressed through a willingness to pay money for it in the marketplace. Market demand is the sum of all individual consumers' demands for a particular good or service. There is an inverse relationship between market demand and the price of a good or a service. The higher the price, the lower the quantity of the good or service demanded. [*WTF?*]

Supply originates with the producer. It is the quantity of a good or service that a producer is willing to offer at any given price. Market supply is the sum of all the supplies that individual producers will offer in the marketplace at all possible prices over a given period. There is a direct relationship between market supply and price—the higher the price, the greater the supply of goods or services that will be provided.

The interaction of demand and supply determines the price for a good or service in the marketplace. The equilibrium price is the price that equates the quantity demanded with the quantity supplied in a market. It is the one price that will clear the market. At any price above the equilibrium price, supply is greater than demand, and the price must fall. At a price below the equilibrium price, demand is greater than supply, and the price must rise. In the following example, the equilibrium price is $3.00 per pound.

Market Demand	Price per Pound	Market Supply
180 pounds	$0.50	40 pounds
140	1.00	50
100	2.00	65
80	3.00	80
60	4.00	100
40	5.00	120

The forces of supply and demand acting through the price mechanism can send effective signals to the marketplace. For example, an increase in demand means that buyers will be willing to purchase more at any price than they were formerly. An increase in demand, with supply remaining constant, would result in an increase in price. The increased price would cause producers to supply more, so quantity would increase also. A decrease in demand would have the opposite effect.

Conversely, an increase in supply with demand remaining constant would result in a decrease in price. The lower price would lead to an increase in the quantity purchased. A decrease in supply would have the opposite effect. Consumers have to pay more for a smaller amount of a good or service.

Figure 2-1 illustrates the determination of prices and output in a free market. Both are determined at the intersection of the demand and supply curves. The equilibrium price is p_0, and q_0 is the quantity supplied. At any price above p_0, the quantity supplied is greater than the quantity demanded, and the price will fall. At any price below p_0, demand is greater than the quantity supplied, and prices will rise.

An increase in demand to D_1 with supply remaining constant will result in an increase in both price and quantity. The new equilibrium price will be p_1 and the quantity will increase to q_1. The increase in demand to D_1 will eventually result in an increase in supply (the supply curve shifts to the right) as producers react to the potential for higher profits. New producers will enter the market, and resources

FIGURE 2-1 *Determination of Equilibrium Price and Output*

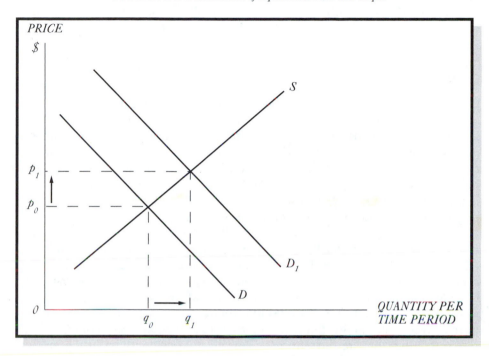

will be shifted from other areas into the market in anticipation of a greater rate of return.[1]

Freedom of Enterprise (right to do any line of economic activity)

Another basic institution of capitalism is freedom of enterprise. It refers to the general right of each individual to engage in any line of economic activity that appeals to that individual. However, there are limits placed on the choice of an activity. People cannot engage in activities that are deemed socially immoral (e.g., child pornography) or that may harm others (e.g., driving while intoxicated). As far as the government is concerned, the individual is free to move to any part of the country, work in any chosen occupation, and find and operate a business unit in virtually any field of lawful economic activity. By comparing market indicators—prices and costs—the individual is supposed to be able to select a field of activity that promises to be remunerative. The institution of private property furnishes the social sanctions necessary for the use and control of the factors of production vital to the chosen field of activity.

The theory used to justify the existence of freedom of enterprise is quite simply one of social welfare. That is, in choosing fields of economic activity in which they will be the most successful from the point of view of private gain, individuals will also be selecting fields in which they presumably will be most productive to society.

Competition

Given the institutions of private property and freedom of enterprise, and given the scarcity of resources and the reliance on a market to allocate them, the attempts of individuals to further their economic self-interest result in competition. Competition is an indispensable part of a free enterprise system. In economic life, self-reliant individuals must struggle and compete for economic rewards—good jobs, high pay, promotions, desirable goods and services, and security in old age. There is the element of social Darwinism in competition: Life is a competitive struggle in which only the fittest, in terms of resources, get to the top.

Certainly, *competition* is one of the "good" words in the American vocabulary. From a very early age, schoolchildren are told that the distinguishing characteristic of the historically successful U.S. economic system is competition and that other economic systems have inefficiencies because, to some degree, they lack that magic ingredient in the particular and unique context in which it exists in our economy. It is, therefore, not surprising that by statute and common law our legal system has been actively concerned with the maintenance of a competitive system.

Certain benefits are thought to be derived from competition in the marketplace. A competitive market will:

1. Allow the price mechanism to reflect actual demand and cost and thus maximize efficiency in the use of capital and other resources.
2. Encourage product innovation and long-run cost reduction.
3. Result in the equitable diffusion of real income.
4. Provide consumers with a wide variety of alternative sources of supply.

Individualism

Individualism is linked to a set of related institutional values of capitalism. Again there is social Darwinism—life seen as a competitive struggle where the fit survive and those who are unfit do not. Individualism also involves competition, which, when combined with social Darwinism, is supposed to provide some guarantee of progress through the inexorable process of evolution. Individualism is also related to equality of opportunity—the right of each person to succeed or fail on his or her own merit.

The institutions of private property ownership and individualism are related from two standpoints. First, private property ownership provides the spur for individual initiative, a reward to be gained through competition and hard work. Second, it provides some guarantee of individual rights against the encroachments of the state. It follows that a requisite for individualism is a limited state role. The rights of the individual would have precedence over those of the state, for the latter is a fictitious body composed of individual people who are considered to represent its members. The idea of individualism can therefore be a safeguard against the tyranny of the state.

Consumer Sovereignty

In a capitalistic market economy, consumer sovereignty is an important institution because consumption is supposed to be the basic rationale of economic activity. As Adam Smith said, "Consumption is the sole end and purpose of all production; and the interest of the producer ought to be attended to only as far as it is necessary for promoting that of the consumer."[2] Consumer sovereignty assumes, of course, that there is a competitive market economy. Consumers are able to vote with their money by offering more of it for products that are in greater demand and less of it for products that are not in demand. Shifts in supply and demand will occur in response to the way in which consumers spend their money.

In competing for consumers' dollars, producers will produce more of those products that are in demand, for the prices will be higher, and less of those products that are not in demand, for the prices will be lower. Production is the means; consumption is the end. Producers that effectively satisfy the wants of consumers are encouraged by large monetary returns, which enable them in turn to purchase the goods and services required for their operations. On the other hand, producers who do not respond to the wants of consumers will not remain in business very long.

Freedom of choice is linked to consumer sovereignty. In fact, one defense of the market mechanism is the freedom of choice it provides consumers in a capitalistic economy. Consumers are free to accept or reject whatever is produced in the marketplace. The consumer is king because production ultimately is oriented toward meeting the wants of consumers. Freedom of choice is consistent with a laissez-faire economy. It is assumed that consumers are capable of making rational decisions, and in an economy dominated by a large number of buyers and sellers this assumption has some merit. Since the role of the government is minimal, the principle of *caveat emptor* ("let the buyer beware") governs consumer decisions to buy.

The Protestant Work Ethic

The Protestant work ethic is an ideological principle stemming from the Protestant Reformation of the sixteenth century and is associated with the religious reformer John Calvin. Calvin preached a doctrine of salvation that later proved to be consistent with the principles of a capitalist system.[3] According to Calvin and the Puritan ministers in early New England, hard work, diligence, and thrift are earthly signs that individuals are using fully the talents given to them by God for his overall purposes. Salvation is associated with achievement on this earth. Thus, work and economic gain have come to have a moral value. According to this view, it is good for the soul to work; rewards on this earth go to those who achieve the most. Moreover, salvation in the world to come is a reward that is in direct proportion to a person's contribution during life.

The Calvinist doctrine of work and salvation became an integral part of the ideology of capitalism. The hard work of merchants and traders often produced profits, and their thrift led to saving and investment. Saving is the heart of the Protestant work ethic. With Adam Smith's idea of parsimony (or frugality) and Nassau Senior's idea of abstinence, it was established that saving multiplied future production and earned its own reward through interest.

Carried into American society in the nineteenth century, the Protestant work ethic came to mean rewards for those who were economically competent and punishment for those who were incompetent or unambitious. Work was put at the center of American life. Most of the industrial capitalists of the last century belonged to fundamentalist Protestant churches. John D. Rockefeller, who became the richest man of his day, attributed his success to the "glory of God." (Skeptics, however, attributed his success to much more mundane factors than God's beneficence.)[4]

Limited Government

For many years, the idea prevailed that the government in a capitalist system, however it might be organized, should follow a policy of *laissez-faire* with respect to economic activity. That is, activities of the government should be limited to the performance of a few general functions for the good of all citizens, and government should not attempt to control or interfere with the economic activities of private individuals. Laissez-faire assumes that individuals are rational and better judges of their own interests than any government could possibly be.[5] The interests of individuals are closely identified with those of society as a whole. It is only necessary for government to provide a setting or environment in which individuals can operate freely. This the government was supposed to do by performing only those functions that individuals could not do for themselves: provide for national defense, maintain law and order, carry on diplomatic relations with other countries, and construct roads, schools, and public works.

In a free enterprise market economy, competition is regarded as a virtue rather than a vice. The proper use of resources in a free enterprise system is ensured by the fact that if a firm does not use resources efficiently, it goes broke. If the market is to function effectively, it must operate freely. If there is intervention in any form, then there is no effective mechanism for weeding out inefficient enterprises. Nevertheless, government has always participated to some extent in business activity of capitalist countries. From the very beginning, the government of the United States was interested in the promotion of manufacturing, and it passed tariff laws very early to protect American business interests. Subsidies were used to promote the development of canals, roads, and railroads. Business was a direct beneficiary of those subsidies.

INCOME DISTRIBUTION IN A CAPITALIST ECONOMY

Once goods and services have been produced, the next important question in any economic system is the manner in which these goods and services are to be divided or apportioned among the individual consumers of the economy. The distribution of income does not refer to the processes by which physical goods are brought from producers to consumers, but rather to the distribution of the national income, first in money and then in goods and services, among the owners of the factors of production—land, labor, and capital.

Income distribution in a market economy is based on institutional arrangements, such as the pricing mechanism, associated with this type of system. The demand for a factor of production is derived from the demand for the goods the factor helps to produce. High prices are set on scarce factors of production and low prices on plentiful factors. In terms of rewards to labor, workers whose skills are scarce relative to demand enjoy high income, while those whose skills are not scarce relative to demand do not. Professional football and baseball players receive high salaries because they possess a scarce talent and people are willing to pay to see them perform.

Measurements of Income Inequality

There are various measures of income inequality, including the Lorenz curve and the Pareto and Gini coefficients. Of these measures, the Lorenz curve is the most commonly used. The Lorenz curve involves the use of an arithmetic scale that begins with an assumption of income equality as a starting point. Equality in the distribution of income is found when every income-receiving unit receives its proportional share of the total income. If incomes were absolutely uniformly distributed, the lowest 20 percent of income earners would receive exactly 20 percent of the total income; the lowest 80 percent would get exactly 80 percent of the total income; and the highest 20 percent would get only 20 percent of the income. In using a Lorenz curve, the curve of absolute equality would actually be a straight line extending upward at a 45° angle from left to right, showing that 20 percent of income earners on the horizontal axis receive 20 percent of the income on the vertical axis, 40 percent of income earners receive 40 percent of the income, and so on. Any departure from this line is a departure from complete income equality.

Figure 2-2 illustrates the Lorenz curve. The straight line 0*AF* is the line of perfect equality. The line 0*BF*—the Lorenz curve—shows a departure from equality. The farther 0*BF* is from 0*AF*, the greater the inequality. There are certain weaknesses in the use of the Lorenz curve as a measure of income distribution. First, one cannot tell by inspecting a curve how unequal the distribution of income is. The use of percentages conceals the number of income-receiving units in the different income brackets. It is also true that the slope of a curve at various points gives no more information than the curve itself. On the other hand, the Lorenz curve is an excellent device for visual presentation of inequalities in the distribu-

http://

Check the Economic Statistics Briefing Room for data on income at www.whitehouse.gov/fsbr/esbr.html

FIGURE 2-2 *The Lorenz Curve*

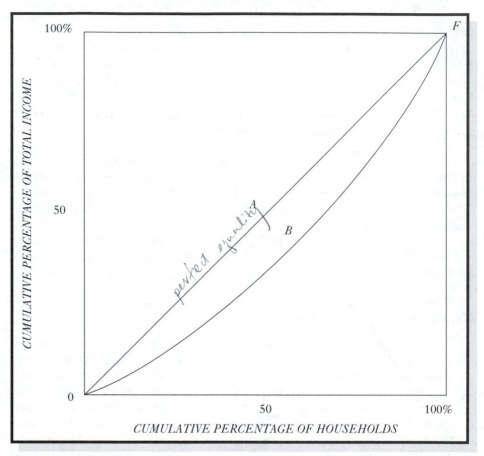

tion of income. It can also illustrate the effects on the distribution of income of changes in taxes and government spending.

Table 2-1 presents the Gini coefficients and compares ratios for the highest and lowest tenths and the highest and lowest quintiles of income distribution for the most important developed countries of the world. It confirms the Luxembourg study done by the Organization for Economic Cooperation and Development (OECD) that income inequality is the highest in the United States and lowest in the social welfare states of Scandinavia. The difference between the highest tenth and lowest tenth of income earners in Sweden is 6 to 1 and the Gini coefficient is 25.0 compared to a difference between the upper and lower tenth of income earners in the United States of 19 to 1 and a Gini coefficient of 40.1. The only other country whose income inequality is anywhere near comparable to that of the United States is Switzerland.

It is possible to avoid relying solely on visual comparisons of Lorenz curves to draw inferences about various income distributions. In a Lorenz diagram the Gini

Quintile *xGinix*

TABLE 2-1 *Income Distribution for Selected Developed Countries (percent)*

Country*	Gini Coefficient	Lowest Tenth	Lowest Quintile	Highest Quintile	Upper Tenth
Canada	31.5	2.8	7.5	39.3	24.7
Denmark	24.7	3.6	9.6	34.5	20.5
Finland	25.6	4.2	10.0	35.8	21.6
France	32.7	2.5	7.2	40.1	24.9
Germany	28.1	3.7	9.0	37.1	22.6
Italy	31.2	2.9	7.6	38.9	23.7
Netherlands	31.5	2.9	8.0	39.9	24.7
Norway	25.2	4.1	10.0	35.3	21.2
Sweden	25.0	3.7	9.6	34.5	20.1
Switzerland	36.1	2.9	7.4	43.5	28.6
United Kingdom	32.6	2.4	7.1	39.8	24.7
United States	40.1	1.5	4.8	45.2	28.5

inequality

Total incomes are needed! GDP's are needed.

*No data given for Japan

Source: The World Bank, *World Development Report, 1998/99* (New York: Oxford University Press, 1998), 198–99.

concentration coefficient is the ratio of the area between the diagonal and the Lorenz curve to the total area below the diagonal. For a perfectly equal distribution, the Gini coefficient is zero. The size of the Gini coefficient is tied to the concavity of the Lorenz curve—the greater the concavity, the greater the coefficient. The coefficient, however, is basically an average and does not tell anything about the extent to which inequality of distribution may be marked in various segments of the income distribution.

Another measure of income inequality is to compare the shares of total income earned by different quintiles in a country—the share received by the poorest 20 percent and that received by the top 20 percent. Perfect equality in the distribution of income would mean that each quintile would receive 20 percent of the income, and the quintile ratio between the top and bottom quintiles would be 1. The larger the ratio, the greater the amount of income inequality.

$$\text{Quintile Ratio} = \frac{\text{Percentage of income received by the highest 20 percent}}{\text{Percentage of income received by the bottom 20 percent}}$$

explanation

Rationale for Income Inequality

The primary rationale for income inequality in a capitalist economy is economic motivation, which means that individuals are usually motivated by the desire for monetary gain in their economic activities. That is, individuals attempt to follow their economic self-interest and try to acquire as many goods as possible for themselves, without much regard for the effects of their actions on other people. The

http://

Global income data can be found at another Yardeni site, www.yardeni.com/country.html.

desire for gain is supposed to make people work harder and longer than any other motive that could be substituted for it. Monetary gain also can be tied to such factors as the desire for power and prestige, which can be reflected in private property ownership and freedom of enterprise. Income inequality is also assumed to result in efficient resource allocation, in that people are pulled into those occupations for which the demand is the highest.

The famous baseball player Babe Ruth was once asked if he deserved a salary three times greater than that of the president of the United States. His answer was that people come to see him play baseball, not to see him be president. Today, many athletes, movie stars, and musicians make at least ten times the amount paid to the president of the United States. The chief executives of many American firms make from forty to two hundred times as much as the average American worker. For whatever it is worth, the United States leads the world in the number of billionaires (it used to be millionaires) with Bill Gates, the founder of Microsoft, reportedly the world's richest person.[6]

The Luxembourg Income Study

A study of income distribution commissioned by the OECD and published in 1995 indicated that the gap between rich and poor in the developed countries grew wider during the 1980s (Table 2-2).[7] The largest increase in the income gap was in the United Kingdom, followed by the United States and Australia. There was a parallel increase in inequality of earnings in most countries due to the varying numbers of working women, the extent of self-employment, and increased early retirement. On the average, the poorest 20 percent of households paid less than 5 percent of all direct taxes in the countries included in the study, while the richest 20 percent paid 50 percent of all direct taxes. Income transfers provided 30 percent of the median income to the poorest 20 percent in Belgium, the Netherlands, and Sweden compared to 14 percent of median income to the poorest 20 percent in the United States. The United States had the most unequal distribution of income, while Finland had the most equal.

SAVING AND CAPITAL FORMATION UNDER CAPITALISM

In a capitalistic system, large amounts of savings are made by individuals on the basis of the relationship between interest rates and other prices. The necessary condition for such savings is that the interest rate be sufficient to overcome the time preference of the savers. Time preference is the desire to consume income in the present as opposed to sometime in the future. A certain amount of savings, however, is independent of the interest rate. Some savings are made to provide for certain financial emergencies or to obtain the power an accumulation of income can bring. People with very large incomes may save almost automatically because of the difficulties involved in finding enough consumption uses for their incomes.[8] Other savings, such as those that result when corporations retain their earnings

Country	Poor[1]	Rich[2]	Ratio of Rich to Poor
Finland, 1987	59	153	2.59
Sweden, 1987	56	152	2.72
Belgium, 1987	59	163	2.79
Netherlands, 1987	62	175	2.85
Norway, 1987	55	162	2.93
Germany, 1984	57	170	2.98
Switzerland, 1982	54	184	3.43
France, 1984	55	193	3.48
United Kingdom, 1986	51	194	3.79
Australia, 1985	47	187	4.01
Canada, 1987	46	184	4.02
Italy, 1986	49	198	4.05
Ireland, 1987	50	209	4.23
United States, 1986	35	206	5.94

TABLE 2-2
The Gap between the Incomes of Rich and Poor Individuals (percentage of median income in each country)

[1]*Relative income for individuals that are poorer than 90 percent of the individuals in the country and more affluent than 10 percent of the individuals, expressed as a percentage of national median income.*
[2]*Relative income for individuals that are more affluent than 90 percent of the individuals in the country and poorer than 10 percent of the individuals, expressed as a percentage of national median income.*

Source: OECD, *Income Distribution in OECD Countries* (Paris: OECD, 1995), 155.

instead of paying dividends to stockholders, do not depend on the voluntary decisions of the individuals (stockholders) whose earnings are being saved. Finally, there may be forced savings in the form of taxes that government may use directly or indirectly for capital purposes.

The use of capital goods in production clearly involves the existence of savings. Savings are translated into investment in a capitalist system through the market mechanism of supply and demand, with interest rates performing an allocative function. To be able to afford to pay interest on a loan and ultimately to repay the principal, the borrower must be able to put the funds to good use. This tends to exclude less productive uses and thus rations savings to more productive uses.

Under capitalism, saving and investment are carried out in large part by different sets of people for different reasons. Investment is the purchase of capital goods and as such is undertaken largely by businesses. The act of saving is undertaken by both individuals and businesses. With large numbers of scattered savers and borrowers who want to obtain funds for investment purposes, there is clearly a need for some type of intermediary or go-between to bring the savers and borrowers together. This function is performed to a large extent by commercial and investment banks that are privately owned and operated for a profit. These banks underwrite securities issues for governmental units as well as businesses. The investment bankers bring together the business and governmental units that desire short- and long-term funds and the individuals and institutions that have these funds to invest.

MODIFICATIONS OF PURE CAPITALISM

Various elements have combined over time to transform pure market capitalism into what might be called "state-guided" capitalism. In fact, the term *mixed economic system* is used in later chapters to describe countries that were at one time purely capitalistic. Part of this transformation has been the development of the welfare state, which resulted from the extremely unequal distribution of income that developed during the Industrial Revolution. A growing concentration of economic power in the hands of a few people created extremes of wealth and poverty. In the United States during the 1890s, for example, the department store magnate Marshall Field had an income calculated at $600 per hour; his sales clerks, earning salaries of $3 to $5 a week, had to work three to five years to earn that amount.[9] Working conditions for most workers in the Western industrial world were deplorable: The twelve-hour workday and seven-day workweek were not uncommon. There were no child labor laws; children of 8 and even younger worked in the coal mines and textile mills in the United States and England.

Government and the Decline of Laissez-Faire

Government has always played some role in Western society, even during the zenith of capitalism. In the historical development of the United States, government policy was primarily a mixture of measures that provided equality of opportunity for the common man, such as public education, and generous favors for those who knew how to help themselves, such as railroad and canal builders. Tariffs were enacted to protect American business firms from foreign competition. In France, where state participation in the economy had always been important, much of the railroad system was state owned by the 1850s, and the state also had a monopoly over the sale of such products as alcohol, tobacco, and tea. State ownership of certain industries also existed in Prussia.

The Depression of the 1930s was probably the catalyst for increasing the role of government. On the basis of experience during the Depression, organized labor, farmers, business firms, and consumer groups turned to government for assistance in improving their incomes and ensuring economic security. The satisfaction of these demands made for a new concept of government. An increase in the power of the state has become the central fact of modern Western society. Crucial decisions about production and distribution have come to be made through the political process rather than through the marketplace.

Restrictions on Competition

firms= corporation .

Competition is one of the basic institutions of capitalism. Its justification, like that of other institutions, is found in the notion that it contributes to the social welfare. It is a regulator of economic activity and is thought to maximize productivity, prevent excessive concentration of economic power, and protect consumer interests. *Competition* may be used to describe the economic structure of a nation, applicable to all economic units—individuals, farmers, and business firms. Economic success goes to efficiently operated firms, and failure eliminates inefficiently and wastefully operated firms. The impersonal market system does not lock in products or skills that have become obsolete and therefore nonproductive.

But competition is a hard taskmaster, for there are losers as well as winners. Since losers don't think they should lose, they take action to prevent losing and thus the rules of the game are altered. The market system has been changed in many ways by government action to prevent or cushion the effects of losing. Through subsidies and restraints on foreign competition, uneconomic production methods and job skills have been maintained by governmental intervention.

Business firms have formed various combinations, cartels, trusts, and holding companies to prevent competition. Workers have joined labor unions to avoid individual competition, and obsolete job skills have been preserved. In the United States, obsolete jobs have been preserved in the construction industry and elsewhere through federal building codes, and inefficient firms, such as Chrysler, have received financial support from the government when otherwise they would have been eliminated by the forces of competition.

Antitrust Laws *(regulate business monopoly)*

Antitrust laws are based on two premises. The first is the English common law as it evolved through court decisions over a long time. In general these decisions held that restraint on trade or commerce is not in the public interest. The second premise is the belief that competition is an effective regulator of most markets and, with a few exceptions, that monopolistic practices can be stopped by competition. This premise is based on the economic theory espousing pure or perfect competition as the ideal, since according to the theory competition forces firms to be efficient, cut costs, and receive no more than normal profits. The theory assumes that in a state of pure or perfect competition, economic decisions will be made by prices and price changes, both of which are determined by the market forces of supply and demand.

Social Regulation

Social regulation came into being because the market mechanism has not been effective in eliminating certain social problems. In a market economy, the price mechanism gives people no opportunity to bid against the production and sale of certain commodities and services that they regard as undesirable. Many people would be happier if they could prevent the production and sale of, for instance, tobacco products or the emission of noxious fumes from a chemical plant, and would pay the price if given the opportunity to do so. But there seems to be no way the market price mechanism can take these negative preferences into consideration, except through government controls on the output of goods deemed deleterious to the public interest. A prime example is government laws protecting the environment.

Social Security

Perhaps as a reflection of a belief in individual responsibility, the United States lagged well behind other countries in adopting a program of social insurance that would protect individuals against the misfortunes of life such as unemployment, illness, and old age. Germany, for example, had a comprehensive program of health insurance in place before the end of the last century. Insurance against unemployment in the United States was provided by the Social Security Act of 1935. It also provided for a system of annuities for workers over sixty-five years of age who had contributed regularly to the building up of a fund for this purpose. The reason for the passage of the Social Security Act was the Depression, which had no parallel in American history. Prolonged unemployment became the norm, and individual responsibility didn't mean much when there were no jobs to be had.

A COMPARISON OF CAPITALIST SYSTEMS: ONE APPROACH

Since capitalism has become the sine qua non of the world's present and future existence, what is left to compare? The answer is to compare various types of capitalism. One way in which capitalism can be compared is by distinguishing between individualistic Anglo-Saxon capitalism and communitarian European and Japanese capitalism. This two-pronged comparison, which is based on a distinction made by George C. Lodge, forms part of the foundation of Lester Thurow's *Head to Head: The Coming Economic Battle among Japan, Europe, and America.*[10] The Anglo-Saxon variant of capitalism dominated the last two centuries, with the United Kingdom dominant in the nineteenth century and the United States in the twentieth century. Who, then, will dominate the twenty-first century? According to Thurow, it will be the communitarian capitalism of Europe.

Individualistic Capitalism

Individualistic capitalism is associated with the writings of John Locke and Adam Smith. It was Locke who developed the argument that the right to govern rests in the hands of the governed, not the governor. Prior to Locke, it had been assumed that the king, not the people, had the right to rule. According to Locke, the individual is a fulcrum of society and has certain inalienable rights, including the right to own property.[11] According to Adam Smith, the individual, if permitted to pursue his or her self-interest, will promote the well-being of all. This will not result from charitable motives, but from the inexorable logic of the free market—the "invisible hand." Stated simply, if all people are motivated to work at full capacity, whether as laborers, artisans, or executives, the net supply of goods and services available for consumption by all will be increased.

According to Thurow, individualism in the United States and other Anglo-Saxon countries takes a number of forms: large income differentials, brilliant entrepreneurs such as Bill Gates, the founder of Microsoft and the richest man in America, and short-term profit maximization. In the tradition of individualism each person is responsible for his or her own personal success. Life is a competitive struggle where the fit survive and those who are unfit do not. Individuals owe no particular loyalty to a company; they are free to leave for higher-paying jobs. Conversely, companies feel no loyalty to their employees; they can be laid off when times are bad or for that matter when times are relatively good, as witnessed by the downsizing of many American corporations. Neither employers nor employees owe each other anything.

Communitarian Capitalism

The term *communitarian* has a number of connotations, but basically it means deriving satisfaction from being part of a group process as opposed to functioning as an individual. The role of the state is greatly expanded under communitarian ideology. It plays roles in stimulating economic growth and providing social welfare programs, and it also is involved in public investment expenditures for such things as job training. There is less job changing and more loyalty to the employer in communitarian capitalistic countries. Employers think more in terms of job retraining and teamwork. Companies think in terms of long-term strategies and often function as part of a group. Close cooperation between companies and the government can also exist. Communitarian capitalism is the result of different cultural and historical developments in Europe and Japan, where governments often as a matter of necessity played an important role in economic development.[12]

Germany and Japan are examples of communitarian capitalist countries. In Germany the state has played an important role since the time of Bismarck. There is codetermination between labor and management, with labor representatives sitting on the boards of directors of German companies. German banks are major shareholders in German companies. Job training is also the responsibility of companies and the government. In Japan the overwhelming emphasis is on the group and one's responsibility to it. Companies (including banks) are often part of a group of companies. Employees are loyal to a company, and there is very little job switching. There is cooperation between business and government and between business and labor. Business thinks in terms of long-term objectives as opposed to short-term profit maximization.

A Comparison of Capitalist Systems: An Alternative Approach

Although there is some validity to comparing capitalist systems according to the previously discussed two-pronged approach, the author prefers a second approach, which divides capitalist systems into three types. The first is the relatively free market system of the United States, where government intervention in the economy has been more regulatory than distributive.[13] The second is the social market capitalism of Europe, where governments play a major role in income distribution through elaborate social expenditure programs. The final type is the state-directed capitalism of Japan and other East Asian countries. The characteristics of each of these three types of capitalism are presented in the following sections.

U.S. Market Capitalism

Although there is no such thing as a completely free market economy, the United States comes closer than either Europe or Japan to this form of economy. The role of the federal government is smaller than in other capitalist countries. Taxes and government spending in relation to gross national product (GNP) are lower in the United States than in other countries. There is also very little state ownership of industry.[14] However, some government intervention is necessary in even the freest type of economic system. The very atmosphere for the conduct of business is created by the ability of the government to establish and maintain private property, freedom of enterprise, money and credit, and a system of civil laws for adjudicating the private disputes of individuals. Such institutions make possible an elaborate system of private planning in which individuals, rather than government, organize and direct the production of goods and services in response to the desires of consumers.

Social Market Capitalism

Social market capitalism, as represented in Germany and other Western European countries, includes an elaborate system of social welfare programs ranging from national health insurance to family allowances. In these countries a higher percentage of total government expenditures than in the United States go toward transfer payments, which are payments such as unemployment compensation or retirement benefits to individuals who provide no goods or services in exchange. Corporations in these countries are far more circumscribed in their treatment of employees. In Germany codetermination gives workers the right to choose members who will sit on the boards of directors of many German companies. The role of government in Germany and other Western European countries is pervasive in several ways—through ownership of shares in private companies, subsidies to industries, and partial ownership of industries. There is also some reliance on economic planning of the indicative type.[15]

State-Directed Capitalism

This variant of capitalism exists in Japan and other East Asian countries. There is a far closer relationship between government and business in such countries as Japan and South Korea than in the United States and Europe, particularly in the allocation of capital and the role of industrial policy in the economy. Cultural differences between Japan and the United States and Europe make for a much more group-oriented form of capitalism based on consensus among various Japanese groups than in the more individualistic capitalism of the West. There is no welfare state in Japan; the function of social provider falls to business firms. There is indicative planning, but it is based in government consensus with other groups. Finally, there is an industrial policy in which industry representatives working with the Japanese Ministry of International Trade and Industry (MITI) discuss strategies regarding where the economy should be going and key industries are targeted for capital allocation.

Public Sector Expenditures and Taxation

These three types of capitalism can be compared on the basis of the extent of government involvement in the economy. Two ways to compare this involvement are through the relationships of government expenditures to GNP and of taxes to GNP. The relationship of expenditures to GNP indicates the extent to which resources have been diverted from private to public use. These expenditures involve use of transfer payments as an instrument for the redistribution of income from one group to another. They include family allowances, old-age pensions, and unemployment compensation. Such expenditures also involve the provision of a broad array of goods, such as roads. On the other hand, the relationship of taxes to GNP indicates the extent to which governments have control over economic resources and the degree to which the cost of public activity is borne by the tax-payers of a nation.

CAPITALISM AND DEMOCRACY

Francis Fukuyama wrote a book called *The End of History and the Last Man*.[16] By the "end of history" he meant that an ideal economic and political system was now in place for the present and future. Communism was a thing of the past and there is no place else to go. He maintains that the free market has clearly emerged as the most efficient system for producing and distributing goods and that Western democratic ideals have triumphed. According to Fukuyama, the human race has one common destiny, democracy. This destiny began with the French Revolution and its ideals of liberty and equality, which Napoleon exported to other parts of Europe, and ended with the victory of the democratic state. In his view there will be minor problems here and there, such as the rise of religious fundamentalism and ethnic and national tensions, but they will disappear over time.

Perhaps because various noncapitalistic systems have usually operated under dictatorial governments, there is a tendency to make capitalism synonymous with democracy. Actually, the government of a capitalist economic system does not have to be democratic in the strict sense of the word. In a large and heavily populated capitalist system like the United States, it would be impossible for all citizens to participate in the democratic process as they might have in the old New England town meetings. It is also doubtful whether the citizens of a capitalist economy could participate in any case since they differ so much as individuals with respect to such matters as wealth and income, economic opportunities, education, and social status.

Democracy is rising throughout the world. In Latin America, where dictators ruled many countries, there are now free elections. In Mexico, where one political party has ruled for almost seventy years, free elections have occurred and representatives of other political parties hold either state or municipal government offices. The former satellite countries of the Soviet bloc—Poland, Hungary, the Czech Republic, the Slovak Republic, Bulgaria, and Romania—have political parties and free elections. Even the Russian Federation and the other countries that comprise the former Soviet Union have achieved some semblance of democracy. But democracy is fragile, and in an increasingly interdependent world, the United States has a growing stake in how other countries govern—or misgovern—themselves.

SUMMARY

Capitalism is an economic system characterized by a set of institutional arrangements. The centerpiece of capitalism is a freely competitive market where buyers satisfy their wants and sellers supply those wants to make a profit. The price mechanism determines resource allocation, and freedom of enterprise and private property ownership provide incentives to save and produce. Individualism is also at the core of the capitalist or free market ideology. It was assumed by Adam Smith and others that people were rational and would try at all times to promote their own personal welfare. The individual, in promoting his or her self-interest, was viewed as promoting the interest of society at the same time.

The advanced capitalist countries of today have modified the institutions of capitalism. In the operation of capitalist economies, problems arose that seemed impossible for private individuals to solve. Their impact brought a demand for government intervention. As a result, government intervention and regulation are common features of life under capitalism. Consumers are not left to depend solely on competition to furnish them with foods and drugs of acceptable quality and purity; there are laws that provide certain standards in these matters. Capitalistic societies have never been willing to extend complete freedom of enterprise to any individual. That is, it has always been recognized that an individual, in selecting the most profitable field of activity, might well choose something that would be clearly antisocial. In such cases, government has not hesitated to step in with restrictions. But government has also altered the economic institutions of capitalism through, for example, subsidies to farmers and protection of inefficient business firms from competition.

QUESTIONS FOR DISCUSSION

1. In which ways can different types of capitalism be compared?
2. What is the function of profit in a market economy?
3. What is the function of prices in a market economy?
4. How are incomes distributed in a market economy?
5. It can be said that a true market economy exists in the United States. Do you agree?
6. How can the enormous differences in income in the United States be justified? Are these differences consistent with democracy?
7. Is it possible to have capitalism without democracy?
8. Do you agree with Francis Fukuyama that capitalism and democracy represent the end of history?

RECOMMENDED READINGS

Friedman, Milton, *Capitalism and Freedom*. Chicago: University of Chicago Press, 1962.
Fukuyama, Francis. *The End of History and the Last Man*. New York: Basic Books, 1998.
"The Future of the State." *The Economist*, A Survey of the World, September 20, 1997, pp. 5–20.
Landes, David S. *The Wealth and Poverty of Nations*. New York: Norton, 1998.
Okun, Arthur M. *Equality and Efficiency*. Washington, D.C.: The Brookings Institution, 1975.
Smith, Adam. *An Inquiry into the Nature and Causes of the Wealth of Nations* [1776]. Indianapolis: Liberty classics, 1981.
Thurow, Lester. *Head to Head: The Coming Economic Battle among Japan, Europe, and America*. New York: Morrow, 1992.
The World Bank. *World Development Report 1997. The State in a Changing World*. New York: Oxford University Press, 1997.

ENDNOTES

1.   For example, as student enrollment in a college town increases, the demand for housing will increase. Townspeople will be willing to rent more rooms, and existing housing will be fully used. Rents will increase, and someone will decide to build apartments for students. The supply of housing will increase as available resources are shifted into housing construction.

2.   Adam Smith, *An Inquiry into the Nature and Causes of the Wealth of Nations* [1776] (Indianapolis: Liberty Classics, 1981), 660.

3.   Richard H. Tawney, *Religion and the Rise of Capitalism: A Historical Study* (New York: Harcourt, Brace, and World, 1926); and Max Weber, *The Protestant Ethic and the Spirit of Capitalism* (New York: Scribner's, 1930).

4.   See, for example, Matthew Josephson, *The Robber Barons* (New York: Harcourt, Brace, and World, 1934); and Ida M. Tarbell, *The History of the Standard Oil Company* (New York: McClure, Phillips, 1904).

5.   The term *laissez-faire* originated in the eighteenth century. It was a reaction to the stringent French government restrictions imposed on all phases of economic activity.

6.   Bill Gates was worth $100 billion in 1999. His wealth was greater than that of the bottom half of all American families together.

7.   Organization for Economic Cooperation and Development, Income Distribution in OECD Countries (Paris: OECD, 1995).

8.   However, there seem to be endless ways to spend money. Savings do not necessarily rise for those in the high-income categories, nor do charitable contributions.

9.   Otto Bettman, *The Good Old Days—They Were Terrible* (New York: Random House, 1974), 67.

10.   George C. Lodge, *The New American Ideology* (New York: Knopf, 1975). Lester Thurow, *Head to Head: The Coming Economic Battle among Japan, Europe, and America* (New York: Morrow, 1992). The battle never occurred.

11.   John Locke, *Second Treatise on Civil Government, 1681*. Government comes into existence, said Locke, because of property. If there is no property, there is no need for government.

12.   An example is Germany. Massive government intervention occurred prior to World War I when Germany was trying to catch up with England as a major economic power.

13.   Examples are antitrust laws, environmental laws, and consumer protection laws.

14.   Privatization has occurred throughout the world in the 1990s. Diverse countries such as the Russian Federation, Poland, Hungary, Germany, Argentina, and Mexico have privatized state-owned industries.

15.   France has relied on indicative economic planning since the end of World War II. Although most of French industry is privately owned, the government developed four- or five-year plans to indicate what economic areas should be developed and credit was allocated accordingly.

16.   Francis Fukuyama, *The End of History and the Last Man* (New York: Basic Books, 1991).

CHAPTER 3

The United States

Based on the individualistic-communitarian approach to capitalism, the United States would score high on individualism.[1] Along with Canada, Australia, the United Kingdom, and New Zealand, the United States has an Anglo-Saxon heritage and a part of that heritage is the degree to which people prefer to act as individuals rather than members of a group. Four of the five countries mentioned were colonies of England and were settled by people willing to strike out on their own to achieve success. There are thousands of entrepreneurs in the United States who want to become their boss. Some become very wealthy; most do not. With individualism comes competitiveness and the United States produces a society that is competitive in everything it does.

When capitalist systems are classified on the basis of market capitalism, Euro-capitalism (social market capitalism), and state-directed capitalism, the United States is an example of market capitalism. Again, its system is a product of its culture and history. The United States had a quick start in the Industrial Revolution of the nineteenth century; it did not have to play catch-up with other nations as Japan did, and it was separated by the Atlantic Ocean from European wars. Government had a limited role in the development of the United States.[2] The Anglo-Saxon view of government was that it should protect private property rights and be responsible for national defense. When it came to resource allocation, the market was superior.

Even though the United States, Japan, and Germany may differ considerably in their cultures and economic systems, they possess the requisites for success presented in both the books by Landes and Porter. In the book by Landes, *The Wealth and Poverty of Nations*, climate and culture determine economic success.[3] The three countries possess a favorable geography, which has created a social and political form of organization conducive to growth. In fact, the three countries produce 50 percent of the world's GNP and are responsible for 30 percent of world trade. In *The Competitive Advantage of Nations*, Porter identified the fundamental determinants of national competitive advantage and how they work together as a system.[4] Companies can extend a nation's competitive advantage over other nations provided that four broad attributes of a nation are available. These attributes are: factor conditions, demand conditions, related and supporting industries, and firm strategy, structure, and rivalry. The countries he deems successful—including the United States, Japan, and Germany—are all located in a temperate climate.[5]

http://

For economic comparisons of these three countries, go to ww.dismal.com/economy/economy.stm.

U.S. MARKET CAPITALISM

There never has been a purely free market economy in the United States. From its beginning in 1787, the federal government has been involved in promoting manufacturing, and it passed tariff laws to protect U.S. business interests. Subsidies were used to build canals, roads, and various forms of transportation from which private enterprises benefited greatly. As industrialization and business concentration increased during the latter part of the nineteenth century, the federal government passed laws to regulate specific sectors of business—for example, railroads—or to control various forms of anticompetitive business practices, such as price fixing and division of markets. Government participation in the U.S. economy increased during the Depression of the 1930s, when minimum wage and social security legislation were passed, and regulatory agencies were created to regulate banks, communications, and the securities market. During the 1960s and early 1970s government regulation was extended to cover consumer product safety, the employment of women and minorities, the environment, and occupational safety.

U.S. Capitalism and Culture

http://

Compare some cultural aspects of Japan with the United States by visiting www.mofa.go.jp/j_info/index.html.

U.S. capitalism is a reflection of U.S. culture, just as Japanese capitalism is a reflection of Japanese culture. In the United States, individualism is a carryover from the last century, when the West opened to settlement and large numbers of immigrants entered the United States. Most of these immigrants came from European countries, fleeing government oppression or economic hardship. The United States was viewed as a land of opportunity where an individual had an opportunity to get ahead through his or her own efforts and each generation would have the opportunity to be better off financially. The West provided opportunities for immigrants, particularly in agriculture, and this is where individualism flourished. It was the individual against the elements of nature, where the fittest survived and the weakest fell by the wayside.[6]

A second facet of U.S. capitalism is the emphasis placed on wealth and consumption. Role models for wealth accumulation date back as far as the nineteenth century, when the new industrial aristocracy was made up of wealthy entrepreneurs and business leaders whom some called "robber barons." The prototypical self-made capitalists were millionaires John D. Rockefeller and Andrew Carnegie. It was the wealthy who often set consumption standards that others tried to follow. It is interesting to note that the wealthy in the United States have never stirred up the class resentment that has existed in more class-conscious societies such as England. Microsoft chairman and CEO Bill Gates, the richest billionaire in the United States, inspires admiration and the belief that anyone with a good idea can succeed in the United States.

Competition.   Whether in business or sports, the United States is a competitive society. Its justification for this emphasis on competition is that it contributes to the welfare of society. When the industries and markets of an economy are organized competitively, certain supposedly desirable things will happen. First, competition is supposed to provide consumers with a wider variety of choices at lower prices. It is supposed to encourage innovation—the firm that builds a better mousetrap than its competitor succeeds. Finally, competition should bring about efficiency in the operation of business and industry by granting economic success to those firms efficiently operated and by relentlessly eliminating those inefficiently operated.

Government Intervention in the U.S. Economy

Government intervention in the U.S. economy has occurred for several reasons:

1. When there is a breakdown in competitive market forces, monopoly, oligopoly, and otherwise imperfectly competitive market structures cause inefficient resource allocation and socially undesirable market performances. Antitrust policies are designed to deal with industry conduct, such as price fixing, as well as aspects of industry structure that might foster monopolistic powers.
2. In a market economy, the price mechanism gives people no opportunity to bid against the production and the sale of commodities and services they regard as undesirable. Many people would be happier if they didn't have to breathe cigarette smoke in public places or noxious fumes from a chemical plant, but there is no way the marketplace can take these negative preferences into account, except through government control.
3. Technological advances have created market externalities. The mass production of automobiles had an enormous impact on the development of the U.S. economy during the early part of the twentieth century. Thousands of jobs

were created not only in the automobile industry but also in related industries, such as steel and rubber. However, the automobile became the prime source of air pollution. Air transportation also became an important form of transportation, and airplanes also create noise pollution.

4. Unemployment compensation and social security pensions were introduced into the United States later than in most other industrial countries. The rationale is to provide a measure of protection for persons who fall through the cracks through no fault of their own. It should be noted, however, that social welfare programs are by no means as comprehensive in the United States as in other countries. The provision of affordable health insurance has become a major domestic issue in the United States. Some 37 million Americans are without any form of health insurance.

Historical Background of Government Intervention

Government intervention in the U.S. economy can be divided into three time periods. The first lasted from 1870 to 1930. During this time, government intervention was essentially microeconomic and took the form of laws to regulate railroads and curb the power of monopolies. Only when the competitive, self-adjusting mechanism broke down did the government undertake the correct its most serious failings. The first laws to protect consumers were passed during this period. Laws regulating railroads and monopolies usually were initiated by state governments and only later adopted by the federal government. Laws were also passed to improve the working conditions of laborers, and taxes were imposed on income and wealth. But, for the most part, the laws directed against industrial concentration and the accumulation of wealth did not have much effect.

The second period, the Depression of the 1930s, marked the end of laissez-faire and the beginning of an increased role of government in the U.S. economy. During this time much legislation was passed to stimulate business recovery. Because people believed that certain defects in the business system were at least partly responsible for causing the Depression, laws were enacted regulating business in a number of areas, including banking, transportation, electric power, and the securities market. The Fair Labor Standards Act of 1938 enacted minimum wages and maximum hours for workers engaged in interstate commerce. The Social Security Act of 1935 provided for federal pensions for persons over 65 years of age. The federal debt, which was around $2 billion in 1929, had increased to $40 billion by 1939.[7] Mechanisms for the government's macrointervention began to be put in place during the 1930s and were consolidated with the passage of the Employment Act of 1946.

The third period of government intervention in the U.S. economy extended roughly from 1964 to 1975. This intervention was more broad-based in that it did not deal with specific economic issues such as monopoly power, pricing, industrial concentration, corporate economic power and its use and abuses, or unemployment. Instead, its focus was on attaining certain social goals such as environmental protection, consumer protection, employment of women and minorities, job safety, and so forth. These goals were associated with a change in societal values that has been characterized by such terms as *rising entitlements* and *quality of life*. Examples of government legislation during this period include the Civil Rights Act of 1964, the Clean Air Act of 1970, the Consumer Product Safety Act of 1972, and the Age Discrimination in Employment Act of 1967. These and similar laws created a new form of government regulation that has become comprehensive in its control over business activity.[8]

PRIVATE ENTERPRISE

Private enterprise is one of the basic institutions of the U.S. economy. There is very little government ownership of industry. There is freedom of ingress and egress in the marketplace. Anyone with an idea and capital is free to start his or her own business. There is the right to succeed and the right to fail. The United States consists of some very large corporations and hundreds of thousands of smaller ones.

Large Corporations

The concentration of many industries in the hands of a few firms is a fact of life in the United States and other industrial nations. The trend toward industrial concentration in this country began in the nineteenth century, when many industries came to be dominated by large firms. In the 1920s corporate largeness was stimulated by changes that were occurring in the economy, in particular the mass production of automobiles. Size came to have an advantage from the standpoint of using modern marketing and production methods. World War II also contributed to the trend toward largeness. Large corporations produced the airplanes and tanks used by the United States and its allies in the war. During the 1960s and 1970s the trend increased, facilitated by a new type of merger called the conglomerate merger, which represented a union of disparate companies.

Table 3-1 presents a comparison of the assets of large corporations to the total assets of the industries they represent. In the table corporations with assets of $250 million or more are considered to be large corporations.

Large corporations may also be global corporations. As modern technology has increased, it has become an internationally marketable commodity because it is readily transferable through the operations of global corporations. This has resulted in the globalization of production. Coupled with the globalization of production is the globalization of financial markets. The pool of saving is worldwide, and intermediaries that mobilize savings for investment know no international boundaries because they have the technological sophistication to access markets worldwide. Finally, there has been a globalization of markets for goods and services. Thus, the global corporation—United States and foreign—does business all over the world and has no particular allegiance to a given country.

http://

A variety of economic information can be found at www.census.gov.

TABLE 3-1 *A Comparison of the Assets of Large Corporations to Total Corporate Assets by Industries, 1995 ($millions)*

Industry	Total	Asset-Sized Class ($250 million and over)
Agriculture, forestry, and fishing	86,299	10,888
Mining	268,690	212,063
Construction	265,813	43,677
Manufacturing	4,941,073	4,214,995
Transportation and public utilities	1,903,214	1,733,237
Wholesale and retail trade	1,919,718	1,081,317
Finance, insurance	15,677,267	14,074,066
Services	950,737	502,757

Source: U.S. Department of Commerce, Bureau of the Census, *Statistical Abstract of the United States, 1998* (Washington, D.C.: U.S. Government Printing Office, 1998), 546.

Small Enterprises

There are also thousands of small and medium-size business firms that provide employment for the majority of U.S. workers as well as much of the innovation necessary for international competitiveness. The number of small companies is increasing, in part as a result of executive downsizing by many large corporations.[9] Former executives create new companies that find a niche in areas once dominated by corporate giants. In addition, small family-owned companies use new technology to carve out market niches in many industries, exploiting the latest technology, employing highly skilled workers, and utilizing sophisticated managerial and financial techniques. Moreover, as the United States becomes a more service-oriented economy, opportunities have increased for consulting firms. More people are also self-employed. A breakdown of employees and payrolls by employment size is presented in Table 3-2.

UNIONS

Unions provide the third part of the business, government, and union triumvirate. Workers in the United States and other capitalist countries have not been content to rely solely on market forces to determine their economic status. Instead, they have banded together to form labor unions for the purpose of bargaining collectively with employers. The worker's need for a job is not reduced, but under collective bargaining an employer must deal with labor as a unit, not as separate individuals. Labor unions vary in strength and importance in the world's major industrial nations. In Germany they participate in their employer's decision-making process through the policy of codetermination; in England they are directly involved in the political process through membership in the British Labor Party.

Unions in the United States hit their peak in terms of membership during the 1940s and 1950s and then began a slow decline as the country shifted from a goods-producing to a service society. This shift represents a change in the type of

Employment Size Employers (thousands)		TABLE 3-2
Employees, total	100,335	*Employees and Payrolls by*
Under 20 employees	25,785	*Employment Size Firms,*
20 to 99 employees	29,202	*1995*
100 to 499 employees	25,364	
500 to 999 employees	7,021	
1,000 or more employees	12,962	
Annual Payroll ($billions)		
Total	2,666	
Under 20 employees	608	
20 to 99 employees	696	
100 to 499 employees	675	
500 to 999 employees	219	
1,000 or more employees	467	

Source: U.S. Department of Commerce, Bureau of the Census, *Statistical Abstract of the United States 1998* (Washington, D.C.: U.S. Government Printing Office, 1998), 547.

work people do, from physically intensive labor to knowledge-intensive labor. In 1945 almost half the American labor force was employed in manufacturing jobs; in 1997 the number of manufacturing jobs was around 17 percent. Conversely, the number of persons employed in service-producing jobs has doubled since 1945. The majority of jobs today are knowledge-based white-collar jobs, not blue-collar jobs, and white-collar workers tend to identify more with management than with labor. Many union jobs were lost in the auto and steel industries, which laid off more than a million blue-collar workers during the 1980s as foreign competition began to erode U.S. markets. This downsizing of employment has continued into the 1990s.

GOVERNMENT

For many years, the idea persisted that the government of a capitalistic system should follow a policy of laissez-faire. This idea was based on the concept of natural liberty. Each individual was assumed to be a more or less rational human being and a better judge of his or her own interest than any government could be. In the natural order of things, people's pursuit of their own interests would inadvertently benefit others as well. Government had a limited role to play in society. Its activities should be limited to the performance of a few general functions. Examples of those functions would be the administration of justice, the construction of public works, and the protection of citizens from foreign invasion.

It has been realized, however, that the institutions of capitalism are man-made, not the product of some natural order. In the operation of a capitalist economy, economic and social problems arise that do not lend themselves to ready solutions by private individuals. U.S. government intervention in the American

TABLE 3-3
Estimated Federal Government Expenditures—Fiscal Year 1998 ($ billions)

Category	Outlays
Discretionary	
National defense	260
International	19
Domestic	268
Total discretionary	547
Mandatory	
Social Security	
Medicare	
Medicaid	
Other means-tested entitlements	
Except Medicaid	
Total	946
Less offsetting receipts	56
Total mandatory	890
Net interest	250
Total outlays	1,687
Total revenue	1,567
Deficit	−120

Source: Executive Office of the President, Office of Management and Budget, *A Citizen's Guide to the Federal Budget, Fiscal Year 1998* (Washington, D.C.: 1997), 12.

economy increased the most during the Depression of the 1930s and World War II. Some of the types of government expenditures listed in Table 3-3 reflect this point. Social security, which accounts for the single largest expenditure in the federal budget, is a product of the Depression. It was designed to provide some form of income security for older persons when millions of Americans were out of work. Probably the bulk of veterans' benefits applies to those persons who served during World War II.

Public Finance

http://

Statistics on the federal budget can be seen at www.fedstats.gov/index20.html.

Public finance is an indicator of the extent of government participation in a modified market economy. Taxes serve two purposes: they provide government with a source of revenue, and they can be used to effect a redistribution of income and wealth. The personal income tax is the most important source of income to the federal government, the sales tax is the most important source of income to the states, and local governments rely on property taxation. Government expenditures for goods and services account for around 20 percent of the U.S. GNP and provide a source of demand for many business products, and government transfer payments redistribute income from one economic group to another.

The Composition of Taxes and Expenditures.   The three main sources of revenue to the federal government are individual income taxes, social insurance receipts, and borrowing. The three most important types of government expenditures are direct benefit payments to individuals, national defense, and interest payments on the national debt. The largest component of total federal government payments is social security, which accounts for around 40 percent of total government expenditures. Table 3-4 and Chart 3-1 present a breakdown of federal government revenue by source, and Table 3-3 and Chart 3-2 present a breakdown of federal government expenditures by types.

Source	Amount
Personal income tax	691
Corporate income tax	190
Payroll taxes	558
Excise taxes	61
Estate and gift taxes	19
Customs duties	18
Miscellaneous	30
Total Revenue	1,567

TABLE 3-4
Estimated Federal Government Revenue by Source—Fiscal Year 1998 ($ billions)

Source: Executive Office of the President, Office of Manpower and Budget, *A Citizen's Guide to the Federal Budget, Fiscal Year 1998* (Washington, D.C.: October, 1997), 8.

CHART 3-1 *The Federal Government Dollar—Where It Comes From*

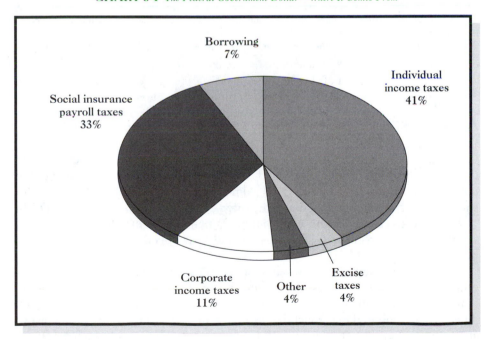

Source: Executive Office of the President, Office of Manpower and Budget, *A Citizen's Guide to the Federal Budget, Fiscal Year 1998* (Washington, D.C.: 1997), 9.

CHART 3-2 *The Federal Government Dollar—Where It Goes*[1]

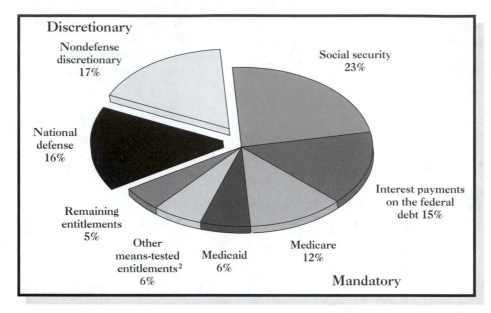

Source: Executive Office of the President, Office of Manpower and Budget, *A Citizen's Guide to the Federal Budget, Fiscal Year 1998* (Washington, D.C.: 1997), 13.
[1]In calculating federal spending, the government deducts collections (revenues) generated by the government's business-like activities, such as fees to national parks. These collections will total an estimated $209 billion in 1998. Without them, spending would total an estimated $1.9 trillion in 1998, not $1.7 trillion.
[2]Means-tested entitlements are those for which eligibility is based on income. The Medicaid program is also a means-tested entitlement.

A COMPARISON OF GOVERNMENT EXPENDITURES BY COUNTRIES

Government expenditures represent a transfer of resources from the private sector of an economy to the public sector, and they also represent the contribution of the government sector to the total gross domestic product (GDP).[10] As Chart 3-3 shows, total government spending amounted to 31 percent of the U.S. GDP in 1996, while private spending contributed 69 percent. The federal government spent about 21 percent of GDP, and state and local governments contributed 10 percent.

However, as Table 3-5 shows, in comparison with other countries, total government expenditures expressed as a percentage of GDP are much smaller in the United States than in other major industrial countries with the exception of Japan. This can be attributed to the fact that income transfer payments in these countries are much higher than they are in the United States. They would include family allowances, free medical care, paid maternity leave, old-age pensions, unemploy-

http://

Good sources of economic statistics are the United Nations at www.un.org and the World Bank at www.worldbank.org.

CHART 3-3 *Government Spending as a Share of GDP, 1996*

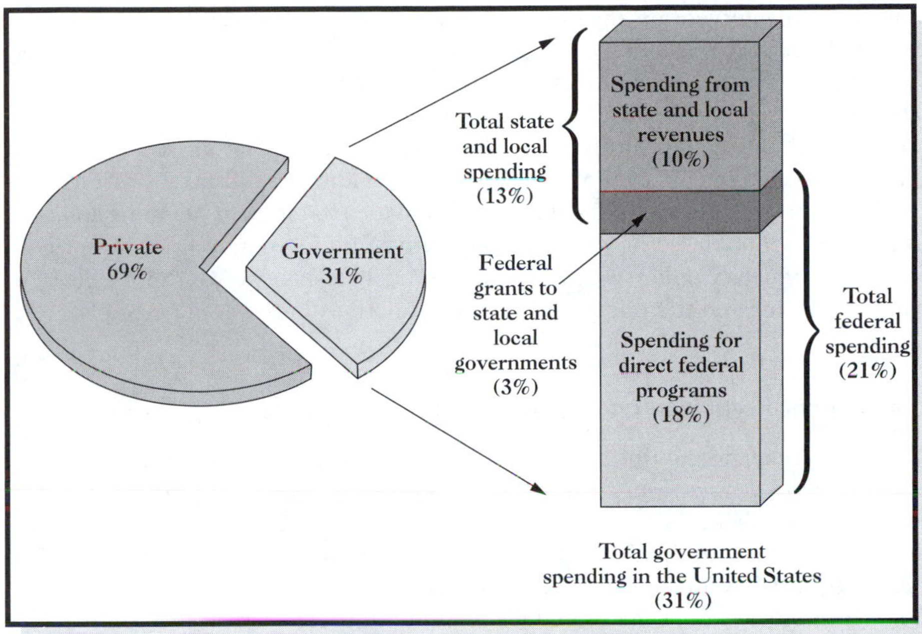

Total government spending accounts for about one-third of the national economy. Federal spending is about two-thirds of this amount, or 21 percent of the GDP.
Source: Executive Office of the President, Office of Manpower and Budget, *A Citizen's Guide to the Federal Budget, Fiscal Year 1998* (Washington, D.C.: 1997), 2.

Country	Percent
Canada	44.7
France	54.5
Germany	49.0
Japan	36.2
Italy	52.9
Sweden	64.7
United Kingdom	41.9
United States	33.3

TABLE 3-5
Government Spending as a Percentage of GDP for Selected Countries, 1996

Source: "A Survey of the World Economy: The Future of the State," *The Economist*, September 20, 1997, p. 8.

ment compensation, free college education, and accident benefits. There is also a reverse side to these expenditures; somebody has to pay for them. Thus, the level of taxation in these countries is much higher than it is in the United States. In such countries as France and Sweden, it is over half of their GDP.

Economic Stabilization Policies

Government intervention includes fiscal and monetary policies that are implemented by its use of taxation and transfer payments, by its purchases of goods and services, and by the Federal Reserve's control of the money supply and interest rates. Fiscal policy refers to the tax and expenditure policies of the federal government.[11] Its objective is to increase or decrease the level of aggregate demand through changes in the level of government expenditures and taxation. The federal budget is the fulcrum of fiscal policy. It provides a system of planning and control over government activities by the executive and legislative branches of government. Monetary policy is used by the Federal Reserve to control the level of national income and the price level through variations in the money supply.

Government Regulation and Control of Business

The regulation and control of business are a second area in which the U.S. government has become firmly entrenched. This became necessary for several reasons, all of which are associated with some failure of the market system. One failure is its inability to furnish individuals or society with a satisfactory means for achieving certain wants, for example, the desire for a clean environment. Initiative for a clean environment therefore falls to public agencies, which use controls that inevitably have a major impact on the operation of business firms. The distribution of income and wealth can be considered a second flaw in the market system. It became apparent that large incomes often accrue to some people not on the basis of their contribution to output but through inherited wealth or the exercise of special privilege.

Antitrust Laws. The rationale for antitrust laws is to promote market competition by preventing the formation of business combinations, such as trusts, that could work against the public welfare. American antitrust laws are encapsulated in the Sherman and Clayton Acts. The Sherman Act prohibits the formation of monopolies and other business combinations that restrain interstate or foreign trade. It also prohibits various anticompetitive business practices such as group boycotts and price fixing. The Clayton Act prohibits mergers whose end result is to substantially lessen competition and prohibits price discrimination whose intent is to ruin competitors. The Clayton Act also restricts the arrangement of interlocking directorates: it provides that no person shall be a director in two or more corporations if they are competitors.[12]

Social Regulation. The government also engages in social regulation of business in such matters as hiring the disabled, occupational safety, consumer protection, environmental protection, and affirmative action. The rationale for social regulation is that the market system does not work to solve such problems as sex and race discrimination, or negative externalities created by rising living standards. For example, as quality-of-life demands increase, there is public pressure for government regulation to provide clean air, clean water, and safe disposal of toxic waste. Expanded definitions of equality give rise to new entitlements, which in turn result in government regulations to provide them. An example is equal employment opportunity.

Government Ownership of Industry

Government ownership of industry is quite limited in the United States, but all levels of government do own and operate government facilities of many kinds. One example is the Tennessee Valley Authority (TVA), a major public enterprise for the production and distribution of public power in the southeastern part of the United States. The TVA was created to erect dams and hydroelectric power plants, to provide electric power, to improve navigation on the Tennessee River, to promote flood control, and to prevent soil erosion. Other government units own local transportation systems and own and operate water, gas, and electricity plants. Government also produces directly or indirectly atomic power and other goods and carries out projects connected with slum clearance and housing.

AN EVALUATION OF THE AMERICAN ECONOMY

The United States dominated the twentieth century, which has been called the American century, and is also expected to dominate the twenty-first century pretty much by default (Table 3-6). It began the twentieth century with a real GDP of $346 billion, and it will end the century with a real GDP of close to $6.5 trillion, based on Maddison's Study of the World Economy, 1820–1992. By comparison, the United Kingdom, which ranked second to the United States with a real GDP of $177 billion in 1900, will finish the century with a real GDP of around $1 trillion. Table 3-7 compares the positions of the United States, Japan, and other major countries at the beginning of the twentieth century. The greatest overall gain was made by Japan, which had a real GDP less than one-third of that for the United Kingdom and around one-sixth that for the United States.

Just back in the mid-1980s Japan and Germany were regarded as the new and seemingly invincible economic superpowers. Thanks to currency realignments, corporate restructuring, deregulation, and flexible labor markets, the United States during the 1990s enjoyed a resurgence in its competitive position. It has regained or reextended its world market share leadership in high-value industries like aerospace, pharmaceuticals, software, and telecommunications. The structural rigidities in Japan and Germany are so deeply entrenched, and many experts believe that these nations will be forever mired in a state of uncompetitiveness. But it is inevitable that the United States will eventually be challenged because there are so many intangibles at work. The European Union, with a common currency, the Euro, could create a European turnaround. A strong dollar and the risk of higher labor costs could erode many of the present U.S. advantages.

http://

For information on federal economic indicators, visit www.whitehouse. gov/fsbr/esbr.html.

TABLE 3-6   *Economic and Social Data for the United States, 1997*

Population in thousands	125,761.0
Population growth 1990–1997 (%)	1.0
Land area, thousands of square kilometers	9,151.9
Real GDP ($ billions)	7,690.1
World rank	1st
Average annual real growth rate in GDP (%)	
1980–1990	2.9
1990–1997	2.5
Foreign trade ($ millions)	
Exports	848,664.0
Imports	956,004.0
Total	1,800,668.0
World rank	1st
Percent of world trade	12.8
Central government revenues (% of GDP)	19.3
Central government expenditures (% of GDP)	20.7
Human development index, rank out of 174 countries	8th
Adult literacy rate (%)	
Males	99.0
Females	99.0
Share of earned income (%)	
Males	65.9
Females	34.1
Gini coefficient of income inequality (%)	40.1

Sources: The World Bank, *World Development Report, 1998/99* (New York: Oxford University Press, 1998), 191, 195, 199, 211, 219; The World Bank, *1998 World Bank Atlas* (New York: World Bank Publications, 1998), 25, 33, 43; United Nations Development Program, *Human Development Report, 1998* (New York: Oxford University Press, 1998), 129, 133.

TABLE 3-7 *A Comparison of Real GDP for Major Industrial Countries in the Twentieth Century ($ billions)*

Countries	1900	1920	1940	1960	1980	2000[1]
France	115.6	124.0	198.9	341.5	807.1	1,300.0
Germany	99.2	114.2	241.1	469.2	946.3	1,500.0
Italy	58.8	94.6	151.1	290.6	739.0	1,100.0
Japan	50.0	91.1	201.8	364.8	1,531.6	2,600.0
Russia	154.0	—[2]	420.1	843.4	1,709.2	—[3]
United Kingdom	176.5	203.3	315.7	448.9	719.5	1,100.0
United States	312.9	594.1	930.8	2,022.2	4,161.0	6,300.0

[1]*Estimates based on a projection of the data.*
[2]*In 1920 the civil war in Russia was still going on, and the country that was to become the Soviet Union had not been created.*
[3]*The Soviet Union was dissolved in 1990 and was formed into a number of new countries. The Russian Federation, which is basically the Russia of 1900, would have a real GDP of $550 billion in 2000, about that of Canada.*

Source: Angus Maddison, *Monitoring the World Economy, 1820–1992* (Paris: OECD Development Centre Studies, 1995), 148, 149, 150, 151, 154, 155.

Strengths of the American Economy

In his book *The Wealth and Poverty of Nations*, David S. Landes addresses the question of why some nations are rich and others are poor. Climate and culture are the major factors. The United States has a temperate climate and a culture conducive to economic growth. Added to these factors is the fact that the United States is more favorably endowed with natural resources than most countries, including Japan and Germany.[13] No country in the Western hemisphere had iron and coal in proximity; no other had comparable ways of transportation and communication. Coupled with this, land was abundant and available to just about anyone who wanted to use it. Society was not divided between a few privileged landowners and a larger mass of laborers as it was in Europe. This created a sense of self-reliance and individual responsibility.

In the *Competitive Advantage of Nations*, Michael Porter attempted to explain why some nations succeeded and other nations failed in international competition.[14] Countries have to possess four broad attributes to be successful. These are factor endowment, demand conditions in the home market, related and supporting industries, and firm strategy and rivalry. These are formed into the shape of a diamond, where they reinforce each other. All facets of the diamond have favored the United States.[15] World demand, mass consumption, and mass marketing have created a demand for American consumer goods in other countries. The United States excels in providing services based on the fluid transmission of information around the world. It also has an unequaled university system and makes substantial investments in research and development.

Application of Competitive Advantage. Morgan Stanley, a U.S. multinational banking firm, published a study called *The Competitive Edge*, which was based on the analytical framework provided by Michael Porter.[16] Their conclusion was that national characteristics shape company-specific opportunities. The study contends that three factors are decisive in shaping the competitive position of both nations and companies: currency values, relative labor cost disparities, and technological prowess. The United States used the currency factor most effectively to its competitive advantage during the 1990s. It also has an advantage in labor costs over Europe and Japan, and it has outdistanced other countries when it comes to adapting to the new technology of the Information Age. Morgan Stanley identified 238 companies that have a competitive edge in global competition, a majority of which were American, and the United States had a majority of companies that dominate a particular industrial sector.

The twenty-first century has already been called "the American century" before it even arrived. Europe and Japan have largely been written off as major world competitors. Both suffer comparative disadvantages relative to the United States that are unlikely to change in the immediate future because they are too beset by structural rigidities. Of all of the paeans to the new American century, one of the most interesting is a book, *America the Wise*, written by Theodore Roszak.[17] Discounting the hyperbole, the author speculates on a demographic shift that is taking place in the United States, namely, the aging of the population. As people grow older, they will have more vitality and wealth relative to previous generations and become more of a collective asset to society. They will be compassionate, wise, and powerful, and with more time on their hands, will perform good deeds. There will be a new social ethic of altruism and hope.

Weaknesses of the American Economy

The United States is not without its weaknesses. It is the world's leading debtor nation, and it has had a deficit in its merchandise trade and current accounts since 1986. In 1997 foreign assets in the United States exceeded U.S. assets abroad by $1.2 trillion.[18] A major part of this debt takes the form of foreign holdings of U.S. Treasury debt obligations, such as Treasury bills.[19] The merchandise trade account, which involves U.S. exports of goods and U.S. imports of foreign goods, was a negative $114 billion for 1997. The current account, which consists of four accounts—the merchandise trade account, the service account, the income receipts and payments on assets account, and unilateral transfers—was a negative $100 billion in 1997. The relationship of the U.S. dollar to other currencies can have a beneficial or adverse effect on American foreign trade and on the American economy.[20]

Income Inequality.   The United States has the greatest income and wealth inequality of any developed country in the world, and this inequality has increased since the 1980s. This is attributed to the development of what has been called "The winner-take-all Society."[21] A growing number of markets have come to be dominated by a few superstars. It is relative, not absolute, performance that is rewarded. A small difference in talent or skill, or just plain luck, can result in vastly different rewards for a few people. Although the competition for top positions in winner-take-all markets attracts talented workers, it generates two kinds of waste. First, it attracts too many contestants. Second, it gives rise to unproductive patterns of consumption and investment.

Tables 3-8 and 3-9 compare income inequality in the United States for selected years beginning in 1970. As Table 3-8 indicates, income inequality has increased. The lowest 20 percent of American families have seen very little increase in their real incomes since 1970 and the second 20 percent have seen only a small increase in their real incomes, averaging around $100 a year. The greatest gain was made by families in the top 5% of income earners, whose average real incomes increased by more than $1,000 a year. Table 3-9 shows that income inequality expressed in terms of percentages has also increased considerably. In 1970 the lowest fifth of families received 5.4 percent of real income compared to 40.9 percent of the highest fifth of families, a ratio of about 7.8 to 1. In 1996 the lowest fifth of families received 4.2 percent of real income compared to 46.8 percent for the highest fifth of families, a ratio of about 11.2 to 1. The top 5 percent of families made less than the bottom 40 percent of families in 1970; in 1996 they made more.

International comparisons of income inequality can be made among the developed nations of the world. Income inequality is greater in the United States than

TABLE 3-8   *Share of Aggregate Income Received by Each Fifth and Top 5% of Families for Selected Years (Income in Constant 1996 Consumer Price Index Dollars)*

	Upper Limit of Each Fifth				
Year	Lowest	Second	Third	Fourth	Top 5%
1970	19,375	31,608	42,925	59,003	92,127
1975	19,506	32,120	44,669	61,847	96,876
1980	19,827	33,382	47,280	66,344	104,854
1985	19,372	33,372	48,342	70,326	115,145
1990	20,223	24,866	50,467	73,816	122,877
1991	19,584	33,535	49,535	72,564	116,451
1992	18,690	33,185	49,206	71,628	118,555
1993	18,426	32,574	48,894	72,526	122,894
1994	18,993	33,137	49,759	74,107	127,090
1995	19,633	33,959	50,431	74,394	127,307
1996	19,680	34,315	51,086	75,316	128,000

Source: U.S. Department of Commerce, Economic and Statistical Administration, Bureau of the Census, *Statistical Abstract of the United States, 1998* (Washington, D.C.: U.S. Government Printing Office, 1998), 473.

TABLE 3-9   *Percent Share of Aggregate Income Received by Each Fifth and Top 5% of Families, 1970–1996*

Year	Lowest Fifth	Second Fifth	Third Fifth	Fourth Fifth	Highest Fifth	Top 5%
1970	5.4	12.2	17.6	23.8	40.9	15.6
1975	5.6	11.9	17.7	24.2	40.7	14.9
1980	5.3	11.6	17.6	24.4	41.1	14.6
1985	4.8	11.0	16.9	24.3	42.5	16.1
1990	4.6	10.8	16.6	23.7	44.6	17.4
1991	4.5	10.7	16.6	23.8	44.3	17.1
1992	4.3	10.5	16.5	24.1	44.2	17.6
1993	4.1	9.9	15.7	24.0	47.0	20.3
1994	4.2	10.0	15.7	23.3	46.9	20.1
1995	4.4	10.1	15.8	23.2	46.5	20.0
1996	4.2	10.0	15.8	23.1	46.8	20.3

Source: U.S. Department of Commerce, Economic and Statistical Administration, Bureau of the Census, *Statistical Abstract of the United States, 1998* (Washington, D.C.: U.S. Government Printing Office, 1998), 473.

it is in the social market economies of Europe. Table 3-10 compares income distribution for selected European countries and the more market-oriented economies of the United States, Canada, and Australia. The greatest income equality exists in Denmark and Sweden; the greatest income inequality exists in the United States. The Gini coefficient, which measures the extent of income inequality, is 40.5 percent in the United States compared to 24.5 percent in Den-

TABLE 3-10   *A Comparison of Income Inequality in the United States and Other Countries (%)*

Country	Gini Coefficient	Lowest 10%	01	02	03	04	05	Highest 10%
Denmark	24.7	3.6	9.6	14.9	18.3	22.7	34.5	20.5
France	32.7	2.5	7.2	12.7	17.1	22.8	40.1	24.9
Germany	28.1	3.7	9.0	13.5	17.5	22.9	37.1	22.6
Italy	31.2	2.9	7.6	12.9	17.3	23.2	38.9	23.7
Netherlands	31.5	2.9	8.0	13.0	16.7	22.5	39.9	24.7
Sweden	25.0	3.7	9.6	14.5	18.1	23.2	34.5	20.1
United Kingdom	32.6	2.4	7.1	12.8	17.2	23.1	39.8	24.7
United States	40.1	1.5	4.8	10.5	16.0	23.5	45.2	28.1
Canada	31.5	2.8	7.5	12.9	17.2	23.0	39.5	23.8
Australia	33.7	2.5	7.0	12.2	16.6	23.3	40.9	24.8

Source: The World Bank, *World Development Report, 1998/99* (New York: Oxford University Press, 1998), 198–99.

TABLE 3-11   *Family Mean and Median Net Worth for 1995 (thousands of constant 1995 dollars)*

Family Income	Percent of Families	Mean Net Worth	Median Net Worth
Less than $10,000	16.1	43.6	4.7
10,000 to 24,999	26.9	77.2	30.0
25,000 to 49,999	30.6	117.7	53.4
50,000 to 99,995	19.8	256.0	121.1
100,000 and more	6.5	1,435.3	483.0

Source: U.S. Department of Commerce, Economic and Statistical Administration, Bureau of the Census, *Statistical Abstract of the United States, 1998* (Washington, D.C.: U.S. Government Printing Office, 1998), 482.

mark. The difference in income received by the highest 10 percent and the lowest 10 percent is 19 to 1 in the United States to around 5.5 to 1 in Denmark.

Wealth Inequality.   Inequality in the distribution of wealth is always greater than that in the distribution of income. Wealth accumulates over a period of time and is inherited. As Table 3-11 shows, the bulk of wealth in the United States is held by the 6.5 percent of families with incomes of more than $100,000 a year. Bill Gates, whose wealth was reported to be $100 billion in 1999, is wealthier than the bottom 50 percent of all American families.[22] He is the wealthiest man in the world and his wealth is greater than the GDP of Nigeria, a country of 115 million people.[23] As income inequality has widened, particularly during the 1980s and 1990s, so has wealth inequality.

Poverty.   Poverty is at the opposite end of the spectrum from wealth. Although the number of persons living in poverty has decreased from 22.2 percent of the

TABLE 3-12   *Poverty in the United States, 1960–1996*

	Number below Poverty Level (1,000)			Percent below Poverty Level		
	White	Black	Hispanic	White	Black	Hispanic
1960	28,039	—	—	17.8	—	—
1970	17,484	7,548	—	9.9	33.5	—
1975	17,770	7,545	2,991	9.7	31.3	23.0
1980	19,699	8,579	3,491	10.2	32.5	21.8
1985	22,860	8,926	5,236	11.9	31.3	28.4
1990	22,326	9,837	6,006	10.7	31.9	26.2
1991	23,747	10,242	6,339	11.3	32.7	28.1
1992	25,259	10,827	7,592	11.9	33.4	29.6
1993	26,226	10,877	8,126	12.2	33.1	30.6
1994	25,379	10,196	8,416	11.7	30.6	30.7
1995	24,423	9,872	8,574	11.2	29.3	30.3
1996	24,650	9,654	8,697	11.2	28.4	29.4

Source: U.S. Department of Commerce, Economics and Statistics Administration, Bureau of the Census, *Statistical Abstract of the United States, 1998* (Washington, D.C.: U.S. Government Printing Office, 1998), 477.

population in 1960 to 13.7 percent in 1996, the number of people living in poverty amounted to 36.5 million in the latter year. Of that total, 13.8 million were children. As Table 3-12 shows, the poverty level is greater among blacks and Hispanics than it is for whites. Since 1967 the proportion of female-headed families increased from 28 percent to 47 percent among black families and from 9 to 14 percent among white families. This has an impact on poverty rates for children because many single parents lack the skills to get high-paying jobs. In 1996 about 20.5 percent of all children lived in poverty. The poverty rate for female-headed families was 49.3 percent. Forty percent of black children lived in poverty. Table 3-13 presents children with family incomes below poverty in 1996.

Criticisms of Income and Wealth Inequality.   Many American supporters of market capitalism regard inequality in the distribution of income and wealth with great respect and enthusiasm and consider its acquisition as admirable and exhilarating as Sir Galahad's pursuit of the Holy Grail. From an economic standpoint, income inequality is justified on the grounds that people will flock to those fields that pay the highest incomes and leave those fields that don't pay as well. Thus, the market mechanism is effectively doing its job of allocating resources to those areas in which demand is the greatest. It also encourages entrepreneurship, an area in which the United States is very strong in comparison with other countries.[24] The United States leads the world in the number of Nobel prize winners and the number of patents.

However, the extent of income and wealth inequality in the United States can be criticized on several grounds. First, it distorts the democratic process based on the idea of equal rights for all and special privileges for none. The buying of the

TABLE 3-13   *Children with Family Incomes below the Poverty Line, 1996*
(% of children in each category)

Demographic Category	Family Income	
	Less than half of poverty line[1]	Less than poverty line[2]
Age of child		
Under 6	10.5	22.7
6–17	7.4	18.3
Race/ethnicity of child		
White	6.6	16.3
Black	20.6	39.9
Hispanic	14.7	40.3
Family status		
Female-headed	25.8	49.3
Married couple	2.8	10.1
All children	9.0	20.5

[1]*For two persons, it would have been $5,100; three persons, $6,200; and four persons, $8,018.*
[2]*For two persons, it would have been $10,233; three persons, $12,516; and four persons, $16,038.*

Source: U.S. Department of Commerce, Economics and Statistics Administration, Bureau of the Census, *Statistical Abstract of the United States, 1998* (Washington, D.C.: U.S. Government Printing Office, 1998), 478.

White House and other forms of campaign contributions subvert the democratic process. Wealth gives power and the ability to afford an overnight stay at the White House for $250,000. Second, families whose incomes are in the top 20 percent nationally have increased their share of the total income pie while everyone else's share fell correspondingly. The upper middle class keeps setting the consumption bar higher, while the majority of Americans are finding it more difficult to clear it.[25] The end result is a debt-ridden society.[26]

The Future of the American Economy: Beautiful or Boastful?

Many experts feel that American dominance of the twenty-first century is preordained. This euphoria is largely based on the performance of the U.S. economy in the 1990s compared to Europe and Japan. They point to the American technological lead in global competition. It is the rugged individualism of Americans that breeds success. American history has encouraged the development of an American management culture that is superior to all others. The American financial system is also superior to all others when it comes to providing capital to finance entrepreneurs. The slowdown in military spending after the end of the Cold War has eliminated the federal deficit, lowered nominal interest rates, and increased the supply of savings. Public policy has promoted the deregulation of railroads, airlines, power companies, and telecommunications, thus fostering competition. The litany of other attributes is endless.

However, this self-congratulatory jubilation also has its critics. For one thing, this optimism is based on the performance of the U.S. economy during the 1990s and the premise that Europe and Japan are too inflexible to catch up with the United States. Also, during the twentieth century, the performance of the U.S. economy as measured by the average annual increase in real per capita GDP is no better or worse than that of many industrial countries.[27] Japan remains a competitor, particularly in exports, and runs a trade surplus compared to a deficit in U.S. foreign trade. It is also argued that the United States and Europe are operating at the same technological level, with each having a small edge in some areas of technology.

SUMMARY

The United States has an individualistic market capitalistic system compared to the communitarian social welfare capitalism of Germany and the communitarian state-directed capitalism of Japan. Income and wealth inequality is much greater in the United States than it is in either Germany or Japan. The role of government is different in the United States from what it is in other countries. In the United States the private sector makes the overwhelming majority of strategic and tactical decisions. Unlike Japan, the government is not involved in formulating industrial policy or in mandating funding or other support to specific industries or companies. Unlike Germany, the government is not involved in a wide variety of rules and regulations covering everything from store hours to plant closings.

QUESTIONS FOR DISCUSSION

1.   Income and wealth inequality increased in the United States during the 1980s and 1990s. Discuss some of the reasons why it happened.
2.   What are some of the factors responsible for poverty in the United States?
3.   To what extent can the development of large corporations in the United States be regarded as a departure from a free-market system? Is this good or bad?
4.   Is wealth inequality compatible with democracy?
5.   From an ethical standpoint, is income and wealth inequality good or bad?
6.   What are some of the reasons for the success of the American economy during the 1990s?

RECOMMENDED READINGS

Evans, Harold. *The American Century.* New York: Knopf, 1998.
Frank, Robert H. *Luxury Fever: The New Middle Class Luxury Boom.* New York: The Free Press, 1998.
Krugman, Paul. "America the Boastful." *Foreign Affairs*, Vol. 77, No. 3 (May–June 1998): 32-43.

Landes, David S. *The Wealth and Poverty of Nations*. New York: Norton, 1998, chap. 19, 292–309.

Porter, Michael E. *The Competitive Advantage of Nations*. New York: The Free Press, 1990, 288–95, 508–19, 723–33.

Roszak, Theodore. *America the Wise: The Longevity Revolution and the True Wealth of Nations*. Boston: Houghton-Mifflin, 1998.

Schor, Juliet B. *The Overspent American*. New York: Basic Books, 1998.

Zuckerman, Mortimer B. "A Second American Century." *Foreign Affairs*, Vol. 77, No. 3 (May–June 1998): 18–31.

ENDNOTES

1.   Gert Hofstede, "Cultural Constraints in Management Theories," *Academy of Management Executive*, Vol. 7, No. 1 (1993): 81–94. The United States scored 91 on individualism, the highest of all countries used in the study, while Japan scored 46, which was low, but not the lowest of the countries in the study.

2.   During the early stages of economic development from 1790 to 1860, the United States used protective tariffs to protect American industry from foreign competition. It also subsidized the building of railroads, turnpikes, and canals by providing financial assistance and land grants.

3.   David S. Landes, *The Wealth and Poverty of Nations* (New York: Norton, 1998).

4.   Michael E. Porter, *The Competitive Advantage of Nations* (New York: Free Press, 1990).

5.   The other countries were Denmark, Italy, South Korea, Singapore, Sweden, Switzerland, and the United Kingdom. Singapore, according to Landes, is successful because of its work ethic and because it has been a center of international commerce for hundreds of years.

6.   Willa Cather's novel, *O Pioneers*, is an excellent example. Set around the turn of the century, the novel is about a Scandinavian family that comes to Nebraska to find opportunity in farming. The father can make violins, but knows very little about farming and fails like most of his neighbors. After his death, his daughter, who has far more business sense, becomes the family leader, buys the right property, farms the right crops, and enables the family to become prosperous.

7.   *Economic Report of the President, 1992* (Washington, D.C.: U.S. Government Printing Office, 1992), 385.

8.   The Americans with Disabilities Act (ADA) of 1990 is a very important act that must be added to the other acts.

9.   In 1997 a total of 564,093 new businesses were incorporated in the United States.

10.   Gross domestic product (GDP) measures the total value of goods and services that are produced and consumed each year in a country.

11.   Fiscal policy is associated with what is called Keynesian economics, which holds that government purchases of goods and services and changes in tax rates can affect the level of aggregate demand.

12.   Interlocking directorates are permitted in both Germany and Japan.

13.   Landes, *Wealth and Poverty of Nations*, 295.

14.   Porter, *Competitive Advantage*.

15.   They also favor Germany and Japan.

16.   Morgan Stanley Equity Research, *Global Investing: The Competitive Edge* (New York: Morgan Stanley & Co., 1996).

17.   Theodore Roszak, *America the Wise: The Longevity Revolution and the True Wealth of Nations* (Boston: Houghton-Mifflin, 1998).

18.   U.S. Department of Commerce, Bureau of Economic Analysis, *International Transactions, 1997* [or (www.bea.doc.gov/bea/ai1.htm)], 34.

19.   In 1997 foreigners held $614 billion in U.S. Treasury bills, notes, and bonds.

20.   The East Asian currency crisis of 1997 had an adverse earnings effect on American companies operating in Indonesia, Thailand, South Korea, and other East Asian countries.

21.   Robert H. Frank and Philip J. Cook, *The Winner-Take-All Society* (New York: The Free Press, 1995).

22.   *Time*, July 26, 1999, p. 17.

23.   The GDP of Nigeria was $27 billion in 1997.

24.   This is a result of American culture, which has been conducive to the development of entrepreneurship going back to the nineteenth century. Other cultures tend to stultify entrepreneurship through taxes and restrictions. Germany is an example.

25.   One-half of those families making $100,000 a year report that they don't make enough to live on.

26.   The American economy is built on consumption. The U.S. culture is a materialistic culture par excellence. Our credit card debt doubled between 1990 and 1996; credit card debtors pay an average charge of $1,000 a year in interest and fees. Nearly 40 percent of all baby boomers have less than $10,000 set aside for retirement.

27.   Angus Maddison, *The World Economy in the Twentieth Century* (Paris: OECD Development Centre Studies, 1991), p. 36.

CHAPTER 4

Japan

In his 1988 bestseller *The Rise and Fall of the Great Powers,* Paul Kennedy stated: "The only answer to the question increasingly debated by the public of whether or not the United States could preserve its leading position in the world is *no,* because it simply has not been given to any one society to remain permanently ahead of others."[1] He cited examples of some of the great empires of Europe that have come and gone, beginning with Spain, the dominant world power for some two hundred years. Spain was followed by Holland, which became the financial center of Europe and the leading seapower. Holland was followed by England, which dominated the nineteenth century and created the largest empire ever known. The United States dominated the twentieth century, but who will dominate the twenty-first century? The answer, according to Kennedy, was Japan.

Clyde V. Prestowitz, Jr., was even more unequivocal. He named the time and date the United States and Japan would trade places. He wrote a book called *Trading Places: How We Allowed Japan to Take the Lead* and stated: "Monday, October 19, 1987, marked the end of the American century twelve years before its time. This date signaled as clear as any bugle call the most serious defeat the United States has ever suffered."[2] By trading places, Prestowitz was referring to Japan. In industry after industry, the United States had ceded first place to Japan. Japan had transformed itself into a world superpower through hard work and a social organization

http://

A myriad of statistics on many aspects of Japanese economy and culture can be found at www.jinjapan.org.

so cohesive and well managed that it was the envy of the world. It was the world's leading creditor nation and the yen would replace the dollar as the world's leading currency.

However, the 1990s proved Kennedy, Prestowitz, and many other "Japan will win" authors wrong.[3] During the 1990s the Japanese economy collapsed. Real GDP, which had increased by 5.1 percent in 1990, fell to 1.0 percent, 0.3 percent in 1993, and 0.6 percent in 1994.[4] A main reason was the collapse of the "bubble economy," which was based on unregulated real estate loans by Japanese banks to borrowers who speculated in property not only in Japan but also in the United States and other countries.[5] Money was also borrowed to speculate in the Japanese stock market. When the real estate and stock markets collapsed in the early 1990s, Japanese banks and other financial institutions were stuck with debts amounting to $1.5 trillion. The Japanese government deserved much of the blame for the financial excess and economic stagnation that followed. Both bureaucrats and politicians were slow to initiate reforms that might have eliminated much of the instability that occurred.

Nevertheless, when one considers the economic base from which the country has had to operate, the performance of the Japanese economy in the twentieth century was remarkable. It started the century with a real per capita GDP of less than one-fourth of that of the United States; in 1997 its real per capita GDP was 85 percent of that of the United States and its money per capita GDP was $12,000 higher.[6] The land area of Japan is small, the natural resources are limited, and its population is large. Its economy was virtually destroyed during World War II, and its real per capita GDP was one-sixth of that of the United States in 1950. It was very much a feudal society until the middle of the nineteenth century and had to build a set of institutions on which to create a modern economy. It is vulnerable to natural disasters, as witnessed by the earthquake in Kobe in January 1995 that caused billions of dollars in damage to the economy.

THE JAPANESE ECONOMY

Japan is an example of state-directed capitalism with an interplay between government policy, private enterprise, and industrial development. An industrial policy that has been linked to export development has been used by Japan for the latter half of the twentieth century. At first, Japan followed a labor-intensive policy based on the creation of light industries to export low-cost Japanese products such as textiles. The government provided financial support in the form of low-cost loans to business firms and followed a policy of import substitution to protect these industries against foreign competition.[7] Later the government encouraged the development of heavy industry, particularly shipbuilding and autos. Priorities were established and monetary and other forms of financial assistance were provided by various government agencies (Table 4-1).

David S. Landes in his book *The Wealth and Poverty of Nations* argues that climate and culture explain why some nations are rich and other nations are poor.[8] In the case of Japan, climate and culture have been favorable to its development as a

TABLE 4-1   *Economic and Social Data for Japan, 1997*

Population (1,000s)	125,761.0
Population growth rate, 1990–1997 (%)	0.3
Land area, thousands of square kilometers	376.5
Read GDP ($ billions)	2,950.7
World rank	3rd
Average annual real growth rate in GDP (%)	
1980–1990	4.0
1990–1997	1.4
Foreign trade ($ millions)	
Exports	468,002.0
Imports	446,679.0
Total	912,681.0
World rank	3rd
Percent of world trade	7.0
Central government revenues (% of GDP)	17.6
Central government expenditures (% of GDP)	18.4
Human development index (rank out of 174 countries)	8th
Adult literacy rate (%)	
Males	99.0
Females	99.0
Share of earned income (%)	
Males	65.9
Females	34.1
Gini coefficient of income inequality (estimate in %)	27.8

Sources: The World Bank, *World Development Report, 1998/99* (New York: Oxford University Press, 1998), 190, 194, 198, 210, 218; The World Bank, *1998 World Bank Atlas* (New York: World Bank Publications, 1998), 24, 32, 42; United Nations Development Program, *Human Development Report, 1998* (New York: Oxford University Press, 1998), 128–32.

world economic power. Its climate is similar to that of Europe and the United States, and the religious aspect of its culture is similar to that of European Calvinism, with its emphasis on the work ethic. This ethic can be summed up in the statement of a prominent Japanese merchant of the eighteenth century: "Never waste your time on matters that have nothing to do with work."[9] A Buddhist monk of the sixteenth century is quoted as saying: "All occupations are Buddhist practice; through work we are able to attain salvation." This is very similar to the Protestant work ethic that carried over to the United States from Europe.

THE DEVELOPMENT OF MODERN JAPAN

Contrary to popular belief Japan was not a benighted country when in 1853 Commodore Matthew C. Perry and his U.S. naval squadron forced it against its will to open itself to the West.[10] It had a prosperous merchant class that specialized in various forms of trade. Monopolies were created to produce sugar and cotton, and craft guilds existed by the seventeenth century. Foreign trade was carried on with Chinese and European merchants and knowledge of Western ideas and practices had spread over Japan long before Perry appeared on the scene.[11] After he compelled Japan to grant trading rights to American nationals, other countries followed suit, forcing the Japanese government to grant trading rights to their nationals. Five Japanese ports were opened to foreign shipping; and extraterritorial rights were granted to foreigners. Foreign aggression demonstrated the need for Japan to change and modernize its economy.[12]

The Meiji Period, 1868–1913

The Meiji Restoration of 1868 marks the beginning of the development of Japan as a modern industrial nation.[13] In the first years after the Restoration, the most important development in Japan was the creation of an environment conducive to economic growth. To survive the economic encroachments of Western powers, Japan, by national policy, had to master the secret of industry. To gain the necessary knowledge, Japanese students were sent to study the technology of Western nations. Also, Western engineers and technicians were temporarily employed in Japan to teach the Japanese the techniques of production. The Japanese learned to adapt the technology of the West for their own purposes.

http://

Facts on Japan's government can be seen at www.jinjapan.org/today/gover.html.

The Role of Government. The government became a major operator of key industries. The modernization of Japan during the latter part of the nineteenth century included the nationalization of key sectors of the economy such as the postal service, telephone and telegraph communications, and railways. The government also built and operated iron foundries, shipyards, machine shops, and factories. Tobacco, salt, and camphor became government monopolies.[14] The government provided technical and financial assistance to private interests in other industries.

The financial and monetary base for the economy was established in 1882 when the Bank of Japan was formed. Tax policies were designed to stimulate capital formation. Taxes were levied on agricultural land and the sale of farm products. The proceeds provided for public capital formation, which went into the development of roads and educational facilities. Expenditures on arsenals, navy yards, warships, and the like provided a military underpinning for the process of economic development.

The Role of Private Enterprise. While the government was involved in producing the conditions requisite to economic growth and industrial development, private enterprise also flourished and developed during the Meiji period. An important development during the Meiji period was the displacement of the samurai, or warrior caste, which had dominated Japan for centuries. The samurai were integrated into Japanese society, and some went into business. Therefore, in Japan businesspeople were drawn from the upper classes of society and enjoyed immediate respect and prestige. In this regard Japan started at an advantage, for in most developing countries, the business class is composed largely of people in lower social classes or from racial and religious minorities not respected by the population. In addition, by building up export industries based on low-cost labor, Japan was able to obtain foreign exchange to purchase food and raw materials needed by the economy.

Japanese capitalism was characterized by the development of concentrated economic power in the form of business combines called *zaibatsu*. Each combine consisted of twenty to thirty major firms, all concentrated around a large bank. These major firms represented each of the important industrial sectors in the economy, so that a group would typically include a shipping company, a steel company, an insurance company, and so forth. Zaibatsu combines were larger than any U.S. corporation and were under the control and management of a few family dynasties. The Mitsui combine, for example, employed 1,800,000 workers prior to World War II, and Mitsubishi employed 1,000,000 workers.[15] There was a working relationship between the zaibatsu and the Japanese government in that the latter, through military force or otherwise, provided penetration of new markets.

Post–World War II Development of Japan

With Japan's defeat in World War II and its subsequent occupation by the United States came problems of reform and reorganization for the economy. A new constitution, which incorporated Western principles of democratic parliamentary government, was promulgated by the United States for Japan in November 1946.[16] The dissolution of the zaibatsu into a number of independent business enterprises was another part of U.S. occupation policy. Antitrust laws molded after the U.S. Sherman and Clayton Acts were imposed on the Japanese. Later, however, the Japanese government enacted various laws to exempt certain industries from antitrust legislation. These exemptions were designed to improve Japan's position as a world exporter by allowing certain types of export cartels.[17] The U.S. occupation of Japan also resulted in the introduction of consumer technology, which the Japanese readily assimilated. The Japanese became wards of the United States and received gifts, low-interest loans, and machinery that restored productive capacity in a number of industries, especially textiles.[18]

However, Japanese economic development policy could not depend on U.S. largesse alone. Local needs had to be satisfied first. The shipbuilding industry had been destroyed during the war and, as a small island country, Japan needed ships of every type for survival. With government aid, the shipbuilding industry developed rapidly; by 1956 the Japanese had become the world's largest producer of ships.

Japan also developed an export strategy to achieve industrial development. For exports, the country's leaders recognized that they would have to depend on handicrafts, textiles, and other small-scale industries in which Japan enjoyed the advantage of low-cost labor. Human capital was an important factor in the early postwar period. Veterans were absorbed in the labor-intensive industries. Earnings from exports were used to finance the acquisition of machine tools that would help

Japan produce modern machinery. This led to the development of other industries, notably Honda, which developed from a one-man operation in 1951 to the largest motorcycle company in the world.

The Role of the Japanese Government.   The Japanese government has played and continues to play an important role in the development of the Japanese economy. The postwar development of Japanese industry was facilitated through government grants and low-interest loans. There has also been extensive use of fiscal and monetary policies to stimulate economic growth. Special tax incentives are used to promote high rates of saving, investment, and capital formation, as well as the introduction of new products and technology. Probably most important to the success of the Japanese economy has been the development of a close working relationship between government and business.[19]

ORGANIZATION OF INDUSTRY

Japanese industrial organization is a product of the culture and the unique economic development of the country. Its industrial groups have no parallel in other countries. Although it is half the size of the United States in population and one-twenty-fifth the size in land area, it ranks second only to the United States in the number of large corporations. Even though it has a limited resource base, it is one of the three largest trading nations in the world. Its economy is based on industrial clusters called *keiretsu*, which are a unique product of Japanese culture. These clusters possess the following characteristics:

1.   Personal relationships between executives based on schooling and marriage. Japan is small and has few universities.[20] It also has little upward social mobility. Chances are that most executives knew each other in college and married into each other's families.
2.   Loyalty to the group. It is the group, not the individual, that is important in Japan.[21]
3.   There are norms of behavior such as a belief in continuity and long-term relationships between people. Friends count and seniority count.[22]
4.   Patriotism and a belief in the superiority of the Japanese culture are very important to the Japanese.[23]
5.   Interlocking directorates, which are basically prohibited in the United States, are common and play a role in the decision-making process. These directors know each other, have gone to the same schools, and have intermarried.

The Keiretsu

The Keiretsu dates back to the latter part of the nineteenth century when family-owned enterprises began to dominate the Japanese economy.[24] Unlike the United States, where antitrust laws were passed to prevent the creation of monopolies, these enterprises, with the support of the Japanese government, produced 90 percent of the Japanese GNP. They remain today and can be divided into two types, horizontal and vertical. There are six horizontal keiretsus in Japan consisting of a family of corporations spanning numerous industries centered around a bank. Figure 4-1 presents the organization of the Sumitoma keiretsu, which consists of firms in banking, electronics, glass, and other industries plus a trading company. Table 4-2 presents the revenue and assets for the Mitsubishi keiretsu, the largest of its type in the world, for 1997. It is necessary to point out that the companies are only those included in *Fortune*'s international 500 largest corporations.

There are thirty-nine vertical keiretsus, each consisting of one industrial group and its subsidiaries. Many are located in industries such as automobiles and electrical equipment. Toyota affords an excellent example of this type of keiretsu. It has financial ties with all of its suppliers. For example, at one time it owned 41 percent of the company that makes its tires, 33 percent of the company that manufactures its upholstery, and 21 percent of the company that makes its body frames.[25] Members of a vertical keiretsu, as is also true for a horizontal keiretsu, own shares in each other's companies, exchange information, and cooperate in new ventures.

The Sogo Shosha

Another important form of business organization in Japan is the trading company, or sogo shosha. There are a half-dozen trading companies, and they are among the largest enterprises in the world. Most of Japan's foreign trade is done through trading companies, each of which is represented in every country in the world. A trading company. may be part of a keiretsu (Sumitomo is an example). Trading companies operate diverse businesses on their own while providing many services to member firms. They procure raw materials, distribute products, and finance some activities of member firms. They are involved in both exporting and importing and can absorb foreign exchange risks for their groups. Moreover, they engage in overseas transactions for Japanese firms as well as for buyers and sellers in other countries. Handling most of Japan's exports and imports, sogo shoshas serve as screening mechanisms to filter out any imports that might be damaging to members of a keiretsu. For example, if soda ash can be imported more cheaply than it could be made in Japan, a trading company could limit its importation to protect the Japanese company. Table 4-3 shows the size of the Japanese trading companies.

The Dual Nature of Japanese Industry

The giant industrial combines dominate the foreign trade of Japan. But it must not be forgotten that a large part of the goods and services produced in Japan remains particular to that county. Along with the development of new industries of Western style, there continue to flourish numerous small-scale industries that provide for the special wants of Japanese consumers. Examples would be the food producing

FIGURE 4-1 *Sumitomo Group*

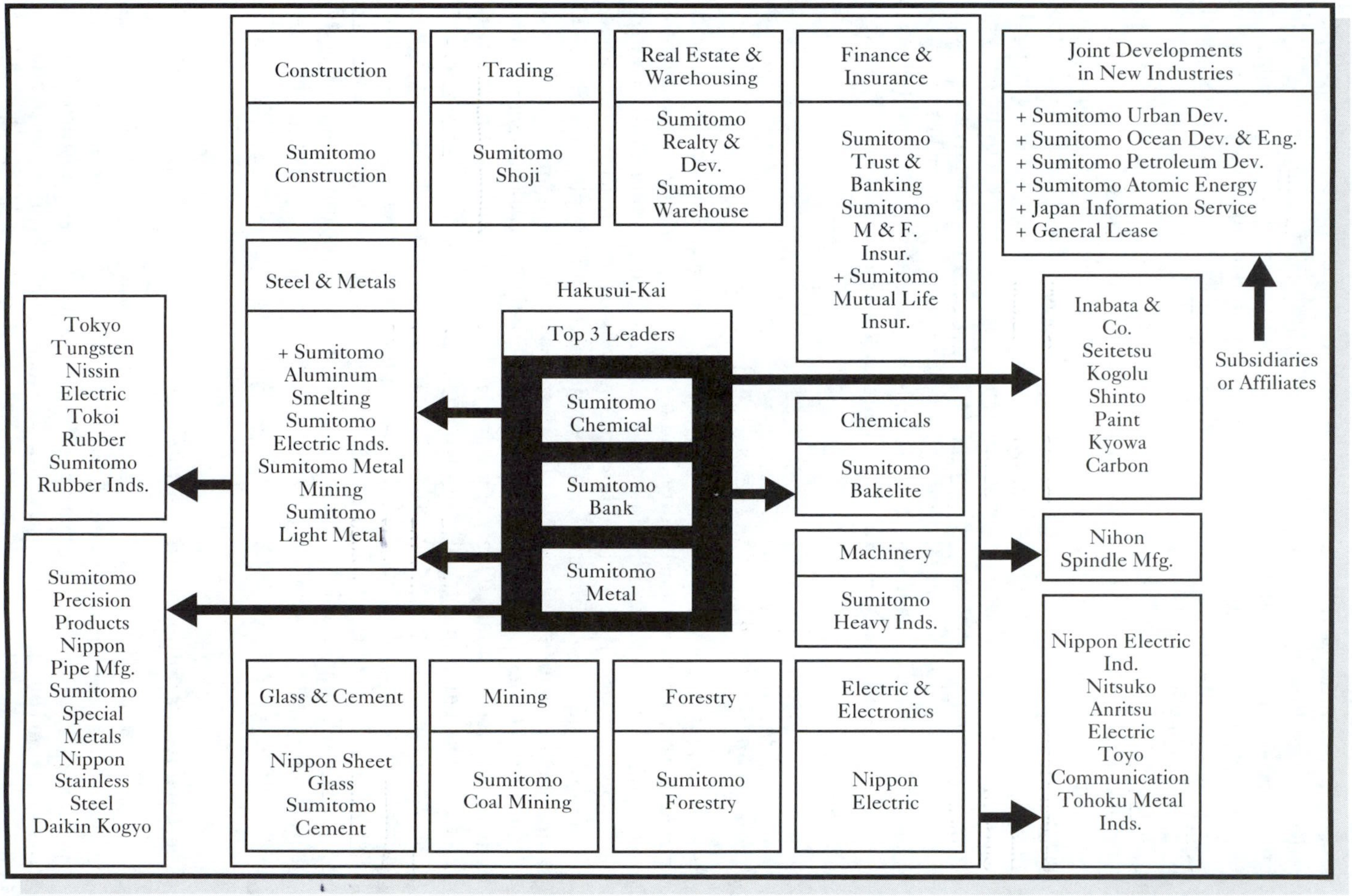

Hakusui-Kai

Top 3 Leaders
- Sumitomo Chemical
- Sumitomo Bank
- Sumitomo Metal

Construction
- Sumitomo Construction

Trading
- Sumitomo Shoji

Real Estate & Warehousing
- Sumitomo Realty & Dev.
- Sumitomo Warehouse

Finance & Insurance
- Sumitomo Trust & Banking
- Sumitomo M & F. Insur.
- + Sumitomo Mutual Life Insur.

Joint Developments in New Industries
- + Sumitomo Urban Dev.
- + Sumitomo Ocean Dev. & Eng.
- + Sumitomo Petroleum Dev.
- + Sumitomo Atomic Energy
- + Japan Information Service
- + General Lease

Subsidiaries or Affiliates

Steel & Metals
- + Sumitomo Aluminum Smelting
- Sumitomo Electric Inds.
- Sumitomo Metal Mining
- Sumitomo Light Metal

Chemicals
- Sumitomo Bakelite

Inabata & Co.
Seitetsu Kogolu
Shinto Paint
Kyowa Carbon

Machinery
- Sumitomo Heavy Inds.

Nihon Spindle Mfg.

Electric & Electronics
- Nippon Electric

Nippon Electric Ind.
Nitsuko
Anritsu Electric
Toyo Communication
Tohoku Metal Inds.

Glass & Cement
- Nippon Sheet Glass
- Sumitomo Cement

Mining
- Sumitomo Coal Mining

Forestry
- Sumitomo Forestry

Tokyo Tungsten
Nissin Electric
Tokoi Rubber
Sumitomo Rubber Inds.

Sumitomo Precision Products
Nippon Pipe Mfg.
Sumitomo Special Metals
Nippon Stainless Steel
Daikin Kogyo

74

Source: Clyde V. Prestowitz Jr., *Trading Places: How We Allowed Japan to Take the Lead* (New York: Basic Books, 1988), 158.

	Revenues	Assets
Mitsubishi Trading Co.	$107,184	$92,630
Mitsubishi Electric	29,682	35,365
Mitsubishi Motors	27,480	34,992
Mitsubishi Heavy Industries	22,748	40,076
Mitsubishi Chemical	11,983	16,771
Bank of Tokyo—Mitsubishi	30,929	663,628
Nippon Oil—Mitsubishi	214,291	24,608
Total	444,297	908,070
General Motors	161,315	257,389
Exxon	100,697	92,630
Chase Manhattan	32,379	365,875
Total	324,391	615,894
Country	GNP	Population
India	357,391	962,378
Pakistan	64,638	128,457
Nigeria	33,393	117,897
Total	455,422	1,208,732

TABLE 4-2
Revenues and Assets of the Mitsubishi Keiretsu, 1998 ($ millions)

Source: "The World's Largest Corporations," *Fortune,* August 2, 1999, pp. F1–F10; The World Bank, *1999 World Bank Atlas* (Washington, D.C.: The World Bank, 1999), pp. 24, 25, 42, 43.

Company	Revenues	World Rank
Mitsui	109,372	3
Itochu	108,749	6
Mitsubishi	107,184	7
Marubeni	93,569	12
Sumitomo	89,020	13
Nissho Iwai	67,742	20
General Motors	181,315	1
Ford	144,416	2
Wal-Mart	139,208	4
Exxon	100,697	8
Toyota	95,137	10

TABLE 4-3
The Six Major Japanese Trading Companies Ranked by Revenues, 1998 ($ millions)

Source: "Fortune's 500 Largest International Corporations," *Fortune,* August 3, 1998, pp. F1–10.

and retail industries. Productivity is generally low in these industries, but they are protected from foreign competition by the Japanese government. There are also a number of family-owned companies employing from two to one hundred workers. They typically manufacture parts or provide a service only to their major customers, which makes them dependent on their customers' success.

THE PUBLIC SECTOR

The public sector in Japan consists of the national government, local governments, and public enterprises. Unlike the United States and Germany, local governments in Japan have little fiscal autonomy and depend on transfers of income from the national government. Also unlike the United States and Germany, the role of the public sector is different in Japan in that it is characterized by a small share of government consumption, a large share of government investment, and a significant control over private sector funds through the use of government intermediaries. Entitlement expenditures by the Japanese government would be far less in Japan than either in the United States or Germany. For example, most private employees participate in their employers' pension insurance program, which provides an earnings-related retirement benefit, and other workers belong to mutual aid associations.

But the most important way in which Japan is different from the United States and Germany is the role of the bureaucracy and the ministries. The well-spring of all legislation in Japan is the bureaucracy, which formulates economic and political policies. Practically all new legislation begins at some low level within a ministry. It then works its way up until it is judged polished enough to be presented to the Japanese Diet (Parliament). The result is that a Japanese prime minister has very little political power. Heads of the all-important Japanese ministries have even less political power. They are handed out to politicians who have served a long period of tenure with a political party.[26] They serve usually no more than a year before being replaced so that others can have their turn. The bureaucrats and the ministries dominate Japan.[27]

http://

A site containing links to information on Japanese economy, business, government, culture, and many other aspects of Japan is at www.anderson.ucla.edu/research/japan/mainfrm.htm.

The Banking System

The Japanese banking system is dominated by giant commercial banks that are typically part of a keiretsu. They have been a standard part of Japanese government development policy going back to the latter part of the nineteenth century. These banks provide loans to keiretsu members and buy their common stock. They function globally. Other private banks are much smaller and typically specialize in financing small and medium-size enterprises. In addition, there are government-owned financial institutions that supplement the functions of the private financial institutions. Included are the Japan Development Bank, which provides long-term loans at low-interest rates to basic domestic industries; Postal Savings, which is the prime vehicle for savings in Japan; and the Export-Import Bank, which provides long-term loans at subsidized interest rates to exporters of Japanese products.

The banking system collapsed during the early 1990s. Many bad debts were run up by the banks in the 1990s. Loans were made by bankers to friends who invested money in Japanese real estate and in properties in the United States and other countries. Real estate values were enormously inflated, creating what is known as a "bubble economy" that eventually collapsed. Unlike American banks, Japanese banks were unregulated and the loans they made were largely unsecured. When the "bubble economy" collapsed, the stock market collapsed. Speculators, using money borrowed from the banks, also played the stockmarket. The banks never made provisions for bad debts, which continue to remain on their balance sheets. As Table 4-4 shows, the top five money losers in the world in 1997 were Japanese banks.

The Ministry of Finance.   The Ministry of Finance, which controls Japan's financial system, and the Ministry of International Trade and Industry (MITI) are the two elite ministries in the government. The Ministry of Finance is the repository of all revenues coming into the Japanese government and it determines how they are going to be spent. Japan relies on this ministry to create fiscal policy. It is responsible for changes in the rates of the personal and corporate income taxes, and it initiates provisions in the tax laws to stimulate the introduction of new products and technology. The prime minister and the legislature have no real control over the Ministry of Finance; they can only take the advice of its bureaucrats. The Ministry of Finance also controls the Japanese banking system.

The Ministry of International Trade and Industry (MITI).   MITI is probably the most important and powerful government agency in Japan, at least as far as Japanese business is concerned. Created in the late 1940s to guide industrial modernization and promote exports, its mandate was to determine a basic course of action to improve Japan's future comparative advantage and to mobilize each sector to contribute to the whole. Building a steel industry was one of Japan's most important postwar priorities. MITI encouraged Japanese banks to supply the capital that purchased steel-producing equipment and technology from the West,

Sumitomo Bank	4,451
Sakura Bank	3,749
Sanwa Bank	3,681
Dai-Ichi Kangyo Bank	3,484
Fuji Bank	3,302
Tokai Bank	2,243
Industrial Bank of Japan	1,418
Bank of Tokyo—Mitsubishi	680

TABLE 4-4
Top Money Losers among Japanese Banks, 1998 ($ millions)

Source: "The World's Largest Corporations," *Fortune*, August 2, 1999, p. F1–F10.

mostly from the United States. Tax incentives, low-interest loans, and other financial incentives were also given to the steel industry. MITI has continued to restructure industry by concentrating resources in areas where it thinks Japan needs to be competitive in the future.[28]

MITI has a number of functions. Its primary role is to offer guidance to Japanese industry. Providing the "big picture," so to speak, of where it thinks Japan as a nation should be heading, it develops an industrial policy for Japan and formulates and guides its implementation. It serves in a consultative capacity to other government agencies and is responsible for the flow of funds to favored industries. It has the power to grant licenses and patents and to determine which firms will get them. No plant, supermarket, or department store in Japan can be built without notification to and authorization from MITI. It has the power to suspend the antitrust laws and create cartels, either to aid industries in recession or to develop particular target industries. It has authority over electric power rates and other energy prices in Japan.

The Agency of Industrial Science and Technology (AIST).   AIST is a semi-independent agency under the jurisdiction of MITI that is responsible for the promotion of technology. It monitors scientific and technical developments abroad and identifies new technology that will be important to Japanese industries. One of the strengths of Japanese industry is that it is well informed about worldwide scientific and technological developments. AIST consults with Japanese industry to encourage the use of new technologies that will further the national interest; it sponsors research that would make the needed technology available. It is also responsible for the development of patents.

Government Financial Institutions.   The government itself is engaged in substantial financial activities through its ownership of a number of specialized credit institutions. Loans are provided for long-term industrial development, export financing, and agriculture as part of government policy for stimulating economic growth in an economy where capital is scarce. These institutions obtain loanable funds from the special counterpart fund in the national budget and from individual savings in the form of postal savings, postal annuities, and postal life insurance. These savings and the surplus funds from special budgetary accounts are deposited in a trust fund bureau that can use the funds for loans to public enterprises and financial institutions. Loans are also made to the private sector, particularly to industries that are export related. However, as a rule, private sector financing is undertaken in cooperation with private lending institutions.

The Export-Import Bank.   The Japan Export-Import Bank provides long-term loans at subsidized interest rates to exporters of Japanese products. For example, loans have been provided for the construction of tankers, textile machinery, and railroad cars. Loans have also been provided to finance projects such as the development of iron ore mines in India and the construction of textile mills in South America. In addition, the bank provides financing and debt guarantees to attract foreign capital into Japan. To stimulate economic development in Southeast Asia, the government set up a special account with the bank called the Southeast Asia Development Corporation Fund. Funds were provided out of the national budget. The fund was eventually transformed into an independent corporation and currently finances long-term investment in Southeast Asia.

Japan Development Bank.   Another important government-owned financial institution is the Japan Development Bank. The bank provides long-term loans at low interest rates to basic domestic industries. Through its control over loanable funds that are in the hands of official financial agencies like the Japan Development Bank, the government is able to exercise some control over national investment. It can thereby exert some influence with respect to its national economic plans.

http://

Visit the Web site of Japan Development Bank at www.jdb.go .jp/index_e.html.

Another financial institution directly owned and operated by the government is the Small Business Finance Corporation, which provides long-term loans to small businesses when financing by ordinary financial institutions proves difficult. The government-owned Agriculture, Forestry, and Fisheries Finance Corporation provides long-term, low-interest loans for investment in agricultural equipment by agricultural cooperatives and individual farming enterprises. Loanable funds for both corporations are obtained from the national budget and from earnings on investments in securities and call loans.

The Ministry of Posts and Communications (MPT).   This is the prime savings institution in Japan, with total savings of over $1 trillion. Every housewife in Japan saves through the postal service, giving her savings to the mail carrier in her district for deposit in the post office. This money then goes to finance such government agencies as the Japan Development Bank. But the MPT does more than collect savings; it also regulates and structures the Japanese telecommunications industry.

Monetary Policy.   The Bank of Japan has three instruments used to control the volume of credit and money—bank rate policy, open market operations, and reserve requirements. Bank rate policy involves the lowering or raising of discount rates and interest rates. The alteration of these rates is the most important monetary policy instrument in Japan because city banks rely heavily on loans from the Bank of Japan, and industries, in turn, rely heavily on bank loans. Costs in general and the availability of bank funds are highly responsive to changes in the discount and interest rates on commercial and export trade bills, overdrafts, and general secured loans. In addition, the Bank of Japan can place a ceiling on borrowing for each bank above which it can impose a penalty rate or refuse to make loans.

Open market operations are inhibited by the lack of a well-developed capital market and are not important as an instrument of monetary policy. Legal reserve requirements are far below the standard of reserve requirements in other major countries, and manipulation of these requirements by the Bank of Japan is a supplementary instrument of monetary control.

Labor–Management Relations

The distinctive feature of Japanese trade unions is that they are usually company unions. The typical Japanese labor union is made up of employees of a single company or of a single operational unit within a company, regardless of their occupation. Approximately one-fourth of the Japanese labor force belong to trade unions, with each union loosely tied to one of four central labor organizations. However, the central organizations have little authority over the company unions, which carry on the bargaining with employers. Negotiations between labor and management are conducted within each enterprise; however, the negotiations are conducted within the context of certain Japanese labor practices that differ from those in many other countries.

Some Japanese firms, in particular the larger ones, provide lifetime employment for their employees, which makes for a very different balance of power between union and management in Japanese firms. Employees know that their future depends on their company's future and that labor work stoppages could hurt their company's competitive position. Since it is difficult to obtain employment by leaving one company for another, the union will rarely press its demands so far as to seriously damage the company. Forcing a company into bankruptcy, for example, would put workers at the mercy of the labor market.

Positions within a company are determined largely on the basis of age and length of service, and Japanese companies routinely provide a number of fringe benefits for their employees. As a result, negotiations between labor and management in Japan are limited primarily to wages. During February through April each year, unions begin what is called the *shunto*, "spring wage struggle," with their respective companies. If agreement is not reached, the union may go out on strike, but since there is one union for each company, industrywide strike efforts are rare. Unions may also resort to public demonstrations to make the community aware of their demands.

Japanese employers are also organized into several confederations, the largest of which is the Federation of Economic Organizations (*Keidanran*). It is made up of financial, industrial, and trading associations that include almost all of Japan's largest business firms. Membership in the federation is institutional, and its work is carried out by standing committees. Keidanran wields considerable influence in government economic policies because many business and political leaders share a common educational background and family ties. The federation provides the Japanese with a mechanism for reconciling industrial policy objectives with political and social goals.

AN EVALUATION OF JAPAN

Not long ago, foreigners went to Japan to see how things were done. The Japanese economy was the envy of the world, and its financial markets the source of stupendous wealth. Countries scrambled for Japanese investment. Much of it poured into the United States—to buy bonds, real estate, and companies and to build factories for Japanese manufacturers who had reinvented entire industries, such as consumer electronics and carmaking. Japanese firms were studied as models of efficiency and innovation and their ideas of employee involvement, quality control, and design were put to work around the world. The Japanese were supposed to be smarter than anyone else, and Japanese politicians said that Americans were lazy and decadent and should take lessons from the Japanese on how to work.[29]

How times have changed! Nowadays, foreigners do not look to Japan for answers. Instead, they tell Japan how to run its economy, which has serious problems and could drag down the world economy, if not properly addressed. The Japanese economy and political system unraveled during the 1990s. The growth rate in GDP is forecast at −2.6 percent for 1998 and −0.8 percent for 1999, and industrial production fell by 7.6 percent in 1998.[30] The Japanese economic and political machinery no longer appears to function as smoothly as it once did. There has been a wave of political, bureaucratic, and business scandals in Japan during the 1990s, where prime ministers have had to resign. It is argued by some persons that excessive homogeneity and conformity, a weakening of the Japanese work ethic, and a diminishing sense of public spirit have contributed to the problems of the Japanese economy.[31]

The Performance of the Japanese Economy in the Twentieth Century

When the twentieth century is divided into specific time periods, the Japanese economy performed the best of all major industrial countries. Its greatest gain in real per capital GDP was made during the period 1950–1987, when its average annual compound growth rate increased by 7.1 percent and its average annual compound growth rate in real GDP increased by 6.0 percent. No other industrial country was even close. For the period 1980–1990 the Japanese growth rate was 4.0 percent compared to 2.2 percent for Germany, 2.9 percent for the United States, and 2.4 percent for France.[32] The decline in the Japanese growth rate occurred in the 1990s. The Japanese real growth rate declined to an average of 1.2 percent for the period 1990–1996. Table 4-5 presents the average annual percent change in real GDP for Japan from 1990–1999.

Strengths of the Japanese Economy

There is a long history of efforts to explain the international success of nations in the form of international trade. Adam Smith is credited with the notion of absolute advantage, in which a nation exports an item if it is a low-cost producer compared to another country.[33] David Ricardo refined this concept to that of comparative advantage, contending that market forces will allocate a nation's resources to those industries where it is relatively most productive.[34] Heckscher and Ohlin developed the factor endowment theory of international trade based on the idea that nations differ in their endowments of land, labor, natural resources, and capital.[35] Nations would export those goods in which they have a comparative factor advantage and

http://

Economic information, statistics, and articles can be found at www.jei.org.

TABLE 4-5
Performance of the Japanese Economy, 1990–1999 (Average Annual Percent Change in Real GDP)

Year	Percent
1980–1989 (average)	3.8
1990	5.1
1991	3.8
1992	1.0
1993	0.3
1994	0.6
1995	1.5
1996	3.9
1997	0.8
1998	−2.5
1999	0.5

Source: International Monetary Fund, *World Economic Outlook, October 1998* (Washington, D.C.: IMF, 1998), p. 172.

import those goods in which they have a comparative factor disadvantage. Nations with abundant low-cost labor, such as China, will export labor-intensive goods such as textiles; nations with abundant land, such as Argentina, will export cattle.

Exports.   When one thinks of Japanese success, it is in terms of its exports. Their products are sold all over the world, from Sony walkmans to Nissans and Toyotas. Only Canada exports more goods to the United States than Japan. But prior to 1900 it had no history as a trading nation. It began the twentieth century by ranking 23rd among the world's leading exporting nations compared to 12th for China. Its exports were less than 2 percent of those of the United Kingdom, the world's leading exporting nation. In 1997 Japan ranked third in the world in exports, which were $150 billion larger than the exports of the United Kingdom.[36] In 1997 Japan had a surplus of $73 billion in its merchandise trade account compared to a deficit of $114 billion in its trade account, approximately one-half of which was with the United States.[37]

Japan as a Leading Creditor Nation.   Japan is the leading creditor nation in the world.[38] It has financed most of its holdings of foreign assets through successive surpluses in its merchandise trade account, which for the past twenty-five years has amounted to $2.2 trillion. A part of this money is invested in U.S. assets ranging from U.S. Treasury bonds to automobile plants. Japan has far more money invested in the United States than the United States has invested in Japan. Earnings from the holdings of Japanese assets in the United States flow back to Japan, while earnings from the holdings of U.S. assets in Japan flow back to the United States. The U.S. government has financed a major part of its expenditures since the late 1970s from borrowing and this has contributed to its debtor position in the world. Japanese holdings of U.S. government debt makes them a creditor.[39]

Japanese Industry. One strength that is associated with Japanese industry is its emphasis on quality.[40] In fact, Japanese products sell in the United States no matter if exchange rates are favorable or unfavorable because to Americans, Japanese goods, particularly automobiles, are associated with quality. Another determinant of Japanese success is research.[41] Earnings from exports have been poured back into research and development. A third factor is the highly skilled labor force of the country and the stock of machinery and equipment per worker. In 1992 Japan ranked first in the value of machinery and equipment per worker and third in years of education per person compared to the other major industrial countries.[42] A fourth strength is the existence of strong domestic demand for Japanese products. The domestic market has usually led industrial development in most industries.

Weaknesses of the Japanese Economy

The Japanese economy faces serious problems as it enters the twenty-first century. It remains to be seen whether or not it will be capable of solving them before it drags down a substantial part of the world with it. It is said that a national malaise grips Japan,[43] which is why the Japanese political and administrative machine has ceased to function. It is also said that the Japanese have caught the "Japanese disease," which means a weakening of the Japanese work ethic; excessive homogeneity and conformity; a loss of creativity; and a diminishing sense of public spirit. The wave of political, bureaucratic, and business scandals that hit Japan during the 1990s are offered as proof that Japan has lost the special glue that has held it together for centuries.

An Aging Society. Japan has one of the world's oldest populations, and during the first quarter of the twenty-first century, it will grow even older at a faster rate. Life expectancy in Japan is the highest among all major countries and is expected to increase in the future.[44] Moreover, there has been a drop in the fertility rate accompanied by a decrease in the working population. But unlike the United States and Germany, there are two problems with which Japan has to contend. The first is a resistance to immigration. Japan is racially homogeneous and wants to keep it that way. Immigrants who would provide a source of labor are not welcome. The second problem is the role of women in Japan. There is a huge resistance to tapping the productive potential of women, thus lessening the tax base.

Financial Problems. The Japanese economy is in the midst of a financial mess. Its banks have $1.5 trillion in bad debts, an amount equal to the GDP of France.[45] Its major banks lost money and other banks failed and had to be taken over by the government. Total government debt and interest payments are larger than the GDP of Japan.[46] Japanese financial institutions made investments based on personal relationships, and favored investors at securities firms were given guaranteed loans on their investments. Loans went to individuals and small businesses for speculation in the stock market and real estate. Ministry of Finance officials told banks when inspections would occur in return for lavish entertainment and other favors.[47] The banks were also involved with Japanese racketeers. Finally, Japanese banks lent heavily to South Korea, Indonesia, and Thailand, three countries that also have serious financial problems.

SUMMARY

During the 1980s Japan was regarded as an economic juggernaut that would dominate the twenty-first century. It invited admiration and everyone looked to it for answers to such problems as economic growth and education. Its conformist and disciplined society was greatly admired, while America's self-centered and individualistic society was not. So, how could a country once lauded for its efficiency get itself into so much trouble in one decade? Is it a result of a collapse of national character and a decline in the vaunted Japanese work ethic, as some would say? Certainly, there is a decline in Japan's sense of public spirit and civic morals, but the problem is deeper than that. These are two major interrelated problems. The first is the collapse of the Japanese financial system, and the second is the ineptitude of the Japanese government to do something about it. This ineptitude is based on interest-group privilege, which has resulted in corruption on a massive scale. It remains to be seen what the future holds for Japan.

QUESTIONS FOR DISCUSSION

1. Discuss some of the factors responsible for the collapse of the Japanese economy in the 1990s.
2. What is a keiretsu? What is a Sogo Shosha?
3. Discuss the relationship of Japanese culture and climate to the economic development of Japan.
4. What are the roles of the Ministry of Finance and the Ministry of International Trade and Industry in the Japanese economy? Do similar agencies exist in the United States?
5. What impact will an aging population have on the Japanese economy of the future?
6. What impact will Japanese financial problems have on the United States and Europe?
7. Compare Japanese economic development in the twentieth century to the economic development of other major industrial countries.
8. What is meant by the "bubble economy"? Why did it collapse?
9. What are the strengths and weaknesses of the Japanese economy?
10. Would American-style capitalism work in Japan?

RECOMMENDED READINGS

Endo, Yukiko, and Eiji Katayama. "Population Aging and Japanese Economic Performance." In Barry Bosworth and Gary Burtless, eds., *Aging Societies*. Washington, D.C.: Brookings Institution, 1998, 240–67.

"The Japan Puzzle." *The Economist*, March 21, 1998, pp. 23–28.

Landes, David S. *The Wealth and Poverty of Nations*. New York: Norton, 1998, 350–391.

Lincoln, Edward J. "Japan's Financial Mess." *Foreign Affairs*, Vol. 77, No. 3 (May–June 1998), 57–66.

Porter, Michael. *The Competitive Advantage of Nations*. New York: The Free Press, 1990, 384–421.

Wood, Christopher. *The Bubble Economy*. London: Sidgwick and Jackson, 1992.

Yoshihara, Kuneo. *Japanese Economic Development*. New York: Oxford University Press, 1994.

ENDNOTES

1.   Paul Kennedy, *The Rise and Fall of the Great Powers* (New York: Random House, 1987).

2.   Clyde V. Prestowitz, Jr., *Trading Places* (New York: Basic Books, 1988).

3.   Kennedy and Prestowitz were hardly alone in their predictions of Japanese success. See Ezra F. Vogel, *Japan as No. 1: Lessons for America* (Cambridge: Harvard University Press, 1979), and Daniel Burstein, *Yen! Japan's New Financial Empire and Its Threat to America* (New York: Simon and Schuster, 1988).

4.   The World Bank, *1998 World Development Indicators* (Washington, D.C.: The World Bank, 1998).

5.   This would be prohibited in the United States.

6.   Angus Maddison, *Monitoring the World Economy, 1820–1992* (Paris: OECD Development Center Studies, 1995), 196, 197.

7.   Tariffs were kept high to make foreign imports expensive, while local producers were subsidized by the Japanese government so that they could sell at lower prices.

8.   David S. Landes, *The Wealth and Poverty of Nations* (New York: Norton, 1998).

9.   Ibid., 350.

10.   Landes, *Wealth and Poverty of Nations*, 345–50.

11.   The Dutch and Chinese established commercial contact with Japan in the early part of the seventeenth century.

12.   Foreign aggression was primarily U.S. aggression. Commodore Perry appeared a second time and had his fleet bombard Japanese seaports to make Japan open its ports to American traders. The United States used this approach in Mexico and other countries. It came to be known as "gunboat" diplomacy.

13.   The Meiji Restoration was called a "restoration" because the powers of the government that the Tokugawa Shogunate had usurped were restored to the emperor of Japan, who came to be known posthumously as the Emperor Meiji.

14.   The government also financed the development of experimental or pilot plants to train Japanese workers and to adapt Western production techniques to Japanese conditions. These plants became models for private industry to follow.

15.   Corwin Edwards, "The Dissolution of Zaibatsu Continues," *Pacific Affairs* (September 1946): 8–24.

16.   The U.S. military occupation of Japan ended in 1952.

17.   Japanese antimonopoly laws permitted the development of cartels and other forms of business combinations to a far greater extent than is permitted by U.S. antitrust laws.

18.   Jean-Jacques Servan-Schreiber, *The World Challenge* (New York: Simon and Schuster, 1981), 178–84.

19.   The downside is that it has resulted in corruption and political scandals.

20.   It has 485 colleges and universities compared to 3,300 in the United States. A few elite universities dominate the educational system. The University of Tokyo is an example. Its graduates usually go to the elite Japanese industries.

21.   This is diametrically opposite to the United States, where the individual counts.

22.   This is good and bad. Much of the corruption in Japan is based on doing friends a favor, and seniority prevents the advancement of younger, more qualified people.

23.   The Japanese believe in divine ancestry. Foreigners are not accepted into Japanese society.

24.   They became known as zaibatsu. The largest of them, the Mitsubishi zaibatsu, was created in 1870. During World War II Mitsubishi produced the planes that were used to fight the Americans. It is still the largest combine in Japan today.

25.   "Japan: All in the Family," *Newsweek*, June 10, 1991, pp. 38–39. The figures are dated, but the principle remains the same.

26.   The United States often does that with its politicians, except they are likely to stay around longer.

27.   "The Japan Puzzle," *The Economist*, March 21, 1998, p. 24.

28.   The U.S. equivalent of MITI would include the Departments of Commerce and Energy, the Office of the U.S. Trade Administration, the Export-Import Bank, the Small Business Administration, the National Science Foundation, the Overseas Private Investment Corporation, the Environmental Protection Agency, and parts of the Departments of Commerce and Justice.

29.   They also said intermarriage with other nationalities made America weak.

30.   U.S. Exports and Imports. *The Economist*, November 28, 1998, p. 108.

31.   We used to say the same thing about the British. It was called the "British disease." Next it was called the "American disease." Now it is called the "Japanese disease."

32.   The World Bank, *1998 World Bank Indicators* (Washington, D.C.: The World Bank, 1998), 176–178.

33.   Adam Smith, *The Wealth of Nations* (New York: Random House, 1937).

34.   David Ricardo, *The Principles of Political Economy and Taxation* (New York: Dutton, 1948).

35.   Bertil Ohlin, *Interregional and International Trade* (Cambridge: Harvard University Press, 1933). Eli Heckscher, "The Effect of Foreign Trade on the Distribution of Income." Reprinted in *Readings in the Theory of International Trade*, eds. H. S. Ellis and L. A. Metzler (Homewood, IL: Irwin, 1949).

36.   World Bank, *1998 World Bank Indicators*, 189–90.

37.   U.S. Department of Commerce, *Business America* (1998), 31.

38.   The United Kingdom was the leading creditor nation of the nineteenth century. The United States was the world's leading creditor nation from 1914 to 1986. The Japanese, despite their economic problems, will continue to be the leading creditor nation for some time to come.

39.   It is estimated that the Japanese hold about 5 percent of the U.S. government debt. Interest payments on the debt flow to Japan and are a plus item in its current account.

40.   Ironically, quality control was taught to the Japanese after World War II by Edward Deming, an American expert on quality control who was ignored by American companies.

41.   Michael E. Porter, *The Competitive Advantage of Nations* (New York: The Free Press, 1990), 390–91.

42.   Angus Maddison, *Monitoring the World Economy, 1820–1992* (Paris: OECD Development Center Studies, 1995), p. 41.

43.   Jimmy Carter said the same thing when he was president of the United States.

44.   Life expectancy at birth is 79.9 years in Japan, the highest in the world. It is 76.4 years in the United States.

45.   Edward J. Lincoln, "Japan's Financial Mess," *Foreign Affairs,* Vol. 77, No. 3 (May–June 1998): 57.

46.   *The Economist,* "The Japan Puzzle," p. 22.

47.   Lincoln, "Japan's Financial Mess," 58.

CHAPTER 5
Germany

Germany represents a third type of capitalism, social market capitalism. Instead of reliance on Adam Smith's "invisible hand" of competition and self-interest to lead to the common welfare, social market capitalism relies on the visible hand of the state. Friedrich List, a nineteenth-century German writer, argued that wealth creation depended on education, transportation, and other elements of infrastructure provided by the state, not by the invisible forces of the market. The German sociologist Max Weber argued that cultural factors were a determinant of wealth, and Werner Sombart contended that the period of unbridled, unrestricted capitalism ended with World War I. The profit motive and pure competition as the sole sources of reference were to be supplemented with rules and regulations, economic cooperation, and the development of a social market economy (*Soziale-marktwirtschaft*).[1]

Germany has never had what can be called a free-market economy; the state has always ensured both order and free enterprise. Its capitalism differs from the free market or individualistic capitalism of the United States in several ways.[2] In the United States, free enterprise and free markets create wealth; in Germany a mixture of state control and private sector autonomy creates wealth. Income and wealth inequality are far more pronounced in the United States than in Germany. There are no German equivalents of Bill Gates. In the United States growth and productivity are prime goals in themselves; in Germany growth and productivity are balanced by social equity. In the United States emphasis is placed on consumption and short-term profit maximization; in Germany emphasis is on long-term goals and production. Finally, the state in the United States ensures law and order and provides basic infrastructure, while the German state creates economic order and develops socioeconomic culture.

Germany's social market capitalism also differs from the state-directed capitalism of Japan. One major difference is the almost complete absence of social welfare programs in Japan compared to the cradle-to-the-grave welfare programs that exist in Germany. Certainly, there are major cultural differences between Japan and Germany that explain the difference in economic systems. In Japan the family or group is responsible for the welfare of the individual. A second major difference is a weak small-business sector in Japan compared to a strong small-business sector called *Mittelstand* in Germany. Again, the difference can be explained by culture and history. A third difference between Japan and Germany is financial. The Japanese financial system, as witnessed by the collapse of the "bubble economy" of the late 1980s and the subsequent banking crisis of the 1990s, is unstable and unregulated. By contrast, Germany has the most stable financial system in the world. Finally, Japanese society is insular and does not open to the outside world.[3]

GERMAN REUNIFICATION

http://

The site of the German Institute for Economic Research at www.diw-berlin.de provides links to a variety of related sites.

One of the most mesmerizing events of the last half of the twentieth century was the reunification of Germany in 1990. The Berlin Wall, which was the consummate symbol of the division between East Germany and West Germany, was torn down and its parts sold as souvenirs to remind people of the past. For forty years the two countries had coexisted side by side with totally different political economic systems. The unification was brought about by the collapse of the Soviet Union. Under tremendous pressure by the East German population, which wanted to benefit from the prosperity of the West, East Germany (or the German Democratic Republic as it was called) dissolved almost overnight and was reunited with West Germany.[4] Despite a common heritage, the two Germanies developed over a period of a generation into two very different cultures.

East Germany and West Germany were a result of the dismantling of Hitler's Third Reich after the end of World War II. East Germany, which was in the Russian zone of occupation, was created out of the provinces of Prussia, Thuringia, Pomerania, Brandenburg, and Upper Saxony. Much of East Germany was agriculture, made up of large estates owned by the Junkers, the land-owning aristocracy of Prussia. West Germany, which consisted of the provinces of Bavaria, Westphalia, Mecklenburg, Hesse, and Lower Saxony, was in the Western zone of occupation. It contained two-thirds of the German population and much of the German industrial base as represented by heavy industry. The German Democratic Republic, or East Germany, became an independent country in 1949, while the Federal Republic of Germany, or West Germany, became an independent country in the same year. The two countries, one communist and the other capitalist, went their separate ways for forty years.

A Comparison of East Germany and West Germany

East Germany and West Germany afford the best comparison between a communist country and a capitalist country because they existed side by side for forty years and had a common heritage. As Table 5-1 indicates, East Germany was better off than West Germany in terms of per capita income before World War II. It was the locus of much of Germany's chemical industry and produced office, textile, and precision machinery and a wide variety of automobiles. All of Germany's production of electrical goods was centered in East Germany. World leadership in the production of optical equipment was held by the Carl Zeiss firm of Jena, which became a part of East Germany.[5] Per capita industrial output was 16 percent higher and per capita GDP was 5 percent higher in East Germany than in West Germany.

Agriculture. As Table 5-2 indicates, East Germany was the leader in agricultural production before the war. It was the food base for Germany, and it produced products for export, including grain, sugar, and potatoes. After the war, the area became a perennial grain importer and a major food deficit region. East Germany also had

TABLE 5-1 *Breakdown of German GDP, Population, and per Capita GDP, 1936–1990*

	1936		
	GDP (million RM)[1]	*Population (thousands)*	*Per Capita Income (RM)*
Federal Republic	41,757	42,208	989
GDR	16,159	15,614	1,035
East of Oder-Neisse[2]	6,968	9,514	732
Total 1936 territory	64,884	67,336	964
	1990 (second half year)		
	GDP (million DM)[3]	*Population (thousands)*	*Per Capita Income (DM)*
Federal Republic	1,216.9	63,527	19,864
Former GDR	97.7	16,111	6,064
Total	1,359.6	79,638	17,007

[1]*The reichmark was the German currency unit in 1936.*
[2]*This would include East Prussia and Lower and Upper Silesia, which are now parts of Russia and Poland.*
[3]*The Deutsche mark was the West German currency unit in 1990. The mark replaced it and the euro replaced the mark in 1999.*

Source: Angus Maddison, *Monitoring the World Economy, 1820–1992* (Paris: Organization for Economic Cooperation and Development, 1995), 131.

TABLE 5-2
Agricultural Production in East and West Germany for Selected Years

Year	FRG	GDR
All Grains[1]		
1935–1938	22.4	23.9
1970	33.4	28.2
1984	53.6	45.1
Potatoes[1]		
1935–1938	185.0	194.3
1970	272.3	195.7
1984	331.5	224.0
Sugar Beets[1]		
1935–1938	327.2	301.2
1970	444.2	320.1
1984	494.7	325.3
Milk[2]		
1935–1938	2,436.0	2,549.0
1970	4,126.0	3,314.0
1984	5,120.0	4,187.0

[1]*Doppelzentners: 1 doppelzentner = 100 kilograms.*
[2]*Kilograms.*

Source: Deutscher Bundestag, *Materialien zum Bericht zur Lage der Nation im geteilten Deutschland,* 1967 (Bonn: Verlag Dr. Hans Heger, 1967), 412; *Materialien zum Bericht zur Lage der Nation im geteilten Deutschland, 1987* (Bonn: Verlag Dr. Hans Heger, 1987), 441–42.

advantages in land fertility, particularly in the north, where the soil is sandy. Table 5-2 compares agricultural productivity in the pre–World War II areas of East Germany and West Germany and during the time they were separate countries. Agricultural productivity was higher in East Germany than in West Germany before the war, but when they became separate countries, West German agriculture became more productive than East German agriculture, despite the fact that West German farms were much smaller than East German farms, averaging around 44 acres compared to 24,000 acres for the average East German state farm and 3,000 acres for the average collective farm.

Industry.   East German industry was very much overrated by Western experts. It may have been the best of the Eastern bloc countries, but it was uncompetitive by Western standards. Industrial production amounted to one-fourth of that of West Germany. Because the service sector was weak, the industrial sector accounted for two-thirds of national output compared to 40 percent in West Germany.[6] Even the elite industries, those into which the state poured the most money, were outmoded by Western standards. Particularly weak was the transportation system, most of which was built before World War II. Only 16 percent of the railroad system was electrified, compared to 98 percent in West Germany, and the rolling stock (locomotives and freight and passenger cars) were old.[7]

Economic planning was the be-all and end-all of the East German economic system, and thus everything had to be centralized and implemented from the top down.[8] East German industrial production was concentrated in large state-owned enterprises, which were integrated both horizontally and vertically. Enterprises in a particular sector and their suppliers were formed into combines (*kombinat*). An East German combine was responsible for developing its long-range and annual production plans and coordinating the plans of all of its member enterprises. In 1988 there were 126 national combines, 95 regional combines, and 3,408 state enterprises.[9] The combines accounted for 98 percent of industrial employment, production, and exports, but they and the firms they represented became top-heavy with managers and bureaucrats and thus inflexible. Moreover, as Table 5-3 indicates, East German industry was far more concentrated and labor-intensive than West German industry.[10] Table 5-4 compares worker productivity in East Germany and West Germany.

Living Standards. Although East Germany had the highest living standards of all of the Soviet-bloc countries, it was well below that of West Germany. Moreover, the living standards grew farther apart during the 1980s. When money wages were translated into real wages, some goods cost less in East Germany than in West Germany while other goods cost more. However, it is necessary to remember that basic necessities, particularly goods, rent, and transportation, were subsidized by the East German government. The price charged by the state to consumers bore little or no relationship to production costs or procurement costs paid to farms. Many consumer goods were priced well below cost, but prices for such items as coffee and fruit were maintained at high levels.[11]

Table 5-5 compares the amount of work time in East Germany and West Germany required to earn enough money to buy consumer goods such as television

TABLE 5-3 *Industrial Employment Structures in East Germany and West Germany, 1988*

	East Germany	West Germany
	(Employees per Enterprise)	*(Employees per Enterprise)*
Chemical industry	1,419	296
Metal industry	3,209	474
Construction materials	712	71
Electronics, electrical engineering	1,554	333
Automotive industry	838	217
Textile industry	1,301	169
Food industry	480	125

Source: Gerhart Fels and Claus Schnabel, *The Economic Transformation of East Germany: Some Preliminary Lessons* (Washington, D.C.: Group of Thirty, 1991), 13.

TABLE 5-4 *Industrial Worker Productivity in East and West Germany (GDR as percentage of FRG = 100), 1970–1988*

Industry	1970	1980	1988
Power and fuels	61	37	45
Chemicals, synthetic fiber, rubber	34	44	55
Metallurgy	41	39	—
Construction	44	44	40
Water production and use	62	56	—
Steel, machinery, vehicles	44	46	45
Electronics, precision, and optics	38	43	50
Textiles	53	57	55
Consumer goods	55	58	56
Food, beverages, and tobacco (average)	60	43	40
Average	48	44	48

Source: Deutscher Bundestag, *Materialen zur Lage der Nation im geteilten Deutschland, 1987* (Bonn: Verlag Dr. Hans Heger, 1987), 392; Deutsche Bank, Economics Department, *Special: East Germany* (Frankfurt: 1989), 8–11.

TABLE 5-5

Purchasing Power in East and West Germany as Measured by Work Time Necessary to Earn Money to Purchase (hours and minutes)

Type of Purchase	West Germany	East Germany
Men's shirt	1.22	7.19
Men's shoes	5.20	24.01
Men's suit	10.49	59.30
Women's pantyhose	0.12	2.40
Women's dress	4.44	21.30
Children's shoes	2.35	7.21
Radio-cassette	13.36	207.09
Color TV	81.34	1,008.56
Washing machine	59.09	491.04
Refrigerator	29.54	272.19
Vacuum cleaner	13.32	82.09
Car	694.33	4,375.00
Railroad fare, 15 km	1.46	0.27
Dark bread, 1 kg	0.12	0.07
Sugar, 1 kg	0.07	0.17
Butter, 1 kg	0.36	1.39
Eggs, dozen	0.10	0.36
Milk, litre	0.05	0.07
Cheese, 1 kg	0.52	1.43
Pork cutlets, 1 kg	1.01	1.47
Apples, 1 kg	0.09	0.15
Lemon, 1 kg	0.16	0.54
Coffee, 250 g	0.21	4.20

Source: Bundesministerium für Innerdeutsche Beziehungen, *Zahlenspiegel Bundesrepublik Deutschland/Deutsche Demokratische Republik*, Ein Vergleich (Bonn: 1989), 77–78.

sets and cars.[12] As the table indicates, the West German worker clearly had superior purchasing power in terms of time invested. Moreover, the difference widened over time, with the East German worker becoming worse off and the West German worker becoming better off. East German consumer goods were far inferior in terms of quality.[13] Selections were limited to what the planners thought the population should have rather than what they actually wanted.[14] It often took several years of waiting before cars or refrigerators could be obtained.

Economic and Social Costs of Reunification

"Verraten und Verkauft!" (deceived and sold!). This is a common slogan written on walls in the former East Germany, which shows that the euphoria of unification has given way to frustration. West German politicians, like their American counterparts, had promised all gain and no pain. Former Chancellor Helmut Kohl promised that flowers would bloom, grass would grow, and living standards between East Germans and West Germans would be equalized in four years at no expense to the German taxpayer. Even allowing for hyperbole, things didn't exactly work out the way he said they would. Reunification has proved to be more expensive than anticipated, and the economic and social costs have been borne primarily by the East Germans, hence the slogan on the walls.

The deep penetration of communism into the economic and social life of East Germans was underestimated. For more than forty years, East Germans were taught the socialist dream that would promote the elimination of poverty by the controlled distribution of wealth. Incomes were more equally distributed in East Germany than in West Germany; unemployment was virtually nonexistent; jobs were available for everyone. The end result was the inefficient use of labor by factories.[15] Hard work was not rewarded by any material means and therefore was avoided wherever possible. Rents were low and housing was provided by the state. As long as one was playing by the rules of the system, the future was secure and predictable. To ensure conformity, an elaborate network of spies was set up, and those persons who didn't conform were turned in to the state police.[16] The system bred dependency on the state, and the psychology of dependency remained long after reunification.

Monetary Union.   On July 1, 1990, the West German mark became the legal tender for the united Germany, and the West German deutsche mark exchanged at a ratio of 1 to 1 with the East German mark.[17] This proved to be a mistake, but Chancellor Kohl ignored the advice of the Deutsche Bundesbank and his advisors by promising an exchange rate of 1 to 1. At the time the unofficial rate was 20 East German marks to 1 West German mark. What happened after the 1 to 1 exchange is that wages in East Germany went up to 65 percent of West German wages, while productivity was a third of West Germany's. The result was mass unemployment in East Germany as firms had to cut costs. Most small firms shut down after being privatized and larger firms responded with layoffs.

http://

Current economic data for Germany, including U.S. comparative data, can be found at www.germany-info.org/facts/germecon.htm.

Environmental Problems.   East Germany was one of the most polluted countries in the world, but little was known about the environmental damage that was caused by the socialist system until after reunification. What was once called the agricultural breadbasket of Germany before World War II became a contaminated region and remains so today. The forests were, and still are, dying, and many rivers were contaminated and could not be used for drinking water. In many areas the soil was toxic up to ten feet deep. As a result, soil had to be excavated and replaced, water purification plants were built, and major coal-using power plants—a prime cause of pollution—were shut down. The clean-up costs have been enormous, in terms of both investment costs and lost jobs.[18]

The Role of Women.   No one group has been affected more adversely by reunification than East German women. Under socialism, they were guaranteed job equality, which, however, did not mean that they got the better-paying jobs. They were entitled to abortion on demand, and they were provided with day-care centers for their children.[19] All of this changed as a result of reunification. Abortion is not legal on demand in Germany and job equality is not guaranteed. As a result, many East German women are jobless and stay at home, which increases social tensions. The unemployment rate nine years after reunification is 30 percent higher for women than it is for men.[20] Many East German women, particularly the younger ones, have migrated to West Germany to search for jobs.

Property Rights.   One of the most complex results of reunification involves property rights. Most East German property was privately owned before East Germany became a communist country. Some of this property had been in the same family for generations, while other property, particularly if owned by Jews, had been expropriated by the Nazis and distributed to Nazi bigwigs such as Goering and Goebbels.[21] A Repossession Law was passed after reunification that allowed former property owners to reclaim property expropriated by the communists even though a period of thirty or more years had elapsed. Dissension occurred when a West German who had lived in freedom and prosperity for thirty years would come and boot an East German off his property.[22]

Unemployment.   In 1988, a year before the collapse of the East German nation, approximately nine million East Germans were employed out of a total population of 17 million.[23] Everyone was guaranteed a job, even though the end result was inefficiency in the use of labor resources as state enterprises were overstocked with workers. Women as well as men were fully employed. Three years later, some four million East Germans had lost their jobs. Once reunification took place, the true state of the East German economy was revealed for the world to see. Although it had been rated as perhaps the world's tenth or eleventh largest industrial producer, East Germany turned out to be a junk heap of industries that were obsolete by Western standards and turned out products that could not compete with Western ones. Unsalable and unusable plants were shut down, and those plants that were of some value were sold to West German and foreign firms, with the end result of cutting employment by one-half or more.

Even after eight years of reunification, the East German rate of unemployment rate is more than twice as high as the West German rate of unemployment. Many East Germans have retired from the labor force, while others have been put to work on public works projects. One result has been increased violence against immigrants and by a growth of political support for right-wing political parties. German immigration laws grant legal immigrants immediate housing and financial support, creating more competition for housing and employment at a time when the unemployment rate was rising. Table 5-6 compares unemployment in Western Germany and Eastern Germany for the period 1992 through October 1998. As a comparison, in the second quarter of 1990 a total of 83,300 East Germans were unemployed; in the same quarter of 1991 834,900 East Germans were unemployed.[24]

Table 5-7 presents a comparison of real per capita income and the average rate of unemployment for the states (länder) of West Germany and East Germany for 1997. The unemployment rate was much higher in the eastern part of Germany

TABLE 5-6 *Unemployment Rates in Western Germany and Eastern Germany, 1992–1998*

	Employed (thousands)	Unemployed (thousands)	Unemployment Rate (%)*
Western Germany			
1992	29,223	2,243	7.7
1993	29,221	2,320	8.0
1994	28,665	2,556	8.2
1995	28,482	2,565	8.3
1996	28,186	2,796	9.1
1997	27,884	3,022	9.8
1998 (Jan.)	27,571	3,236	10.8
1998 (May)	28,861	2,826	9.2
1998 (Oct.)	28,232	2,690	8.8
Eastern Germany			
1992	7,534	835	10.1
1993	6,845	1,122	13.9
1994	6,314	1,142	15.2
1995	6,386	1,047	14.0
1996	6,279	1,169	15.7
1997	6,078	1,363	18.1
1998 (Jan.)	5,918	1,588	21.1
1998 (May)	6,000	1,469	18.1
1998 (Oct.)	5,910	1,267	17.6
1999 (Jan.)	—	1,430	18.9

Relative to the total labor force.

Source: Deutsche Bundesbank, *Annual Report, 1998* (Frankfurt am Main, Germany: March 1998), 63; *Monthly Report*, September 1998, 65; *Monthly Report*, February 1999, 58.

TABLE 5-7   *Real per Capita Income and Unemployment in the States of East and West Germany, 1997 ($ and %)*

	*Real per Capital Income**	*Unemployment*
West Germany		
Hamburg	46,153	13.0
Schleswig-Holstein	23,137	11.2
Bremen	34,216	16.8
Lower Saxony	22,832	12.9
North Rhine-Westphalia	25,200	10.3
Rhine-Palatinate	22,400	12.2
Hesse	33,565	12.2
Saarland	23,775	13.6
Baden-Wurttemburg	28,420	8.7
Bavaria	28,870	8.7
East Germany		
Mecklenburg-Pomerania	11,833	20.3
Berlin	24,327	17.3
Brandenburg	13,179	18.9
Saxony	12,102	18.4
Saxony-Anhalt	11,457	21.7
Thuringia	11,516	19.1

*Estimates made by taking the average exchange rates of the dollar and the mark for 1997, which was approximately 1.55 marks = $1.

Source: OECD Economic Surveys, *Germany* (Paris: Organization for Economic Cooperation and Development, 1998), 86.

than it was in the western part. Real per capita income in the eastern part was about half of what it was in the western part. In addition, there are more retirees in the East than in the West because of a lack of job opportunities, and more workers are working part-time. Younger and more productive workers moved to West Germany right after reunification.

Benefits of Reunification

Reunification is expected to cost close to one trillion marks ($650 billion) by the beginning of the twenty-first century, but there are also benefits. The standard of living for East Germans has increased. Almost every family has a car, and, although wages are lower than they are in West Germany the average worker earns from six to ten times as much as the typical Polish or Hungarian worker receives. Moreover, once upgrading is complete, East Germany will have one of the world's most modern and advanced roads, ports, rail lines, airports, and telecommunication networks. Infrastructure investment in East Germany has cost the German government $550 billion since reunification, but East Germany will develop into a region more modern and better developed than any other area in Europe. Its telephone system is more up-to-date than West Germany's.

In 1999 the German government moved its capital from Bonn to Berlin, where it was prior to World War II. Since Berlin is in the heart of East Germany, this move may help integrate the different cultures of the two areas. Many West Germans hold prejudices about their eastern counterparts, referring to them as louts and blockheads.[25] West German taxpayers also resent the fact that they have had to pay most of the cost of reunification, particularly after the politicians told them it would be painless. The renewal of Berlin has brought about construction projects, new apartments, and hotels and has brightened up East Berlin from the dull and drab appearance it showed visitors before reunification.[26]

THE GERMAN ECONOMY

Germany has a population of 82 million, which is actually declining because the death rate exceeds its birth rate (Table 5-8). Its currency unit, the mark, not only has dominated the currency system of Europe, but also has been one of the strongest currencies in the world. When the European Monetary Union is created

TABLE 5-8 *Economic and Social Data for Germany, 1997*

Population (thousands)	81,912.0
Population growth, 1990–1997 (%)	0.5
Land area, thousands of square kilometers	349.3
Real GDP ($ billions)	1,748.3
World rank	4th
Average annual growth rate in GDP	
1980–1990	2.2
1990–1997	0.7
Foreign trade ($ millions)	
Exports	604,277.0
Imports	576,283.0
Total	1,180,560.0
World rank	2nd
Percent of World trade	10.1
Central government revenues (% of GDP)	29.4
Central government expenditures (% of GDP)	32.1
Human development index, rank out of 174 countries	19th
Adult literacy rate (%)	
Males	99.0
Females	99.0
Share of earned income (%)	
Males	65.2
Females	34.8
Gini coefficient of income inequality (%)	28.1

Sources: The World Bank, *World Development Report, 1998–1999* (New York: Oxford University Press, 1998), 190, 194, 198, 210, 218; The World Bank, *1998 World Bank Atlas* (New York: World Bank Publications, 1998), 32, 34; United Nations Development Program, *Human Development Report, 1998* (New York: Oxford University Press, 1998), 128–32.

http://

For current eco-
nomic data on
Germany, visit
www.commerzbank
.com.

in 2002, the euro will replace the mark, the franc, and other European currencies as the sole currency, but its value is weighted in favor of the mark. Moreover, the influence of the German financial system will be felt in the financial system of the European Union (EU) because the Central Bank of the EU will be based in Frankfurt, the home of the Deutsche Bundesbank, for years the central bank of Germany. The Central Bank of the European Union will follow the same mone-tary policies that were established by the Deutsche Bundesbank over the last forty years, with emphasis placed on price stability.

The German economy is a product of its history, society, culture, and collective psyche. Its individual economic components, such as Mittelstand, are simply a part of a system that dates back for centuries. Martin Luther provided a religious ration-ale for German capitalism. He said: "Men are born to work, just as the birds are born to fly" and thus founded a work ethic that came to be called the Protestant work ethic.[27] By working hard, the individual adds to the total wealth of the group (*Gemeinde*) and the state. This is a communitarian, rather than an individualistic, ethic that emphasizes loyalty to the group and the state. It is diametrically opposite to the Adam Smith concept of individual self-interest benefiting society as a whole.

Mittelstand

Mittelstand, or "middle estate," is an important part of the German economy. As an institution, it dates back to the Middle Ages when craftsmen's guilds dominated the economies of the German principalities. They set strict regulations that defined quality in craftsmanship and rewarded with the title of master (*meister*) those who had been through the training and achieved the prescribed standards. Even today, craftsmanship remains important in Germany and provides an iden-tity to those who possess it. In comparing Germany to the United States and Japan, *Mittelstand* plays a uniquely German role. It contributes to the German economy in two different ways. First, it accounts for almost two-thirds of total employment, half of all business sales, and over 40 percent of all investment. Second, it plays a very important role in perpetuating the German system of vocational education, which is considered by many experts to be the best in the world.[28]

Mittelstand companies belong to employers associations that act as informal car-tels. They are far better organized than they are in the United States. They are responsible for collective bargaining with the German trade unions. In addition, there are the German chambers of commerce and their trade association, the Deutsche Industrie und Handelstag (DIHT). Membership is obligatory for all Ger-man firms, regardless of their size. A major responsibility of the German chambers of commerce is involvement in vocational training programs. As public law bodies, they set store hours, issue business licenses and work permits, resolve disputes between business firms, and interact with government institutions at all levels.[29] Thus, their functions are central to the operation of the German economic system.

Banking

The financial power of German banks is far greater than that of banks in the United States. They are the major source of capital to German industry and are the largest stockholders. They also provide most of the brokerage service in Germany. There is no enforced separation of investment and commercial banking as there is in the United States and Japan.[30] German bankers sit on the board of directors of companies in which they own stock or to which they lend money, a practice that is illegal in the United States. It is estimated that the major German banks, all privately owned, directly or indirectly, own one-fourth of the voting stock in 25 percent of Germany's largest corporations and are the source of 28 percent of their supervisory boards.[31] Then there are state and regional commercial banks, also privately owned, that are the sole source of capital for small German business firms. The German banks control at least half of the German economy; hence the emphasis on long-term goals and monetary stability.

A cultural characteristic of the Germans is their love of order, which is reflected in their banking system. There are no loose ends. The power of German banks is a product of the nineteenth century when the Deutsche Bank and the Commerzbank were created by the Prussian state to finance the development of the chemical industry. When Germany was unified, the Deutsche Bank became the key bank of both the government and business, with representatives of both serving on its board of directors. It still remains the most powerful bank in Germany. The order has been maintained through bank linkages with major German firms. For example, the linkage of the Deutsche Bank with the German chemical company BASF dates back to the nineteenth century, when the bank provided the start-up capital for the company. Through control of voting rights, the bank exercises the same control over the company today.

Codetermination

A unique feature of labor-management relations in German industries is codetermination of business policies on the part of labor and management. Its purpose is to give workers a voice in determining public policy. As a principle codetermination dates back to the development of trade unionism in the nineteenth century. It was tied into the idea of a just social order, which permeated German trade unions at that time. The first relevant legislation was passed in World War I, when the Law on Auxiliary Services for the Fatherland made workers' committees obligatory in all enterprises with fifty or more workers engaged in war contracts. However, after Germany lost the war, codetermination did not become a labor-management issue again until the passage of the Works Constitution Act of 1952, which was applied to workers in the iron, steel, and coal industries. Subsequent acts have broadened the application of codetermination to cover all German firms with five or more workers.[32]

Codetermination takes place through two structures—supervisory boards and works councils.[33] The supervisory board must have one-third worker representation in firms between 500 and 2,000 employees and one-half worker representation for firms with 2,000 workers or more. For public corporations, there must be equal representation of labor and management; for private corporations, there must be equal representation between labor and management plus one representative who is supposed to be neutral. This neutral representative, who is elected by both groups, is supposed to serve as a tiebreaker. Supervisory boards make investment and other long-term decisions for companies. Membership on a supervisory board gives employees a voice in personnel policy matters but not operational issues, which are the domain of management.

Functioning at the factory level, the works council exists in most German firms and covers all aspects of job conditions. All individual worker dismissals must be brought to the works council before notice can be given, and it may intervene by filing suit in a labor court against the dismissal. It deals with other issues of immediate concern to workers, such as plant closings or new production processes. It cannot block major investment decisions by employers or interfere with large-scale capital transfers; it is basically restricted to making the best out of general working conditions. In some respects, works councils are more important than supervisory boards in that they involve greater worker participation in issues of more immediate concern.

Vocational Education

The educational system of Germany is one of its major strengths in that it has created a skilled labor force capable of handling new industrial technologies. This may be contrasted with the United States, where the high school dropout rate is eight times higher than that of Germany and where in international student achievement comparisons, U.S. students usually rank near the bottom in math and sciences. This means that many U.S. workers are unable to compete for jobs that require technical skills. The German labor force, on the other hand, annually receives vocational training in some four hundred occupations. Training, often with a preselected employer, will usually last for two or three years. There are also

a number of short, or refresher, courses available to workers.

Each year around one-half of German teenagers between the ages of 15 and 19 receive vocational training within a range of four hundred occupational specialties, including crafts, carpentry, car repair, electronics, sales, office or banking work, medical technician work, and secretarial work. Vocational training is administered by the German state governments, trade unions, and business firms in conjunction with the German school system.[34] The trainee normally is assigned to a company and then works for it two or three days a week. The remainder of the week is spent at a state vocational school.[35] Vocational training programs cost industry an estimated DM35 billion ($22 billion) annually, but the end result is that the labor force is well trained and unemployment among teenagers is low. Germany has the highest share of world trade in goods with a high skill content.

Social Security and Other Welfare Measures

Social security programs in Germany date back to Bismarck's opposition to socialism and his dislike of trade unions, which led him to sponsor the health insurance law of 1883. By 1911, when the Insurance Consolidation Act brought all German insurance systems under one statute, the majority of German workers were insured against sickness and invalidism. Unemployment insurance, which had originated in the United Kingdom in 1911, was introduced into Germany in 1927. War and war-related pensions and financial assistance comprise an important component of German social welfare pensions. Included are various measures for the creation and maintenance of transit and reception camps for refugees.[36] Then there is the family allowance, or children's allowance (*Kindergeld*) as it is commonly called, which is separate from the social insurance system and is financed out of general government revenues.

The bulk of social security expenditures are kept in the social budget (*Sozialbudget*), which is administered by the federal government but separately from the federal budget. The bulk of the German social security system is financed by payroll taxes levied on both employers and employees, other contributions, and the general revenues from the federal budget. The revenues from payroll taxes are never adequate to cover all expenditures by the system. Thus, some proportion of all taxes paid by individual taxpayers is used to help finance the social security system. In 1997 total social security payments amounted to DM758 billion ($348 billion), which represented about 24 percent of the German GNP. There was a deficit of around DM35 billion ($11 billion) in the social security budget.[37]

AN EVALUATION OF THE GERMAN ECONOMY

The performance of the West German economy was good, particularly during the period immediately after the end of World War II and continuing up to 1960. It was helped to some extent by Marshall Plan aid from the United States and from NATO expenditures.[38] Postwar German economic policy revolved around the combination of personal freedom and social welfare within the framework of a competitive market economy. Social welfare programs became among the most comprehensive in Europe. Tax incentives were designed to stimulate investment of the part of German enterprises. Postwar German monetary and fiscal policies were oriented toward increasing production. The social market economy established in Germany after World War II remains the policy of Germany today.

Strengths of the German Economy

Germany has its strengths. It will be the dominant economy in the European Union, and monetary policy will follow the same philosophy as followed by the Deutsche Bundesbank for the last forty years, with emphasis placed on price stability. Germany is strong in the automotive, chemical, textile, and machinery industries. In addition, Germany enjoys a competitive advantage over other nations in the production of optical-related products and in household goods, including certain segments of ceramic and porcelain-related products and in household goods and equipment. Its banks are among the most competitive in the world. With respect to the European Union, the long-term effect on Germany will be positive because of its location at the center of Europe. Seven member countries of the European Union border on Germany, such as Poland and the Czech Republic, who hope eventually to become full-fledged members.

http://

Learn more about the economic effects of reunification at www .germany-info .org/facts/qafiles/ QAch3.htm, part of the German Information Center's site at http://www .germany-info .org/index.htm.

Despite two major world wars that were of disastrous consequence to the German economy and the German people, Germany performed well during the twentieth century. Tables 5-9 and 5-10 provide different comparisons of growth rates for the major countries for selected time periods. Table 5-9 presents the average annual compound growth rates in real per capita GDP for seven major countries, including Germany, for the period 1900–1913 before World War I; the period 1913–1950, which included World War I, the Depression of the 1930s, and World War II; the period 1950–1973; and the period 1973–1987. Table 5-10 presents a comparison of the same countries, using real GNP growth rates for a different set of time periods.

Weaknesses of the German Economy

Unemployment.   The results of national elections often turn on the amount of unemployment a country has. This was true in France in 1997 and Germany in 1998, and both countries changed political leaders. Reeunification increased the German unemployment rate, as East German factories were shut down and workers lost their jobs. Even after eight years of unification, the unemployment rate remains high, particularly in eastern Germany among women and youths. One result has been an increase in violence against immigrants accompanied by a growth in political support for right-wing political parties. The composition of unemployment has changed; long-term unemployment has increased, as has the share of the unemployed accounted for by old workers. There is also considerable

TABLE 5-9   *Per Capita Real GDP Growth Rates for Selected Countries, 1900–1987 (average annual compound growth rates in percent)*

Country[1]	1900–1913[2]	1913–1950[3]	1950–1973[4]	1973–1987
Canada[5]	3.3	0.7	2.5	1.5
France	1.5	1.1	3.8	1.7
Germany	1.6	0.7	4.9	2.0
Italy	2.0	0.7	4.8	2.0
Japan	1.2	0.9	8.0	2.8
United Kingdom	0.7	0.8	2.5	1.5
United States	2.0	1.6	2.2	1.5

[1]*Countries were not at the same stage of economic development in 1900. Japan's real per capita GDP in 1900 was $677 compared to $2,911 for the United STates; in 1987 it was $9,756 compared to $13,550 for the United States.*
[2]*Period prior to World War I.*
[3]*Period including World War I, the Depression, and the World War II.*
[4]*1973 marks the Arab oil embargo, which resulted in the end of the Bretton Woods exchange standard based on the U.S. dollar, which was backed by gold. The currencies of the other countries in the table were pegged to the U.S. dollar.*
[5]*Canada was a part of the British empire until after World War II.*

Source: Angus Maddison, *The World Economy in the Twentieth Century* (Paris: OECD Development Center Studies, 1991), 35.

TABLE 5-10   *Real GNP Growth Rates for Selected Countries, 1950–2000 (%)*

Country	1950–1955	1960–1973	1974–1979	1980–1991	1992–2000
Germany	8.2	4.4	2.4	2.3	1.7
France	4.6	5.6	2.8	2.2	2.3
Italy	5.6	5.3	3.7	2.3	2.0
United Kingdom	2.8	3.3	1.5	1.9	2.2
United States	3.3	3.9	2.6	2.1	2.6
Japan	8.8	9.6	3.6	4.1	2.6
Canada	4.0	5.3	4.2	2.4	3.3

Note: Figures for 1992–2000 include East Germany.

Source: OECD Economic Surveys, *Germany* (Paris: Organization for Economic Cooperation and Development, 1994), 70.

TABLE 5-11   *Relative Disposable Income of Individuals and Population Share by Age of Household Head for Selected Countries, 1997 (%)*

Country	Canada	France	Germany	Japan	United States
Below 30					
Relative income	87.7	78.7	78.5	75.9	75.0
Population share	11.3	10.5	9.8	5.0	13.4
30 to 50					
Relative income	101.5	101.7	100.9	94.2	101.5
Population share	48.3	52.7	45.7	52.5	53.4
50 to 65					
Relative income	111.9	110.1	113.0	120.7	120.0
Population share	23.9	22.1	25.1	30.3	18.9
Retirement age, above 65					
Relative income	87.3	95.0	89.3	93.1	91.9
Population share	16.6	14.7	19.4	12.2	14.2

Source: Organization for Economic Cooperation and Development, *Maintaining Prosperity in an Aging Economy* (Paris: OECD, 1998), 57.

"hidden unemployment," which covers those in early retirement on account of unemployment.

An Aging Population.   Aging is a major problem in Germany, as it is in the United States and other developed countries. At the same time the population is aging, the number of workers in the German labor force is decreasing.[39] The end result in Germany, as well as in other countries with aging populations, is a shift of resources across generations, as Table 5-11 shows. In Germany there is an additional problem. When reunification took place, millions of East German pensioners who had not contributed to the West German social security system were nonetheless given pensions. To make matters worse, the German labor force is declining in number and the death rate now exceeds the birth rate. This means that in the future, fewer German workers will have to pay more to support an ever-increasing number of pensioners.

The German National Election of 1998

Since reunification many economic and political changes have occurred. After sixteen years of continuous rule by Chancellor Helmut Kohl and the Christian Democrats, Gerhard Schroeder was elected the new chancellor of Germany and the Social Democrats became the dominant political party. One of the most significant results of this election was a rise in the strength of the ex-communist Party of Democratic Socialism. Table 5-12 presents a breakdown of the popular vote as expressed as a percentage of the total vote cast and the number of seats each German political party has in the Bundestag, the German equivalent of the U.S. House of Representatives.[40] Neither major political party received a majority of the popular vote, or had a majority of seats in the Bundestag.[41]

TABLE 5-12
The Results of the German National Election of 1998

Parties	Votes Cast (%)	Seats in the Bundestag[1]
Social Democrats	40.9	298
Christian Democrats/CSU[2]	35.2	245
Greens[3]	6.7	47
Liberals[4]	6.2	44
Ex-communists[5]	5.1	35
Others[6]	6.0	0
Total	100.0	669

[1]*A party can only become a national political party with representation in the Bundestag if it receives 5 percent or more of the popular vote.*
[2]*The CSU is the Christian Social Union of Bavaria.*
[3]*The Greens are the environmentalist party of Germany.*
[4]*The liberals are the Free Democratic Party. The name is a misnomer; actually, the Free Democrats are a center-right party.*
[5]*The ex-communists got 19 percent in Eastern Germany and less than 1 percent in Western Germany.*
[6]*Representation in the Bundestag is based on the percentage that each political party receives times the number of seats in the Bundestag. The ex-communists got 5.1 percent of the national votes in the election and received thirty seats. This would not be true in the United States. Ross Perot got approximately one-fifth of the popular vote in the 1992 national election; yet his party got no seats in congress.*

Source: "Germany's Election," *The Economist*, October 3, 1998, p. 55.

SUMMARY

Germany was the dominant economic power in Europe for most of the twentieth century, and will probably continue to dominate even though it is a member of the European Union. It will shape monetary policy in the European Union. East Germany and West Germany are now united into a nation of 80 million people, and Germany is the second largest trading nation in the world. Its strengths include a high level of education and vocational training that will continue to be a factor supporting high living standards and a high technological base. A major weakness is the set of rules and regulations, particularly in the service sector, that inhibit competition and market entry. Another problem is the aging of the German population and the increasing costs of the welfare state.

QUESTIONS FOR DISCUSSION

1.   Is the eastern part of Germany, which was formerly the German Democratic Republic, better off now than when it was as a separate country? Discuss.
2.   What is *Mittelstand*?
3.   What is the relationship between banking and industry in Germany? Would this be legal in the United States?
4.   Who has borne the cost of German reunification?
5.   What are the strengths and weaknesses of the German economy?
6.   Distinguish between the social market capitalism of Germany and the free-market capitalism of the United States. Can it be said that one system is superior to the other?
7.   In what ways is the social market system of Germany different from the state-directed economy of Japan?
8.   What is codetermination? Would it work in the United States?

RECOMMENDED READINGS

Gazdan, Kaevan. *Germany's Balanced Development*. Westport, Conn.: Quorum Books, 1998.

"Germany's Election." *The Economist*, October 3, 1998, pp. 55–57.

Landes, David S. *The Wealth and Poverty of Nations*. New York: Norton, 1998, Chaps. 18 and 25.

Maier, Charles S. *Dissolution: The Crisis of Communism and the End of East Germany*. Princeton: Princeton University Press, 1997.

OECD Economic Surveys. *Germany*. Paris: Organization for Economic Cooperation and Development, 1998.

———. *Maintaining Prosperity in an Aging Society*. Paris: Organization for Economic Cooperation and Development, 1998.

Porter, Michael E. *The Competitive Advantage of Nations*. New York: The Free Press, 1990, 337–82.

Zelikow, Philip, and Condoleeza Rice. *Germany Unified and Europe Transformed*. Cambridge: Harvard University Press, 1997.

ENDNOTES

1. Kaevan Gazdar, *Germany's Balanced Development* (Westport, Conn.: Quorum Books, 1998), 5; Max Weber, *The Protestant Work Ethic and the Spirit of Capitalism* (New York: Scribner's, 1930); Sombart's view is found in *Gazdar*, 5; *Socialemarktwirtschaft* (social market economy) was formulated during World War II by a group of economists at Freiburg University. They advocated market competition along with social welfare.

2. Lester Thurow, *Head to Head: The Coming Economic Battle among Japan, Europe, and America* (New York: Morrow, 1992), 13–20. As Thurow has acknowledged, America has won the battle.

3. This works to the disadvantage of Japan. As the population ages, immigrants will have to enter the labor force. But unlike the United States and Germany, Japan discourages immigration.

4. The German Democratic Republic was East Germany; the Federal Republic was West Germany.

5. The Zeiss firm was privatized after reunification and is still in existence.

6. *Statistiches Jahrbuch der DDR, 1989* (Berlin: Staatsverlag der DDR, 1989), 181. This was the last statistical yearbook of East Germany.

7. The author once took the train from East Berlin to Poland. The cars were pre–World War II cars, the road bed was not well maintained, and the railroad station was poorly lit.

8. There were two types of economic plans, the five-year plans and the one-year operational plans.

9. *Statistisches Jahrbuch der DDR, 1989*, 138–39.

10. Many plants had twice as many workers as were needed. The end result was absenteeism and inefficiency.

11. This was to discourage consumption of nonessentials.

12. Bundesministerium für Innerdeutsche Beziehungen, *Zahlenspiegel Bundesrepublik Deutschland: Ein Vergleich* (Bonn, 1989), 77–78.

13. The major car produced in East Germany was called the Trabant. It was a small two-cycle car that was poorly made and often broke down. When the wall came down, many East Germans abandoned their Trabants to buy West German cars.

14. This changed somewhat during the 1980s when marketing research was used to determine consumer preferences.

15. Worker productivity in East Germany was about half that of worker productivity in West Germany.

16. East Germany had a very efficient secret police called the Stasi. It functioned like the Gestapo in Nazi Germany. In addition, neighbors were encouraged to spy on each other.

17. The East German valuta mark was not convertible into the West German mark or any Western currency.

18. East Germany and the other communist countries placed the main emphasis on industrialization and economic growth. Environmental costs were ignored. Brown coal, which was abundant in East Germany, was used in industry and was the major cause of air pollution. Cost estimates for cleanup run as high as $500 billion.

19. West Germany prohibited abortions and they are prohibited in Germany today.

20.   *Monthly Report of the Deutsche Bundesbank* (Frankfurt am Main, September 1998), p. 7.

21.   The Goebbels estate was expropriated by the Nazis. It was owned by a Jewish department store magnate. The estate, even though it has passed through several owners, belongs to the heirs of the original owner.

22.   The East German has to be given the option of renting.

23.   *Statistisches Jahrbuch der DDR, 1989*, 67.

24.   *Monthly Report of the Deutsche Bundesbank* (Frankfurt am Main, February 1993), 58.

25.   Germany is no different from other countries. Snobbery based on region also exists in the United States.

26.   Apartments were gray and drab outside and cramped inside.

27.   Actually, the Protestant work ethic is associated more with John Calvin and Calvinism.

28.   Michael E. Porter, *The Competitive Advantage of Nations* (New York: The Free Press, 1990), 368–69.

29.   Gazdar, *Germany's Balanced Development*, 79.

30.   The Glass-Steagall Act of 1933 separated investment banking from commercial banking in the United States.

31.   *Forbes*, July 18, 1994, 232.

32.   There have been five laws on the subject. The last passed in 1976.

33.   Firms can have both structures depending on their size.

34.   John Ardagh, *Germany and the Germans* (London: Hamish Mailton, 1984), 112–15.

35.   According to Porter, this is one of Germany's major competitive advantages and one of the weaknesses of the United States.

36.   This is a major cause of social unrest in Germany.

37.   *Monthly Report of the Deutsche Bundesbank* (Frankfurt am Main, September 1998), 54.

38.   Marshall Plan aid to Germany was in excess of $5 billion.

39.   Employment has decreased from 36.3 million workers in 1989 to 33.9 million workers in 1997.

40.   A political party must receive 5 percent or more of the popular vote to have representation on the Bundestag.

41.   A coalition government consisting of the left-wing parties will have to be formed.

PART III

Nonmarket Mechanisms and Socialism

CHAPTER 6
Socialism as an Economic System

The standard Marxist postulate was that communism was the inevitable concomitant of the crises of capitalism within industrialized society. The twentieth century was supposed to be the century of communism, during which there would be a continuous defection of countries from capitalism, with the instability and decay of the capitalist countries manifested in low rates of economic growth and chronic unemployment. World War I contributed to the advent of communism in Russia, and mass unemployment during the 1930s convinced many people that communism was the wave of the future. After World War II the two major superpowers, the United States and the Soviet Union, ruled over a divided world, part capitalist and part communist. As late as 1989 countries ruled by the Communist Party accounted for around 34 percent of the world's population and 31 percent of the world's land area.[1] Included were two major countries, the Soviet Union and China. Of the twenty-six countries headed by the Communist Party, only four remain—China, Cuba, North Korea, and Vietnam—although the future status of Cuba is in doubt. The Soviet Union is gone and China, although still headed by the Communist Party, now has a dual economy, part state-owned and part privately owned. Czechoslovakia, Hungary, Poland, and other countries that were formerly a part of the Soviet bloc are now in the process of transforming their former socialist economies into capitalist economies. Communist parties are gone, and many of their former members have transferred their allegiance to a new political and economic system.

Before beginning a discussion of the political and economic systems of countries that were formerly communist, it is necessary to distinguish between communism and socialism. To the West, the former Soviet Union was communist, but that is not what it called itself. It called itself a socialist country (Union of Soviet Socialist Republics—USSR). In Marxist terminology there were two stages of communism. The first stage, socialism, was to be a transitional stage during which some elements of capitalism were to be maintained. The second stage, communism, was to be a higher stage marked by an age of plenty, distribution according to needs, the absence of money and the market mechanism, the disappearance of capitalism, and the withering away of the state. The political system of the former Soviet Union was communist; the economic system was socialist.

In a non-Marxist form, socialism is an economic system that would modify, but not eliminate, many of the institutions of capitalism. The extent of modification is something that has never been completely delineated by socialists because there are many variations of socialism. Some socialists favor the complete elimination of private property, with replacement by public property ownership. Other socialists favor placing maximum reliance on the market mechanism while supplementing it with government direction and planning to achieve desired economic and social objectives.

Socialism today has also come to be associated with the concept of a welfare state, where the state, through a wide variety of transfer payments, assumes responsibility for protecting its citizens from all the vicissitudes of life. Private ownership of the agents of production is permitted, with state ownership of those facets of production and distribution considered vital to the interests of society. In reality Western society has incorporated many of the principles of both capitalism and socialism.

http://

Biographical information and links to writings on Marx can be found at www.marx.org or www.spu.edu/ ~hawk/marx.html.

HISTORICAL DEVELOPMENT OF SOCIALISM

The terms *socialist* and *socialism* identify relatively new concepts. They first came into use in England and France in the early part of the nineteenth century and were applied to the doctrines of certain writers who were seeking a transformation of the economic and moral basis of society by substituting social for individual control of life and work.[2] The term *socialism* was popularized as the antithesis of *individualism*. However, precursors of socialism can be found among medieval writers and even going as far back as Plato. For example, Thomas Aquinas believed that property ownership should be private, but that the use of goods should be in common. Whatever goods a man possessed should be shared with the poor. He considered poverty undesirable because it led to sin, and he proposed that both church and state should help poor people bring healthy children into the world.

The Renaissance Utopias

During the Renaissance a number of scholars turned their attention to the construction of imaginary communities, or utopias, in which society was organized so as to remove all of the evils of the day. These utopias were primarily economic and social rather than religious. For the most part, they followed a definite pattern, the authors placing a group of regenerated people on an isolated land area where they could be free from contamination by the rest of the world. Rigid conditions would then be set up by means of which an ideal state would be attained. For example, in Sir Thomas More's *Utopia*, everything is owned in common and there is no money.[3] In the middle of each city is a marketplace to which each family takes the things it produces; from these central marketplaces products are distributed to central warehouses from which each family draws what it needs. Women and men have equal rights, and households are arranged so that women are relieved of some of their most time-consuming domestic duties.

French Utopian Socialists

French utopian socialism was associated with the French Revolution and later with the Industrial Revolution. The French Revolution created a great economic and political upheaval whose impact was felt all over Europe. In France every political and social division became rooted in the alignment of the revolution. Commercial business interests, as represented by a merchant class, replaced the aristocracy, who had gone to the guillotine. A large class of urban workers who had helped make the revolution found that their living conditions were largely unchanged. The fact that a great political revolution had taken place in France and that socially the results of this revolution were largely unsatisfactory set the stage for a new group of reformers, the French utopian socialists.

In general, the ideas of the utopian socialists were based on the theory that nature had ordained all things to serve the happiness of humankind and that every person had natural rights due at birth.[4] Furthermore, it was believed that in the original state human beings were perfect. At various times in the past, however, people had tampered with the natural order of things by establishing customs and institutions that ran contrary to it. As a result, people in the existing state were not happy, enjoyed few, if any, rights, and certainly were far from being perfect. Having discovered the cause of human difficulties, the utopian socialists proceeded to the obvious solution of the problem of social regeneration. If people had lost their natural perfection through the establishment of unnatural customs and institutions, the thing to do was to discover the nature of the original state of goodness and then reorganize society so as to give nature's forces full play, unhampered by the conventions and institutions of the existing social environment.

However, the French utopian socialists could not agree on how to reorganize society. Some advocated the elimination of private property, considering it the main reason for human degeneracy. Others favored complete income equality.

Babeuf proposed that production be carried out in common, distribution be shared in common, and children be brought up in such a way as to prevent the growth of individual differences. Saint-Simon, one of the better-known early French utopian socialists, rejected the whole idea of equality, arguing instead that people were naturally unequal and that any attempt to make them equal would involve greater injustices than actually existed at the time. However, differences were to be based on talent, rather than the inheritance of wealth. Saint-Simon favored an economic mechanism that would require each person to labor according to his or her capacity and would provide rewards on the basis of service. Charles Fourier worked out a plan for cooperative living in small communities that he hoped would lead to a transformation of society. These communities were called *phalanxes*, and each phalanx was to be self-sufficient. The highest pay would go to those performing the most necessary work, as determined by the members of the phalanx.

Socialism and the Industrial Revolution

The Industrial Revolution was in due course to revolutionize the economic life of the whole Western world. The availability of new technology encouraged the formation of real capital with which the technology might be put into widespread use. The availability of resources for use in capital formation encouraged the search for new technology that, once discovered, could be embodied in the real capital. The new technology enabled gross national product to be large enough to provide sufficient consumer goods to satisfy the minimum subsistence needs of the population and still have some resources left over. Population growth provided labor to use the enlarged amounts of real capital to increase total national output.

However, there was a darker side to the Industrial Revolution. Working conditions in factories were unpleasant. Equipment was sometimes dangerous and caused workers to have serious accidents. Average wages of industrial workers were low, largely because the rapid expansion of population provided a large number of workers for the labor force. These workers concentrated in the industrial cities and competed with each other for jobs.

The cities that grew up or expanded to house the workers were unattractive and unpleasant. Many of them consisted of slums with houses of poor quality when constructed and in a constant state of disrepair thereafter. Charles Dickens, the great chronicler of English society in the nineteenth century, has a rather graphic description of the squalor of the London slums in his novel *Bleak House*.

Jo lives—that is to say that Jo has not yet died—in a ruinous place known to the like of him by the name of Tom-all-Alone's. It is a black, dilapidated street, avoided by all decent people, where the crazy houses were seized upon, when their decay was far advanced, by some bold vagrants who after establishing their own possession took to letting them out in lodgings. Now, these tumbling tenements contain by night, a swarm of misery. As on the ruined human wretch vermin parasites appear, so these ruinous shelters have bred a crowd of foul existence that crawls in and out of gaps in walls and boards; and rocks itself to sleep in mag-

got numbers, where the rain drips in; and comes and goes, fetching and carrying fever and sowing more evil in its every footprint.[5]

Modern Socialism

Modern socialism, as opposed to utopian socialism, had its genesis during the Industrial Revolution. It developed as a social reform movement to protest the seamy side of the Industrial Revolution. Robert Owen, an early English socialist, was considered a utopian socialist in that he developed a scheme for social regeneration: change society, you change the person. He believed that true happiness is found in making others happy. Unlike many other social reformers, Owen had the money to carry out his plan of social regeneration. He created a textile mill at New Lanark in Scotland in 1800, reducing the hours of work to 10 1/2 hours per day and raising wages.[6] He did not employ children under the age of 10. Education and playgrounds were provided for the children of mill workers. The experiment made money, and Owen was able to get a factory reform bill introduced in Parliament. However, other mill owners were not willing to adopt similar measures. Subsequent experiments by Owen were unsuccessful. Coming to the United States, he created a community called New Harmony in Indiana, but attempts to create a perfect community failed there as well.

Socialism coalesced into a political movement in England around the middle of the nineteenth century. A contributing factor in its development was mass unemployment created by business recessions. One of the basic defects of capitalism was the constant recurrence of recessions. In England and in other countries, unemployment and labor unrest began to occur more frequently, and a working-class movement developed in these countries.

The movement found its support in labor unions and among intellectuals who were not of the working class but felt that the political and economic structure of society had to be reformed for the benefit of the workers. A split developed between Marxist and non-Marxist socialists; the former preached class revolution and the overthrow of the existing political and social order; the latter urged the attainment of economic, political, and social reforms by working within the existing system. Political parties representing both Marxist and non-Marxist points of view had been formed in France and Germany by 1900.

http://

A site containing numerous links to writings on socialism and communism can be found at http://gate.cruzio .com/~marx2mao.

INSTITUTIONS OF SOCIALISM

Socialism developed into a viable political force in Western Europe around the latter part of the nineteenth century and continued to develop during the twentieth century. Socialist parties captured control of the governments of France and Greece in elections held in 1981. Socialism is no longer an important political force today. There are certain institutional arrangements that set socialism apart from capitalism and communism. These arrangements represent a modification in most of the institutions of capitalism, since socialism developed in opposition to some of the worst abuses of capitalism.

Private Property

Under ideal socialism, the rights of private property would be limited to consumption goods; productive wealth, land, and capital would in general be owned by society as a whole. Socialists today say that the social ownership of the means of production would be limited to the land and capital used in large-scale production. For example, the socialist government of former French President François Mitterrand proposed the nationalization of some French banks (the more important ones have already been nationalized) and some key industries, such as aluminum. In France, one car company (Renault) is state-owned, but another car company (Peugeot) is not.

Most socialists would permit private individuals to own and operate small farms, stores, and repair shops. Some even contend that certain industries, operating satisfactorily under private ownership and unsuited to government ownership and operation, be left alone to function in the hands of individuals. Modern socialists thus do not adhere to ideal socialism when it comes to the right of private property ownership.

The Price System

According to many socialists, the ideal socialist system would retain money and the price system, but it would not rely on price movements and price relationships in making important economic decisions to nearly as great an extent as a capitalist system does. Decisions as to the kinds and quantities of goods, particularly public goods, would be made by the government. A major socialist criticism of the price mechanism in a market economy is that prices do not reflect the nonmarket wants of the people, such as the desire for economic security. Nor can negative wants be expressed through the price mechanism.[7] Also, individuals with large sums of money can express their wants through prices and thereby channel resources to the production of goods that the mass of consumers cannot afford. Socialism would divert productive resources to satisfy basic wants of all of the people before the relatively less important wants of the few with large incomes are satisfied.

Socialism and Government

Perhaps because various noncapitalistic economic systems have so often operated under dictatorial governments, there is a tendency in popular discussion to link capitalism with democracy and to link socialism and communism with dictatorship. However, this is not the case with socialism. European social democratic parties have operated within the framework of democracy. The 1981 elections of socialist governments in France and Greece illustrate the point.

By the early 1960s many of the European social democratic parties severed completely whatever remaining ideological ties they had with Marx and communism. They abandoned their traditional opposition to private property and their goal of social ownership and turned their attention to improving the public mix of total goods and services. Thus, what have developed in Western Europe are mixed capitalist-socialist economies. When socialists come into power, the tilt is toward socialism; there is still reliance on a market economy, but also heavy governmental direction and planning to achieve desired social and economic objectives.

COMMUNISM

Early hints of communism can be found in Plato's *Republic*.[8] Plato's criticisms of the economic and social structure of his time led to his proposal for an ideal state. The state described in the *Republic* is a city-state, a type of political organization quite common in Greece at the time (431–351 B.C.E.). Among other things, Plato's ideal republic is a communist society in which all things are held in common, at least as far as the upper classes are concerned. The upper classes, or guardians of the state, eat in common dining rooms and live in common quarters, receiving their support from contributions made by the citizens at large.[9] Members of the group never consider their own personal interests but always work for the good of the whole state. To ensure their disinterest, Plato does not make any provision for private interest, not even a private family life. However, Plato's communism was not for the masses, who were excluded from political life in his republic. Instead, it was communism of the select.

Karl Marx and Das Kapital

Both modern communism and socialism began in England as reactions against capitalism. As mentioned, unequal incomes, squalor, and poverty were characteristic of industrial life in England. The winds of revolution that had blown in from France had died away, and rank and privilege were firmly entrenched. The upper class was all-powerful over a tenantry for the most part unenfranchised.

Flattered, adulated, deferred to, the English aristocracy reigned supreme, with incomes enormously increased by the Industrial Revolution and as yet untaxed. The aristocracy was subject to no ordinary laws and held the government firmly in its hands. However, an entrepreneurial class had begun to emerge as a result of the Industrial Revolution, and the two classes clashed over government control. This conflict did very little to ameliorate the working conditions of the industrial masses.

This was the general economic and social milieu in which Karl Marx wrote *Das Kapital*. It is necessary to remember that Marx was a product of his time and that the activities of other persons in England, as well as in other countries, had attracted widespread attention to the problem of poverty. Marx is important because in *Das Kapital* he presented a dynamic theory of economics that still serves as the basis for much of communist dogma. The most important elements of the theory are summarized as follows.

The Marxist Theory of Income Distribution.   According to Marx, the way in which people make a living at any given time is conditioned by the nature of the existing productive forces. There are three productive forces: natural resources, capital equipment, and human resources. Since people must use these productive forces in the process of making a living, some sort of relationship between people and the productive forces is necessary. Specifically, the property relation is involved. People may own certain productive forces individually, as in a capitalist society, or they may own them collectively, as in a socialist society. Under capitalism, there were people who owned property or capital and there were people who owned only their own labor. Marx called the former the capitalists or the *bourgeoisie* and the latter the workers, or the *proletariat*.

The Labor Theory of Value. Many economists of the eighteenth and nineteenth centuries, including Adam Smith and David Ricardo, believed that labor supplied the common denominator of value.[10] Marx adopted this idea and made it the basis for his own theory of income distribution. He stated that the one thing common to all commodities is labor and that the value of a commodity is determined by the amount of socially necessary labor required for its production. *Socially necessary labor,* as defined by Marx, is the amount of time necessary to produce a given product under existing average conditions of production and with the average degree of skill and intensity of labor.[11] The relative prices of two products will be in the same proportion as the amount of socially necessary labor required to produce them. If two hours of labor are required to make a pair of shoes and five hours of labor are required to build a cart, the price of shoes in the market will be two-fifths that of the cart.

The price of labor is the wage rate. The wage rate determines the income of those who own their own labor. Marx asserted that the wage rate itself is determined by the labor theory of value. How much a worker receives in income in return for working for an employer depends on how many labor hours are required to produce the necessities of life for that worker. If the necessities can be produced with five hours of labor per day, a worker can produce and be available to the employer for work if five hours' wages are paid to the worker each day. Even if the worker actually works twelve hours each day for an employer, the pay will be for only five hours because that is all it takes to sustain the worker. That is all the pay can be, under a labor theory of value. In effect, Marx believed in a subsistence theory of wages in a system of market capitalism.

Theory of Surplus Value. Although all value is created by the workers, it is expropriated by employers in the form of *surplus value,* which can be defined as the difference between the value created by the workers and the value of their labor power. When a worker sells labor power to an employer, the worker gives up all title and claim to the products of that labor. Income in the Marxist scheme is divided into two categories—surplus value, which is the source of all profit, and labor income. Value in the Marxist rubric can be expressed in the formula $C + V$

+ S, where C represents raw materials and capital consumption, V represents various outlays on wages, and S represents surplus value in the form of rent, interest, and profit. The C component, raw materials and capital, although clearly not labor, is explained away by Marx, who regarded it as stored-up labor from past periods. Thus the remainder, $V + S$, represents net output, which consists of the two basic income shares, wages and profit.

How much a worker gets as a wage is based on the amount of labor time socially necessary to produce subsistence or maintenance for the worker and the worker's family. Assume that this subsistence requires only five hours of socially necessary labor time for its production. If the worker worked only five hours for the employer, the worker would be fully paid and there would be no surplus value. However, it is the employer's right to set the length of the working day, and it will normally be set at a number of hours greater than that required to produce the worker's subsistence. The difference between the actual hours worked and the labor time needed for subsistence is surplus value.

The Dynamic Weaknesses of Market Capitalism.

Marx believed that the market distribution of income between workers and property owners was bound to be a source of increasing difficulty for capitalist economies.

Crises and Depressions. For one thing, it would sometimes be difficult to sell the output being produced. The workers received money income enough to buy only part of the total output. This part would necessarily take the form of subsistence or consumer goods. The capitalists received the rest, an amount sufficient to buy the remainder of the output of goods and services. But would they buy it? Of course they would buy some of it to satisfy their own consumption desires. The rest they might purchase in the form of capital goods with which to carry on production and to expand productive capacity if they found such a purchase profitable. However, from time to time there would be periods of months or even years when they would not find it profitable to expand capacity. These would be periods of crisis and depression. During these times there would be sharply increased financial losses for business, unsold output, business bankruptcies, falling prices, and unemployment.

Worsening Trends. Marx suggested that these crises and depressions would become increasingly severe. In each successive crisis, the weakest firms would disappear, being absorbed or replaced by a smaller number of larger firms. In the long run the number of firms and the number of capitalists would decline both absolutely and relative to the size of the economy and of the population. The proletariat would be absolutely and relatively enlarged.

The capitalist employers would be impelled by competition among themselves to substitute machinery or capital for labor, even though it was labor that provided surplus value and profits. The capitalists would be impelled to discover and introduce into use new technology because it would reduce the cost of subsistence needs for labor and thereby enlarge the amount of surplus value and profit. The increasingly severe crises, the substitution of capital for labor, and the introduction of new technology would create a larger and larger volume of unemployment among the workers. There would be an ever-increasing *industrial reserve army* of unemployed.

Marx felt that the rate of profit on capital would fall continually lower, primarily because of the replacement of laborers with machines. The laborers were the source of all surplus and hence of all profits. Machines produced no surplus and, therefore, did not contribute to profits. The capitalists, desperately seeking to sustain profits, would seek ways to increase the surplus value by greater exploitation of the workers. They would resort to longer working hours, more intense work, and the employment of children.

There would be more and more severe crises, fewer and fewer capitalists, larger and larger unemployment, lower and lower profit rates, bigger and bigger amounts of unsold goods, and ever more outrageous exploitation of the workers by the capitalists. These trends would ultimately lead, in the Marxist view, to the end of market capitalism. It would be replaced with a new economic system, or rather, with a whole new society. In Marx's view, economic arrangements were causally determinant of all else in society, and capitalism's inevitable demise would mean a complete change of everything else in society.[12] Because Marx felt that the character of a society depended wholly upon its economic system, his philosophy is labeled *materialism*.

Economically Determined History.   To reiterate, Marx contended that economic conditions were the basic causal forces shaping the nature of society. All other aspects of society—political, religious, and philosophical—depended on the economic system of the society.

Materialism. For example, in a primitive nomadic society where horses might be of particular importance in enabling the people to gather food and to exist in general, the ownership of horses would be important to the people. Those persons who owned the horses would be able to control the others. That is, those who possessed the principal means of production would also possess the ability to rule. The religion and philosophy of the nomadic society would revolve about horses and those who owned them. The patterns of marriage and inheritance would be heavily influenced by considerations regarding the use and ownership of horses.

In a society that had amassed considerable real capital and technology, the capital would be the principal means of production. The society would be organized around the existence, ownership, control, and use of the capital. Political power would reside with the owners and controllers of capital, the capitalists. Religion and philosophy would sanctify the ownership and rationalize the social dominance of the owners.

In some advanced societies with great real capital, all ownership and control might be exercised by the government. It would act on behalf of all the people. Political power would rest with all the people. A philosophy of altruism would develop among them.

In the most advanced society, so much capital and such advanced technology would exist that enough goods and services would be produced to more than completely satisfy the desires of everyone. The ownership of the means of production would cease to matter. Political control over others would cease to have significance. Interpersonal animosity, based on the covetousness of each for the material goods and services of others, would disappear. Government, no longer necessary as the instrument by which some controlled others or by which some were protected from others, would gradually wither away.

The Dialectic. Marx's view of philosophy and history is called a dialectic. From the philosopher Hegel, Marx adopted the notion that everything that happened in the world could be explained by the clash of opposites. In simple terms, Hegel claimed that a proper understanding of the world could be achieved if all change were viewed as a result of clashing ideas. First, there is an idea, such as a scarcity. Then there emerges an opposite idea, such as abundance. Finally, the two opposing ideas are combined into a new and superior idea, such as economy, which is a means to achieve abundance out of scarcity.

Marx adopted the notion of the clashing of opposites to produce a successor synthesis. However, he rejected the view that this clashing and synthesis took place basically and most significantly in the realm of ideas. Rather, according to Marx, the basic conflict and synthesis took place, as his philosophy of materialism suggests, in the real world of economic events, economic classes, and economic systems.

Dialectical Materialism. Marx welded together his views of the primacy of economic arrangements and of history as a progressive conflict into the doctrine of dialectical materialism. According to this doctrine, a society, such as that of Europe during the Middle Ages, is based on an economic system, such as manorial agriculture. A political structure, such as feudalism, and a philosophical and religious structure, such as medieval Catholicism, grow up in harmony with the economic base. There are three socioeconomic classes: landed nobility, clergy, and serfs. The economic system is successful in filling the material needs of the people. In fact, it is too successful for its own permanence.

The increasing productive ability of the manorial system makes it possible for some people to leave agriculture and become traders or craftsmen. Others have sufficient time to make economically useful discoveries and innovations. Gradually the techniques of production and other economic arrangements change. Local economic self-sufficiency decreases as trading increases. First guilds and then factory workers carry on production in place of the manorial serfs or craftsmen. There begins to grow up a new socioeconomic class made up of the shopkeeping proprietors, the factory managers and owners, and the merchant traders.

In the meantime, the political power remains, in an increasingly outmoded way, with the hereditary landed aristocracy. The religious rules grow more and more inappropriate for the economic system. For example, doctrines against usury and in favor of just prices become obsolete. Finally, the economic system and the seat of real power have changed enough that the new class, the bourgeoisie, is able to wrest political power from the landed nobility. They do so either by forceful revolution, by new laws, or by influence with the sovereign. They also reshape the religious code, perhaps by replacing Catholicism with Protestantism.

Capitalism thereby replaces feudalism. Then, because of its inherent nature, capitalism under the bourgeoisie unintentionally promotes its own replacement.

Capitalism brings together the working proletariat and infuses in them a unity born of misery and exploitation. The class conflict between the proletariat and bourgeoisie sharpens with conditions increasingly favorable to a proletarian victory. The political superstructure of government is in the hands of the bourgeoisie, who use it to perpetuate their power. However, it fails to reflect the underlying economic reality of bourgeoisie weakness and proletarian strength. Religion has been used as a device for cowing the workers, for justifying their exploitation, and for drugging them with visions of heaven so that they will accept their earthly misery. However, religion becomes more and more obviously a sham.

Eventually, the workers topple the bourgeoisie government, seize the means of production, abolish private property, and set up a socialist state under the dictatorship of the proletariat. The economic system is thus converted to socialism. Then, because all else follows from economic change, the society becomes ultimately a communist one, without government, scarcity, conflict, or classes.[13]

The Weaknesses of Marxism

Each of Marx's main ideas can be disputed on a number of grounds.

The Labor Theory of Value.   The labor theory of value, as an explanation of what determines relative prices of goods and services, is extremely vulnerable to criticism. Marx anticipated some of these criticisms and tried to deal with them.

Exceptions to the Theory. A piece of fertile land may exist and command a high price without any human labor at all having been expended on its creation. Such nonreproducible goods, Marx said, fall into a special category. The prices or values of this category are determined without reference to amounts of labor. Then what about a durable good that was produced some time ago and for whose production a technological improvement has been discovered in the meantime? The value of such a good will fall, Marx would say, in the meantime. It is not the amount of original labor expended but the amount necessary to replace a good that is the determining variable.

What about a unit of good much like many other units of the same good except that it embodies a much greater amount of labor because it was turned out by a very slow, inept worker? Will it on that account be much more valuable than the other units? No, it will not, because it is the actual amount of *socially necessary* labor that determines values and prices, Marx would answer. What about a good, like a hideous piece of sculpture, whose production required a great amount of labor but which cannot be sold for any price because no one wants it? Can it, all in all, be said to be of great value? No, Marx might answer, because labor expended on a useless product is not socially necessary labor. What about a good produced by a monopolist and sold at a high price? Is its price in proportion to the labor in it? Admittedly it is not, for monopoly may distort prices from true values.

The Problem of Diverse Kinds of Labor. What about two goods, one embodying four hours of unskilled labor and the other, four hours of skilled labor? Will the two goods sell at the same price? Do they have equal value? No, in creating and determining value, one hour of skilled labor counts for more than one hour of unskilled labor. To compute value, one must convert skilled labor into unskilled labor by multiplying the number of hours of skilled labor by an appropriate conversion number. How can the appropriate number be known? It is determined, in part, by the number of hours of labor socially necessary to produce the goods and services needed to sustain the skilled laborers through the period of training. It is also determined, in part, by the number of hours required for every laborer, skilled or unskilled, to produce the goods needed to rear that person from infancy and for subsistence during working years.

Unfortunately, too many qualifications and exceptions spoil the attraction of a generalization. The labor theory is of limited value after all the necessary modifications are taken into account. Furthermore, the modifications suggested are incomplete. In the last case, for example, the number of labor hours necessary to sustain a worker consists itself of some hours of unskilled labor and some of skilled labor. To add the two together, a conversion number must be available. It is not available, however, for it is precisely what the whole procedure is set up to find.

Alternative Modern Theory. Modern economic theory, developed since Marx, explains values or prices in terms of degree of scarcity. According to this theory, the value of a thing in exchange for something else depends on how scarce it is. Its scarcity in turn depends on the state of its supply and the state of demand for it. Behind supply and demand lie a great many interdependent determinants. The scarcity theory is a complicated one, but it provides a more satisfactory explanation than the labor theory of value. The scarcity theory treats not only labor but also capital and natural resources as productive and value-creating.

Owing to the weaknesses of Marx's labor theory of value, his use of it as a basis for arguing against the capitalistic market society's distribution of income makes that argument weak. One might still question market capitalism or market capitalism's distribution of income. However, one would probably do so on grounds other than because one believed that only labor had the power to create value and that all value was in proportion to labor used.

The Subsistence Theory of Wages.

Another element in Marx's theory of market capitalism is the subsistence theory of wages. Marx alternated between two explanations of this theory. One is that the wage rate will tend to fall until workers receive only enough income to provide a minimum physical existence for themselves. The other is that the wage rate will tend to fall until workers receive only enough to provide a psychological or culturally determined minimum level of living for themselves.[14] The latter minimum might change as attitudes changed. It might vary from place to place, depending on the attitudes prevailing in the society of each place. Marx did not give a satisfactory causal explanation of why the wage rate under market capitalism tended toward a subsistence minimum, however defined.

The Malthusian Explanation. Marx rejected the explanation offered by such people as Thomas Malthus. Malthus had argued that any wage higher than subsistence would reduce the death rate or raise the birthrate. These changes would cause the population and the supply of labor to increase. The increase would depress the market for labor and force the wage rate down. Perhaps Marx rejected the Malthusian explanation because it seemed to place the blame on the workers or to suggest that any economic system, not just market capitalism, would produce the same undesirable result.

Lopsided Bargaining Power. Marx did contend that the bargaining power of each individual worker would be small relative to that of a capitalist employer in the negotiations on wage rates. A worker sometimes has no real alternative, other than unemployment, to accepting a job from one accessible employer. On the other hand, most employers either can offer work to any one of a number of different workers who are competing with each other for jobs or can withhold work entirely by shutting down operations.

Critics of Marx have pointed out that, at least sometimes, workers have considerable bargaining power. Their power arises because of their unusual skills, because they band together in labor unions, because there is competition among employers for their services, or because without their labor real capital is unprofitable. Even with weak bargaining power, there is no proof that the wage rate will fall to the subsistence level.

The Reserve Army of the Unemployed. Marx also contended that there usually would be substantial numbers of unemployed workers. They would always be ready to compete with those who had jobs. They would also furnish an inexhaustible supply of labor at a minimum subsistence wage rate, no matter how strong the demand for labor.

Critics of this argument emphasize that Marx never really convincingly demonstrated that capitalism creates unemployment. Indeed, if Marx were right that only labor creates surplus value and profits, capitalist employers would seek out and employ every available worker because, by so doing, profits could be maximized. Actually, real wages in countries heavily dependent on market capitalism have risen substantially in the long run. A Marxist may choose to dismiss this evidence by claiming that it merely reflects a rising psychological minimum subsistence level. But one can reasonably rejoin that capitalism is performing well, not badly, in this respect. It has raised both aspirations and the means to fulfill them.

The Theory of Surplus Value.

The theory of surplus value asserts that workers usually produce more goods and services than are needed for their subsistence. This assertion seems acceptable. It is probably equally acceptable, however, to assert that land is capable of producing more crop than that needed to reseed the land adequately in the next growing season. Likewise, a labor-saving machine may spare more labor hours than were required to make it. As the basis for an argument against market capitalism, the theory of surplus value is not a strong argument unless supplemented by a labor theory of value and a subsistence theory of wages.

Actually, land, labor, and capital cooperate in most production activities, regardless of the economic system. The complete removal of any one of these three factors would cause production to cease almost entirely. As long as they do cooperate, the productive output is usually more than enough to replace the worn equipment, maintain the natural resources, and provide for the subsistence needs of the workers. The excess may take the form either of suprasubsistence consumer goods or of capital goods that increase the society's stock of real capital.

The Theory of Crises and Trends.   Another element in Marx's argument against market capitalism is the crisis or business cycle. These do occur in many forms of capitalistic economic systems. They had been the object of economists' inquiries and theories before Marx, and they have continued to be. Marx's explanation of them was incomplete and questionable, and we have not yet achieved a complete understanding of them. However, as a result of economic studies undertaken since the Great Depression, most economists believe that mixed economic systems can avoid severe crises and cycles by accepting rather modest government economic intervention. In any case, crises and cycles have not yet forced the complete collapse of market capitalism and its replacement by Marxist socialism or communism.

Many of the trends Marx predicted would bring the downfall of capitalism have not been corroborated by subsequent history. Most striking has been the failure of the capitalist owners to become a smaller and smaller percentage of the population and the proletariat a larger and larger percentage. An increasingly greater portion of the people of Western Europe and North America possess property in the form of savings accounts, shares of corporate stock, government bonds, houses, automobiles, and durable consumer goods. The proletarian proportion of the populace has diminished as skilled white-collar and service workers have come to outnumber unskilled, manual workers.

The percentage of the labor force unemployed has not increased in the long run, as Marx predicted it would. The quality of life of the majority of the population has not become increasingly miserable. Working conditions have improved, not deteriorated, on the average at least. In the long run, the rate of profit on capital has not fallen as much as Marx predicted. Technological and social changes have provided new, profitable opportunities for the use of machinery and other capital goods. The governments of most capitalist countries have not resolutely blocked every attempt by the majority of the people to obtain legislation to improve their lot. It is not the case that for most noncommunist, developed countries the government is used as the instrument by which an increasingly small number of capitalists keep subjugated an ever more preponderant working class.

The Theory of Economic Determinism and Dialectical Materialism.   Marx's emphasis on the economic system of a society as determinant of all else about society can also be criticized.

Economics as Only One of Many Interdependent Forces. The economic system is as much a result as a cause of the general character of society. Religion and philosophy, for example, help to determine economic organization. A people's religion may emphasize the evil of the accumulation of material goods and the virtue of asceticism. In consequence, the economic system is likely to remain a traditional one, and economic growth will not occur. Alternatively, religion may stress individual responsibility and working hard, saving much, and investing productively. As a result, the economic system is likely to become a market one with rapid change. A people's philosophy may accord great prestige to those who are very successful in military, spiritual, or governmental affairs and little prestige to those who are economically successful. Then the economic system of the people is likely to remain organized around the principle of tradition, and what modern Westerners regard as economic progress will probably be slow.

The political system of a society may place and keep in power those who wish to maintain the status quo. Then economic change will probably occur only slowly. The cultural heritage of a people may include a great accumulated stock of technological knowledge. The economic system of that people will probably be very different from that of a people with little such knowledge. The physical environment of a people is also likely to shape their economic system. The tropics may offer no challenge to traditional economic organization, which remains underdeveloped. The arctic may offer too great a challenge, which prevents economic organization from being anything but traditional and underdeveloped.

Monocausal Theories of History. It is implausible that human history is simply a sequence of economic changes that bring about other changes. Such a theory of history is as questionable as every other monocausal explanation of history. For example, one other such theory is the *hero theory*, which claims that the shape of history is the result of the appearance from time to time of extremely influential people such as Plato, Jesus, Caesar, Charlemagne, Columbus, Luther, Marx, and Lenin. Another is the *idea theory*, which stresses the great historical influence of ideas such as monotheism, asceticism, altruism, capitalism, democracy, and communism. Another is the *war theory*, which claims that conflicts of arms provide the key to the understanding of history. There is also the *political theory*, which claims that history is the sequence of governments.[15]

The Merits of Marx

Marx's theory was not totally without merit. He did indicate some of the weaknesses of the market capitalism of his time and place. The inequality of income, wealth, and power of nineteenth-century European capitalism was too great to be permanently tolerated by the populace and too great by twentieth-century Western standards. Marx correctly predicted some of the trends in market capitalism. Recurrent and sometimes severe business fluctuations have taken place. Unemployment has been a persistent problem. Inordinate political and social power has accrued to the economically most successful. Control, if not ownership, has been concentrated in the hands of those who guide the great private corporations.

Marx was perhaps the first to try to explain why history had occurred as it had rather than merely to describe what had occurred. He attempted to integrate economic theory with history. He was one of the few of his time to do so.

THE POLITICAL AND ECONOMIC SYSTEM OF THE SOVIET UNION AND EASTERN EUROPE

Control of the government machinery in the former Soviet Union and the former communist countries of Eastern and Central Europe was in the hands of the Communist Party, the only political party permitted.[16] Membership in the Communist Party was limited to a small minority of the population, as Table 6-1 indicates. It maintained firm control over every aspect of life through its well-organized, disciplined organization. Communists held key positions in all institutions and enterprises in society. In factories, offices, schools, and villages, primary units called *cells* operated. Consisting of at least three party members, each cell was responsible for recruiting members and selecting delegates to local party conferences, which in turn selected delegates to conferences covering a somewhat wider geographic area. This process continued to the highest body of party authority.[17]

http://

Soviet economic history and other related links can be found at http://lcweb2.loc.gov/frd/cs/sutoc.html.

Organization

The organization of the Communist Party took the form of a pyramid. At the top of the pyramid was the Central Committee, which was elected at the meeting of the National Party Congress. It had no effective role as a decision maker; its main function was to disseminate leadership aims and objectives of the leaders to officials in the various central government agencies, and downward to party officials at lower administrative levels. The Politburo was the supreme instrument of political power, responsible for all phases of national life—foreign policy, domestic economic policy, and military policy. The Secretariat of the Central Committee was responsible for the administration of the Communist Party. It was also responsible for providing leadership for the party organization, which consisted of a hierarchy of subordinate secretariats at lower administrative levels.

Country	Party Members (thousands)	Party Members (% of population)
Bulgaria	932	10.4
China	44,000	4.2
Czechoslovakia	1,675	10.8
East Germany	2,304	13.8
Hungary	871	8.2
Poland	2,126	5.7
Romania	3,557	15.6
Soviet Union	18,500	6.6
Yugoslavia	2,168	9.3

TABLE 6-1
Proportion of Party Members in Selected Countries, 1986

Source: Richard F. Staar, "Checklist of Communist Parties in 1986," *Problems of Communism*, Vol 36, No. 2, March-April (Washington, D.C.: U.S. Government Printing Office, 1987), 45–47.

Party and Government Structure

The Communist Party was a part of the government bureaucracy, not independent from it as would be the case in the United States and other democracies. Party and government structure paralleled each other. For example, in the former Soviet Union the basic party administrative units were the Central Committee, Politburo, and Secretariat; the basic governmental units were the Supreme Soviet and the Council of Ministers. Party leaders were members of both units. This interlocking relationship continued at all levels of government even down to rural areas. This interconnection of party and government provided unity of control and uniformity of ideological perspective. This did not mean, however, that party and government organs functioned as two perfectly synchronized parts of a smoothly working administrative machine. To the contrary, power rivalries and disputes were common.

The Nomenklatura System

All major appointments, promotions, and dismissals were the prerogative of the Communist Party. This prerogative of selection covered offices in government administration and all major managerial positions in the economy. There was an ideological imperative that party leaders had to maintain a monopoly of political, ideological, and economic power. This was done through the nomenklatura system, which was simply patronage designed to ensure party loyalty. Being a member of the nomenklatura elite carried with it a number of benefits—better apartments, access to the best schools, foreign travel, shopping at state stores that carried quality products from Western countries, and many other perquisites not available to the masses. Supposedly workers were "first among equals" in the former Soviet Union and the other socialist countries, but that was hardly the case.[18]

THE ECONOMIC SYSTEM OF SOCIALISM

The socialist countries had the same type of economic system. One thing that immediately comes to mind is economic planning, which gave control over resource allocation to the state rather than the free market. Under the socialist system, private firms employing hired labor either did not exist or were restricted to a small segment of the economy.[19] The almost total elimination of private property and other forms of capitalism was considered the main criterion of socialism. Control by the state over resource allocation was supposed to be more efficient and equitable than it was under capitalism. There would not be the waste of resources and conspicuous consumption that existed in the capitalist countries.

A major criticism of the capitalist market mechanism is that it produces too many things that have no social value. If there is a demand for a product, no matter how frivolous, then it is going to be produced. Socialism, by eliminating both private ownership of the means of production and the anarchy of the market, would allow organization on a national scale through economic planning. Such questions as what to produce, how to produce, and to whom goods would be distributed would be decided through economic planning. Saving and investment decisions, which would be determined by the supply of and demand for loanable funds in a market economy, would be determined by planning. With economic planning, the role of money and prices would become far narrower and more restricted than it was under capitalism.

Economic Planning

In the socialist economies production and distribution were implemented through economic plans. The plans represented an attempt to balance the supply of and demand for resources to achieve an equilibrium. Planning not only was concerned with every branch of economic activity, but also embraced many other aspects of economic life. It was not content with merely making the socialist system operate; it also had such objectives as increasing national wealth or the industrialization of an economy. In other words, economic planning could have both short- and long-term goals. It relied on commands for its implementation; it was controlled by a central planning agency, by financial organizations such as the state bank, but above all by the political authorities. Economic planning was divided into several categories as follows.

Planning with a Time Horizon. Economic plans were divided into several time categories:

1. General plans laid down for a period of fifteen to twenty years were primarily concerned with long-term problems of structural changes on a national scale, technology, and the like.
2. Medium-term plans, usually covering a period of five years, were concerned mostly with changes in the capacity and rate of production of different industries and enterprises.
3. Annual plans within each five-year plan provided a detailed description of production plans for the year and served as a control mechanism by all state-owned enterprises.[20]

Physical Input-Output Planning and Financial Planning. The basic planning in the socialist economies was in real terms and involved physical output targets of the most important industrial and agricultural commodities and the allocation of labor at the national level, the balancing and transfers of important types of raw materials and equipment, and total national capital investment. Financial planning was used as a control mechanism over the execution of the physical input-output plan, a control which was imposed by the banking system. It was also used to maintain a balance between consumer disposable income and the volume of consumer goods available. It consisted of three parts—the state budget, the credit plan, and the cash plan of the central bank. The credit and cash plans controlled the outlay of short-term credit and the cash and currency issued by the central bank.

The Use of Material Balances.   Physical input-output planning relied on the use of material balances, which presented an intended relationship between supplies and their allocation for special commodities. Material balances were drawn up for all of the important types of industrial and agricultural products. An example of the use of material balances can be presented as follows:

Resources	*Distribution*
Physical stocks at the start of the planning period	Production and operating needs
Production	Capital construction
Imports	Replenishment of state inventories
Mobilization of internal resources	Exports
	Stocks at the end of the planning period
Total	Total

State Budget

In terms of the relationship of expenditures to gross domestic product, the state budgets of the socialist economies were much larger than the budgets of the major capitalist economies.[21] About half of the gross domestic product of the former Soviet Union, Poland, and other socialist countries flowed through their budgets. The reason for the size of the socialist state budget is obvious: many things financed by private enterprise in a capitalist economy were financed by the government. For example, investment expenditures, which in the United States would be financed by private enterprise, were financed to a considerable degree out of the state budget. Many other expenditures, such as expenditures on health and research that would be financed at least in part by private enterprise in a market economy, were financed out of the state budget.

The state budget was an integral part of economic planning, particularly the financial plan, which was the financial counterpart of the physical input-output plan. It involved cash, credit, and investment financing necessary to try to reach the physical output goals spelled out in the national economic plan. It was through the state budget that taxes and other fiscal resources of the government were collected and distributed. The state budget was a prime vehicle for allocating resources for various purposes. In a market economy, the market is a device for the organization of economic activity by transmitting preferences to producers, who adjust output to direct resources into alternative uses.

Table 6-2 compares budgetary expenditures of selected socialist and capitalist countries in relationship to GDP. The major difference is the percentage of economic expenditures financed out of socialist budgets as compared to capitalist budgets. Economic expenditures include state investments in state-owned enter-

	Total Budgetary Expenditures	Economic Expenditures of the Budget	TABLE 6-2
Socialist countries			Size and Economic Expenditures of Government Budgets, 1981 (% of GDP)
Czechoslovakia	53.1	22.8	
Hungary	63.2	26.9	
Poland	53.2	32.5	
Soviet Union	47.1	25.8	
Capitalist countries			
Australia	33.6	2.8	
France	46.4	4.6	
United States	34.8	3.5	
West Germany	49.8	4.8	
Low-income capitalist			
India	21.3	6.8	
Kenya	29.2	8.6	

Source: Janos Kornai, *The Socialist System: The Political Economy of Communism* (Princeton: Princeton University Press, 1992), 135–36.

prises and state subsidies, which would include price supports to agricultural cooperatives and state-owned enterprises.

Money and Banking

Money in a socialist economy possessed many of the same functions as money in a capitalist economy. Within and outside the state sector, money served as a unit of account, that is, all goods and services that were bought and sold were valued in monetary units.

Money also functioned as a medium of exchange in that wages and salaries were paid in currency and receivers of money could use it to buy goods and services. The ownership of money, however, did not give individuals command over the allocation of resources as it did in a capitalist economy because resource allocation was determined by the economic plan and not by the price system.

Banking was centralized as a monopoly of the government in the socialist economies. Control over the money supply was vested in the state bank: in the Soviet Union, Gosbank, and in the German Democratic Republic, Staatsbank der DDR. Through the direct operation of the state bank, the government could control the volume of credit and hence the money supply. The state bank also played an integral part in the implementation of economic planning. It was responsible for implementating the credit and cash plans. The credit plan regulated the granting of credit by the state bank to state-owned enterprises during a stipulated period of time; the cash plan controlled the amount of money the state bank could put into circulation. In addition to the state bank, there were banks that specialized by functions: foreign trade, agriculture, and savings.

Prices

The problem of pricing in a socialist economy was of a different nature from that under capitalism. For one thing, prices did not determine the allocation of resources to the extent that they do in a market economy. Moreover, pricing was a question not merely of economics but also of ideology and politics: the socialist rationale for prices was the law of value, the amount of labor time embodied in the creation of goods and services. Labor was the only factor of production credited with the capability of producing value. So the price or value of anything was determined by the amount of labor required to produce it. The relative value of two products would be in the same proportion as the amount of labor required to produce them.

A dual price system operated in the socialist economies: prices paid to producers and prices paid by consumers for retail goods. Producers' prices were those received by producing enterprises from other producing enterprises and from trading entities. Producer prices were normally based on an average cost for the entire branch of industry producing a product. Included in average costs were not only wage payments and material costs but also capital charges. In some cases producer prices were set by the state at levels below average cost, so that enterprises operated at a loss with the loss subsidized by state revenues.

Consumer retail prices consisted of all the components that made up the prices charged by the producer to the retailer plus a retail price markup. There was virtual isolation between producer and retail prices; what happened to the former had little to do with the latter. Retail prices were set by the state to keep supply and demand in balance within the guidelines of the economic plan. The setting of prices was based on the macrosocial preferences of the planners rather than on the true interaction of supply and demand affected by consumer preferences, but a certain amount of flexibility in retail prices was permitted within limits. For example, "free prices" set by supply and demand operated in the purchase and sale of certain agricultural products.

Income Distribution

The communists deplored the great differences in the distribution of income and wealth in the capitalist system. The end result of communism was supposed to be a society in which income differentials would be eliminated and social classes based on wealth distribution would disappear. This, of course, did not happen and would not have happened in the former Soviet Union and the other socialist economies. Given the existence of the Communist Party and the nomenklatura elite, there was no such thing as a "classless" society. Moreover, the socialist system lagged behind numerous capitalist countries in the qualitative improvement

TABLE 6-3 *Comparison of Net Household Incomes in East Germany and West Germany by Quintiles (%)*

	1970		1983	
	West Germany	East Germany	West Germany	East Germany
Quintile 1	8.3	9.7	9.8	10.9
Quintile 2	12.7	16.1	14.7	16.3
Quintile 3	16.8	19.7	18.3	19.7
Quintile 4	22.3	23.4	22.9	22.9
Quintile 5	39.9	31.1	34.3	30.2

Source: Deutscher Bundestag, *Materialien zum Bericht zur Lage der Nation im geteilten Deutschland, 1987* (Bonn: Bundesminister für Innerdeutsche Beziehungen February 1987), 503.

of living standards. Economic security, including the guarantee of full employment, and a social security safety net that covered everyone, was considered the major accomplishment of the socialist economies, but even here a price was paid in the curtailment of political, social, and economic liberties.

Table 6-3 compares income distribution in the former German Democratic Republic (DDR) and West Germany before reunification. In the socialist system of the DDR, income distribution was determined by the state rather than the marketplace. Income distribution had clear-cut aims within the scope of the state economic plan. Wages constituted almost all of the income distributed in the DDR and was determined by the government rather than by the forces of supply and demand. Wages were set within the framework of the state economic plan. In West Germany, a capitalist economy, wages were determined by supply and demand. Table 6-3 breaks down net household income by quintiles for the two countries for 1970 and 1983.[22]

Organization of Industry and Agriculture in the Former Soviet Union and Eastern Europe

In a socialist economy most productive and distributive enterprises came under the jurisdiction of the state, which exercised virtually monopolistic control over all economic resources. It owned and operated large-scale industries, mines, power plants, railways, and other means of communication. It was a monopoly in banking and foreign trade, and it controlled the domestic channels of distribution in its role as manufacturer, farmer, merchant, and banker. It engaged in farming on its own account through the institution of the state farm, and it largely controlled agriculture through the institution of collective farming. In the field of labor relations, it was the sole employer of note and as such dominated bargaining between itself and its employees.

Organization of Industry. The organization of industry in the socialist economies was complex because an extensive bureaucratic structure was neces-

http://

See the Library of Congress site, http://lcweb2.loc .gov/frd/cs/sutoc .html, chapter 12, Industrial Organization, for more information.

sary to plan and administer production and distribution policies. To facilitate top-down planning, industrial organization was strongly skewed toward large state enterprises that were integrated both horizontally and vertically. Firms in a particular sector were grouped together in large industrial combines, which were national or regional. The extent of industrial concentration was much higher in the more developed socialist economies than in the United States. For example, in the former East Germany, which was the most developed country in the Eastern bloc, the largest one hundred enterprises, or about 1 percent of all enterprises, produced half of industrial output in 1988.[23] Within industry, preferred treatment was given to producer or capital goods that would produce other producer goods.

Organization of Agriculture.   The organization of agriculture was similar to that of industry in that it, too, was considered a basic part of the economic and political organization of the state, and there was a constant effort to combine agricultural enterprises into larger units to increase output. The two basic units of agricultural production were state farms and collective farms. State farms were owned and operated by the government and operated as regular industrial establishments with managers and hired workers. The budgets and operating plans of state farms were subject to government control. State farms were typically extremely large and received most of the capital investment allocated to the agricultural sector. Collective farms represented a form of agricultural organization in which individual farms pooled their resources and farmed on a collective basis.

http://

For more information, see http://lcweb2.loc.gov/frd/cs/sutoc.html, chapter 13, on agriculture.

Summary

Socialism, as it existed in the former Soviet Union and the Soviet-bloc countries of Eastern and Central Europe, is a thing of the past even though it continues to exist in a diluted form in China. The development and the breakup and the decline of the socialist system amounted to the most important political and economic phenomena of the twentieth century. At the height of its power, more than a third of the world's population lived under it. But the system had a great impact on the rest of the world as well. For more than forty years the United States and the Soviet Union were the major superpowers of the world in direct ideological conflict with each other. Millions of people all over the world feared that if war broke out, they would have to encounter the military might of the Soviet Union.

So what then was the socialist system? It was the economic structure developed in the Soviet Union that was developed under Lenin and Stalin, but particularly by Stalin. It also emerged in China, in the countries that became a part of the Soviet bloc after the end of World War II, and in several Asian, African, and Latin American countries. The political system of these countries was run by the Communist Party, but the political and economic systems overlapped, with the party responsible for both. The main economic characteristic of socialism was state ownership of the means of production. Most natural resources and capital were state-owned, including land, manufacturing industries, finance, and domestic and foreign trade. A second characteristic was central economic planning, which was responsible for resource allocation. The third characteristic was the distribution of income by the state.

QUESTIONS FOR DISCUSSION

1.   In the Marxist framework, what was the difference between socialism and communism?
2.   What was Marx's labor theory of value? How can this theory be criticized?
3.   What was Marx's theory of surplus value? Is it a valid theory?
4.   What was the role of the Communist Party in a socialist system?
5.   What was the function of economic planning in a socialist system?
6.   Compare the allocation of resources in a market economy with that in a socialist economy.
7.   Compare the distribution of income in a market economy with that in a socialist economy.
8.   How were prices determined in a socialist system?

RECOMMENDED READINGS

Balinsky, Alexander. *Marx's Economics: Origin and Development.* Lexington, Mass.: Heath, 1970.
Kornai, Janos. *The Socialist System: The Political Economy of Communism.* Princeton: Princeton University Press, 1992.
Lichtheim, George. *Marxism: A Historical and Critical Study.* New York: Praeger, 1961.
Marx, Karl. *Das Kapital.* New York: Modern Library, 1906.
Pryor, Frederic L. *A Guidebook to the Comparative Study of Economic Systems.* Englewood Cliffs, N.J.: Prentice-Hall, 1985.
Wilczynski, Joseph. *The Economics of Socialism.* London: George Allen and Unwin, 1970.

ENDNOTES

1.   Janos Kornai, *The Socialist System: The Political Economy of Communism* (Princeton: Princeton University Press, 1992).

2.   *Socialist* seems to have been used first in England to describe the followers of Robert Owen. The word *socialism* was used in France to describe the writings of Saint-Simon and Fourier.

3.   Lewis Mumford, *The Stories of Utopias* (New York: Boni and Liveright, 1992), 23–37.

4.   Richard T. Fly, *French and German Socialists in Modern Times* (New York: Harper, 1883), 37–51.

5.   Charles Dickens, *Bleak House* (New York: Signet Books, 1964), 232–33.

6.   By the standards of those days, these provisions were not harsh.

7.   For example, there may be a number of people whose total satisfaction would be much increased if they could prevent the publication and sale of pornographic books or the production and sale of cigarettes. They might well be glad to pay a price to obtain that satisfaction of their negative preferences if the opportunity could be given them to do so. But there seems to be no way, short of government edict, in which the market mechanism can take these negative preferences into account.

8.   In Irwin Edman, ed., *The Works of Plato* (New York: Modern Library, 1956), 397–481.

9.   In Plato's republic there are three social classes—the rulers or guardians, the auxiliary guardians, and the artisans. The ruling class is selected from the auxiliary class and is composed of philosophers who have been selected after a long course of study. The artisans make up the largest group of the republic but have little status.

10.   *Value* may be defined as the worth of a commodity or service as measured by its ability to command other goods and services in return. It is, in short, exchange value, which is the power to command exchange in the market.

11.   Karl Marx, *Das Kapital* (New York: Modern Library, 1906), 198–331.

12.   A brief, clear, and entertaining explanation of Marx's theories appears in Sir Alexander Gray, *The Development of Economic Doctrine: An Introductory Survey* (New York: Wiley, 1931), chap. 11. A more technically difficult account that assumes more knowledge of economic analysis can be found in Mark Blaug, *Economic Theory in Retrospect*, rev. ed. (Homewood, Ill.: Irwin, 1968), chap. 7.

13.   A readable account of world history, including the Industrial Revolution, as seen by a modern Marxist, is Leo Huberman, *Man's Worldly Goods: The Story of the Wealth of Nations* (New York: Monthly Review Press, 1952).

14.   See Thomas Sowell, *Marxism* (New York: William Morrow, 1985), 136–37.

15.   A brief elaboration of this kind of criticism of Marx can be found in William Ebenstein, *Today's Isms: Communism, Fascism, Capitalism, and Socialism*, 7th ed. (Englewood Cliffs, N.J.: Prentice-Hall, 1973), chap. 1.

16.   The Communist Party permitted minor parties to exist to provide token opposition.

17.   This was called democratic centralism, which meant that all members of all legislative bodies from the lowest to the highest were elected. There were no opposition parties of any strength.

18.   There is a famous quote in George Orwell's classic *Animal Farm*: "All animals are equal, but some are more equal than others." In the beginning when the animals took over the farm from its owner, the plan was that all would run it and share equally, but the pigs took over. The Communist Party was much like Orwell's pigs; it purported to rule in the name of the people.

19.   Some form of private enterprise existed in all of the socialist countries. In Poland most agriculture was privately owned. In East Germany, the most ideologically rigid of all of the socialist countries, small privately owned firms existed.

20.   There were also quarterly plans within each annual plan.

21.   The state budget is similar to the national budget of the United States, only far more comprehensive.

22.   There are a number of caveats regarding this table. First, only wage incomes are included. Excluded are incomes from property ownership, which would affect West German income but not East German income. Also it does not reflect the fact that West German income could buy a wider variety of goods and services at a lower price than East German income. However, housing, transportation, and food were subsidized in East Germany. The quality of social services was far better in West Germany.
23.   *Statistisches Jahrbuch der DDR* (Berlin: Rudolf Haufe Verlag, 1990), 138.

CHAPTER 7

The Rise and Fall of Communism

Decades of communist rule left a complex economic and social legacy in the former Soviet Union and the Eastern European countries that were a part of the Soviet bloc. One legacy is the extent to which environmental pollution, a by-product of an emphasis on industrial development, has become a costly expense that now has to be dealt with. Communist rule destroyed traditional institutions of civil society and inhibited open exchange on ethnic group rights and aspirations. Ethnic strife has now become a serious problem in the former Soviet Union, which was a multinational empire put together and ruled by the czars and then, after the Revolution of 1917, by a centralized communist government. With the communists came centralized control of economic planning and production, ambitious plans for rapid industrialization, the neglect of agriculture and the consumer sector, isolation from the world, and a lack of concern over the social impact of economic policies.

The Soviet Union imploded from within, and the promise of the creation of a utopian society that once appealed to many people never materialized. At the end it was hard to remember that for most of the seven decades of its existence, it was far from a foregone conclusion that Soviet communism would perish while American capitalism survived and not the other way around.

It is also hard to believe that the Soviet Union, to a considerable degree, shaped American politics for most of this century, beginning with U.S. and Allied intervention in the Russian civil war of 1919–1920, continuing with the alliance with the Soviet Union to defeat Hitler in World War II, and ending with the Cold War.

THE RISE OF COMMUNISM IN RUSSIA

The Russian Revolution of 1917 is often thought of as the work of a small group of radicals called Bolsheviks who took advantage of Russia's defeat in World War I, murdered the czar, and seized power.[1] The Bolsheviks had very little to do with the making of the revolution; their leaders, including Lenin, were not in the country when it occurred. Like the French and American Revolutions, the Russian Revolution was in the making for many years before it actually broke out. No one can understand the success of communism in Russia, which was a backward country compared to industrialized England and Germany, without some knowledge of the factors that made the revolution and the eventual seizure of power by the communists possible. These factors were as follows:

1. First among the causes of the revolution was the existence of an autocratic government in which one person, the czar, was the supreme ruler—a dictatorship as complete as that of its successor, the communists. Although from time to time some reforms were made, the czars were complete autocrats, and as a result the condition of the Russian people was the most backward in Europe. The last czar, Nicholas II, simply did not have the ability or the inclination to implement reforms that might have prevented the revolution.
2. The second factor that caused the revolution was the condition of the Russian peasants, who constituted 70 percent of the population and lived in poverty. Even though serfdom had been abolished in Russia in 1861, the majority of peasants had no land and had to hire themselves out as farm laborers. Other peasants who owned land found it too small to cultivate and sold it to the large landowners.
3. Poor labor conditions also contributed to the revolution. Wages were low and paid irregularly, hours were long, the employment of women and children common, and factory conditions unsafe. Attempts to use strikes to improve working conditions were put down by the cossacks, and strikers were sent to Siberia.[2] Labor unions were illegal, and legislation designed to protect workers was not enforced.
4. Another factor that contributed to revolution was a very complicated racial problem that has flared up today. Much of Russia was populated by non-Russians: Poles, Ukrainians, other Europeans, and a wide variety of Asiatics. Non-Russians made up over half of the total population of the Russian empire. Efforts were made to make them Russian by forbidding the use of other languages than Russian. Resistors of russification were shot or sent to Siberia.

World War I

World War I was the catalyst that brought about the Russian Revolution. Russia had already lost a major war, the Russo-Japanese War of 1904. This defeat was followed by the Russian Revolution of 1905, which began when workers demonstrated for safer working conditions. This demonstration was put down by the Russian army, and many lives were lost. A wave of strikes eventually forced the czar to make political concessions. A constitutional monarchy was created, and freedom of speech and assembly were granted to the people. However, the reforms were too little and too late. Discontent was further exacerbated by Russian defeat during World War I, and in 1917 the revolution occurred, bringing about a complete economic, social, and political change.

The Russian Revolution

The first phase of the revolution began in March 1917, when a series of riots over food shortages led to strikes in Petrograd.[3] Soldiers sent in to suppress the strikes joined the strikers. Czar Nicholas then abdicated, and a provisional government was created. At the same time workers and soldiers who had participated in overthrowing the czar formed the Soviet (council) of Workers and Soldiers Deputies. The provisional government proved to be ineffectual in implementing needed economic and social reforms, while the Petrograd soviet grew in influence and became a model for similar organizations that sprang up all over Russia. A reform program was developed that included labor legislation and land distribution.

In October 1917 the second and final phase of the Russian Revolution began. The Bolshevik faction, led by Lenin, had played only a minor role in the March revolution but was able to take advantage of the chaos in Russia.[4] They came out with a radical program calling for worker ownership of the factories and distribution of land to the peasants. In what could be called a coup d'état, the Bolsheviks seized control of power by persuading elements of the Russian army and navy to revolt.[5] Then they seized control of the Petrograd soviet and forced the provisional government to surrender. The revolution was over and the communists were in power.

http://

For a brief synopsis of events leading to the October Revolution, go to www.pitt.edu/ ~mmbst35/ october.html.

LENIN AND COMMUNISM

In 1918 the Bolsheviks formally formed the Communist Party and the machinery that was to run the Soviet Union for seventy-four years was put in place. A decree declared all land to be the property of the state, and industrial and commercial enterprises were given to committees selected by workers. The expectation of the Bolshevik leadership in October 1917 was that the Russian Revolution would trigger a revolution that would bring about the collapse of capitalism throughout Europe. A corollary to this belief was that once capitalism collapsed, socialism would automatically appear. In Lenin's view the total organization required to wage World War I represented that rational organization of economic life that was the essence of socialism.[6] However, capitalism did not collapse, and socialism did not automatically appear once the war was over.

The Creation of a Party State

One characteristic of the former Soviet Union was a dual Communist Party and government administrative structure. Lenin said the proletariat should be led only by a small, dedicated core of communists who would direct society like an orchestra, dictating who should play each violin and hearing if someone played a false note. One way to ensure complete control over the machinery of government was to put it in the hands of the Communist Party. This system of dual administration, first developed in the army to ensure loyalty, was eventually applied to any function in Soviet society, including government.[7] The function of the party was to realize a political and economic vision; its vocation was not to exercise techniques and professional competence but to see that everything conformed to the vision. The functional government bureaucracy was monitored by a parallel party administration.

The New Economic Policy, 1921–1928

A state of chaos existed in Russia after the Russian Revolution was over. A civil war broke out between the communists and their opponents. This war, which was eventually won by the communists, lasted until 1920 and did much property damage. One outcome of the war was the creation of the Red Army, which became the mainstay of Soviet military power up to the time of the collapse of the Soviet Union. The communists encountered a number of problems after the war was over. The whole economy was on the verge of collapse. To feed factory workers the government ordered the peasants to hand over their grain above a certain minimum for feed and seed. When peasants refused to do this, their produce was requisitioned by military force. This led to a decline in agricultural production, food shortages in the cities, and a decline in industrial production.

Lenin introduced the New Economic Policy (NEP) in March 1921. The government kept its control over such areas of economic activity as large-scale industry, transportation, banking, and foreign trade. Many other sectors were opened to private enterprise. Markets were restored, and peasants were allowed to sell their surplus grain at market prices. Small business firms were returned to their former owners. Forced labor was abolished, and money wages were generally adopted as a medium of exchange. To attract foreign capital the government offered foreign companies concessions for trade and manufacturing and for the exploitation of natural resources. The NEP was generally quite successful. Industrial production regained its 1913 level by 1927 and agricultural production also increased. The NEP saved the Soviet economy from collapse and enabled the communists to maintain and consolidate their power. However, after Lenin's death in 1924,

Joseph Stalin assumed power. In 1928 a decision was made to industrialize rapidly and to convert workers and peasants into the proletariat. Stalin was able to achieve the complete socialization of industry and agriculture.

Stalin and the Development of Communism

Stalin's main objective was to industrialize the Soviet Union as soon as possible. To do this, he collectivized agriculture, killed off the more prosperous farmers who resisted, and inaugurated a series of five-year plans. The First Five-Year Plan (1928–1932) marked an attempt to convert all available resources into industrial development, with targets of production set for every sector. Priority was given to the production of steel, which was supported at the expense of agriculture. By collectivizing agriculture into state farms and collective farms, Stalin was able to siphon off what otherwise would have gone into consumption and divert it to industry. The Soviet Union was able to attain a rapid rate of industrial growth during the 1930s, but it came at a high price, particularly in the neglect of agriculture.

A Second Five-Year Plan (1933–1937) followed the first, and a third, intended for the years 1938–1942, was greatly modified with the approach of World War II. Both plans continued the emphasis on development of capital goods industries, particularly steel. The three plans strengthened Soviet industry and set the nation on the road to modernity, but at a price. Consumers and peasants paid for progress—the former in terms of the capital that was withheld from their standard of living, and the latter in terms of loss of freedom to own land and produce crops. There was always a shortage of consumer goods, but they were regarded as expendable at a time when it was considered necessary to build the Soviet Union into an industrial power.

Party Purges.   It is estimated that some twenty million Russians lost their lives during Stalin's purges of the 1930s. Among those executed were most of the generals in the Soviet army, many leading Communist Party members, and millions of ordinary citizens. It was officially stated that the accused had either plotted with foreign powers for an invasion of the Soviet Union or had in some other way conspired against the welfare of the state. Any disagreement within the party became a challenge to Stalin and ultimately a crime. A system of terror, implemented by the secret police, left no individual secure during Stalin's long reign as the dictator of the Soviet Union. No one, not even Politburo members, was free from the possibility of death or deportation to Siberia.

The Party Elite.   Any pretense of creating a classless society vanished with Stalin. Instead, the state became highly bureaucratized, and those who were part of the bureaucracy gained power and privilege. It was Stalin who created this class of persons, the *nomenklatura* elite, who were absolutely subservient to him and would carry out his orders. Once a person became part of the nomenklatura elite, his or her position was assured for life. The elite was self-perpetuating in that members' privileges were extended to their children, who also eventually became part of the system. This vast structure of overlapping privileges, controls, rewards, and vested interests remained in place until 1990.

The Soviet Union After World War II

The Soviet Union became one of the two major military superpowers after the end of World War II, a position it maintained until 1991. It extended its economic and political control over the Eastern and Central European countries of Poland, Romania, Bulgaria, Hungary, Czechoslovakia, and Yugoslavia, and a part of the defeated Germany, which became the German Democratic Republic (East Germany).[8] Since these countries became miniature versions of the Soviet Union, economic planning also became a way of life for them. In successive stages, each country moved toward the nationalization of industry, banking, trade, and agriculture. After 1948 each government launched long-term economic plans, consciously modeled after the Soviet five-year plans, with emphasis placed on rapid industrial expansion, especially in the production of steel. As industry and agriculture were almost completely nationalized by this time, planning represented the final step toward developing a command economy designed to direct the productive effort of each country.

The Post-Stalin Period

Joseph Stalin was the leader of the Soviet Union from 1924 until his death in 1953. He left a mixed legacy in that he made the Soviet Union into an industrial nation but at a high cost to society. During the 1930s industrial output rose rapidly and exceeded 10 percent growth annually.[9] For example, the production of pig iron increased from 13.0 million tons in 1932 to 48.2 millions tons in 1940, the production of steel from 6.2 million tons in 1932 to 14.9 million tons in 1940, and the production of tractors from 23,900 in 1932 to 147,100 in 1940. The Soviet economy continued to grow after World War II, maintaining its emphasis on industrial production, which came at the expense of agriculture and consumer living standards. Moreover, Stalin's rule continued to be based on a system of terror after World War II.

Nikita Khrushchev.   Stalin was replaced by Nikita Khrushchev, who introduced a number of policy changes. To improve efficiency in production, more decentralized responsibilities for ministries, administrators, and plant managers were introduced through the creation of *sovnarkhozy*, which were administrative units generally based on the territorial and economic significance of an area. Economic plans continued to favor investment in producer goods and heavy industry at the expense of the consumer. Nevertheless, economic life in the Soviet Union during the Khrushchev period improved, with shorter lines for foods and increased availability of consumer goods. However, Khrushchev was deposed as party leader and premier in 1964 and replaced by Leonid Brezhnev, who remained in power until his death in 1982.[10]

Leonid Brezhnev.   Under Brezhnev's regime, Soviet troops invaded Czechoslovakia and Afghanistan, and the concept of the Brezhnev doctrine was born. This doctrine held that the Soviet Union would fight to keep its Eastern European satellites within its sphere of influence. Living standards improved during the Brezhnev years, particularly for the nomenklatura and for Brezhnev himself, but even the masses benefited to a certain extent. More emphasis was placed on the development of agriculture, particularly in the area of livestock production. This commitment extended to the use of grain imports to help cover shortfalls in livestock feed output and to an acceptance of external debts to make possible such imports. Soviet imports of grain increased from a low of 600,000 tons in 1969 to around 46 million tons by 1981. The process of economic and social decay began during the Brezhnev era and accelerated during the latter part of it.[11]

Brezhnev was followed into office by Yuri Andropov, who died in 1984 and was replaced by Konstantin Chernenko, who died in 1985. The 1980s witnessed a decline in economic growth in the Soviet Union. It began to lag farther behind the West in technology, particularly in the production of computers and software. For example, in 1987 the Soviet Union possessed around 200,000 microcomputers, compared to over 225 million in the United States.[12] It also lagged far behind in fields that required large and sophisticated supplies of laboratory equipment. The quality of nearly all Soviet products was poor by world standards and declining. Because of low quality, few Soviet manufactured goods could be exported to the West. The Soviet Union was losing out to the newly industrialized countries in manufacturing exports to the West. The same was also true of the Eastern European countries.

GORBACHEV, PERESTROIKA, AND GLASNOST

General Secretary Mikhail Gorbachev was named *Time* magazine's "Man of the 1980s" and rightfully so, because no man had a greater impact on the decade than he. He was responsible for the developments in Eastern Europe; no Eastern European country would have dared to break away from his predecessors, particularly Leonid Brezhnev because of the Brezhnev doctrine, which justified Soviet intervention in the internal affairs of the Eastern European countries, beginning with the Soviet invasion of Czechoslovakia in 1968. Relations between the United States and the Soviet Union improved immensely; armaments were reduced; and the prospect of a third world war was virtually eliminated. When Gorbachev replaced Chernenko in 1985, the Soviet economy was in a mess, so he initiated broad economic and political reforms to revitalize the Soviet economy. However, they failed to produce economic gains for the population. Food and other goods remained in short supply and social unrest increased. In 1989 the Communist governments in Eastern Europe fell, and in 1990 Lithuania, Latvia, and Estonia declared their independence from the Soviet Union.[13] A coup attempt in August 1991 to depose Gorbachev failed, but his time in office was drawing to an end. He resigned as leader of the Soviet Union in December 1991.

http://

Read more about Gorbachev and his views at http:// keirsey.com/ gorbachev.html.

Perestroika

The Russian word *perestroika* means restructuring. The concept did not begin with Gorbachev; rather, it was first put forth before the revolution of 1917 by some political groups that wanted a restructuring of Russian society. It was also a concept used in the early Stalinist period, when it meant some form of reorganization in culture, education, and economics. Under Gorbachev, it represented an attempt to modernize Soviet society, which meant less bureaucracy, central planning, and coercion in the economic field; more reliance on private initiative and incentive; and an attempt to rekindle the spirit of the masses to build a better and more energetic socialist society within the Marxist-Leninist framework.[14] The old economic system—where only quantity of output counted and where payment was made according to whether the plan was fulfilled, not whether the products were needed by anyone—was simply inefficient.

Perestroika, 1985–1987.   Perestroika consisted of three major elements—tighter economic discipline, industrial modernization, and economic reform. It was first used to improve rather than to change the economic system.[15] Efforts were made to improve quality control by setting higher standards for Soviet industrial products. Also, a major effort was made to modernize and retool Soviet industry by providing more investment funds from the state budget and from foreign loans. There was also what was called the "human factor" campaign, an effort to increase personal accountability and productivity. Gorbachev replaced party chairmen and head officials of many government ministries to improve discipline and initiated an anti-alcohol campaign to reduce worker absenteeism. To do this, he either shut down or curtailed the hours of the state liquor stores. To improve the productivity of workers, he increased the wage base by 20 percent for blue-collar workers and 30 percent for specialists.

The effects of the first stage of perestroika were mixed at best. The anti-alcohol campaign, although well-intentioned, did not work because drinkers simply made their own "bathtub" vodka. In addition, the state lost money from declining sales of alcohol, thus increasing the deficit in the state budget.[16] The quality control program worked well in that some 18 percent of output was rejected on first inspection, but output stalled, production targets were missed, and bonuses were reduced. Restrictions on the power of state ministries led to a reduction in their bureaucracies from 1.6 million employees in 1986 to 871,000 by 1989, but the result was an increase in the bureaucratic power of the fifteen union republics and autonomous regions.[17] Finally, measures designed to increase the role of private activity in the Soviet economy largely failed.

Perestroika, 1987–1989.   New reforms were implemented, the cornerstone of which was the Law on State Enterprises announced on July 1, 1987. It abolished the traditional mandatory output targets, it allowed enterprises to contract directly with their suppliers and customers, and it gave them greater latitude in decisions concerning investments and the distribution of profit. Enterprises were given centrally determined profit norms and were subject to rules determining prices, but were free to produce and trade as they wished. The Law on State Enterprises also affected wages, in that enterprises were given more latitude to increase wages and bonuses out of their wage funds. Workers were allowed to form councils to elect managers. In 1988 prices were reformed, permitting enterprises to negotiate contract prices for new goods, within limits that varied by industry and time period.[18] Private enterprise activities were liberalized in March 1988, permitting collective farms and family cooperatives to engage in private selling and buying. Joint venture legislation was passed to attract foreign capital.

Failure of Perestroika.   The major reason perestroika failed was that it encompassed too many reforms that were uncoordinated and came too late to save the Soviet economy. There was a multiplicity of economic decision-making centers. Many of the administrative methods traditionally used to direct the Soviet economy from the center were abandoned without waiting for the mechanisms needed to guide decentralized decision making to be put in place. Even though enterprises were given more latitude in production, they produced goods with high profit margins that, in the absence of market competition, were often not what consumers wanted. Although wages were raised, the production of consumer goods did not increase; black marketeering, on the other hand, did. Consumer discontent increased, and strikes and ethnic unrest occurred.[19]

Glasnost

Glasnost means openness about public affairs in every sphere of life.[20] When the concept was introduced by Gorbachev in 1985, it involved an exposé of bureaucratic inefficiencies and waste and mismanagement in the economic system. Glasnost encouraged perestroika because, through popular support, Gorbachev was able to initiate a series of changes that focused on restructuring the Soviet economy. Glasnost was considered an effective form of public control over the activities of all public entities and a lever in correcting shortcomings. It marked an enormous step forward over the dismal state of affairs that prevailed before Gorbachev. If nothing else, it allowed Soviets to let off steam and give vent to their frustrations. But in the end, it was the catalyst that brought about the collapse of communism.

Glasnost and the Soviet Economy.   Glasnost had a direct impact on the Soviet economy. It revealed much about the state of the economy, particularly its shortcomings. For example, glasnost attacked official statistics, which had been notoriously untrustworthy. Some attempts were made to supply more valid statistical data, such as grain harvest data, but other data on crime and alcoholism were not published.[21] There was also more openness when it came to discussing the Soviet supply system. Seventy years after the 1917 revolution, the Soviet Union had not created the good life; in fact, conditions had gotten worse. Cars made in the 1950s were better made than cars made in the 1980s. Shoddy goods and the absence of services became a topic for discussion under glasnost.

Glasnost and Soviet Society.   Glasnost revealed the bad side of Soviet society, from alcohol to pollution, failings that the Soviet Union had refused to admit when it held itself up as a country that had solved all social problems. Glasnost was used by Gorbachev as a moral crusade to cut down on alcoholism, corruption, drugs, and prostitution. However, it was expanded to include subjects that were previously considered sacrosanct, including a full airing of the mistakes of the past. Soviet censorship was relaxed, and books, articles, authors, and ideas that were formerly banned began to flood the mass media. The public trial of Stalinism and its excesses was an important part of glasnost. The whole sordid history of Stalin's rule was unveiled in the Soviet press, with the disclosure that between 1935 and 1941 seven million people were shot and thirteen million others were sent to forced labor camps, where most of them died.[22]

Glasnost and Nationalism.   Glasnost and perestroika were linked in that free, public discussion of problems and events and the restructuring of the Soviet economy were compatible ideas and either one led to the other. However, glasnost also led to ethnic nationalism in the Soviet Union. Nowhere was this more apparent than in the Baltic republics of Latvia, Lithuania, and Estonia, which took "openness" literally and demanded independence from Moscow. But nationalism was not limited to the Baltic republics; it had spread to other areas of the Soviet Union as well. By the end of 1990, all of the remaining Soviet republics had declared some form of independence. Gorbachev proposed the Union Treaty to give them more autonomy, but it was too late. The year 1991 marked the end of the Soviet Union and its replacement by the Commonwealth of Independent States.

Democratization

Democratization (*demokratizatsiya*) was the third prong in Gorbachev's approach to reform the Soviet economy. Perestroika was to be reinforced and driven by glasnost, which would in turn be stimulated by democratization. This was designed to encourage pressure from the bottom up to spur reforms, as opposed to traditional Leninist emphasis on total control from above.[23] Gorbachev felt that continued reliance on the traditional approach would doom his reforms for the simple reason that he would be opposed by a party structure of power and privilege. Even limited democratization from above meant concessions that were bound to be repugnant to a ruling elite steeped in the Marxist-Leninist notion that it alone was the repository of tradition and power.

THE PERFORMANCE OF THE SOVIET ECONOMY IN THE 1980s

When Gorbachev took over the leadership of the Communist Party, he stated that his goal would be to reform Soviet economic and political life. While his efforts at political liberalization were enormously successful, probably much to his political regret his attempts to revitalize and reform the Soviet economy were largely ineffectual. Economic reform was supposed to make the Soviet Union more competitive in the production of conventional products, such as machine tools, as well as high-technology products. He also promised to raise the living standards of the Soviet people. He failed on both counts, particularly the latter. The per capita real standard of living showed a decline during the five years (1985–1989) that he was in power. Many goods were in short supply because he did little to stimulate the production of consumer goods.

Economic Growth

Table 7-1 presents the performance of the Soviet economy for the 1980s. In fairness to Gorbachev, he inherited a rather poor economic situation. From 1979 through the early 1980s, there was a drop in the real rate of economic growth and a decline in the production of many industrial goods. But there was little improvement after he was in office, and he had to assume a major share of the responsibility for the poor performance. Investment policies led to a failure of industrial modernization and did not increase the rate of economic growth. Even more important was the Soviet lag in key technologies, such as computers and electronic components and instruments, that offered the promise of future economic growth. Increased international competition using new technologies left the Soviet Union far behind the West.

Foreign Trade

The Soviet Union's lack of export competitiveness was an important impediment to the success of perestroika. Its inability to increase export earnings from manufactured goods was reflected in the commodity composition of exports, which basically consisted of military hardware, crude and refined oil, and natural gas. Import

Year	Real per Capita GNP	Industry	Agriculture
1981–1985	1.0	2.0	1.2
1984	0.5	2.5	−0.5
1985	0.0	2.0	−3.9
1986	3.1	2.7	10.3
1987	0.2	2.9	−4.0
1988	1.5	2.4	−3.2
1989	0.5	0.2	3.1

TABLE 7-1
Soviet Economic Performance, 1981–1989 (annual rate of growth in percent)

Source: Central Intelligence Agency, *Handbook of Economic Statistics 1989* (Springfield, Va.: NTIS, 1990), 34, 58; Central Intelligence Agency and the Defense Intelligence Agency, *The Soviet Economy Stumbles Badly in 1989* (Report to the Technology and National Security Subcommittee, Joint Economic Committee, Congress of the United States, 1990), 4, C11.

TABLE 7-2   *Hard Currency Debt of the Soviet Union to the West, 1980–1989 ($ billions)*

	1980	1984	1985	1986	1987	1988	1989
Gross debt	20.5	22.2	29.0	36.0	40.8	41.7	47.0
Less assets in Western banks	10.0	11.5	13.3	14.9	14.4	14.4	15.0
Net debt	10.5	10.7	15.7	21.1	26.4	27.3	31.0
Net interest	−1.2	−1.2	−1.5	−1.7	−2.2	−2.4	−3.0
Gold sales	1.6	1.0	1.8	4.0	3.5	3.8	3.6

Source: Central Intelligence Agency and the Defense Intelligence Agency, *The Soviet Economy Stumbles Badly in 1989* (Report to the Technology and National Security Subcommittee, Joint Economic Committee, Congress of the United States, 1990), Table C8.

strategy was directed toward running a surplus in the merchandise trade account, which was accomplished through cutbacks in imports from the developed countries. This adversely affected Soviet industry because imports were cut in Western machinery and equipment, impairing Soviet ability to improve the quality and assortment of its manufactured products and to compete in world markets, where it had to earn more hard currency to service the interest on its foreign debt and to purchase advanced technology. The net hard currency debt of the Soviet Union to the West, as indicated in Table 7-2, almost tripled during the 1980s.

Defense and the Economy

The Soviet Union met its Vietnam in Afghanistan and eventually had to withdraw after a useless expenditure of money and human resources. These expenditures as well as those made in response to the military buildup of the Reagan administration drained resources that could have been applied to Gorbachev's economic reforms. Military expenditures increased the deficit in the Soviet state budget from around 2 percent of Soviet GNP in 1983 to around 10 percent in 1989. However, it was more than the military buildup that contributed to the deficit in the state budget. One factor was an increase in consumer subsidies of some 43 billion rubles from 1985 to 1989, which made this the fastest-growing expenditure item in the state budget. State revenues were adversely affected by falling oil prices and a loss of revenue from the sale of alcohol. Table 7-3 presents expenditures and revenues, the deficit, and the deficit expressed as a percentage of GNP between 1985 and 1989.

Food and Other Goods and Services

An abundance of food and other goods and services is the most important measure of living standards. Gorbachev failed to deliver in this area despite his promises to increase availability, especially of food. A Soviet survey in 1988 showed that only 23 out of 211 varieties of foodstuffs were readily available in state stores.[24] Even

TABLE 7-3 *Revenues and Expenditures of the Soviet State Budget, 1985–1989 (billions of rubles)*

Year	Revenues	Expenditures	Deficit	GNP	Deficit as a percent of GNP
1985	367.7	386.0	18.3	770.0	2.3
1986	366.0	415.6	49.6	798.5	6.0
1987	360.1	429.3	69.3	825.0	8.4
1988	365.5	445.9	80.4	875.0	9.2
1989	384.9	480.1	96.8	924.1	10.4

Source: International Monetary Fund, The World Bank, Organization for Economic Cooperation and Development, European Bank for Reconstruction and Development, *A Study of the Soviet Economy*, Vol. 1 (February 1991), 53, 54, 280, 281.

bread was in short supply, and rationing was imposed on products such as meat. Real per capita living standards decreased, and the rate of inflation increased. Even including imports of grain and meat, the availability of consumer goods fell far short of consumer demand, and goods produced in the Soviet Union were of inferior quality. Meanwhile, enterprise reforms allowed for an increase in wages, while shortages of consumer goods increased.

THE END OF THE SOVIET UNION

Communism Is Dead[25]

The Soviet Union lasted two years after the 1980s had ended. By 1991 trying to save it was like rearranging the deck chairs on the *Titanic*, because no matter what was tried, it didn't work. Most of the economic and political institutions that had held the country together in the past were discredited. Six years after Gorbachev launched his program of economic reforms, much of the economic and political system that had been put together by Lenin and Stalin had been undermined. A struggle began between the central government and its constituent republics over the control of resources. There was also a growing fiscal and monetary crisis that contributed to inflation, as the deficit in the Soviet state budget increased to over 100 billion rubles, or 12 percent of the Soviet GNP.[26] Bank credit had to be expanded to support financially troubled enterprises. Decades of mismanagement left many industrial sectors with an aged capital stock that was unable to cope with changing demand.

The Soviet economy continued to decline, but at an accelerated rate in 1991. Real gross domestic product declined by 2 percent in 1990 and 17 percent in 1991.[27] Retail prices, which had increased by 5.6 percent in 1990, increased by 86 percent in 1991.[28] Industrial output fell by 7 percent, and a shortage of imported parts adversely affected the food processing, chemical, and light industries. Agricultural output also showed a decline in 1991, as grain production fell from 211.5

million tons in 1990 to 154.7 million tons in 1991. The energy sector declined in
both 1990 and 1991, in part because of equipment shortages, and coal production
was lower in 1991 than it was in 1980. There was an increase in social and ethnic
unrest, including a coal strike and a civil war in Georgia. The growing decentralization of political power and the regionalization of markets also contributed to a
decline in output.

The year 1991 marked the end for Gorbachev, who had lost most of his power
as the republics broke away to form either separate countries or independent
states. Reforms were still being made, but to little avail. An effort was made to
change the banking system by creating central banks at the republic level. The
December 1990 Law on Banks and Banking permitted commercial banks to carry
on a broad range of banking.[29] Gosbank, which had been the monobank under
central planning, became part of a three-tiered banking system that included
republic central banks and commercial banks. The foreign exchange system
underwent some changes in 1991. Commercial banks were given a more prominent role in foreign exchange transactions, and the ruble was given multiple
exchange rates against foreign currencies.

Prices were liberalized in 1991, and many prices shifted from a state-determined
to a contractual basis where buyers and sellers could set prices within limits. Retail
prices were reformed in April 1991, which reduced the share of state fixed prices
in favor of regulated prices and contractual prices between the producer and the
retailer. Fixed prices on certain goods, such as meat and bread, were raised with
the objective of reducing state subsidies. The April price reforms resulted in an
increase in the retail price level of about 55 percent. Also, before the April price
reforms took effect, much hoarding took place, with the result that retail stores
were short of consumer goods. Also in 1991, agricultural procurement prices were
increased substantially, with the intent of improving production incentives. The
price reforms were followed by an announcement on the part of the national, or
union, government rejecting the old command system in favor of a commitment to
privatization.

Radical changes were made in the area of public finance, which had been centralized in the Soviet state budget and used to enforce plan objectives. Revenue
sharing with republic and local government units served only as an administrative
device to simplify central resource allocation, and expenditures were guided by
the state planning agency called Gosplan. By 1990, however, this began to change
because of pressure from the republic and local levels of government for regional
fiscal decentralization. In 1990 the fiscal relationship was changed, and the
republics and lower-level governments were given much more control over the
preparation of their own budgets. For the first time since the creation of a centrally
planned economy, there were separate budgets. The central government retained
primacy in determining the tax system, but by mid-1991 the republics began to
demand the right to levy their own taxes.

The second half of 1991 witnessed the end of the Soviet Union. In August an
abortive attempt was made to overthrow the leadership of President Gorbachev.
After the failed coup by Communist Party hard-liners, Gorbachev resigned as
Communist Party general secretary, and the whole party apparatus collapsed. The

flow of power to the republics that had already started accelerated after the coup, and Boris Yeltsin, president of the Russian Federation, who had opposed the coup, replaced Gorbachev as the leader of the country. Those republics that had not left the Soviet Union declared their independence, including Russia and Kazakhstan. The power of the union, or national government, slipped away, and the republics began the takeover of properties that had formerly belonged to the union but were located in their territories. On December 8, 1991, three major republics—the Russian Federation, Ukraine, and Belarus—agreed to form a Commonwealth of Independent States (C.I.S.). On December 21, 1991, eight other republics joined the C.I.S. and signed the Alma-Ata Agreement. The Soviet Union was left on the dustbin of history.[30]

WHY DID COMMUNISM FAIL?

The collapse of the Soviet Union represented the greatest social disaster of this century. In its beginning, it offered hope for the creation of a utopian society, but that never came close to reality. Constant coercion held the country together, but coercion could not last forever. Still, no one could have predicted that the Soviet Union would collapse when it did. There was a mystique of invincibility about the country that carried over from World War II after the Red Army defeated the Germans and captured Berlin. It was this army that went into Hungary in 1956 and Czechoslovakia in 1968 to put down uprisings. But the war in Afghanistan destroyed the myth of invincibility. Even though economic sclerosis had set in during the 1980s, there were still no signs that the country was in any imminent danger of collapsing.

But this does not explain why communism collapsed so suddenly. Disproving Marxist predictions that countries would defect from capitalism during the twentieth century, capitalist countries have instead turned out to be more adaptable than communist countries in a rapidly changing world.

Failure of the Economic System

Centrally planned economies could function reasonably well in the age of coal, steel, and manufacturing, but they could not compete in the highly complex and dynamic postindustrial world. The pace of international technological innovation is a driving force in the world economy, and the world's body of scientific technology doubles every decade. The communist world was pretty much isolated from the rest of the world, and its insularity cost it dearly. At the time of its demise, the Soviet Union was not competitive even with such developing countries as South Korea. Moreover, direct comparisons between the Eastern and Western European countries over two different time periods show the Eastern European countries lost ground (Table 7-6).

Economic Planning.   Weaknesses in economic planning in communist countries included the following:

1. State enterprises placed emphasis on plan fulfillment rather than profitability. Product markets were distorted by production, price, and trade controls that insulated domestic prices from international ones. Asset and capital markets were practically nonexistent, with financial flows responding passively to plan demands.

2. Central planning did not promote efficiency and productivity growth. Distorted input and output prices divorced resource use from resource costs. Plans emphasized the heavy industry and resource sectors of the economy at the expense of consumer goods and services. Compressed and arbitrary wage structures and job security were poorly linked to productivity and inhibited worker motivation.

3. Economic planning undervalued natural resources and placed little emphasis on environmental safeguards, which created serious environmental problems. The emphasis on heavy industry and low energy prices resulted in a level of energy use two to three times that of market economies.

4. An important part of the planning legacy common to all socialist countries was the absence or weakness of core market-oriented institutions. Legal and accounting standards were weak and there was no tradition of independent audit. State enterprises lacked marketing and strategic planning capabilities and inventory control, and they had little information about the profitability of the various products they were ordered to produce.

Burden of Defense Expenditures

It can be argued that one thing that caused the collapse of the Soviet Union was an inability to continue matching defense expenditures with the United States, particularly when it came to spending on more sophisticated technology. In 1990 national defense expenditures in the United States amounted to $300 billion, or 6 percent of the U.S. GNP.[31] In the Soviet Union total defense expenditures amounted to around 20 percent of the state budget and around 14 to 18 percent of the Soviet GNP, which was one-third that of the United States.[32] Soviet defense expenditures placed a burden on the economy. For one thing, the best human and material resources were channeled into defense-related activities. The huge amounts of human and material resources claimed by the military and space establishment were particularly detrimental to agriculture. The resources forgone for defense could have resulted in a higher standard of living for the Soviet consumer. The most apparent tradeoff was between defense weapons and producer or durable goods, with decreases in the latter resulting in smaller capital stock, one of the primary ingredients in economic growth.

The Bureaucracy

The bureaucracy and the nomenklatura elite of the Soviet Union and Eastern Europe were obstructions to change.[33] Like bureaucrats all over the world, communist bureaucrats resist change, particularly when they feel threatened. However, communist bureaucrats may be more likely than other bureaucrats to resist change because reforms reduce their power by definition. Therefore, to be successful, reforms must break the power of the bureaucracy, and that is easier said than done. Bureaucratic conservatism and dogmatic orthodoxy tend to reinforce each other, with dogma legitimizing established power and power protecting the established dogma. Coupled with that was the system of nomenklatura, with its vast structure of overlapping privileges, controls, rewards, and vested interests. Since reforms threatened the privileges of the nomenklatura elite, they fought against them. Thus, reformers such as Gorbachev encountered obstacles because to implement reforms they had to rely on the very people they wanted to get rid of.

Glasnost

Glasnost provided the eventual undoing of the Communist system.[34] It meant openness in every sphere of life, something that never would have been possible in the days of Stalin or Brezhnev. Glasnost released the genie from the bottle by reducing fear, the one element that had held Soviet society in check for seventy years. When Soviet coal miners went on strike, it was reported on both Soviet and foreign television, and the miners were interviewed by reporters. In the old days, the miners would have been shot or sent to Siberia. Glasnost contributed to ethnic nationalism in the Soviet Union. Nowhere was this more apparent than in the Baltic republics of Latvia, Lithuania, and Estonia, which took "openness" literally and demanded independence from Moscow.

Reorganization of the Soviet Union.   The former Soviet Union consisted of fifteen separate republics, three of which—Estonia, Latvia, and Lithuania— declared their independence in 1990 and were formally recognized as independent nations by the U.S.S.R. The Soviet Union before its breakup was one of the most ethnically diverse countries in the world, including some ninety nationalities among its 290 million people. The largest nationality group was Russian, comprising around half of the population. The Ukrainians and Belorussians made up another 20 percent, and a number of non-Slavic groups, formed by Turkish Moslem people, accounted for around 15 percent. There were also non-Slavic Christians, including Armenians and Georgians; Moldavians, who were once aligned with Romania; and Estonians, Latvians, and Lithuanians. Other nationalities were interspersed in the mountains and valleys of the Caucasus where they had lived for centuries; still others lived in Siberia and the Arctic Circle. Although Russian was the most common language, some two hundred different languages and dialects were spoken, and racial and religious animosities had existed for centuries.

Table 7-4 presents the population and per capita incomes of the fifteen republics in the year of the dissolution of the Soviet Union. The republics vary enormously in natural resource wealth. Estonia, Latvia, and Lithuania, which are now independent countries, were among the wealthiest republics. The Ukraine

http://

For updated data on the countries in the table, select links at www.un .org/esa/goveast .htm.

TABLE 7-4   *Land Area, Population, and per Capita Incomes for the Republics of the Former U.S.S.R., 1991*

Republics	Land Area (square miles)	Population (thousands)	Per Capita Income ($)
Armenia	11,490	3,360	$2,150
Azerbaijan	33,340	7,219	1,670
Belarus	80,137	10,328	3,110
Estonia	17,413	1,591	3,830
Georgia	27,000	5,478	1,640
Kazakhstan	1,049,155	16,899	2,470
Kirghizia	76,460	4,448	1,550
Latvia	24,595	2,693	3,410
Lithuania	25,170	3,765	2,710
Moldova	13,000	4,384	2,170
Russian Federation	6,600,000	148,930	3,220
Tajikistan	55,240	5,412	1,050
Turkmenistan	186,400	3,748	1,700
Ukraine	231,990	51,999	2,340
Uzbekistan	172,241	20,955	1,350

Source: The World Bank, *The World Bank Atlas 1992* (Washington, D.C.: World Bank, 1992), 8–9, 18–19.

has rich farmland, which made it an important source of food for the former U.S.S.R.; it provided more than a fifth of the U.S.S.R.'s meat and dairy output and around one-quarter of total grain, potato, and vegetable production. Kazakhstan is rich in minerals. The poor republics of Central Asia—Uzbekistan, Turkmenistan, Tajikistan, and Kirghizia (now called the Kyrgyz Republic)—are agrarian, and that region also faces a challenge in meeting its water needs. The Russian Federation encompasses over half of the population, 75 percent of the land area, and 60 percent of net material product and possesses industry and natural resources.

LEGACIES OF COMMUNISM

The attractiveness of communism as an ideology was based on the belief that it could create a society free from exploitation and want. It failed to do this. It proclaimed the building of God's kingdom on earth and the happiness of mankind, but it couldn't deliver on its promises. Instead of the withering away of the state and the emancipation of the proletariat, the state, as represented by the Communist Party, ran a tightly controlled economic and political system. Communism had its successes in the Soviet Union—industrialization, the defeat of Nazi Germany, postwar reconstruction, the space race, and the achievement of military parity with the United States, but a high price was paid for them. It left behind several legacies that are by-products of an emphasis on industrialization at all costs and the achievement of economic self-sufficiency.

Environmental Pollution

Communism left an environmental disaster in the Soviet Union and Eastern Europe. Production at all costs, without regard for the environment, was the basic objective of the economic plans. A major source of pollution involved the burning of soft brown, high-sulfur coal, called lignite, which emits a yellow-brown smog that was often so thick that drivers had to turn on their headlights during the day. Air pollution was particularly bad in East Germany, Czechoslovakia, and Poland. The area around the Lenin steel mill on the outskirts of Krakow in southern Poland and the coal-mining area around Katowice were and remain among the most polluted areas in the world.[35] Katowice is a grimy, soot-laden city where coal dust turns everything brown. In the northern area of the former Czechoslovakia, sulfur dioxide, a by-product of burning brown coal, is often fifty times the maximum safety limit.[36]

Eastern Europe's waterways are fouled by sewage, chemicals, and acid rain. The Vistula River, which runs through Poland, is so laden with poisons and chemicals that its waters are unfit for drinking or even for factory coolants. Acid rain has damaged the forests of Eastern Europe. In former Czechoslovakia groundwater contamination has rendered 50 percent of the water supply undrinkable; twenty-five tons of pollution gas fall on each kilometer of the area each year.[37] Moreover, there is the possibility of a nuclear disaster similar to that at Chernobyl. The Czech and Slovak Republics operate eight Soviet-made nuclear reactors that can and have cracked under pressure. Two nuclear meltdown accidents in 1976 caused several deaths and injuries that were kept a secret until recently.

Efforts to clean up the environment in Eastern Europe have inevitably clashed with the desire to raise living standards by increasing the production and consumption of food and manufactured products. The revolution against the communist system was in part a reaction against a system that could not deliver the goods. However, transformation from a centrally planned economy to a market economy has created unemployment. At least for the time being, employment is more important than the environment. In Poland, rather than risk massive unemployment, the government has kept the steel mills open and still mines lignite, both of which are major causes of pollution. Little has changed in former Czechoslovakia, where steel mills and strip mining continue to pollute the environment.

Poor Infrastructure

The infrastructure in Eastern Europe and the former Soviet Union is a disaster. In Poland most of the major roads were built by Hitler before World War II or by the German army during World War II, and the railroad system was developed by the Germans before World War I. The transportation system in the former East Germany is also outdated; its network of roads was built by Hitler during the 1930s. Because the road system was inadequate, East German railroads had to take on the major share of the transportation of goods; this resulted in considerable cost disadvantages in the use of energy. Telecommunication facilities in East Germany were even less developed than transportation, because the East German government cut telephone communication to the West to keep its people isolated.[38]

Uncompetitive Trade

The Council for Mutual Economic Assistance (CMEA, sometimes referred to as Comecon) was created in 1949. Its European members were the Soviet Union, Poland, East Germany, Czechoslovakia, Hungary, Romania, and Bulgaria. It developed an elaborate institutional framework for planning and implementing bilateral trade between member countries, denominated in transferable rubles. An integral part of each country's five-year plan, CMEA trade was managed by a few foreign trade organizations (FTOs) that operated directly under ministries in charge of foreign trade. The FTOs had a trading monopoly on a wide variety of products. The principal advantage of CMEA to each member was access to low-cost raw materials and assured exports regardless of production costs.

However, CMEA had distinct disadvantages that carry over today to Eastern Europe and the former Soviet Union.[39] The ease of disposing of output in each member country meant that it was not necessary to upgrade output mix and process technologies in line with world market standards. The separation of the domestic economy from changes in world relative prices and from technological innovation over time ossified the industrial structure of each member country, making industries increasingly uncompetitive. The result was that the monopolistic domestic and regional seller's market reduced incentives for producers to keep up with international standards of production and process technology and to develop effective marketing know-how. As a result, CMEA's world export shares declined during the 1980s, while world export share of the Asian newly developed countries (NDCs) increased.[40] Table 7-5 presents shares of Soviet bloc countries in CMEA exports for 1989.

TABLE 7-5
Shares of Soviet Bloc Countries in CMEA Exports for 1989 (%)

Country	Exports of CMEA	U.S.S.R. Share
Bulgaria	83	76
Czechoslovakia	54	62
GDR (East Germany)	42	62
Hungary	39	64
Poland	35	61
Romania	38	59
U.S.S.R.	46	—

Source: Allen H. Gelb and Cheryl W. Gray, "The Transformation of Economies in Central and Eastern Europe," *Policy and Research Series 17*, Policy, Research, and External Affairs (Washington, D.C.: The World Bank, June 1991), 16.

Social Costs

The Soviet Interview Project (SIP) of the University of Illinois interviewed thousands of emigrants from the Soviet Union, most of whom had left during the Brezhnev era, about the desirable and undesirable aspects of living in their former country.[41] The desirable aspects included free comprehensive health care, free public education, control of crime in the streets, job security, subsidized housing, and inexpensive food. These were the main components of a social contract that existed between the Soviet Union and its citizens. Although there were some flaws in the contract—housing was usually substandard, people had to wait in line for goods that were often unavailable, and medical care was often of poor quality—most respondents were generally satisfied. So the Soviet Union did not collapse because of dissatisfaction with living standards. There had to be other causes.

The social contract also had a negative side. Communist Party members and the nomenklatura elite received a superentitlement program that provided special medical care, trips abroad, vacation homes, better-quality food and clothing available at special state stores, and access to the best universities. There was also large-scale corruption, the inevitable by-product of a one-party state. Although the public was aware of special privileges that contradicted the claim of a classless society, special privileges and corruption were not sufficient in themselves to cause the overthrow of the system. There were more important factors, some of which have already been mentioned. One factor was the potential for conflict on the part of diverse nationalities. Some of these nationalities had been acquired by the Soviet Union after World War II.[42] Other nationalities had been a part of a diaspora that forced minority groups to migrate to different regions.[43]

Attitudes and Behavior.   A system that rigidly controlled the lives of people would certainly have had an impact on their attitudes and behavior. One thing that comes to mind is individual initiative. It is difficult for a person who has been guaranteed a job for life to adjust to a market economy and its sink-or-swim philosophy. Adaptation would often depend on the age of the person; the older the person, the more difficult it is to adjust.[44] Also lost are social identities that were once anchored in secure occupations. For example, after the former East Germany merged with West Germany entire university and research institutes were shut down, and many professors who taught Marxist-Leninist economics or the Russian language were suddenly without jobs. Since college professors are held in high esteem in Germany, the blow to their self-esteem must have been enormous. Students also had their college degrees completely eliminated.

Then there is the matter of trust. The Soviet Union and also East Germany, Czechoslovakia, Romania, and Bulgaria were tightly controlled by the police and informers. In East Germany, for example, one out of every three persons in a country of 17 million either worked for the secret police in a full-time or part-time capacity or was an informant. Each apartment complex had a person who would check on the comings and goings of the occupants, and any strange activity was reported to the police. Each block or place of employment had a person or persons who would do the same thing. Distrust that had built up over many years is bound to carry over even though the system has changed.

Loss of Identity.   While many groups have gained a sense of identity they didn't have when they were a part of the Soviet Union, other groups have lost a sense of identity. The Russian ethnic group is an example. In a poll, nearly three-quarters of Russians supported the idea of the restoration of the Soviet Union as a union of sovereign states linked together at least economically and politically.[45] Missing is the sense of what the Soviet Union once was, a superpower to be reckoned with. The Russian ethnic group was the core of the Soviet Union. One can also wonder about the loss of such symbols of past Soviet might as the national anthem (the "Internationale") and the hammer and sickle flag, both of which are no more.

Women.   It has already been pointed out that the one group that lost the most in the reunification of East Germany and West Germany was the East German women. Under communism there was a professed commitment to gender equality because both sexes should contribute to the building of socialism. Women were educated and entered the labor force in large numbers. They were provided various forms of social assistance: guaranteed maternity leaves, guaranteed job security, and child-care facilities.[46] However, women were far from equal in the socialist economies. They had the double burden of income earner and family work at home. There was not equal pay for equal work; women's salaries were lower than men's. They were also concentrated in the service occupations—medicine, law, and teaching—that paid less than occupations dominated by men. The core sectors of socialism—the bureaucracy and heavy industry—were dominated by men. They were in positions of authority, but those positions were largely symbolic.

So the question is, has the position of women improved now that socialism is a thing of the past and capitalism is in? The answer is, probably not. In the political sphere, women have been increasingly marginalized in that they participate far less in the democratically elected parliaments of the post-Communist countries of Central and Eastern Europe. The role of women in society is also being redefined, meaning that their proper role is supposed to be in the home. Social assistance such as child-care centers, once provided under socialism, has been reduced or eliminated. Personal choice with regard to reproduction, which was legal under socialism, has been withdrawn in some countries. There has also been an increase in prostitution. In Moscow and elsewhere, prostitution, pornography, and striptease shows are common.

AN EVALUATION OF THE SOVIET ECONOMY IN THE TWENTIETH CENTURY

Russia started the twentieth century with a real per capita GDP of about one-fourth that of the United States, half of that of Germany and France, but more than that of Japan. It was basically an agricultural country, but some industrial development had taken place. Russian industry had begun a process of development based on czarist economic policies that blocked economic development in the non-Russian areas that constituted most of Russia. Most of Russia's industries were owned by foreign investors, particularly the British and the French. Russian industry lagged far behind American and German industry in terms of development and productivity, but, as Tables 7-6 and 7-7 indicate, there was a gain in real per capita GDP of 3.5 percent that was superior to that of France and the United Kingdom. Nevertheless, Russia was ill prepared for war when it occurred in 1914.

Russia was devastated by the war, which it lost, and the civil war that followed. The year 1928 marked the introduction of communism with the first five-year plan and the collectivization of agriculture. The Soviet Union had formally been created and its real GDP was $1,370, which was about one-fifth of that of the United States. Both the first and second five-year plans placed emphasis on the development of the capital goods industries, with the purpose of making the Soviet Union an advanced industrial country. By 1938 the real Soviet per capita GDP had increased to $2,150, while the real per capita GDP of the United States had shown

	Year	United States	U.S.S.R.
TABLE 7-6 *Real per Capita GDP for the U.S. and U.S.S.R., 1900–1992 (1990 dollars)*	1900	4,096	1,218
	1913	5,307	1,488
	1928	6,577	1,370
	1933	4,738	1,493
	1938	6,138	2,150
	1946	8,896	1,913
	1950	9,573	2,834
	1955	10,948	3,304
	1960	11,193	3,935
	1965	13,317	4,626
	1970	14,854	5,569
	1975	16,060	6,136
	1980	18,270	6,437
	1982	18,027	6,544
	1984	19,957	6,715
	1985	20,050	6,715
	1986	20,426	6,924
	1987	20,880	6,943
	1988	21,463	7,032
	1989	21,783	7,078
	1990	21,866	6,871
	1991	21,366	5,793
	1992	21,558	4,671

Source: Angus Maddison, *Monitoring the World Economy, 1820–1992* (Paris: OECD Development Center Studies, 1995), 196, 197, 200, 201.

TABLE 7-7   *The Performance of the U.S.S.R. during the Twentieth Century (GDP per capita in 1990 international dollars)*

Country	1900	1913	1950	1973	1992
France	2,849	3,452	5,221	12,940	17,959
United Germany	3,134	3,833	4,281	13,152	19,351
Italy	1,746	2,503	3,425	10,409	16,229
Japan	1,135	1,334	1,873	11,017	19,425
United Kingdom	4,593	5,032	6,847	11,992	15,738
United States	4,096	5,307	9,573	16,607	21,558
U.S.S.R.	1,218	1,488	2,834	6,058	4,671
South Korea	850	948	876	2,840	10,010
Taiwan	759	794	922	3,669	11,590
Argentina	2,756	3,797	4,987	7,970	7,616
Brazil	704	839	1,673	3,913	4,637
Mexico	1,157	1,467	2,085	4,189	5,112

Source: Angus Maddison, *Monitoring the World Economy, 1820–1992* (Paris: OECD Development Centre Studies, 1995), 32, 194, 195, 196, 197, 200, 201, 202, 203, 204, 205.

a decline from 1928 to 1938. When World War II broke out in 1939, the real per capita GDP of the Soviet Union was one-third of that of the United States.

World War II also had an adverse impact on the Soviet economy. Much of its industrial base had been destroyed and its casualties were the heaviest of all combatants. In 1946 its real per capita GDP was less than it was in 1938. During the 1950s and 1960s, the Soviet Union began to narrow the difference in real GDP with the United States, and Nikita Khrushchev made his famous boast that they would bury the United States, by which he meant economically. The Cold War was in full swing, and defense expenditures in both countries were increasing. However, during the 1980s the real per capita GDP of the USSR began to level off, as defense expenditures and the Afghan war began to consume an ever-increasing share of the Soviet GDP.

SUMMARY

For more than forty years the United States and the Soviet Union dominated the world in the twentieth century. The world was divided into two major enclaves, one dominated by the United States and the other by the Soviet Union. The armies of both countries held their respective enclaves in order during what was once called the Cold War. The collapse of communism was sudden. No longer could the once-mighty Soviet army hold the empire together as former communist countries went their own ways toward capitalism and democracy. The transition has been anything but smooth, as witnessed by what has happened in the former Yugoslavia. The Soviet Union fragmented into fifteen different countries, but the Russian Federation is by far the largest and most important.

QUESTIONS FOR DISCUSSION

1.   What was the economic legacy of communism?
2.   What was the environmental legacy of communism?
3.   What was the social legacy of communism?
4.   Discuss some of the factors that led to the collapse of the Soviet Union.
5.   What type of life did the average person have under communism?
6.   Compare the economic performance of the U.S.S.R. with that of other countries during the twentieth century.

RECOMMENDED READINGS

Dunlop, John B. *The Rise of Russia and the Fall of the Soviet Empire*. Princeton: Princeton University Press, 1993.

Klegman, Gail. "The Social Legacy of Communism: Women, Children, and the Feminization of Poverty." In James R. Millar and Sharon L. Wolchik, eds., *The Social Legacy of Communism*. New York: Cambridge University Press, 1994, 252–71.

Malia, Martin. *The Soviet Tragedy: A History of Socialism in Russia, 1917–1991*. New York: The Free Press, 1994.

Millar, James R., ed. *Politics, Work, and Daily Life in the USSR*. Cambridge: Cambridge University Press, 1987.

Rennick, David. *Lenin's Tomb: The Last Days of the Soviet Empire*. New York: Random House, 1993.

Roxburgh, Angus. *The Second Russian Revolution*. London: BBC Books, 1991.

ENDNOTES

1.   John Reed, *Ten Days That Shook the World* (London: Boni and Liveright, 1919).

2.   Lenin, Stalin, and other Communist leaders continued the practice of sending political and other opponents to Siberia.

3.   Petrograd (St. Petersburg) was the capital of Russia. In 1924 its name was changed to Leningrad. In 1991 the name again became St. Petersburg.

4.   There were two factions: the Mensheviks, who favored a gradual change to socialism, and the Bolsheviks, who were for immediate change.

5.   As Lenin said: "We found power lying in the streets and picked it up."

6.   Martin Malia, *The Soviet Tragedy: A History of Socialism in Russia, 1917–1991* (New York: The Free Press, 1994), 111.

7.   Ibid., 115.

8.   Yugoslavia split from the Soviet bloc in 1948.

9.   E. J. Simmons, *U.S.S.R.—A Concise Handbook* (Ithaca: Cornell University Press, 1946), 20.

10.   His handling of agricultural production was probably the main reason for his deposal. He raised retail prices on agricultural products and reduced the size of private garden plots.

11.   The Brezhnev period is noted for corruption in high places and the generally poor performance of agriculture.

12.   Anders Aslund, *Gorbachev's Struggle for Economic Reform* (Ithaca: Cornell University Press, 1989), 12–13.

13.   Lithuania, Latvia, and Estonia were created as separate countries after World War I, but were absorbed into the Soviet Union in 1939.

14.   Walter Laquer, *The Long Road to Freedom: Russia and Glasnost* (New York: Scribner's, 1989), 52.

15.   World Bank, *A Study of the Soviet Economy*, Vol. 1, International Monetary Fund (Washington, D.C.: The World Bank, 1991), 21–24.

16.   Anders Aslund, "Gorbachev, Perestroika, and Economic Crisis," *Problems of Communism* (January-April 1991): 26–28.

17.   Ibid., 27.

18.   However, all but a few prices continued to be set by the authorities either at the central, republic, or local level.

19.   Central Intelligence Agency and the Defense Intelligence Agency, *The Soviet Economy Stumbles Badly in 1989* (Report to the Technology and National Security Subcommittee, Joint Economic Committee, Congress of the United States, 1990), 16–22.

20.   Glasnost was not a new concept in Russian history. The term was used in the Russian periodicals of the nineteenth century.

21.   Laquer, *Long Road*, 197–205.

22.   Stephen F. Cohen and Katrina vanden Heuvel, *Voices of Glasnost* (New York: Norton, 1989), 27–28.

23.   This was called democratic centralism. It was predicated on the belief that the Communist Party was the chosen representative of the proletariat; therefore, no elections were necessary.

24.   Marshall I. Goldman, "Gorbachev the Economist," *Foreign Affairs*, Vol. 69, No. 2 (Spring 1990): 26.

25.   Boris Yeltsin in a speech before a joint session of Congress, Wednesday, June 17, 1992.

26.   World Bank, *A Study of the Soviet Economy*, 282–283.

27.   International Monetary Fund, *The Economy of the Former U.S.S.R. in 1991* (Washington, D.C., 1992), 41.

28.   Ibid., 58.

29.   The former specialized banks of the Soviet Union were reorganized into commercial banks.

30.   Georgia did not join, and Estonia, Latvia, and Lithuania were independent states.

31.   Office of Manpower and Budget, *Budget of the United States Government, Fiscal Year 1991* (Washington, D.C.: U.S. Government Printing Office, 1990), 153.

32.   Central Intelligence Agency, National Foreign Assessment Center, *Handbook of Economic Statistics* (Washington, D.C.: U.S. Government Printing Office, 1985), 64.

33.   In former East Germany there were 2.2 million bureaucrats in a country of 17 million people.

34.   Seweryn Bailer, "The Death of Soviet Communism," *Foreign Affairs*, Vol. 70, No. 5 (Winter, 1991–92): 172–73.

35.   The author was in Katowice in October 1991. The pollution from the steel mills was very bad.

36.   *MacNeil/Lehrer News Hour,* January 2, 1992.

37.   Ibid.

38.   The former East Germany now has the most modern phone system in Europe.

39.   Martin Schrenk, "The CMEA System of Trade and Payments," *Working Paper 753* (Washington, D.C.: The World Bank, 1991).

40.   In 1970 Eastern Europe's share in world exports was 6.8 percent compared to 1 percent for the Asian NDCs. In 1987 the East Asian NDCs accounted for 6.8 percent of world trade compared to 4.7 percent for Eastern Europe.

41.   James R. Millar, ed., *Politics, Work, and Daily Life in the USSR: A Survey of Former Soviet Citizens* (Cambridge: Cambridge University Press, 1987).

42.   Examples were Estonia, Latvia, and Lithuania.

43.   Scattering nationalities throughout the country began with Lenin. The purpose was to reduce their potential for troublemaking.

44.   It is necessary to mention that a second economy, often underground, existed in all of the socialist countries.

45.   Peter Juviler, "Making Up for Lost Choice: The Shaping of Ethnic Identity in Post-Soviet States," in James R. Millar and Sharon L. Wolchik, eds., *The Social Legacy of Communism* (New York: Cambridge University Press, 1994), 233–47.

46.   Gail Klegman, "The Social Legacy of Communism: Women, Children, and the Feminization of Poverty," in James R. Millar and Sharon L. Wolchik, eds., *The Social Legacy of Communism.*

CHAPTER 8

The Russian Federation

Russia was the core of the Soviet and czarist empires. It was the first republic to be formed after the Bolshevik revolution of 1917 and was called the Russian Soviet Federated Socialist Republic. In 1922 it was joined by the Ukraine and Belarus to form the Soviet Union. The Russian Federation was by far the largest part of the Soviet Union, accounting for 91 percent of its industrial output and 88 percent of its land area. From a natural resources standpoint, it is the richest country in the world. Large-scale enterprises in the highly monopolized industries in the Soviet industrial sector were based in Moscow, which was and still remains the center of government. Moreover, Russia was and still is the dominant market for all of the newly independent countries that were formerly a part of the Soviet Union. Most scientists and scientific facilities continue to be located in Moscow.

However, turning the Russian Federation into a capitalist market economy has proved to be as difficult as teaching a pig to sing. The performance of its economy during the 1990s has been abysmal. Its average annual real growth rate from 1990 to 1998 was −9.1 percent, and its real GDP per capita of $4,190 in 1997 was less than that for Peru and less than one-third of that for South Korea.[1] Income inequality has increased and 40 percent or more of Russians live in poverty.[2] Russia's market system is run by robber barons, most of whom are former communists, and is permeated by crime and corruption.[3] Scandal after scandal has shown unethical behavior in the financial sector and in government. In August 1998 the government defaulted on its debt. By no stretch of the imagination has Russia become a Western-style market economy, nor is there anything in Russian history and culture to indicate that it will.

THE LEGACY OF RUSSIAN HISTORY

Russian culture is a product of seven centuries of Mongol, czarist, and communist rule. It can be argued that Russia cannot transform itself from a statist to a free-market economy because there are too many adverse cultural forces at work to prevent it, including the influence of collectivist institutions such as the peasant communes and the lack of a native capitalist tradition. On the other hand, it can be argued that there has always been capitalism in one form or other, dating back to Mongol times when there were traders, merchants, small farmers, and lenders. Nevertheless, economic development in Russia has been state-driven going back to the sixteenth century, and ideas and support have always come from other countries, particularly Germany.[4] Modernization rested on forced labor from serfs. A culture of greed and envy was created that still exists today.[5]

Geography has also worked against the development of the economy of Russia. Transportation was difficult. The major rivers flow north–south, but the commerce flows east–west. An adverse climate meant that the waterways were open for a short time each year. Agriculture has always been inefficient and remains so. For centuries, Russian agriculture was based on serfdom and absenteeism. The serfs worked the estates and the nobles lived in the cities.[6] The serfs, until they were emancipated, were tied to the land.[7] Under communism, farm workers worked on state farms and collective farms. They had little incentive to be productive until they were given private plots of their own. Even then there was much waste and inefficiency in agricultural production.

TRANSFORMATION OF THE ECONOMY
OF THE RUSSIAN FEDERATION

The transformation of a communist country into a capitalist country is very difficult. It involves changing the economy from central economic planning to free markets. But as Table 8-1 points out, it involves much more than that. A whole set of institutions must be changed, including culture. East Germany was fortunate in its transformation to capitalism because West Germany was willing to finance the transformation. Even then the cost ran into hundreds of billions of dollars. There was also a common language to bind the countries and a history of capitalism in East Germany before it became communist. Poland, the Czech Republic, and Hungary had exposure to capitalism before they became a part of the Soviet bloc after the end of World War II.

TABLE 8-1   *A Comparison of Centrally Planned and Market Institutional Arrangements*

Type of Institution	Centrally Planned	Market
Economic Institutions		
Resource allocation	Central planning	Free market
Resource ownership	State	Private
Pricing	State	Free market
Income distribution	State	Free market
Profit determination	State guidelines	Free market
Related Institutions		
Money and banking	State owned	Primarily private
Public finance	State budget	More decentralized
Industrial organization	Large combines	Large private companies
Agriculture	State and collective farms	Privately owned farms
Political Institutions		
Government structure	Centralized	Federal (U.S.) or centralized
Political parties	Communist Party	Two or more parties
Legal Institutions		
Laws	Centralized legal system, no business laws or private property laws	Contract law Tort law Bankruptcy law
Social Institutions		
Individual	Cooperation	Competition
Social contract	Extreme paternalism	Varies by country
Labor unions	Controlled by government	Independent of government
Education	Curriculum state-controlled and ideological	Curriculum less ideological and far broader

The Communist Party was formally abolished in 1991 after a coup attempt to restore the old regime failed. The drafting of a new constitution, which had begun in 1989 when Mikail Gorbachev still presided over the Soviet Union, continued under Boris Yeltsin and was ratified in December 1993. Unlike the American Constitution, which separates power among the executive, legislative, and judicial branches of government, the Russian constitution is one-sided in favor of the president, or executive branch, and grants less power to the legislative and judicial branches. In this respect, it follows the history of Russia going back to the time of the czars. The constitution provides for freedom of speech, of assembly, of religion, and of the press. It also guarantees free elections and the formation of political parties, and it created an upper and lower house of parliament.

http://

For facts on the Russian Federation, go to www.odci.gov/cia/ publications/ factbook/rs.html.

Political Change

The Communist Party was the only party permitted in the Soviet Union. This was based on the principle of democratic centralism, which was rooted in the assumption that victory in the Bolshevik revolution of 1917 meant that the people had spoken through their representative, the Communist Party. Consequently, party leaders assumed the right to choose their own successors and subordinates. Thus, rule was by the selected, not by the elected. The Communist Party was the only party permitted in the Soviet Union, and of course this gave its candidates for elected positions an obvious advantage. Only candidates belonging to the party would be considered. Western democratic ideals based on the American and French revolutions had no carryover to the Soviet Union. The right of people to freely rule themselves through the choice of elected representatives was absent. Freedom of religion and freedom of speech were not permitted.

Nomenklatura Elite.   The quote from George Orwell's *Animal Farm*, "All men are equal but some are created more equal than others," was applicable to the Soviet Union and other communist countries. Supposedly, workers were "first among equals" in the Soviet Union, but that was hardly the case. To the contrary, party leaders maintained a monopoly of political, ideological, and economic power. This was done through the nomenklatura system. It involved patronage designed to ensure party loyalty. Party leaders determined the staffing of government and industrial positions beneath them. This ensured control from the top down. Nomenklatura gave a person both power and privileges that were unavailable to the masses. For example, they were able to shop in special state stores, which were off-limits to ordinary citizens, and had larger apartments and cars.

Transformation to a Democracy.   Boris Yeltsin formally abolished the Communist Party in 1991. A new constitution, which was drafted in 1989 when Mikhail Gorbachev was president, was ratified in December 1993. Unlike the American constitution, which separates power among the executive, legislative, and judicial branches of government, the Russian constitution vests most power in the hands of the president and less power to the legislative and judicial branches of government. It also provides for freedom of speech, of assembly, of religion, and of the press and guarantees free elections and the formation of political parties. It created a parliamentary system of government, with an upper house and a lower house called the Duma, which was a parliamentary system also used by czarist Russia. Boris Yeltsin was named president by the Duma after parliamentary elections in December 1993 and was the first leader in Russian history to have been popularly elected.

Democracy is anything but stable in a country that never in its history has been exposed to it. There is uncertainty over who will rule Russia after Yeltsin leaves office. Corruption is rampant in both business and politics, thus circumventing the democratic process. The once-mighty Russian army is discontented and extremist groups would like a return to the glory days of the Russian empire. The old party elite have not only survived, but have advanced their interests, both economically and politically, while the gap between rich and poor has widened. The division between winners and losers poses a threat to political and social stability. Declining living standards and growing wealth and income inequality play into the hands of those politicians who promise order and a return to the good old days of Russian glory.

Legal Framework

It would be impossible to transform a socialist, centrally planned economy into a market economy without changing the legal system. Laws in the former Soviet Union and other socialist countries were circumscribed in their use and involved criminal law and family law. There was no need for property, contract, and bankruptcy laws because the state owned everything and state-owned enterprises were not allowed to go bankrupt. Most civil complaints were heard by a judge with a lawyer representing the plaintiff and another the defendant. Law was held in low esteem, and lawyers were considered to be nonproductive, one of the parasitic classes so despised by Marx. Consequently, lawyers were poorly paid and most, like doctors, were women. Thus, the legal system had no applicability to a market economy.

Conversion of Laws to a Market Economy.   Several major areas of law have to be constructed from scratch during the transition period from socialism to capitalism:

1. Contract law lies at the heart of any business or individual transaction involving performance. The law has to provide remedies for breach of contract. It sets the framework within which parties can legally contract, and it protects vulnerable parties to contracts, such as consumers and tenants.
2. Bankruptcy law involves a decision to close an operation and distribute its assets. The possibility of bankruptcy in a market economy enforces fiscal discipline in an enterprise, something that was not necessary in the socialist economies.
3. The role of property law in a market economy is all-important because ownership has many dimensions, including the right of sale, control, and access. It facilitates title to property and the identification of assets and liabilities necessary to any transaction.
4. Competition law, referred to as antitrust law, is necessary to prevent such anticompetitive business practices as price fixing, division of markets, and group boycotts.[8] It is also designed to prevent the creation of anticompetitive business structures such as monopolies.
5. Securities law is necessary to regulate the sale of stocks and bonds to the public. It involves the creation of a regulatory body to protect buyers of securities against fraud and to require some form of disclosure of information from companies issuing stock.[9]
6. Intellectual property law, which covers patents, trademarks, and copyrights, is necessary to protect owners from any form of legal infringement in both domestic and international commerce.

Before the advent of communism, Russia's legal system was civil law based on the Napoleonic code, which is the legal system of many of the countries of the world and which dates back to Roman law.[10] A civil law nation bases its law and its theory on statutes. Judicial interpretation is not a major factor in civil law nations, and the courts are not concerned with precedents from prior opinions as would be the case under common law. The judge makes the decision and there is no jury system. The Russian legal system is predicated on civil law, but the problem is that there are few lawyers and judges to administer it.[11] Lawyers, like doctors and teachers, were women and were poorly paid when Russia was a communist country. The legal system in Russia today is corrupt, contracts are meaningless, and bankruptcy rarely occurs. It will take many years before the legal system is fully in place.

Shock Therapy versus Gradualism

In the old days before the advent of drugs such as Prozac, people with emotional problems were sent to hospitals where they were strapped to chairs or put into bathtubs and subjected to electrical jolts. This was called shock therapy and it was supposed to chase away their emotional problems—if it didn't kill them first. The term *shock therapy* was used to describe one approach to the conversion of a centrally planned economy to a market economy. At the core of shock therapy is the creation of a new set of institutions designed literally to create a market economy in as short a time as possible. A democratic system would be created to allow everyone to participate in the democratic process.

A more gradual approach would take into consideration the fact that American economic policies are not particularly applicable to an economy that has never experienced them. For example, after the American and French revolutions were over, the legal systems of common law and code law remained in place as a part of the new building blocks. Seventy years of the communist ideal, based on abstract nineteenth-century ideals, were imposed on the economic and political system of the Soviet Union. Gradualists argued that shock therapy is based on American economic policies that have no relevance to Russia. They believed that conversion to a new economic system takes time and should be based on prior experience. An example would be the Marshall Plan, which stabilized Europe at the end of World War II. It was designed to achieve political stabilization through economic stabilization.

In January 1992 Russia embarked on a policy of shock therapy. Prices were decontrolled on most producer and consumer goods. Cuts were made in defense spending and subsidies to industry and agriculture, and a new tax system was introduced. Foreign trade was liberalized, and the ruble, which was inconvertible into other currencies under the old socialist system, could be exchanged with other currencies, but within limits. Prices on many goods were freed to seek a market-determined level. This increased the supply of goods in the marketplace, but prices rose to the point where many Russians could not afford to buy these goods.

The initial impact of shock therapy was an increase in employment and a fall in living standards. For most Russians not much has changed since then.

Privatization

By far the most important problem in converting a socialist centrally planned economy to a market economy is privatization of state-owned enterprises. Privatization can be defined as the general process of involving the private sector in the ownership or operation of a state-owned enterprise. It can refer to the purchase of all or part of a state-owned company; it also covers the privatization of management. State-owned enterprises occupied all areas of economic activity in the socialist economies, and for the most part they never achieved the efficiency, productivity, and related performance levels expected of them.[12] Despite efforts to reform them, their performance level deteriorated during the 1980s.[13] Despite massive government investment in science and technology, state enterprises operated far below existing Western technological standards. To some extent, this resulted from undefined property rights that inhibited those enterprises from acting in an entrepreneurial fashion.

Sequencing of Privatization.   Privatization does not take place in a vacuum. Before property can be privatized, certain preconditions must exist.[14] First, there must be macroeconomic adjustments. There must be a price system that gives correct signals not only about the real value of the assets and companies to be privatized, but also about their chances of survival in an open market exposed to international competition. Second, there must be a proper legal framework that establishes ownership rights, titling procedures, and arrangements for the transfer of property. In addition, labor and social security laws are needed to establish employer and worker rights and labor contracts. Third, there is the matter of asset valuation. In principle, the value of a state-owned enterprise is the price it fetches in the marketplace. One way to value enterprise assets is to use foreign auditors.[15] Fourth, restructuring is necessary. This refers to the breakup of former state monopolies into more salable forms. Also, removing any large or open-ended liability for an enterprise may be necessary before it can be sold.

Methods of Privatization.   There are a number of ways in which state enterprises can be privatized.[16] One way is to distribute to every person a share of equity in the enterprises being privatized. This is called the voucher method, referring to the vouchers, or certificates, that each person receives, giving him or her an entitlement in equity shares. A second method is public auctions. This is typically done in the sale of small enterprises, such as restaurants and dry cleaning establishments. The problem has been that those who have the money to buy them were usually part of the nomenklatura elite of the old communist system. A third way is to give away state-owned enterprises to workers and managers. This is the easiest and quickest way to privatize, but there is a problem in that workers and managers were often the cause of inefficiency in those state enterprises. A fourth way is to sell state enterprises to workers and managers. A fifth way is to sell state enterprises to foreign companies.[17]

Privatization of Industry.   In the former Soviet Union each sector of industry was managed by its own ministry in Moscow, whose bureaucrats picked the managers to run the state-owned enterprises. People were picked who could be relied on to meet the objectives of the economic plan that each ministry was responsible for implementing. Emphasis was placed on physical output planning, and success for a manager was based on fulfilling or overfulfilling the output target specified by the plan. The reforms of the 1980s were designed in part to give managers more latitude in the choice of inputs used in the production process and in the choice of products to be produced and sold within the framework of the economic plan.

The first part of privatization proved to be easy. Small enterprises, such as shops and cafes, were usually bought by their workers. However, it was decided to use a voucher system for larger firms. By the autumn of 1992, every Russian citizen was given a free voucher having a face value of 10,000 rubles, worth about $25 at that time. The voucher holder had three options: to sell it for cash; to put it into an investment fund that would pool vouchers and invest them in large blocks; or to invest it directly at auction in an enterprise. The first auction was held in December 1992. By June 1994, when all vouchers were set to expire, shares in 2,621 medium-sized and large enterprises had been auctioned off.[18] By the end of that month, 86 percent of the Russian industrial labor force was working in the private sector.

The voucher was a liquid security. It was actively traded on organized exchanges throughout Russia. On the Russian Commodity and Raw Material Exchange, the largest exchange in Moscow, around 100,000 vouchers changed hands each day. By the end of 1994, some 8.8 million employees worked for more than 10,000 firms that had been privatized in voucher auctions. These workers represented 45 percent of the manufacturing workforce in Russia.[19] This can be considered good for the reason that the voucher program was conceived in a hostile political environment. It was opposed by the bureaucrats and workers and managers for state firms. One way to get around these constraints was to give local government control over small-scale privatization and the revenues derived from the sale of small shops and enterprises.[20]

Russia's mass privatization program was completed in 1994 and succeeded in transferring around 60 percent of industrial assets and employment. Subsequently, the Russian government's privatization efforts shifted to cash sales of share blocks in partially privatized and wholly government-owned enterprises, with the intent of raising revenue for the budget. However, the sales did not achieve the government's revenue target for 1995. In mid-1995 the government introduced a loans-for-shares auction where it offered ownership in some of the country's most valuable companies. These shares could be used as collateral for loans, which could be used by the government to cover its revenue shortfall. A few banks won most of the auctions, which led to charges of corruption, and the government repaid few of its loans.

In 1997 the government initiated a third stage of privatization focusing on case-by-case sales of large enterprises to attract foreign investors and raise money for the government budget. To achieve this end, the government specified rules and implementation procedures for case-by-case transactions, including the competitive selection of financial consultants, who were supposed to analyze the property value of each piece of property and to make recommendations on the time and means of sale. All information was to be made available to both domestic and foreign investors. By the middle of 1998 some 70 percent of state assets had been privatized, but not in the way the government had envisioned. Much of the properties were bought by the former nomenklatura elite of the Soviet Union.

Privatization of Agriculture. Agriculture was controlled by the government through economic planning. The supply and price of inputs, the share of output marketed, and the prices paid for agricultural output, as well as farm income and expenditure, were regulated by the plan. Overall output goals were established for agricultural products that were to be delivered to the state. Agriculture was notoriously inefficient in the Soviet Union. The distribution system was very poor. As Table 8-2 indicates, less than 10 percent of potatoes produced ever got to consumers. Grain and vegetable products rotted in the fields before they could be harvested. Meat often spoiled because of a lack of refrigeration facilities. There were few storage facilities in which to store the food and few wholesalers to get the food to the retail stores. The best cuts of meat were sold to foreigners or the party elite, while the average citizen spent hours standing in line to get food. There were three types of agricultural production:

1. *State farms.* The state farm was the highest form of socialized production unit and enjoyed a favorable status in Soviet agriculture. State farms were intended to increase agricultural production through economies of scale by utilizing modern agricultural techniques. State farms accounted for one-fourth of total agricultural output in the Soviet Union. They were mostly inefficient.
2. *Collective farms.* Unlike workers on state farms, collective farmworkers were not paid wages but shared in the income of the collective farm. Also, unlike state farms, collective farms were not financed out of the state budget but from the income of the collective farm. However, there was an attempt to shift to a

TABLE 8-2 *Estimated Potato Production and Losses in the Soviet Union (per hectare)*

12-ton yield per hectare
1. Of which 4 tons are lost at harvest or during storage.
2. Eight tons left, of which 4 tons go to seed and 4 tons come out of storage.
3. Two tons used as feed and 2 tons purchased for home use.
4. One ton lost in cleaning and trimming waste and 1 ton actually gets to consumer.

1 hectare = 2.471 acres

Source: European Bank for Reconstruction and Development, *Survey on Pricing Policy in the U.S.S.R./R.S.F.S.R.* (London, September 1991), A-3.

regular cash wage paid on a monthly basis. Collective farms were generally unsuccessful.

3. *Private plots*. Private plots represented the third form of agriculture in the Soviet Union. They were divided into three categories: plots operated by state farmworkers, plots operated by collective farmworkers, and plots operated by workers in urban areas. Although they accounted for less than 3 percent of the land under cultivation, they accounted for approximately one-third of the total Soviet Union production of meat and milk and two-thirds of the eggs and potatoes.

Most of Russian agriculture has experienced the same legal transformation as Russian industry. Collective farms were transformed into closed partnerships owned by their workers. However, subsidies to the agricultural sector have continued, as has bureaucratic control. State farms were broken up and sold at auction. Many were simply unsalable because of their geographic location or because their equipment was obsolete. Moreover, since politicians have retained control, the result has been corruption in the sale of land. There has been an increase in the quality and quantity of agricultural products available to Russian consumers, at a higher cost.

July 1994 Privatization Edict. In July 1994 President Yeltsin issued an edict that changed the process of privatization. First, shares in privatizing companies that had previously been sold for vouchers now could be sold for cash. Second, workers in an enterprise about to be privatized retained their priority rights to acquire shares in the privatized enterprise.

Then on March 7, 1996, Boris Yeltsin signed a decree stating that owners of farmland, including those who own it indirectly through shares in collective farms, can buy, sell, or mortgage their land, provided it stays in agricultural use and in Russian hands. The decree also allows a free market in the small landholdings of some 40 million people, formerly passed on only through inheritance.

As of 1998 more than nine-tenths of Russian agriculture is controlled by large, inefficient, undercapitalized collective farms, which are run pretty much as they were in the old Soviet Union. Most often, they are run by managers who are indifferent to free market forces.

Financial Markets

The development of a financial market is also important in the transition from a centrally planned economy to a market economy. Financial markets have two fundamental functions. The first is to mobilize savings, and the second is to allocate them to the most efficient uses. The role of financial markets in a centrally planned economy was very limited. Individuals had very little influence on the allocation of resources, on the rate of saving, on the level and allocation of investment, or on the rate of interest. The distribution of income was determined directly through the control of prices and wages and by government-imposed obstacles to saving and wealth accumulation. Credit was rarely extended to individuals and when available was directed toward socially approved purchases. Interest served no allocative function as it would in a market economy.

Banking.   The monetary system of the Soviet Union was a tool of the annual plan, which was conceived in physical terms. The plan determined the shares of the total physical resources of the country that would go into consumption and investment. A corollary of the physical plan was the financial plan, divided into the state budget, a credit plan, and a cash plan. Monetary policy, which was exercised by the state bank (Gosbank), was used to control the volume of credit to state enterprises and make available the growth of cash in line with the planned gap between receipts and outlays in the household sector. The state bank monitored the observance of the plan by guaranteeing enterprises credit necessary to carry out planning transactions and seeing that credit was used for these transactions.

Gosbank performed the functions of the central bank and commercial banks and was the repository of funds from the state budget. It was also the collector of taxes.[21] There were also special-purpose banks, one of which was Sberbank, the savings bank in the Soviet Union. It acted as the conduit of household saving to finance the fiscal debt of the Soviet Union. Another bank was Vneshtorgbank, created in 1924. It was responsible for financing Soviet foreign trade and for carrying out a large part of Soviet international financial settlements. It also held the official foreign reserves of the Soviet Union. Another special bank was the Agroprombank, which was responsible for the provision of credit to state and collective farms.

Creation of a Two-Tiered Banking System.   A two-tiered banking system was created in the Soviet Union in 1988 as a result of the perestroika reforms. Gosbank was broken up into two separate entities, a central bank and a group of commercial banks. The central bank assumed some of the functions of a Western central bank, such as the conduct of monetary policy, which involves regulating overall credit and interest rates.

The Central Bank of the Russian Federation was created in 1990 by the Law on the Central Bank of the Russian Federation and parts of the Civil Code. Licensing and regulation of banks fall under the jurisdiction of the Central Bank. It has the sole right to issue and revoke licenses. It can issue licenses of several types, ranging from those that authorize only domestic ruble transactions to general licenses for universal banking and all foreign exchange transactions. Trading in precious metals also requires a license. The Central Bank controls legal reserve requirements for ruble-dominated demand deposits, which have fluctuated from 12 percent to 20 percent from 1992 through early 1998. It also sets reserve requirements for foreign currency accounts. It implements monetary policy by raising or lowering the discount rate on commercial bank borrowing, and it is the primary dealer for government securities.

There are approximately 2,000 commercial banks in the Russian Federation, many of which are poorly capitalized. The majority of these banks fall into one of two categories. The first would be former state banks or branches of state banks, and the second would be banks set up by individual enterprises or organizations. Their primary function is to make loans to industry and agriculture through Central Bank refinancing. Comprehensive deposit insurance of the type that exists in the United States does not exist, so demand deposits are low. There is also a low share of working assets; that is, interest-bearing securities, in the banks' portfolios. Credit is short-term rather than long-term, and loans are usually restricted to the enterprise group to which they belong or to persons who have contacts. They make most of their money by speculating in foreign exchange.[22]

Table 8-3 lists the ten largest commercial banks in the Russian Federation as of 1997 as measured by the value of their assets. All ten are based in Moscow. By far the most important bank in Russia is Sberbank, which was formerly the savings bank of the Soviet Union. It is a major holder of Russian government securities. Vneshtorgbank was the former foreign trade bank of the Soviet Union. The Central Bank of Russia owns a controlling interest in Sberbank and Vneshtorgbank. Other banks are part of Russian conglomerates. The Menatep bank is part of a group that has major investments in the food industry, owns the second largest oil firm, and has interests in textiles, mining, construction, and the mass media. There is cross-shareholding within this group as there are with other banks groups. They are also linked directly to the Russian government in that they are provided loan guarantees by the Ministry of Finance.

Securities Market. The development of a securities market is important in the transition from socialism to capitalism. Financial institutions, including a securities market, mobilize domestic savings by providing a range of instruments (in the case of securities markets, debt and equity instruments) that enhance the efficiency of investment and return to capital. Securities markets also facilitate trading in government debt obligations. In the United States, government debt obligations,

TABLE 8-3   *Net Assets of the Ten Largest Russian Banks, 1997 (trillions of rubles)*

Bank	Net Assets	State Securities	Household Deposits
Sberbank	151.0	52.5	63.9
Vneshtorgbank	25.3	6.9	2.1
Oneksimbank	19.2	0.7	0.7
Inkombank	17.3	12.0	18.1
Rossiiskii Kredit	12.3	6.8	2.6
Stolichnyi Bank	11.6	1.7	11.1
Menatep	11.1	4.9	6.3
National Reserve Bank	9.9	24.7	0.7
MKF*	9.5	2.8	3.4
Mosbusinessbank	8.5	16.3	7.4

Mezhdunarodnyi Finansovaia Korporatsiia

Source: OECD Economic Surveys, *Russian Federation* (Paris: Organization for Economic Cooperation and Development, 1997), 172.

ranging from short-term Treasury bills to long-term Treasury bonds, are bought and sold in various U.S. and foreign securities markets.

Government Capital. Much of the capital of Russian enterprise still comes from government subsidies and directed credit from the central bank. Subsidies take several forms: import subsidies, energy subsidies, and subsidies for making interest payments on already subsidized credits. Agriculture and energy have been the major beneficiaries of the government and central bank's subsidies and credit policies, as are very large manufacturing firms. Firms that get credit from the central bank usually get it at negative real interest rates. In addition, the government often subsidizes the interest payments to the central bank made by enterprises out of the budget. Thus, the combination of subsidies and loans reallocates massive resources to some sectors of the economy, in particular agriculture, which has been hard to privatize. In the allocation of credits and subsidies, no discrimination is made between state-owned and privatized enterprises.

The first Russian stock exchanges were opened in the summer of 1991. The securities market is still unregulated and segmented. The main volume of business has been the purchase and sale of privatization vouchers, gold certificates, and short-term debt obligations. Russian securities markets also deal in commercial paper, promissory notes, currency futures, and hard currency certificates of deposit. Privatization of industry has resulted in an increase in the purchase and sale of stocks and bonds. Outside the securities markets there is also over-the-counter trading in stocks and bonds. Portfolio investment by foreigners is normally done this way. But there are problems that have affected the securities markets, not the least of which was the crash of the Mexican stock market in December 1994, which dampened the enthusiasm foreign investors had for emerging markets.

Public Finance

The operation of any modern state requires the collection of large sums of money to finance public services and pay for the general administrative expenses of government. This was as true of the Soviet Union as it is of any capitalist country. However, there were great differences in the ways in which the two forms of economic system acquired and disposed of their revenues. The most important difference was the role that the national, or state, budget played in resource allocation in the Soviet Union. It was a consolidated budget that provided for the revenues and expenditures of the national, republic, and local units of government. It was also closely related in terms of revenues and expenditures to the national economic plan. It was the major instrument for financing most types of investment and for controlling the use of investment in accordance with planning goals.

Taxation. The role of taxation in the centrally planned economy of the Soviet Union was nominal, because planning determined resource allocation. It was simply the difference between output and what the state chose to release to private households and firms. The turnover tax was the most important source of tax revenue. The basic role of the turnover tax, which has the impact of a sales or excise tax, was to siphon off the excess purchasing power of consumers. It varied in response to supply and demand conditions.

A second important tax was the profits tax levied on state enterprises. It was a mechanism by which the state extracted the financial surplus of enterprises. Since the state was the sole owner of enterprises, there was no need to distinguish between dividends and taxes. Since all pricing and production decisions were made by the state, different taxes had neutral effects on both efficiency and incentives. Moreover, both turnover and profits taxes could be adjusted ex post, making statutory tax rates irrelevant.

Expenditures.   State expenditures were divided into four major categories: expenditures to finance the national economy, social-cultural measures, defense, and administration. Financing the national economy accounted for over half of expenditures in the Soviet state budget. Included were allocations to state enterprises for capital investments and financial capital. Capital goods and construction industries were the major recipients of budget funds for investment purposes. Appropriations from the state budget were used to finance the construction of transportation facilities, investment in state farms, and housing construction.

Fiscal Reforms

The Russian Federation has a three-tiered system consisting of federal, regional, and local governments. There is a division of tax authority between these governments. Under this authority, the federal government sets the rates of a number of taxes, the most important of which are the value-added tax (VAT), profit tax, and excise taxes. Regional and local governments also may levy certain taxes, including property taxes, excise taxes, and fees. There are also three types of budgets— the budget of the federal government, the budgets of regional and local governments, and extra budgets for pensions, social insurance, employment, and medical insurance. The tax system of the Russian Federation is complex and inadequate. There are up to two hundred types of taxes, numerous exemptions, and a narrow tax base. There is also much tax avoidance.

Table 8-4 presents revenues and expenditures for the federal government and regional governments of the Russian Federation. Probably the most important point is the ratio of debt service to GDP. Russia defaulted on its debt in August 1998 and is likely to default again. As the GDP of the Russian Federation has declined, so has federal government revenue. This can also be attributed to a weakness in tax administration. There is a lack of coordination among the various tax collection agencies and the Ministry of Finance. For all practical purposes, the personal income tax is nonexistent. This means that the rich escape payment of the income tax.[23] Another weakness is the acceptance of barter as a way of paying taxes that are in arrears.

Federal revenue		TABLE 8-4
VAT	40.5	*Components of Federal*
Profit taxes	12.9	*and Regional Government*
Excises	18.0	*Budgets in the Russian*
Personal income tax	2.0	*Federation, 1996*
Revenue from foreign economic activity	12.2	*(% share of revenue*
Other	14.4	*and expenditures)*
	100.0	

Regional revenue	
VAT	12.1
Profit taxes	19.5
Excises	2.5
Personal income tax	15.7
Transfers from federal budget	18.4
Property taxes	11.2
Other	20.6
	100.0

Federal expenditures	
Subsidies	8.8
Social and cultural	6.5
Defense	15.0
Debt service	30.4
Transfers to subnational budgets	10.9
Law and order	6.7
Other	21.7
	100.0

Regional expenditures	
Education	21.8
Health	15.8
Housing and municipal services	26.9
Social security	8.1
Other	27.3
	100.0

Source: OECD Economic Surveys, *Russian Federation* (Paris: Organization for Economic Cooperation and Development, 1997), 189.

Foreign Trade

Foreign trade in the former Soviet Union was a part of the economic plan, where the central planning authorities decided export and import goals during the planning period. Each ministry was responsible for its exports and imports. The control mechanism was Vneshtorgbank, which was responsible for financing all of the Soviet foreign trade and for carrying out a large part of Soviet international settlement operations. It was also an agent for Gosbank, the major Soviet bank, in many dealings with regard to gold and foreign exchange. Because the ruble was inconvertible into other currencies, trade had to be done with currencies that were valued in international trade, such as the dollar and mark. It provided the state budget with any surplus of export proceeds.

The Soviet Union belonged to a regional trading bloc called the Council for Mutual Economic Assistance (CMEA). CMEA was a trading bloc consisting of the Soviet Union and the satellite countries of East Germany, Poland, Czechoslovakia, Hungary, Romania, and Bulgaria that formed the Soviet bloc. These countries traded with each other on the basis of each country's economic planning objectives. Trade was basically done on the basis of barter arrangements among countries. Oil from the Soviet Union was exchanged for manufactured goods from East Germany and farm products from Hungary. Prices played no role in the allocation process, nor was there competition between firms for markets. The end result was that trade outside of CMEA was not competitive in world markets because the goods sent from the Soviet Union and the other countries were of inferior quality.

Currency Conversion during the Transition.   One of the first things that had to be done during the transition from a centrally planned economy to a market economy was to make the ruble convertible into other currencies so it would have exchange value outside of Russia. A formal ruble-dollar exchange rate was established in 1992. It has changed over the years. In 1995 the exchange rate of the ruble to the dollar fluctuated from 3,500 rubles to the dollar to 5,100 rubles to the dollar. In 1996 the monetary authorities fixed the ruble-dollar exchange rate at 4,300 rubles to 4,900 rubles to the dollar, with the ruble allowed to fluctuate within these limits. The purpose was to reduce inflation in Russia. This was changed later in the same year to a range of 4,550 rubles to 5,150 rubles equal to a dollar. However, inflation increased and the ruble depreciated against the dollar until it exchanged at a rate of 6,000 rubles to the dollar. In August 1997 the ruble was revalued with one new ruble equal to 1,000 old rubles, or 6 rubles = $1.24.[24]

AN EVALUATION OF THE RUSSIAN FEDERATION

Has the transformation of Russia to a market economy been successful? The answer is, on balance, probably not. Shock therapy has not worked because Russia did not have the history, culture, and institutions to make it work. Poland, Czechoslovakia, and Hungary had some exposure to capitalism before they became communist. They also had more exposure to the West and were able to avail themselves of Western financial aid. The former East Germany was absorbed into a united Germany and was the recipient of massive aid from the government. One has to be a consummate optimist to assume that the problems of Russia will be resolved, for there are too many of them to be solved. They can be presented as follows.

Corruption

Corruption is rampant in Russia and is controlled by Russian Mafia types who are similar to Al Capone and other gangsters who controlled Chicago during the

1920s.[25] Russia has consolidated a semi-criminal oligarchy that was largely in place in the former Soviet Union and has simply changed its appearance, just as a snake changes its skin. Mob rule exists and violence is common. What corruption does is to distort resource allocation, particularly in the area of public investments, which tend to involve large sums of money.[26] High-level officials can manipulate the allocation process to choose a bidder who pays a bribe.[27] The contract goes to the company that pays the bribe, not the company that is the most efficient. Therefore, bribery permeates the whole economic and social structure and subverts democracy.

Wealth and Poverty

There is no middle class in Russia, and the majority of Russians are either rich or poor. Those who are rich are typically former members of the nomenklatura elite, who have maintained contacts and who already made money through bribes when the country was communist. At the other end of the spectrum, the poverty rate is as high as, if not higher than, it is in many less developed countries. Many, if not the majority, of those who are poor are older people. The social safety net that provided pensions and medical care under communism is not working. Pensions as well as living standards in most parts of Russia are lower than they have been in decades.[28]

Unequal income distribution results in unequal wealth distribution in any society. The same people who made the most money in the Soviet Union also had the most wealth. They could lay claim to the best dachas, or country estates, and other properties that were unavailable to the ordinary citizen. Table 8-5 presents the distribution of wealth in the former Soviet Union. It was far from equal. The top 10 percent of households owned more than 40 percent of the total sum of wealth and approximately 45 percent of the total financial assets. Conversely, the lowest 50 percent of the households owned only 8.9 percent of wealth and 5.9 percent of financial assets. Although the data in the table were based on estimates, there probably was not that much difference in wealth distribution in the Soviet Union and the United States.

	Gross Wealth	Financial Assets
Lowest 25%	0.30	0.00
Lowest 50%	8.90	5.90
Highest 1%	7.00	11.50
Highest 5%	28.70	28.60
Highest 10%	42.00	43.10
Highest 25%	69.50	72.80
Gini coefficient	.61	.64

TABLE 8-5
Wealth Distribution in the Soviet Union (%) (1970s)

Source: Aaron Vinokur and Gur Ofer, *Inequality of Earnings, Household Income and Wealth in the Soviet Union in the 1970's* (University of Illinois: Soviet Interview Project, 1987), 43.

Poverty was not supposed to exist under communism, but it did. The ultimate goal of communism was supposed to be the creation of a classless society where each person would receive on the basis of his or her ability and other persons would receive on the basis of his or her needs. Of course, the Soviet Union never came close to achieving the goal of ideal communism, and, despite its claims that poverty existed only in capitalist countries, it did have poverty. Soviet authorities admitted that at least 20 percent of the people lived in poverty.[29] The extent of poverty in Russia today is greater than it was in the Soviet Union. As is true in the United States, there was and still is feminization of poverty in Russia. Single women with children are more likely to live in poverty, as are older persons who have lost their pensions.[30]

Table 8-6 presents estimates of the extent of poverty that exists in the Russian Federation. Prior to transition, Russia and other countries had a system of cash and in kind programs—pensions, family allowances, and housing—that were aimed at complementing low wages and redistributing income but were not designed to prevent poverty. These benefits helped smooth the transition in some countries, but not in others, Russia included. In Russia, the whole social welfare system has been mismanaged and pensions and other benefits have often not been paid, and there has been little assistance directed to help the poor. Some transition countries have performed better than others in dealing with poverty. Russia has not done well, nor have those other countries, with the exception of the Baltic countries, that were formerly a part of the Soviet Union.

Financial Problems

To say that Russia has severe financial problems is an understatement. In August 1998 the government defaulted on $40 billion of ruble bonds. It is in debt to both

TABLE 8-6
Estimates of Poverty in Selected Transition Countries, 1993–1995

Country	Poverty Headcount (% of population)	Total Number of Poor (in millions)
Belarus	22.0	2.3
Bulgaria	15.0	1.3
Estonia	37.0	0.6
Hungary	2.0	0.2
Kazakstan	62.0	10.6
Latvia	22.0	0.6
Poland	14.0	5.3
Romania	39.0	8.9
Russia	44.0	66.1
Ukraine	63.0	32.7
Uzbekistan	32.0	8.3

Source: Branko Milanovic, *Income, Inequality, and Poverty during the Transition from Planned to a Market Economy* (Washington, D.C.: World Bank, 1988).

the International Monetary Fund and the World Bank. It fell behind on its $1.5 billion debt which it inherited from the Soviet Union. Moreover, it is unable to pay the interest on most of its debt. Its credit rating is lower than that of Egypt and Lebanon, and it has been downgraded by Moody's and Standard and Poor's to a noninvestment grade or default grade. The latter would put the world's sixth most populous country, a nuclear superpower, and a permanent member of the UN Security Council in the same category as the Sudan, Congo, Iraq, and Afghanistan. No one expects Russia to repay the entire $17.5 billion debt and interest that is due in 1999.

So how did Russia achieve this sorry state of affairs? The answer is overall government inefficiency. Its current account is positive, meaning that more money from trade is coming into the country than out of it. Little of it reaches the tax collectors because the tax system is very inefficient and tax avoidance is common. The money is reinvested outside of the country.[31] The financial crisis had its origins in deficits in the federal budget and an increase in the foreign holdings of government debt. But political instability and a decline in the world price of oil made it more difficult to sell debt abroad and refinance the debt that came due.[32] Cut off from foreign capital, Russia would face poverty and stagnation, political discontent, and increased crime and corruption.

Political Instability

Boris Yeltsin is supposed to be the leader of Russia, but he is often absent for one reason or another. Although there have been free elections, Russia is far removed from being a Western-style democracy. The country lacks a system of checks and balances, as evidenced by the fact that Boris Yeltsin fired most of his cabinet in 1998. Although political factions exist within the Russian political system, there is not a true political party system of the type that exists in Germany or the United States. No true party acts as the representative of the government. The political power structure is replete with former communists, former members of the KGB, the security organization that once kept order in the former Soviet Union, and ultranationalists who want to take Russia back to the glory days of the past.

Political instability and corruption work against foreign investment in Russia where it is needed for internal economic development. International rankings of political instability and corruptions for countries show that Russia ranks high in each ranking.[33] The Russian default on its debt in 1998 and the possible default on its Eurobonds and its low credit rating also do not help attract foreign capital. When communism collapsed and the Russian Federation was created, it was regarded as a potential gold mine for foreign investors. It is the world's richest country in terms of natural resources. But things have not turned out as well as was expected. Total foreign direct investment in Russia at the end of 1997 amounted to $7 billion compared to $50 billion in China, although there is as much corruption in China as there is in Russia. China is considered to be more stable politically than Russia and has more economic potential in the future. As Table 8-7 indicates, China is far more important to the United States than is Russia.

http://

Fact sheets and a variety of information on Russia in the 1990s can be found at www .state.gov/www/ regions/nis/#facts.

TABLE 8-7
The Relative Importance of Russia and China in International Capital Flows ($ millions)

	Russia	China
Private capital flows		
1990	5,604	8,107
1998	7,454	50,100
Foreign direct investment (FDI)		
1990	0	3,487
1998	2,479	40,180
Portfolio investment flows		
Bonds		
1990	310	−48
1997	21	1,190
Equity		
1990	0	0
1997	5,008	3,406
Bank and trade, related lending		
1990	5,294	4,668
1997	−54	5,264

Source: The World Bank, *1998 World Bank Indicators* (Washington, D.C.: The World Bank, 1998), 334–35.

A Cashless Society

Between 1994 and 1998 the Russian government raised $45 billion by selling securities, and Russian firms ran up additional debts of $20 billion, mostly from the sale of Eurobonds.[34] An estimated $60 billion left Russia in the form of flight capital during the same period. In August 1998 the government defaulted on its debt, ordered private borrowers to default on foreign loans, provoked a collapse of the domestic banking system, and abandoned its support for the ruble. The combined effect of its policies was that almost everyone with rubles lost 75 to 100 percent their money.[35] Moreover, the credit rating of the Russian government was lowered in October 1998 by all of the international bond rating services and given a negative outlook for the future.[36] Its bond ratings were well below such countries as Kazakhstan, Moldova, and Turkmenistan, all formerly a part of the Soviet Union.

So, what has happened in Russia is that prices are charged which nobody pays in cash and where wages are declared and not paid. The end result is some form of barter arrangement where A pays B for the resources it has used by giving B a part of the final product. When wages are in arrears, the workers simply take something in kind. Enterprises settle their tax debts with the government through payment in kind.[37] What Russia is becoming is a noncash economy. The main source of cash in Russia is outside, from export earnings in the world market, and exports have been perhaps the only successful part of Russia's transition to a market economy. In 1997 Russian exports exceeded imports by $16 billion,[38] but much of the earnings have to go to servicing the foreign debt.

TABLE 8-8   *Economic and Social Data for the Russian Federation*

Population (thousands)	147,739.0
Average annual population growth rate, 1990–1997 (%)	−1.0
Land area, thousands of square miles	16,388.5
Real GDP ($ billions)	618.4
World rank out of 133 countries	14th
Real per capita GDP	4,190.0
World rank out of 133 countries	59th
Average annual real growth rate in GDP (%)	
1980–1990	2.8
1990–1998	−9.1
National poverty rate in percent	31.0
Human development index rank out of 174 countries	72
Life expectancy at birth (years)	65.5
Rank out of 174 countries	109
Life expectancy of males at birth (years)	59.2
World rank out of 174 countries	120
Life expectancy of females at birth (years)	72.1
World rank out of 174 countries	88
Adult literary rate (%)	99
Gender related index rank out of 174 countries	72
Share of earned income (%)	
Males	58.7
Females	41.3
Gini coefficient of income equality (%, 1993 estimate)	31.0

Sources: The World Bank, *The World Development Report, 1998–99* (New York: Oxford University Press, 1998), 190–91; United Nations Development Program, *Human Development Report, 1998* (New York: Oxford University Press, 1998), 128–33.

SUMMARY

Russia's economic problems are getting worse, not better. The economy is shrinking, inflation is rising, and foreign financial markets have closed to Russian borrowers. It is one of the most corrupt and politically unstable countries in the world. Regulation of the banking system is poor and tax administration is inefficient. Much of the internal transactions in the country are done on the basis of barter arrangements. The West cannot stand by idly and let Russia collapse into chaos, particularly since it possesses a large nuclear arsenal. Therefore, it has to concentrate on keeping Russia stable in the short run by bailing out its economy. That may only perpetuate the problem. The future of the Russian economy is not bright, unless some unforeseen miracle happens.

QUESTIONS FOR DISCUSSION

1.   How have cronyism and corruption affected the economic and social development of the Russian Federation?

2. What was shock therapy? How was it applied to Russia?

3. What importance does a legal system have in the transformation of Russia to a market economy?

4. What are the best-case and worst-case scenarios for Russia in the future?

5. Discuss the reasons why income and wealth inequality in Russia have increased during the 1990s. Were income and wealth equally distributed when Russia was communist?

6. The situation of women has generally improved in Russia during the transformation from socialism to communism. Do you agree?

7. There was no poverty in the former Soviet Union. Do you agree?

8. How have climate and culture worked against the economic and social development of Russia?

RECOMMENDED READINGS

Dinello, Natalia. "Personal Connections in Russia." *Problems of Post-Communism*, Vol. 46, No. 1 (January–February 1999): 23–33.

Gaddy, Clifford, and Barry Ickes. "Russia's Virtual Economy." *Foreign Affairs*, Vol. 77, No. 3 (May–June 1998): 67–79.

Gregory, Paul R. "Has Russia's Transition Been a Failure?" *Problems of Post-Communism*, Vol. 45, No. 6 (November–December 1997): 13–22.

Leitzel, Jim. "Lessons of the Russian Economic Transition." *Problems of Post-Communism*, Vol 44, No. 1 (January–February 1997): 49–57.

Milanovic, Branko. *Income, Inequality, and Poverty during the Transition from Planned to Market Economy* (Washington, D.C.: World Bank, 1998).

Miller, James R. "Empire Envy and Other Obstacles to Economic Reform in Russia." *Problems of Post-Communism*, Vol 45, No. 3 (May–June 1998): 58–66.

Organization for Economic Cooperation and Development Economic Survey. *Russian Federation 1997*. Paris: OECD, 1997.

Rogov, Sergei M. *The Russian Crash of 1998*. Alexandria, Va.: Center for Naval Analysis, 1998.

Russian Federation–Recent Economic Developments. IMF Country Staff Report 97/63. Washington, D.C.: International Monetary Fund, 1997.

Silverman, Bertram, and Murray Yanowitch. *New Rich, New Poor, New Russia: Winners and Losers on the Road to Capitalism*. Armonk, N.Y.: M.E. Sharpe, 1997.

Yavlinsky, Grigory. "Russia's Phony Capitalism." *Foreign Affairs*, Vol. 77, No. 3 (May–June 1998): 67–79.

ENDNOTES

1. The World Bank, *1998 World Bank Atlas* (Washington, D.C.: The World Bank, 1998), 42–43.

2. One estimate of poverty in Russia places 66.1 million Russians, or 44 percent of the population, as living in poverty. See Branko Milanovick, *Income, Inequality, and Poverty During the Transition from Planned to Market Economy* (Washington, D.C.; World Bank, 1998).

3.   In a survey of corruption in eighty-five countries, Russia ranked in the bottom 10 along with Indonesia and Nigeria.

4.   This was particularly true in the court of Catherine the Great, who was herself German.

5.   As a Russian joke has it, peasant Ivan is jealous of neighbor Boris because Boris has a goat. A fairy offers Ivan a single wish. What does he wish for? That Boris's goat should drop dead.

6.   The nobles rarely saw their properties, but lived off of the earnings. Little effort was made to improve the working conditions of the serfs.

7.   Even after emancipation, they continued to live in servitude. Working conditions were worse in the cities. There was a parallel in the emancipation of blacks who were free but were discriminated against after the Civil War in the United States.

8.   The major laws regulating competition in the United States are the Sherman Act of 1890 and the Clayton Act of 1914.

9.   The Securities and Exchange Commission is the regulatory body in the United States.

10.   Code law originated in Rome around 200 B.C.E. It was applicable to all Romans. Formalized into writing by the emperor Justinian in 534 C.E., these laws were called the Corpus Juris Civilis. There are two types of code law: The French civil code (Code Napoleon) and the German civil code (Burgerliches Gesetzbuch).

11.   The discussion of the Russian legal system is based on the European Bank for Reconstruction and Development, *Transition Report 1995*.

12.   They had no reason to be efficient, for they were subsidized by the government, and the managers were part of the nomenklatura elite.

13.   Barbara Lee and John Nellis, "Enterprise Reform and Privatization in Socialist Economies," *World Bank Discussion Paper 104* (Washington, D.C.: The World Bank, 1991), 3–7.

14.   Guillermo de la Dehesa. *Privatization in Eastern and Central Europe*, Occasional Paper No. 34 (Washington, D.C.: Group of Thirty, 1991), 4–10.

15.   Western accounting firms, such as Price Waterhouse, were used in Russia to revalue state assets in terms of market value.

16.   Eduardo Borenstein and Manmohan S. Kumar, "Proposals for Privatization in Eastern Europe," *International Monetary Fund Staff Papers*, Vol. 38. No. 2 (June 1991): 300–326.

17.   For example, PepsiCo bought the leading candy manufacturer in Poland.

18.   "Russia's Emerging Market," *The Economist*, April 8–14, 1995 Survey, 6.

19.   OECD, Center for Cooperation with the Economics in Transition, *Mass Privatization: An Original Assessment* (Paris: Organization for Economic Cooperation and Development, 1995), 164.

20.   Small shops represent the greatest success with privatization. More than 95 percent are privately owned.

21.   Since producers and retailers had accounts with branches of Gosbank, it was relatively easy for the bank to monitor sales. Each enterprise had an account with a branch of Gosbank and had to make all payments on checks drawn from that branch.

22.   They take in ruble deposits, sell the rubles for dollars or marks, watch the ruble depreciate, then take the foreign exchange profit when depositors ask for their rubles back.

23.   Russia is very similar to the United States of the latter part of the nineteenth century. A few people were able to accumulate vast fortunes because there were no income taxes at the federal level of government.

24.   The U.S.–Russian exchange rate as of February 19, 1999, was 23.5 rubles to $1.

25.   Al Capone claimed he was an honest businessman who gave the public what it wanted, namely, liquor during Prohibition.

26.   Vito Tanzi and Hamid Davoode, *Roads to Nowhere: How Corruption in Public Investment Hurts Growth*, Economic Series 12 (Washington, D.C.: International Monetary Fund, 1998).

27.   An excellent example is the Winter Olympic Committee in Salt Lake City who bribed members of the Olympic Committee to award the Winter Olympic games to Salt Lake City.

28.   *The Economist*, February 6, 1999, 24.

29.   *The New York Times*, January 22, 1989, A3.

30.   Bertram Silverman and Murray Yanowitch, *New Rich, New Poor, New Russia: Winners and Losers on the Russian Road to Capitalism* (Armonk, N.Y.: M.E. Sharpe, 1997), 51–55.

31.   This is true of many developing countries. The political risk factor is high in these countries, so those who are wealthy move their capital to safer havens.

32.   Oil prices reached their lowest point in twenty years in January 1999.

33.   Out of eighty-five countries ranked from least corrupt to most corrupt, Denmark was the least corrupt and Russia ranked 79th.

34.   A Eurobond is a bond issued by a country backed by its currency and sold in the Eurobond market.

35.   The ruble exchanged for around 6 rubles to $1 in September 1998; in February 1999 the exchange rate was 23 rubles to $1; in July 1999, it was 24.3 rubles to $1.

36.   International Monetary Fund, World Economic and Financial Surveys, *World Economic Outlook and International Capital Markets* (Washington, D.C.: IMF, December 1998), 19.

37.   Doctors and lawyers in the United States used to accept eggs, chickens, and other produce when patients and clients were too poor to pay their bills.

38.   The World Bank, *1998 World Bank Indicators* (Washington, D.C.: The World Bank, 1998), 314.

CHAPTER 9

Poland, the Czech Republic, and Hungary

Poland, the Czech Republic (formerly Czechoslovakia), and Hungary were formerly members of the Soviet bloc. They were linked to the Soviet Union in every way. They were ruled by communist parties and relied on central economic planning to allocate resources. Their foreign trade was mostly linked to that of the Soviet Union and other bloc countries through the Council for Mutual Economic Assistance (CMEA). Their foreign and domestic policies were pretty much dictated by Moscow, and any attempt to achieve some modicum of independence brought an invasion by the Soviet army.[1] Of the three countries, Czechoslovakia was the most ideologically rigid and adhered faithfully to Soviet policies. Hungary was the most experimental in terms of economic reforms and had the greatest contact with the West.

The three countries were created by the Treaty of Versailles that ended World War I, and all were once a part of the Austro-Hungarian empire. Czechoslovakia was created in 1918 by combining two different ethnic groups, the Czechs and the Slovaks.[2] Hungary, which lost two-thirds of its territory, became an independent nation in 1919. Poland was created out of territory that had been claimed over time by Germany, Russia, Sweden, and the Austro-Hungarian empire. Historically, it suffered the misfortune of being the common battleground for invaders ranging from the Mongol hordes of Genghis Khan to the Magyars and Swedes to the Germans and Russians—a misfortune that was to continue in World War II and also during the postwar period.

After the war the economies and political system of the three countries were organized along Soviet lines. The first and most important move was the nationalization of industry, banking, and trade. The nationalization of agriculture followed later, with varying degrees of success. Political parties were tolerated at first under the guise of a popular front, but the communists soon seized control. During the period from the early 1950s to the collapse of communism in the late 1980s, the three countries developed in different ways. Czechoslovakia was the most industrialized, a carryover from the interwar period. Poland was the most agrarian, and most of its agriculture remained in private hands. Hungary was the only country to have had prior experience with communism before World War II.[3]

http://

Links to social, political, and economic development of countries around the world can be found at http:// www .worldbank.org/ data/countrydata/ countrydata.html.

LEGACY OF COMMUNISM

The collapse of the Soviet bloc countries occurred in 1988, two years before the end of the Soviet Union. It was sudden and swift—and somewhat unexpected. This was particularly true of East Germany, where the communist leader Erich Honecker had boasted that the wall that separated the two Germanies would last for another 100 years. In less than a year after he made this boast, the wall came down and Germany was reunited. Some governments, including those of Poland and Bulgaria, had borrowed heavily from the West to shore up their declining economies. Others printed more money, which in a system of fixed prices meant queues, shortages, and corruption. In Poland the rate of inflation as measured by a 1985 base year of 100 percent increased to 828 percent by 1989. But discontent and change would have been impossible if change had not been going on in the Soviet Union, with Gorbachev implementing perestroika and glasnost.[4]

The performance of the Soviet bloc countries can be compared to that of the Western European countries by using per capita GNP before World War II and in 1990. As Table 9-1 indicates, in 1938 all of the countries had somewhat similar economic systems. Italy actually had a lower per capita GNP than Czechoslovakia in 1938, and Hungary and Poland had higher per capita GNPs than Spain and Portugal. Czechoslovakia was more industrialized than any of the four Western European countries. All of this changed when the Central and Eastern European countries became communist. In 1990 the four Western European countries were far better off than the Central and Eastern European countries. Austria and Czechoslovakia had the same per capita GNPs in 1938; by 1990 Austria's per capita GNP was six times that of Czechoslovakia's.

Environmental pollution was a legacy of communism in Poland, Czechoslovakia, and Hungary, as it was in the Soviet Union and East Germany. In Poland the rivers and lakes were polluted. The Vistula River, the main waterway of Poland, was so polluted at Warsaw and Krakow that the Poles claimed one could walk across it. The steel mills at Katowice belched sulfuric fumes into the atmosphere which turned into acid rain that corroded everything it touched. Czechoslovakia was more industrialized than Poland, so the extent of its pollution was even worse.

Country	1938	1990
Western Europe		
Austria	1,800	19,200
Italy	1,300	16,800
Spain	900	10,900
Portugal	800	4,900
Eastern Europe		
Czechoslovakia	1,800	3,100
Hungary	1,100	2,800
Poland	1,000	1,700
Romania	700	1,600

TABLE 9-1
Per Capita GNP for 1938 and 1990 for Western and Eastern European Countries (in 1990 U.S. Dollars)

Source: Bartlomiej Kaminski, "The Legacy of Communism," in *East-Central European Economies in Transition*. Joint Economic Committee, Congress of the United States, 103d Cong., 2nd Sess. (Washington, D.C.: U.S. Government Printing Office, November 1994), 17.

Moreover, the breakdown of several of its nuclear reactors threatened to cause a nuclear disaster worse than Chernobyl. The mining areas of Czechoslovakia were also polluted. Hungary, of the three communist countries, was probably the least polluted because there was less of an industrial base. Nevertheless, chemicals used in agriculture did cause soil pollution.

POLAND

Communism did not have the hold in Poland that it had in the other Soviet bloc countries for several reasons. First, Poland had no tradition of communism before World War II. Second, there was a resentment of any outside power, particularly from Germany and the Soviet Union, both of which had made Poland a battleground for centuries. Third, the Catholic Church has always been a viable part of the life of Poland and a bulwark against change. Fourth, many Poles were able to travel to other countries and were aware of what life was like elsewhere. Finally, an aspect of the Polish national character is a romantic fatalism created by many centuries of being a common battleground for Swedes, Germans, Russians, and Austrians. Poles have revolted countless times against their oppressors, usually with disastrous results.

Many Poles used communism as a way to advance their careers; few were ideologically committed to it. For this reason, there were few reprisals after communism collapsed. Most Poles went about their business as if nothing had changed. Party members simply held on to the jobs they had or used their positions to be first in line to buy state enterprises or to acquire private property. They also achieved political success by running for office representing new political parties committed to democracy and free enterprise. This was no different from what happened in

http://

For fundamental facts, figures, and regulations about the economy in Poland, go to http://www .polska.net.

Russia, East Germany, and other former communist countries. The political elite had the contacts and the knowledge to take advantage of their opportunities.

Problems of the Polish Economy

Poland was the only centrally planned economy in the Soviet bloc countries that relied principally on private farming for the bulk of agricultural production.[5] Although there were some state and collective farms, they were of no particular importance. Prior to World War II, Poland was one of the premier agricultural countries in Europe and a net exporter of agricultural goods. By the 1970s agriculture was so inefficient that food products had to be imported. There were several reasons why agriculture was inefficient. First, the government concentrated most of its resources on the development of such industries as iron and steel, heavy machinery, and chemicals and ignored agriculture. Second, most Polish farms were too small to achieve economies of scale, and farmers did not have the money to invest in equipment for mechanizing farm tasks. Third, processing facilities, such as slaughterhouses and meat-producing plants, were run by inefficient state monopolies. Fourth, the distribution system was inefficient, with much waste and spoilage before farm products reached consumers.

Polish industrial policy was based on the Soviet model of economic development. Resources were poured into heavy industries such as iron and steel. This model was not suitable for Poland, because it was totally different from the Soviet Union in resources and size. Profitable industries had to subsidize unprofitable ones and high operating costs made most plants and industries uncompetitive and unprofitable. The consumer sector was neglected while resources went into the development of heavy industry. The end result was the creation of consumer unrest that was attributed to chronic shortages of meat and other consumer goods. This led to food riots, a shakeup in the Communist Party in the early 1970s, and the replacement of the party secretary. Poland borrowed money from the United States, but wasted much of it on inefficient projects.

The Polish economy was similar to other planned economies. Central planning was not guided by a coherent price system. High levels of subsidies accounted for half of Polish government budgetary expenditures. Prices to consumers were based on social considerations, and consumer goods and housing were provided at prices well below their cost. The principal role of the Polish banking system was to prepare the financial plan and to monitor the success of state enterprises in achieving plan targets. Ownership of enterprises was in the hands of the state, and few people had the incentive to concern themselves with managing them successfully. Wages were set by the economic plan and jobs were guaranteed. The result was a high rate of absenteeism and of alcoholism.

Shock Therapy

Poland was the first of the Soviet bloc countries to use shock therapy, which involved a rapid transformation from communism to capitalism. It involved several approaches.[6]

http://

Information on Poland, including its economy, can be found at *http://www.odci .gov/cia/ publications/ factbook/pl.html.*

1. It freed prices from central control and eliminated most subsidies. Prices were allowed to increase, which reduced purchasing power, but increased incentives for farmers and factories to produce and thus to increase supply.
2. The central government balanced its budget to eliminate deficit spending that had contributed to a rapid increase in inflation in the latter part of the 1980s.
3. Poland devalued its currency unit, the zloty, made it convertible into other currencies, and allowed it to float to attain a market-determined level. Devaluation was supposed to make foreign investments in Poland cheaper and Polish exports were competitive in world markets.
4. State enterprises were privatized to create a private ownership group. A Ministry of Ownership was created to oversee the privatization process, and specialized institutions were set up to facilitate it.

Privatization

When Poland began the privatization process, it had a distinct advantage over Russia and most of the other countries involved in the transition from communism to a market economy in that private enterprise had existed under communist rule. Restaurants and other service enterprises had a considerable amount of private ownership and hotels were generally built and managed by foreign chains. Poles were also allowed to travel abroad, make business contacts, learn business techniques, and bring hard currency back to Poland. They were able to exploit Poland's shortage of goods by bringing back items that were in short supply. Many use the hard currency accumulated by working abroad to create their own businesses. In 1989 the private sector share of GNP was 28.6 percent.[7]

Like other countries, the Polish economy was dominated by large state-owned enterprises. Firms with more than 500 workers numbered around 2,000 and accounted for 80 percent of industrial employment in Poland. Firms with more than 1,000 workers numbered 1,000 and accounted for 66 percent of employment in industry. As was the case in Russia and other communist countries, Polish industry was obsolete by Western standards. An example was the Lenin steelworks in the industrial city of Nowa Huta, which employed some 36,000 workers in 1990. Its products were not competitive in world markets. Six years later, the steelworks, now renamed Huta Sendzimira to shed the association with Lenin, was operating with a labor force of 11,000 and was still losing money because it was too politically important to close down.

Privatization of state property in Poland originally took four forms:

1. Sales of entire firms to Polish or foreign investors.
2. Liquidation of firm assets and their sales to private investors.
3. Free distribution of stock shares to investors.
4. Establishment of holding companies.

Privatization has had notable success in Poland. Small pieces of the economy were converted rather quickly into the free market. Nearly 80 percent of retail and wholesale outlets were privatized by October 1991.[8] Half of the nation's trucking industry was in private hands, and more than 1.2 million new private companies were created in the sixteen months after privatization started. Banks were privatized, as were department stores. But the industrial base of Poland proved to be much harder to privatize. Even though many large Polish firms were uncompetitive by world standards, they employed thousands of workers, and few politicians, particularly those who were former communists, wanted to lose votes. But privatization of large Polish firms has continued, and Table 9-2 lists some of the largest firms that have been privatized by the end of 1997.

The privatization process changed a number of times between 1990 and 1997. There have been public offerings, sealed bids, debt-equity swaps, leasing, vouchers, and joint ventures.[9] In August 1996 the Law on Commercialization and Privatization was passed, which gave 96 percent of Polish citizens investment certificates. In 1998 the Privatization Guideline was introduced to further privatization, with the emphasis to be placed on the on privatization of the remaining large state enterprises. As Table 9-2 indicates, privatization in Poland has been a success. The table compares 1990 when the transition to a market economy really got underway to 1997. The transformation is enormous. Table 9-3 shows some of the large state enterprises that have been privatized.

Banking

Prior to transition the national bank of Poland was the central bank. It had a monopoly over both traditional banking functions and commercial bank activities. Its operations, as was true of other socialist countries, were linked to the central economic plan, and monetary policy played a passive role. It was also responsible for the formation of the annual cash and credit plans. In 1988 its functions were changed by two new laws, the Act on the National Bank of Poland and the Banking Law. Nine state-owned commercial banks took over the commercial functions of the National Bank of Poland. In October 1991 the legal status of these com-

TABLE 9-2   *Number of Public and Private Enterprises in Poland, 1990–1997*

	1990	1997
Public sector		
State-owned enterprises	8,453	3,369
Municipal enterprises	32	265
State treasury commercial companies	248	2,056
Commercial companies owned by state	1,135	5,226
Private sector		
Domestic commercial companies	33,239	106,475
Joint ventures	1,645	32,942
Foreign companies	862	518
Individual entrepreneurs (thousands)	1,135	2,090
Cooperatives	18,575	19,775

Source: OECD Economic Surveys, *Poland* (Paris: Organization for Economic Cooperation and Development, 1998), 47.

TABLE 9-3 *Large Polish State-Owned Enterprises That Have Been Privatized*

Company	Sector	Employment	Assets[1]
Bank Handlowy	Banking	4,365	14,696
KGHM	Copper production	25,837	4,346
Elektrocieplownia Krakow	Energy	786	404
Orbis[2]	Travel service	10,524	748
PBK	Banking	5,942	9,244
Polfa Poznan	Pharmaceuticals	1,316	222
ZPT Krakow	Tobacco	4,121	782
DT Centrum	Department store	5,744	164
Undergoing privatization			
TP	Telecommunications	73,506	11,016
Group Pekao	Banking	23,487	42,276
Bank Zachodni	Banking	6,787	5,045
Huta Katowice	Steel	20,332	3,771
Huta Zendzimira	Metallurgy	17,486	2,837
Ruch	Press chain	13,535	497
LOT[3]	Airline	4,265	1,257
CPN	Oil distribution	10,243	1,211
PZU	Insurance	14,396	2,188

[1]*In millions of zlotys (average exchange rate in 1997 was ZL3.28 to $1.00).*
[2]*Orbis ran all but a few of the hotels in Poland and handled overseas travel.*
[3]*LOT was the national Polish airlines. It handled all international and domestic flights. It used Russian-made planes.*

Source: OECD Economic Surveys, *Poland* (Paris: Organization for Economic Cooperation and Development, 1998), 138.

mercial banks was transformed into that of joint-stock companies 100 percent owned by the Polish Treasury. The nine state-owned commercial banks played the same functions as commercial banks in the West. The National Bank of Poland assumed the responsibility of implementing monetary policy.

Bank privatization has been rather slow, but most of the nine state-owned banks have been privatized. Since the transition, one of the largest privatizations took place in 1997. In the privatization of the major state banks in Poland, stocks and convertible bonds were used. There were five types of investors: the state, employers, foreign investors, institutional investors, and individual investors. The Polish banking system as of 1998 was made up of four types of banks: the large, formerly state-owned commercial banks; the state-owned specialized banks, now privatized, which deal with foreign trade; small private banks that were chartered by the banking law of 1989; and approximately 1,500 cooperative banks whose function is to make housing loans.

Public Finance

In Soviet-type economies, including Poland's, resource allocation was regulated by economic planning. The state budget was a key part of planning in that it represented the administration of the entire payment system. Virtually all payments were made through the state financial sector. The two most important taxes were the turnover tax and the tax on enterprise profits. The most important expenditure in the state budget was subsidies, which accounted for 16 percent of the Polish GNP in 1998.[10] The bulk of these subsidies went to support state-owned enterprises. When transition began in 1990 Poland was faced with two major problems. The first was the development of an entirely new tax system more in line with the tax systems of the European Union countries, and the second was a reduction in the federal budget.

Several significant changes were made in the Polish tax system. A personal income tax was introduced in 1992. Marginal tax rates from 1992 to 1996 ranged from 21 percent to 45 percent. They were changed in 1996 and the rates as of 1999 are 20, 32, and 44 percent. In 1989 an enterprise income tax rate of 40 percent was introduced; in 1999 the rate was 34 percent.[11] In 1993 the value-added tax (VAT) was introduced at a standard rate of 22 percent and a minimum rate of 7 percent on necessities, and the rates have not changed much. It is the single most important source of revenue in the Polish national budget. There are also a variety of excise taxes levied on such products as alcohol and tobacco. At the local level, property taxes are the most important source of revenue.[12] Table 9-4 presents a breakdown of revenues and expenditures in the Polish national budget for 1996.

TABLE 9-4

Revenues and Expenditures of the Polish Government, 1996 (billions of zlotys)

Total revenue	99.7
Tax revenues	40.4
Direct taxes	36.9
Personal income tax	26.2
Enterprise income tax	10.7
Excess wage tax	0.0
Indirect taxes	43.9
Value-added (VAT)	27.7
Excise taxes	15.9
Trade taxes	9.4
Customs duties and import surcharge	9.4
Nontax revenue	6.0
Total expenditures	106.7
Current	101.1
Wages	17.7
Social security contributions	5.2
Purchase of goods and services	32.3
Interest	15.0
Transfers to local governments	7.9
Transfers to social security funds	17.9
Capital	17.9
Expenditures and grants	5.6

Source: International Monetary Fund, *Republic of Poland–Recent Economic Development* (Washington, D.C.: IMF, April 1997), 52–53.

TABLE 9-5 *Indicators of the Performance of the Polish Economy, 1991–1998 (%)*

Year	GDP Growth Rate	Inflation	Productivity	Unemployment
1991	−7.0	70.3	−0.6	16.3
1992	2.6	43.0	7.2	15.0
1993	3.8	35.3	6.3	12.5
1994	5.2	32.2	8.0	11.8
1995	7.0	27.8	6.5	13.9
1996	6.1	19.9	5.4	10.4
1997	6.9	14.9	5.5	10.8
1998	5.1	8.6	5.4	10.6

Source: OECD Economic Survey, *Poland* (Paris: Organization for Economic Cooperation and Development, 1998), 150, 151; *The Economist*, February 13, 1999, p. 106.

An Evaluation of the Polish Economy

Unlike the Russian Federation, Poland has performed well during the 1990s. It has performed the best of all the former Soviet bloc countries as measured by growth in real GDP for 1991–1998. Inflation and unemployment have declined, and output growth has been helped by gains in product. Capital inflows have exceeded capital flows, indicating investor confidence in the Polish economy and its political system. Unlike the Russian Federation, corruption is not a major political problem, and Poland's credit rating is far superior.[13] It is hoping to eventually join the European Union, but meeting EU standards will be difficult and expensive, particularly since its agricultural and environmental standards are well below those set by the EU. Table 9-5 presents the performance of the Polish economy during the 1990s.

http://

Data on economic development in Poland are at http://www .worldbank.org/ data/countrydata/ countrydata.html.

THE CZECH REPUBLIC

Czechoslovakia, now the Czech and Slovak republics, had the highest living standard of all of the East Central European countries before World War II. It was created by the Treaty of Versailles and included much of the industrial base of the former Austro-Hungarian Empire. It developed both capitalistic and democratic institutions during the period 1919–1939. When it was occupied by the Soviet Union after World War II, it was reorganized along the lines of the Soviet economic system. With the exception of East Germany, it became the most ideologically rigid of the Soviet bloc countries, and any attempt at economic reform was rigidly suppressed. Under communism 98 percent of the means of production were owned by the state. Prices were set by the state, and wages were tightly controlled. Economic planning stressed the development of heavy industry, and most foreign trade was done with the other CMEA countries.

In 1989 the authoritarian rule of Gustav Husak was toppled by the peaceful "velvet revolution," and Czechoslovakia became an independent country. It had a

http://

Information on the Czech Republic, including economic information, is at http://www .odci.gov/cia/ publications/ factbook/ez.html.

very small service sector, and production of consumer goods was relatively small. It was industrialized with an emphasis on military and heavy industry and collectivized in agriculture. Production facilities were located and developed, according not to domestic needs or comparative advantage in regional markets, but to the needs of the Soviet Union. The end result was an overemphasis on heavy industry and military industry, subsidized energy inputs resulting in inefficient energy use, and environmental problems of the highest order. In addition, marketing and management skills necessary for the transition to a market economy did not exist.[14]

Privatization

Privatization in Czechoslovakia took several forms. One was restitution, which involved the return of property to those who owned it prior to its confiscation or nationalization when the communists took power in 1948. Property was returned to the original owners or to their heirs except in cases where buildings had been constructed on the land after it was nationalized. About 30,000 industrial and administrative buildings, forest properties, and agricultural properties that had been nationalized by the communists during 1948–1955, as well as 70,000 residential properties nationalized during 1955–1959, were returned to their original owners.[15] The value of the assets returned was around $5 billion.

Auctions. Small-scale privatization of small shops and businesses began on November 1, 1990, and was accomplished mainly through public auction. However, few persons could afford to bid on these businesses. Those who could generally fell into two categories. The first category included those who were a part of the nomenklatura elite and anyone who had the opportunity under communist rule to make money illegally. This included those persons who sold any commodity by weight or volume, such as butchers and gas station operators. Also included in this category were persons who exchanged money on the black market for foreign currency. The second category included persons who had financial backing from people in other countries who, by law, could not purchase a business in Czechoslovakia. Auctions were held as often as four times a week, and by November 1992 over 20,000 small-scale enterprises had been sold.[16]

Vouchers. On May 18, 1992, Czechoslovakia decided to sell 1,200 of its larger state enterprises by distributing shares in them to millions of its citizens by issuing vouchers. Every citizen over the age of 18 was entitled to a voucher book with 1,000 investment points that could be bid at auction. Every share in each of the 1,200 companies was priced at the same fixed number of points. Individuals could bid themselves or give all or some of their points to privately run investment funds in exchange for shares in the fund. The managers of the funds would bid the points they collected. The voucher books cost 1,000 koruna ($33), which represented a week's pay for the average citizen. The rationale for the voucher system was to achieve privatization as soon as possible. The scheme also had political advantages in that it spread private property ownership widely.

The privatization process was to occur in three waves, with each wave divided into several rounds. The first wave began in May 1992 and was completed by July 1993. The businesses selected for that wave were those that were most prepared for privatization and had little strategic importance. During that period, 25 percent of the country's assets were privatized. The second wave began in 1993 and was completed in December 1994 after six rounds of share offers. Of the shares offered, 96.3 percent were allocated to individuals and investment funds.[17] The third wave, which began in 1995, included many heavy industries, such as refineries, telecommunications, and utilities. In late June 1995 a partnership of the Dutch and Swiss phone companies was given a 27 percent stake in the Czech phone company, SPT Communications, with a bid of $1.45 billion.

Table 9-6 presents the privatization methods used by the Czech Republic through 1996. As the table indicates, the voucher method was by far the single

TABLE 9-6 *Methods of Privatization and Revenues from Sales in the Czech Republic, 1990–1996*

	Revenues (billions of korunas)*	Percent of Sales
Small-scale privatization (auction)		
Shops	16	48.5
Restaurants	3	9.1
Services	6	18.2
Other	8	24.2
Total	33	100.0
Large-scale privatization		
Nonincorporated enterprises		
Auction	7	1.2
Tender	18	3.1
Direct sale	33	9.0
Free transfer of property	29	4.9
Restitution	4	0.7
Total	91	18.9
Incorporated enterprises		
Vouchers	343	58.4
Public offers and tenders	18	3.1
Direct sales	29	4.9
Unpaid transfers to municipalities	50	8.5
Restitution funds	20	3.4
Other	20	2.7
Total	480	81.1
Total for large-scale privatization	571	100.0

The Koruna in 1997 exchanged at 34.6 korunas = $1.00.

Source: OECD Economic Surveys, *Czech Republic* (Paris: Organization for Economic Cooperation and Development, May 1998), 51.

TABLE 9-7
Share of Nonstate Sector in the Czech Republic in Output and Employment, 1992 and 1996 (%)

	1992	1996
Output		
Total GDP	27.7	63.8
Agriculture	69.4	85.8
Industry	17.6	61.6
Construction	54.4	98.6
Wholesale and retail trade	56.0	91.8
Transportation, storage, and communication	18.6	53.5
Employment		
Total economy	39.8	77.6
Agriculture	68.6	92.3
Industry	31.1	93.0
Construction	61.8	98.1
Wholesale and retail trade	74.2	98.6
Transportation, storage, and communication	16.1	47.1

Source: International Monetary Fund, *Czech Republic: Statistical Appendix* (Washington, D.C.: IMF, April 1998), 16.

most important source of revenue for the Czech government from the privatization of its enterprises. Table 9-7 presents the shift from state ownership to private ownership as measured by output and employment for various sectors of the Czech economy in 1992 and 1998. The greatest shift in output and employment came in industry. But there still is considerable government ownership of various sectors of the Czech economy. One such area is banking.

Banking

The banking system of Czechoslovakia was in every way similar to the banking system of other communist countries. There was a central bank—the Czechoslovak State Bank—that issued money and handled all financial transactions among state-owned enterprises. Three banks, each with limited functions, were directly under the control of the central bank. Two of these were commercial banks with specialized functions, and the other was a national savings bank that collected the savings of the population and transferred them to the central bank. As in other communist countries, the central bank was responsible for implementing the national financial plan, the purpose of which was to adjust the supply of money to the real output goals of the national physical output plan.

Banking reforms in Czechoslovakia were somewhat easier to undertake during the transition period than in Poland and Hungary because it was in better financial shape. It had a low foreign debt and a government deficit of less than 1 percent of GDP.[18] Poland and Hungary had foreign debts amounting to over half of their GDPs and large budget deficits. A problem that confronted banking reform in the three countries was what to do with the bad debt of state enterprises. In 1991 a special bank, the Consolidated Bank, was set up to manage the debt by providing credit to indebted enterprises. Major banking reforms were initiated in the same year with the passage of the Banking Act and the State Bank Act. A new banking system was created and was largely in place when Czechoslovakia split into the Czech Republic and the Slovak Republic in January 1993.

However, having a banking system in place has not meant that the transition has been successful. By 1997 four large state-owned banks—Komercni, Ceska SporaTelna, IBB, and CSOB—had a combined market share of 63 percent of total bank assets.[19] The government had a controlling interest in these four banks, meaning that they had 34 percent or more ownership shares. In July 1997 the government reached an agreement with the Japanese financial firm Nomura so it could buy a controlling interest in IPB. In late 1997 the Czech government approved a strategy for privatizing the three remaining state-owned banks, with the objective of selling at least one of them by the end of 1998. The sale was to be conducted through competitive bidding. However, a change in the political climate of the Czech Republic has delayed the sales.

The remainder of the Czech banking system consists of the State Bank of the Czech Republic, which is responsible for implementing monetary policy and for regulating the Czech banking system. Subsidiaries and branches of foreign banks accounted for 19 percent of total bank assets in 1997, and they have been exerting pressure on domestic banks to improve their efficiency. They have improved the quality of banking services in the Czech Republic and have increased their market share of loans. Medium and small Czech banks are privately owned and have about 10 percent of total bank assets. They lend primarily to private enterprises, are undercapitalized, and at least half of their outstanding loans are of poor quality.[20] Bank regulation in the Czech Republic has generally been poor. Finally, there are three specialized banks, the Commercial Bank, Export Bank, and the Czech and Moravian Guarantee and Development Bank.

An Evaluation of the Czech Economy

Czechoslovakia was more industrialized than either Hungary or Poland before World War II, and it had a higher living standard. It carried these advantages throughout the Communist period and through the transition period from a socialist economy to a market economy. When Czechoslovakia split into the Czech Republic and Slovak Republic, the Czech Republic benefited the most because it inherited most of the industrial base and fewer inefficient state enterprises. Its labor force was skilled and well educated, and it had the heritage of democracy prior to and immediately after World War II. The process of privatization was relatively smooth, with the bulk of industry and agriculture privatized during the transition. But, as Table 9-8 indicates, the performance of the Czech economy during the 1990s has not been particularly good when measured by changes in real GDP.

http://

Data on the economy of the Czech Republic can be seen at http://www.czech.cz/.

TABLE 9-8
The Performance of the
Czech Economy during the
1990s as Measured by
Changes in Real GDP (%)

Average 1980–1989	2.5
1990	−0.4
1991	−15.9
1992*	−8.5
1993	0.6
1994	2.7
1995	6.4
1996	3.9
1997	1.0
1998	−1.5
1999 (estimated)	1.0

**Czechoslovakia split into the Czech Republic and the Slovak Republic on January
1, 1993. The statistical data before 1993 are for Czechoslovakia.*

Source: International Monetary Fund, *World Economic Outlook* (Washington: D.C., IMF, October 1998), 181.

http://

Find data and
statistics on the
Czech Republic at
http://www
.worldbank.org/
html/extdr/data
.htm.

Several factors are responsible for the decline in economic performance of the Czech Republic during the latter part of the 1990s. The first is that wage gains far outstripped worker productivity. In 1994 compensation per employee rose 18.4 percent compared to a 1.8 percent gain in productivity. This increased unit labor costs by an average of 14 percent between 1993 and 1998. Second, this discrepancy has had an adverse impact on the consumer price index, which has averaged around 10 percent during 1993–1998. Third, there has been a deficit in the merchandise trade, with merchandise imports increasing more rapidly than merchandise exports. Finally, there has been a decline in direct and portfolio investments in the Czech Republic. In 1995 total foreign direct investment and portfolio investment in the Czech Republic amounted to 3.9 billion, mostly from Europe; in 1997 total direct investment and foreign investment fell to 1.2 billion.

HUNGARY

http://

Information on
Hungary, including
its economy, can
be found at
http://www
.odci.gov/cia/
publications/
factbook/hu.html.

Hungary was a major part of the old Austro-Hungarian Empire. The Treaty of Versailles created three independent nations—Austria, Czechoslovakia, and Hungary—and Hungary for a brief period was ruled by the communists. Prior to and after World War I, Hungary was an agricultural country dominated by large landed estates, but it also had an industrial base. Hungary had a per capita income of $120 in 1937, which was second only to that of Czechoslovakia among the Eastern European countries. After World War II, Hungary was ruled by a coalition of political parties, but by 1949 the communists were firmly in control, and industry and banking had been nationalized. In 1956 an uprising against the rigid controls of the communist government occurred, and the Soviet Union sent in troops and tanks to put it down. Janos Kadar, who became the leader of Hungary, proved more flexible and willing to experiment with reforms than leaders in the other Eastern European countries.[21]

The New Economic Mechanism (NEM), 1968

The New Economic Mechanism (NEM) introduced the Hungarian reforms. Its objective was to reduce central government intervention in the economy at the enterprise level. Enterprises were made independent economic units with the right to determine the structure of their production and sales. This policy conformed to one basic objective of the reforms, namely, to relieve the planning authorities of the task of preparing intricate economic plans. Instead, broad guidelines were provided for enterprises to follow. They were given latitude with respect to quality, styling, and pricing. They were then given the right to determine their own production mix on the basis of their preferences. A modified market economy was permitted in which enterprises could react to consumer preferences. Nevertheless, the central planning authorities were able to exercise some control over enterprise production through the use of economic levers designed to induce cooperation by making it more profitable to produce certain items.

Later Reforms

Reforms introduced in 1984 and 1985 were aimed at increasing the efficiency of state enterprises. A compulsory reserve fund, introduced in 1968, was eliminated. In its place, reserves held from pretax profits were allowed, based on the decisions of enterprise managers. Bonds could be issued by state enterprises and sold to the general public to raise capital. A new form of management was introduced in 1985. Rather than being chosen by the Communist Party, managers and staff of small and medium enterprises were to be selected by the workers, who were also given the right to recall them. Enterprise councils were introduced in the same year as a new form of management for large state enterprises. They were given the following responsibilities:

1. Approval of capital budgets, major resource allocation decisions, and financial statements of enterprises.
2. Approval of mergers, acquisitions, or any other major reorganization decisions.
3. Election and evaluation of the performance of the managing director.

It can be said that Hungary was much farther on the road to a market economy than the other Eastern European countries when communism collapsed in late 1989. In January 1989 any company in Hungary was given the right to issue and sell stock to the public. The rationale for the sale of stocks and bonds was to end dependence on state subsidies. In 1988 the Hungarian government passed laws to encourage more foreign investment in Hungary, including the formation of joint ventures with Hungarian enterprises. A 1989 law permitted the setting up of 100 percent foreign-owned firms. Restrictions were reduced on the amount of earnings that could be repatriated out of Hungary.

http://

For information on
the Hungarian
economy, see
http://www
.gm.hu/english/
economy/facts/
index.htm.

By 1989 in terms of asset values, about half of the Hungarian state-owned enterprises were managed by enterprise councils, and the other half, mainly transportation and utilities, were managed by the state ministries. However, the privatization process was under way. In June 1989 a law was passed that allowed enterprise managers and workers to initiate the privatization process. The result was a number of spontaneous privatizations, whereby managers and councils more or less confiscated enterprise assets and either became the new owners or arranged sales to foreign investors. This enabled Hungarian managers to become owners without having to pay a fair price. Often the new managers and owners were former members of the Hungarian nomenklatura elite.

Problems of the Hungarian Economy

Despite efforts to convert the Hungarian economy into an efficient market-oriented socialist economy, problems developed, particularly during the 1980s. There was persistent economic stagnation, particularly during the second half of the decade, and the foreign debt almost doubled. The rate of economic growth in Hungary during the 1980s was lower than that in most of the other Eastern European countries, and its current account balance was negative for each year.[22] There was a need to make the Hungarian industrial sector more efficient because, despite reforms, subsidies continued to be paid to state enterprises. Hungary became poorer relative to the OECD market economies. From 1975 to 1989 Hungarian real GDP was estimated to have grown by about 35 percent, compared to 54 percent for the OECD countries, and its per capita income was 50 percent lower than that of Portugal, the poorest OECD country.[23]

Low Productivity.   There was a slowdown in Hungarian economic growth during the 1980s, with real per capita growth in GNP averaging about 1 percent a year. A fall in factor productivity and a misallocation of investment resulted in resource wastage. Modernization attempts were hindered by the fact that an increasing share of resources was allocated to inefficient enterprises in the heavy industry sector. Productivity increases were also retarded by the declining health of the population, which contributed to increased absenteeism and prolonged illnesses. Finally, slow productivity growth was attributed to financial constraints imposed by the large foreign debt, which imposed limitations on the import of investment goods into Hungary.

Foreign Trade.   Although the bulk of Hungarian foreign trade was with its fellow CMEA members, it was more involved with trade to the West than any other Eastern European country. All of the Eastern European countries have lost world market shares to the developing countries of East Asia. This reduced hard currency earnings in many Hungarian export sectors. The bulk of Hungarian exports were raw materials whose prices declined in world markets, and imports consisted in part of manufactured goods whose prices went up in world markets. Hungary had a negative balance of trade during the 1980s. It also lost a major source of hard cur-

http://

World Bank data
on Hungarian debt
can be found at
http://www.oecd
.org/dac/debt/
htm/jt_hun.htm.

rency, namely, its reexporting of Soviet oil. Also, lower world prices for oil during the 1980s meant less hard currency for Soviet purchase of Hungarian products. Hungarian foreign debt also increased in the 1980s.

Privatization

The major initial attempt to privatize industry and agriculture began in 1989, when state-owned enterprises were given the right to transform themselves into either mixed or privately owned companies. However, some state enterprise managers used this opportunity to sell assets to themselves or their friends at bargain prices and without competitive bidding. As a result of public dissatisfaction with this behavior, a government agency called the State Property Agency was created, and state-owned property was transferred to it. It was given authority to value property assets and to handle the process of privatization. It was to select those state companies that would be most attractive to Hungarian and foreign investors. It hired consulting firms to value the assets of state enterprises that were to be sold, usually through bids. In March 1991 the agency started a second round of privatization by selling off state holding companies.

Hungarian privatization has taken several forms. One is restitution for property seized by the communists after 1949. About 1.2 million Hungarians were given compensation coupons that could be used to purchase land, apartments, businesses, or other property that had been expropriated by the communists. The coupons were tradable on the Hungarian Stock Exchange. The most important method of privatization, however, was through direct sale to foreign investors.[24] Small-scale privatization, which involved the sale of stores and restaurants, occurred through direct sales to buyers. Large state enterprises have proved more difficult to privatize. Some have been liquidated, while others were sold to foreign or Hungarian investors. Privatization of agricultural cooperatives involved giving coupons that could be used to purchase the land.[25]

Results of Privatization.   State-owned retail stores, restaurants, and other small-scale enterprises were the first to be privatized. Out of 10,423 state-owned enterprises and shops in 1990, a total of 9,900 had been transferred into private hands by 1995.[26] Larger state-owned enterprises came under the jurisdiction of the State Property Agency (SPA) and the State Holding Company. The State Property Agency owned 1,857 large enterprises, ranging from the large state-owned commercial banks to the state-owned oil company. Many have been sold to both foreign and domestic investors.[27] Table 9-9 presents the results of privatization through May 1997. Some enterprises deemed of strategic importance remain in state hands while the state will maintain a minority interest in other enterprises.

Banking

A two-tiered banking system was introduced in January 1987, and privatization has continued apace through 1997. One characteristic of the Hungarian banking system

TABLE 9-9
Divestiture of Hungarian State-Owned Enterprises, 1990–May 1997

State-owned enterprises on January 1, 1990	1,857
State-owned enterprises established	
since January 1, 1990	399
	2,256
Of which:	
Liquidated	491
Dissolved	187
Fully privatized	968
Under long-term asset management	149
Transformed companies remaining in state	457
Of which:	
More than 50% state-owned	215
Less than 50% state-owned	242

Source: International Monetary Fund, *Hungary-Statistical Appendix* (Washington, D.C.: IMF, October 1997), 17.

is the extent of foreign ownership of Hungarian bank assets, which was over 50 percent in 1997. Another characteristic of the Hungarian banking system is the domination by five large formerly state-owned commercial banks, which held 68.7 percent of bank assets in 1997. The last bank to be privatized was sold to German and Irish banking interests. There is also a number of smaller private banks, most of which are affiliated with foreign banks. Hungarian banks come under the jurisdiction of the State Banking Supervision, which was merged with the State Securities and Stock Exchange in 1997. Such nonbanking financial institutions as domestic insurance companies have also been privatized.

Public Finance

The Hungarian fiscal system is similar to those of the Czech Republic and of Poland because the three countries want to become members of the European Union. The major taxes in Hungary are the personal income tax, which is progressive, with a top rate of 42 percent on annual incomes above 9,000,000 forints.[28] There are two value-added tax (VAT) rates of 12 percent and 25 percent. Excise taxes, particularly on alcohol, gasoline, and tobacco, are also an important source of revenue for the government. Social security contributions are financed by a payroll tax on employers and employees. The respective rates in 1997 were 47 percent for employers and 10 percent for employees, with the funds used to finance pensions, health, unemployment insurance, and vocational education. A third of all contributions are scheduled to be placed with privately managed pension funds. Table 9-10 presents revenues and expenditures of the Hungarian government for 1997.

Revenues	3,228.9
Taxes on income	538.3
Social security contributions	1,140.5
VAT	627.0
Excises	266.3
Customs duties	196.0
Other revenue	460.7
Expenditures	3,566.9
Primary expenditures on government operations	2,825.0
Subsidies	262.7
Transfers to local governments	361.8
Social transfers	1,063.7
Other expenditures	1,136.7
Interest payments*	741.9
Deficit	−338.0

TABLE 9-10
Revenues and Expenditures of the Hungarian Government for 1997 (billions of forints)

Source: International Monetary Fund, *Hungary-Statistical Appendix* (Washington, D.C., IMF, October 1997), 18.

Average 1980–1989	1.5
1990	−3.5
1991	−11.9
1992	−3.1
1993	−0.6
1994	−2.9
1995	1.5
1996	1.3
1997	4.4
1998	5.2
1999 (estimated)	4.8

TABLE 9-11
The Performance of the Hungarian Economy, 1990–1999 (%)

Source: International Monetary Fund, *World Economic Outlook* (Washington, D.C.: IMF, October 1998), 181.

AN EVALUATION OF THE HUNGARIAN ECONOMY

Hungary was the first of the former communist countries to implement a comprehensive transformation of its economic system, implementing price reforms and reducing subsidies to agriculture and industry, enacting new bankruptcy and banking laws, and privatizing state enterprises. As was true in Poland and the Czech Republic, these reforms were followed by a sharp drop in prices and an increase in inflation and unemployment. Between 1989 and 1993, GDP declined by a cumulative 18.5 percent. After four consecutive years of negative output growth during transition, the recovery was slower in Hungary than in Poland and the Czech Republic. Table 9-11 presents the performance of the Hungarian economy, as

http://

Current statistics on Hungary may be seen at http://www.ksh.hu/eng/homeng.html.

measured by real GDP, for the 1990s. The latter part of the decade was marked by considerable improvement in the economy.

A COMPARISON OF POLAND, THE CZECH REPUBLIC, AND HUNGARY

Poland, Czechoslovakia, and Hungary were the most important of the Soviet bloc countries before the transition from socialism to capitalism began.[29] Although all were a part of the Austro-Hungarian Empire, each had developed its own historical, cultural, political, and economic characteristics over many centuries, and they had very little in common with each other—save for countless wars over territory. These factors were reflected in the breakup of Czechoslovakia in January 1993 when the Bohemian and Moravian part formed the Czech Republic and the Slovak part formed the Slovak Republic. Each of the three countries depended on CMEA for the bulk of their foreign trade, but Hungary had the greatest commercial contacts with the West. During the transition to a market economy, the economies of the three countries declined sharply from 1990 through 1992 and then began to rebound. As Table 9-12 indicates, the performance of the Polish economy has been the best between 1993 and 1999.

Table 9-13 presents competitiveness and export performance of the three countries for 1994–1997. On average during this period, productivity growth in the Czech Republic lagged behind that of Poland by a wide margin and was less than in Hungary. Very rapid wage growth in the Czech Republic helped to create this problem as real unit labor costs grew rapidly while they were falling or stable in Poland and Hungary. The Czech competitive advantage in manufacturing eroded when labor costs increased, while imports kept increasing. The Czech Republic

TABLE 9-12

A Comparison of Real GDP in Poland, the Czech Republic, and Hungary, 1990–1999 (% real DGP)

	Poland	Czech Republic*	Hungary
Average 1980–1989	1.4	2.5	1.5
1990	−7.2	−0.4	−3.5
1991	−7.0	−15.9	−11.9
1992	−2.6	−8.5	−3.1
1993	3.8	0.6	−0.6
1994	5.2	2.7	2.9
1995	7.0	6.4	1.5
1996	6.1	3.9	1.3
1997	6.9	1.0	4.4
1998	5.6	−1.5	5.2
1999 (estimated)	5.1	1.0	4.8

Czechoslovakia was split into the Czech Republic and the Slovak Republic in 1993. The statistical data before 1993 are for Czechoslovakia.

Source: International Monetary Fund, *World Economic Outlook* (Washington, D.C.: IMF, October 1998), 181.

TABLE 9-13 *Competitiveness and Export Performance, 1994–1997 (annual change, %)*

	1994	1995	1996	1997	Average
Labor productivity growth					
Czech Republic	1.9	4.4	2.7	1.7	2.7
Hungary	5.0	3.4	1.8	3.9	3.5
Poland	6.8	6.1	4.9	5.4	5.8
Change in real labor unit costs in the business sector					
Czech Republic	11.2	9.8	8.0	5.3	8.6
Hungary	0.2	−14.6	−5.5	−5.0	−6.2
Poland	−3.2	−4.3	6.9	2.1	0.4
Export market growth (manufacturing)					
Czech Republic	8.9	12.0	7.4	8.2	9.1
Hungary	—	9.6	6.4	8.6	8.2
Poland	—	13.0	4.9	8.9	8.9
Export performance (manufacturing)					
Czech Republic	−5.1	−4.3	−0.9	5.3	−1.3
Hungary	—	−6.1	0.9	23.0	5.9
Poland	—	7.4	7.0	−0.2	4.7

Source: OECD Economic Surveys, *Czech Republic* (Paris: Organization for Economic Cooperation and Development, 1998), 55.

lost manufacturing market shares in its most important market, the European Union, while Polish and Hungarian exports to the same market expanded.

Table 9-14 compares total investment and foreign direct investment in the Czech Republic, Hungary, and Poland for 1994–1997. Foreign direct investment was necessary to improve the economic infrastructure in the three countries, which had been ignored by the communists. Transportation and communication were obsolete by Western standards. The roads and railroad lines had been built before World War II. Sizeable initial investments were also needed to upgrade existing plants. There was a relatively lower rate of foreign direct investment in the Czech Republic than in Hungary and Poland, and the average incremental capital output in the Czech Republic was about three times worse than in the other two countries.

Table 9-15 presents the progress made by the three countries in their transition from a centrally planned economy to a market economy. The countries have been more successful than the Russian Federation.[30] However, the categories covered by the transition indicators do not cover all of the relevant aspects of the transition process. One aspect that is not covered is poverty and income distribution. The first phase of transition witnessed an increase in poverty and a growing inequality in the distribution of income. The hardship for substantial sections of the population of the three countries has been severe and for many will continue.

TABLE 9-14   *Productive Investment in Poland, the Czech Republic, and Hungary, 1994–1997*

	Poland	Czech Republic	Hungary
Total investment (growth rate)			
1994	9.2	17.3	12.5
1995	16.9	21.0	−4.3
1996	20.6	8.7	6.3
1997	21.9	−4.9	9.6
Incremental capital output ratio			
1994	0.78	1.43	0.45
1995	0.87	2.21	0.63
1996	0.92	2.75	0.90
1997	—	2.76	—
Average	0.85	2.29	0.60
Foreign direct investment ($ billion)			
1993	0.60	0.65	2.34
1994	0.54	0.87	1.15
1995	1.13	2.56	4.45
1996	2.74	1.40	1.79
1997	3.04	1.28	1.65
Average	1.61	1.35	2.28

Source: OECD Economic Surveys, *Czech Republic* (Paris: Organization for Economic Cooperation and Development, 1998), 56.

TABLE 9-15   *Progress in Transition for Poland, The Czech Republic, and Hungary, mid-1997**

	Poland	Czech Republic	Hungary
Private sector share (% GDP)	65	75	75
Large-scale privatization	3+	4	4
Small-scale privatization	4+	4+	4+
Governance and restructuring	3	3	3
Price liberalization	3	3	3+
Trade and foreign exchange system	4+	4+	4+
Competition policy	3	3	3
Banking reforms and interest rate stabilization	3	3	4
Securities markets and nonbank financial institutions	3+	3	3+

*Scale ranges from 1 to 4+, with a 1 indicating a country has done little to change its economy during the transition and a 4+ indicating a country has achieved the standards and performance norms of advanced industrial countries.

Source: European Bank for Reconstruction and Development, *Transition Report, 1997* (London: EBRD, 1998), 13–15.

Those who have been most adversely affected by transition are farmers, industrial workers, and people who depend on government assistance, while those who have benefited the most are the nomenclature elite and anyone else who had the money to become an entrepreneur.[31]

SUMMARY

A new phase has begun in the process of transformation toward a market economy in the former communist countries of Central and Eastern Europe. The first phase was dominated by a need to replace the legacy of the communist system—central economic planning, state ownership of industry, and a one-party political system. The major achievements of this first phase were the privatization of most industries and banks, the reliance on the market mechanism to allocate resources, the creation of a new monetary system, and the establishment of democratic institutions. The Czech Republic, Hungary, and Poland were quicker to adapt to a market economy than most of the other countries. They were the countries that had some exposure to capitalism and democracy prior to World War II and before their eventual takeover by the communists.

A new transition phase is in the process of beginning. The Czech Republic, Hungary, and Poland have joined NATO and have applied for admission into the European Union. This enlargement of the EU would represent an event of historic proportion for Europe as a whole and a landmark in the process of transition. Major advances in the areas of environmental and health standards, as well as the financial sector, are needed. The early phase of transition brought an increase in poverty and widening disparities in the distribution of income in all of the former communist countries. The task of establishing the governmental, financial, legal, and regulatory framework, which is required for a well-functioning market economy, has not been completed. Taxation administration has been haphazard and arbitrary, and financial systems are fragile.

QUESTIONS FOR DISCUSSION

1. In your opinion, which of the three countries has been the most successful in its transition to a market economy?
2. How has privatization proceeded in the three countries? What problems still remain?
3. Discuss the approaches to privatization used in the three countries.
4. In what areas do Poland, the Czech Republic, and Hungary have to progress before their transition to a market economy is complete?
5. The process of transition is not complete in the three countries. What remains to be done?

RECOMMENDED READINGS

European Bank for Reconstruction and Development. *Transition Report, 1997*. London: EBRD, 1998.

International Monetary Fund. *Czech Republic: Selected Issues*. Washington, D.C.: IMF, April 1998.

———. *Hungary: Selected Issues*. Washington, D.C.: IMF, October 1997.

OECD Economic Surveys. *Czech Republic*. Paris: Organization for Economic Cooperation and Development, 1998.

————. *Poland*. Paris: Organization for Economic Cooperation and Development,
1998.

————. *Hungary*. Paris: Organization for Economic Cooperation and Development,
1997.

Sachs, Jeffrey. *Poland's Jump to the Market Economy*. Cambridge: MIT Press, 1998.

ENDNOTES

1.   The Soviet army invaded Hungary in 1956 when the Hungarians revolted against
communist rule. The uprising was crushed and thousands of lives were lost in the
process. The Soviet army invaded Czechoslovakia during the "Prague spring" of 1969
when the Czechs tried to promote political reforms.

2.   They are now two countries—the Czech Republic and the Slovak Republic. Animosity between the two slavic groups had existed for centuries.

3.   In 1919 and 1920 the Communist Party, led by Bela Kun, ruled Hungary.

4.   In fact, Gorbachev wanted the East Germans to allow more freedom.

5.   Joseph Stalin, who was not known for his sense of humor, once said that it was
easier to rope a bull than impose communism on the Poles. Polish farmers resisted collectivization.

6.   Jeffrey Sachs, *Poland's Jump to the Market Economy* (Cambridge: MIT Press, 1994).

7.   *Maly Rocznik Statystyczny, 1991* (Warsaw: Glowny Urzad Statystyczny, 1990), 125.

8.   "Against the Grain: A Survey of Poland," *The Economist*, April 16–22, 1994, 14.

9.   OECD Economic Surveys, *Poland* (Paris: Organization for Economic Cooperation
and Development, 1998), 46.

10.   International Monetary Fund, *Republic of Poland: Selected Issues and Statistical
Appendix* (Washington, D.C.: IMF, May 1998), 11.

11.   Ibid., 16.

12.   The same is true in the United States.

13.   International Monetary Fund, *World Economic Outlook and International Capital
Markets* (Washington, D.C.: IMF, December 1998), 19.

14.   Heavy industry accounted for 17.3 percent of total employment in Czechoslovakia compared to 3 percent in developed Western countries.

15.   However, former owners of houses were not allowed to evict their tenants.

16.   Joshua Charap and Alena Zemplinova, *Restructuring in the Czech Economy*. Working
Paper No. 2 (London: European Bank for Reconstruction and Development, March
1993), 6.

17.   Data are for the Czech Republic only. The Czech Republic and the Slovak
Republic became separate countries in January 1993.

18.   *Wall Street Journal*, June 29, 1995, p. A-12.

19.   OECD Economic Surveys, *Czech Republic* (Paris: Organization for Economic
Cooperation and Development, 1998), 58.

20.   International Monetary Fund, *Czech Republic: Selected Issues* (Washington, D.C.:
IMF, April 1998), 78.

21.   Janos Kadar ruled Hungary for thirty-two years.

22.   The World Bank, *World Debt Tables, 1988–1989* (Washington, D.C.: The World Bank, 1989), 29.

23.   OECD Economic Surveys, *Hungary* (Paris: Organization for Economic Cooperation and Development, 1991), 11–12.

24.   In 1989 General Electric bought the Hungarian state enterprise Tungsram for $150 million.

25.   This did not work well because buyers and sellers would cut deals to undervalue property.

26.   International Monetary Fund, *Hungary–Statistical Appendix* (Washington, D.C.: IMF, October 1997), 17.

27.   Ibid., 18.

28.   International Monetary Fund, *Hungary–Selected Issues* (Washington, D.C.: IMF, October 1997), 23.

29.   East Germany, the German Democratic Republic as it was known, had a higher standard of living, but it is now a part of a united Germany.

30.   The Russian Federation scored a 70 and Belarus a 20.

31.   In Poland in 1991 the author met a husband–wife entrepreneurial team. The husband, who worked for a state enterprise, was making lamp stands and selling them in Germany. The wife, who taught English at the local university, was an importer of the latest women's fashion clothes—she would travel to Italy, buy the current fashions, and bring them back to sell to Polish women who wanted style and quality, both of which were lacking under communism—and was very successful.

PART IV

Market and Nonmarket Mechanisms in Developing Economies

CHAPTER 10

Problems of the Less Developed Countries

The countries of the world can be generally classified as more developed and less developed, or as haves and have-nots, and a few are somewhere in between. Unfortunately, many countries can be classified as less developed—and they have around a third of the world's population. Mass poverty exists in the less developed countries (LDCs) and basic consumption needs remain unfulfilled. The magnitude of poverty is all too apparent. We read about it in newspapers and see it on television. A drought in Ethiopia and other parts of Africa was responsible for the death by starvation of thousands of people. Anyone who has been to a less developed country is struck by the squalor and the number of beggars in the large cities. The enormous gap between more and less developed nations increases the potential for social conflict in the world.

This chapter is divided into several parts, the first of which examines the subject of economic development. The second part discusses the characteristics of the less developed countries. It looks at population—the causes and consequences of population growth and its link to economic development and performance. The third part explores some theories of economic development. Many economists are concerned with the conditions necessary for economic development confronting the less developed countries, and there are many. Possible solutions to the problems

http://

Find background information and economic data on least developed countries at www.unctad.org/en/subsites/ldcs/ldc11.htm.

of economic development make up the last part of the chapter—but solutions will not come easily. The problems of the less developed countries can be attributed in part to the economic and financial policies of the developed countries.

ECONOMIC DEVELOPMENT

Although the terms economic growth and economic development are often used interchangeably, they have different meanings. *Economic growth* can be defined most simply as the ability of a nation to expand its capacity to produce the goods and services its people want. It represents an increase in the real output of goods and services. *Economic development* means not only more real output but different kinds of output than were produced in the past.[1] It includes changes in the technological and institutional arrangements by which output is produced and distributed. There can be economic growth without economic development. For example, a country that relies on the production of oil for export can have its growth rate increase as greater inputs lead to greater output of oil, while its economic development may be minimal. However, the process of economic development almost necessarily depends on some degree of simultaneous economic growth.

A number of factors must exist before economic development can take place in any country. Most of the developed countries in the world have at least several of them:

1. The quantity and quality of a country's labor force have an impact on its economic development. However, the existence of a large labor force does not guarantee economic development. India is an excellent case in point. A labor force has to have education and job skills, both of which are lacking in India because it is a poor country.

2. The quantity and quality of real capital are important for economic development. Real capital is capital goods or inventories in the form of raw materials, machines, and equipment used for the ultimate purpose of producing consumer goods. The supply of real capital depends on the level of savings in a country, which is the difference between its income and its consumption. In countries at a subsistence level, there is little difference between income and consumption.

3. The level of technological attainment in a country must be considered. Technology as a concept deals more with the productive process than with the introduction of new goods. It involves the relationship among inputs of economic resources of land, labor, and capital. The combination of these inputs will determine both the level and type of technology.

4. The quantity and quality of a country's natural resources are also important. Great natural resources contributed to the economic development of the United States. However, it is possible for a country to develop without adequate natural resources. Japan has attained a high level of economic development by importing what it needs.

5. Sociocultural forces also affect economic development. Religion is an example. The role of religion as an economic force can vary considerably among countries. The theocratic society of Iran offers a case in point, where modern ways are resisted. Other sociocultural forces are the underlying competitive nature of an economy, the distribution of income and wealth, the pattern of consumer tastes, the dominant forms of business organization, and the organization of society.

CHARACTERISTICS OF THE LESS DEVELOPED COUNTRIES

Three-fourths of the world's population live in the less developed countries. Most of the nations of Latin America, Africa, and Asia fall into this category.[2] However, the less developed countries are by no means all alike; some countries are in different stages of economic development from others. There is a vast degree of difference between the lives of, say, the typical slum dweller of Mexico City and an average peasant in Bangladesh or Ethiopia. Although Mexico's per capita income is one-sixth that of the United States, it is twenty times that of Bangladesh or Ethiopia. Nevertheless, the less developed countries possess some common characteristics, and a discussion of each is in order.

http://

State Department country reports provide economic and other information on LDCs at www.state.gov/www/issues/economic/trade_reports/97_toc.html.

Per Capita Income

Whether a country can be classified as developed or less developed, rich or poor, or in between can be determined by the size of its per capita gross national product (GNP), a rough measure of the value of goods and services produced and available on the average to each country. Among the poorest countries of the world are India, Pakistan, Bangladesh, and Nigeria. These have one-fourth of the world's population and less than 1 percent of the world's GNP. The per capita incomes of each of these countries is less than 5 percent of the annual U.S. figure, which was $28,740 in 1997, and the average of $25,870 for the rich developed countries.[3] Nigeria had a per capita income of $260 in 1997, which was less than 1 percent of the per capita income for the United States. The poverty this figure represents shows up in nutritionally inadequate diets, primitive and crowded housing, an absence of medical facilities, and a high rate of illiteracy.

In 1997 there were 63 countries with a per capita income of $785 or less. These countries accounted for 35 percent of the world's population, but only 5 percent of the world's GNP. Their average per capita GNP was $490. At the opposite end of the spectrum were the wealthy countries of the world, those countries with a per capita GNP of $9,635 or more. These countries had only 16 percent of the world's population, but 80 percent of the world's GNP. The countries in between rich countries and poor countries are classified as lower-middle income countries if they have achieved some stage of economic development and upper-middle income countries. China would be an example of a lower-middle income country, and Poland would be an example of an upper-middle income country. Table 10-1

TABLE 10-1 *Money per Capita GNP and Real per Capita GDP for Selected Countries, 1997*

Income Groups	Money per Capita GNP	Real per Capita GNP	Country Rank*
Low income			
Bangladesh	$270	1,050	106
Ethiopia	110	510	122
India	390	1,650	92
Nigeria	260	880	114
Pakistan	490	1,590	94
Lower middle			
China	860	3,570	65
Philippines	1,220	3,670	63
Russian federation	2,740	4,190	59
Ukraine	1,040	2,170	82
Upper middle			
Brazil	4,720	6,240	47
Hungary	4,430	7,000	39
Mexico	3,680	8,120	35
Poland	3,590	6,380	46
High			
Canada	19,290	21,860	10
France	26,050	21,860	11
Japan	37,850	23,400	6
United States	28,740	28,740	2

*Rank out of 123 countries in terms of real per capita GDP measured in purchasing power parity relative to the U.S. dollar.

Source: The World Bank, *World Development Report, 1998/99* (Washington, D.C.: The World Bank, 1998), 190–96.

presents a breakdown of some countries, based on money income. The table also shows real income, or purchasing power.

Overpopulation

Although the overall rate of population growth in the world had been declining since the late 1970s, annual world population figures have increased at an average of around 100 million a year. Almost all of this increase is occurring in the poor countries of the world, where birth rates remain high and mortality rates are declining. Conversely, in the rich countries of the world, birth rates are declining to the point where the population is not replacing itself. An aging population is a major problem in the poor countries of the world. In either situation, there is a drain on monetary resources. Table 10-2 presents the population average annual growth rate for selected countries for 1980–1997.

Poverty.   More than one billion people out of the world's population of 5.8 billion people live on less than $1 a day and around two billion people live on less than $2 a day. Poverty is the greatest among African and Asian countries, where twelve

TABLE 10-2 *Population Growth for Selected Rich and Poor Countries, 1980–1997*

| | Population (millions) | | Average Annual Growth Rate (%) | |
	1980	1997	1980–1990	1990–1997
Rich nations				
Canada	25	30	1.2	1.2
France	54	59	0.5	0.5
Germany	78	82	0.1	0.5
Italy	56	57	0.1	0.2
Japan	117	126	0.6	0.3
United States	227	268	0.9	1.0
Poor nations				
Bangladesh	87	124	2.4	1.6
China	981	1,127	1.5	1.1
Ethiopia	3.8	6.0	3.1	2.3
India	687	961	2.1	1.8
Nigeria	71	118	3.0	2.9
Nepal	14	23	2.6	2.7
Pakistan	83	127	3.1	2.9
Viet Nam	54	77	2.1	2.1

Source: The World Bank, *World Development Report, 1998/99* (Washington, D.C.; The World Bank, 1998), 194–95.

Country	Population (millions)	International Poverty Line (%)
Brazil	161	23.6
China	1,227	22.2
Ethiopia	60	46.0
Guatemala	11	26.3
India	961	52.5
Kenya	28	50.2
Nigeria	118	31.1
Pakistan	137	11.5
Philippines	73	28.6
Uganda	20	69.3
Zambia	9	84.6
Nepal	23	50.3

TABLE 10-3
Percentage of the World's Population below the International Poverty Line of $1 or Less a Day, 1997

Source: The World Bank, *World Development Report, 1998/99* (Washington, D.C.: The World Bank, 1998), 196–97.

countries that possess over half of the world's population account for 80 percent of the world's poor. India and China alone account for close to 50 percent of the world's poor. Table 10-3 presents the poverty rates for selected countries, using the international standard of poverty as $1 or less a day. Poverty and population increases are linked. The poorest countries typically have the highest birth rates.

India is a case in point. Its population is increasing at a faster rate than growth in real income. It has a population of close to one billion people, 52.5 percent of whom live on $1 or less a day.

Illiteracy.   Some 275 million children throughout the world are illiterate because they live in poor countries that cannot afford to build enough schools to educate them. They will grow up to be adults without the requisite skills to compete in a world that relies more and more on technical skills. Close to one-third of the world's population is illiterate, and two-thirds of those who are illiterate in many countries are women, as far fewer women receive an education than men. Table 10-4 presents the adult illiteracy rate for countries with an illiteracy rate of 40 percent or more of the population. In India close to 50 percent of the adult population is illiterate; in Pakistan 62.2 percent of the adult population is illiterate. In India 38 percent of children have not reached a grade 5 level of education.

Gender Disparity

In the poor countries of the world most of the activities of women take place in the non-wage sector of the economy for household consumption. Women work longer hours than men. For example, in rural Kenya women work on average 56 hours a week compared to 42 hours for men. This disparity also extends to girls who work on an average of 41 hours a week compared to 35 hours for boys. In household work, including firewood and water collection, women put in ten times the hours of men, and girls 3.7 times the hours of boys. Almost 80 percent of men's work, but only 41 percent of women's, involves earning income. Girls spend 10 times the

TABLE 10-4
The Adult Illiteracy Rate in Selected Countries, 1997

Country	Percent
Bangladesh	61.9
Burkina Faso	80.8
Egypt	48.6
Ethiopia	64.5
Gambia	61.4
Haiti	55.0
India	48.0
Iraq	42.0
Morocco	56.3
Nepal	72.5
Niger	86.4
Nigeria	42.9
Pakistan	62.2
Senegal	66.9
Sudan	53.9
All less developed countries	50.8
All industrial countries	1.4

Source: United Nations Development Program, *Human Development Report, 1998* (New York: Oxford University Press, 1998), 146–47.

hours of boys in income-related activities outside the household. Self-employed urban women are the worst off of all Kenyan women, working more than 75 hours a week. Kenyan men are more likely to earn cash wages for work, and they are less likely than women to spend it on life's necessities.

The role of women in Kenya is no better or no worse than that of women in the other poor countries of the world. They are less likely to be educated than their male counterparts. They usually have fewer legal rights regarding marital relations, the division of property, or land tenure. In some countries, men can divorce their wives, but not the other way around; also, it is often difficult for the woman to get any form of alimony. Inheritance of property in many countries is limited to male relatives. What this does is to institutionalize poverty for women, because they have no control over resources. Control over property conveys power, but it is usually males who control property. There is also a carryover into such areas as education and health.

Table 10-5 presents a gender-related development index for developed and less developed countries. As the table indicates, the poorer the country, the lower

http://

See reports on women in development in several countries at www.census .gov/ipc/www/ publist.html#WID.

TABLE 10-5 *Gender-Related Development Index for Developed and Less Developed Countries, 1997*

	Life Expectancy at Birth (years)		Adult Literacy Rate (%)	
	Female	Male	Female	Male
Developed countries				
Canada	81.8	76.3	99.0	99.0
Chile	78.0	72.2	95.0	95.4
Denmark	78.0	72.7	99.0	99.0
Germany	79.5	73.0	99.0	99.0
Italy	81.0	74.7	97.6	98.6
Sweden	80.8	75.9	99.0	99.0
United Kingdom	79.4	74.2	99.0	99.0
USA	79.7	73.0	99.0	99.0
Less developed countries				
Bangladesh	57.0	56.9	26.1	49.4
Egypt	66.1	63.6	38.8	63.6
Ethiopia	50.3	47.2	25.3	45.5
Haiti	56.3	52.9	42.2	48.1
India	61.8	61.4	37.7	65.5
Kenya	55.1	52.5	70.0	86.3
Nepal	55.6	56.3	14.0	40.9
Niger	49.2	45.9	6.7	20.9
Nigeria	53.0	49.8	47.3	67.3
Pakistan	63.9	61.8	24.4	50.0
Sierra Leone	36.3	33.3	8.2	45.6
Sudan	53.6	50.8	34.6	57.7

Source: United Nations Development Program, *Human Development Report, 1998* (New York: Oxford University Press, 1998), 132–33.

the life expectancy for both sexes and the lower the rate of literacy, particularly for women.[4] In Pakistan only 24.4 percent of the women are literate; and in India only 37.7 percent of women are literate. Two-thirds of the world's illiterate are women, and two-thirds of those who live in poverty are illiterate. The main factor in causing the high rate of illiteracy and poverty among women is the lack of equal educational opportunities. The smaller the percentage of females attending school, the greater the female–male gap; the closer the female percent is to the male percent, the smaller the gender gap.

Human Development

In 1990 the United Nations Development Program (UNDP) introduced its human development index (HDI) as a broad measure of economic and social progress. The HDI contains a number of economic and social indicators of well-being, including life expectancy, income, adult literacy, infant mortality rate, enrollment in primary, secondary, and tertiary education, health and sanitation facilities, and the status of women. The 174 countries that are included in the index are placed in three categories: (1) countries with a high level of human development; (2) countries with a medium level of human development; (3) and countries with a low level of human development. Table 10-6 presents the HDI for selected countries in each of the three categories. In the high level of human development, Canada ranks first and the United States fourth.[5] The Russian Federation and China are ranked in the medium human development category, at 72 and 106, respectively.[6] The low level of human development category consists of 44 countries, 33 of which are in Africa, and contain one-third of the world's population.[7]

In addition to literacy, mortality, and income as measures of social indicators in human development, access to health care, potable water, and sanitation are also vital. According to the WHO's revised definition, *access to health care* means the ability of citizens to reach services and drugs within one hour's walk or travel. In 1992, 83% of the population of developing countries had such access; however, this says nothing about the quality of medical services. Potable water was available to 76% of the population of low- and middle-income countries in 1995, but only 37% had access to adequate sanitation, based on World Bank statistics.

OBSTACLES TO ECONOMIC AND SOCIAL DEVELOPMENT

Economic and social growth and development have been slow or nonexistent in most of the less developed countries of the world. In Nigeria, the largest country in Africa in terms of population, the average annual growth rate in per capita GNP between 1965 and 1996 was 0.1 percent compared to an average annual population growth rate of 2.8 percent for the same period. Per capita income in Nigeria declined from $900 in 1979 to $260 in 1997, reflecting a weakness in many of the less developed countries, namely a dependence on the export of one or a few commodities. In Nigeria's case it is oil. Economic and social development is an

http://

Read on social development, economic, background, and other issues for countries around the world in the World Factbook at www.odci.gov/cia/publications/factbook/index.html.

TABLE 10-6   *Human Development Index for Selected Countries, 1997*

	Life Expectancy at Birth (years)	Adult Literacy Rate (%)	Real GDP per Capita (ppp*$)	HDI
High human development				
Argentina	72.6	96.2	8,498	0.885
Canada	79.1	99.0	21,977	0.960
Germany	76.4	99.0	2,370	0.925
Hungary	68.9	99.0	6,793	0.857
Italy	78.0	98.1	20,174	0.922
Japan	79.9	99.0	21,930	0.940
Medium human development				
China	69.2	81.5	2,935	0.650
Iraq	58.5	58.0	3,170	0.547
Peru	67.7	88.7	3,940	0.729
Russian Federation	65.5	99.0	4,531	0.769
South Africa	64.1	81.8	4,334	0.717
Less human development				
Bangladesh	56.9	38.1	1,382	0.371
Ethiopia	48.7	35.5	455	0.252
Haiti	54.6	45.0	917	0.340
India	61.6	52.0	1,422	0.451
Nigeria	51.4	57.1	1,270	0.391
Pakistan	62.8	37.8	2,209	0.453
Sierra Leone	34.7	31.4	625	0.185
Sudan	52.2	46.1	1,110	0.343
Uganda	40.5	61.8	1,483	0.340

*purchasing power parity

Source: United Nations Development Program, *Human Development Report, 1998* (New York: Oxford University Press, 1998), 150–54.

extremely elusive objective in the less developed countries. The obstacles to their achievement are many, and the task of converting illiterate, poor people into at best moderately well-off ones is far from being easy. There are many obstacles to development, and a review of some of them is in order.

Corruption

Corruption is endemic in most countries of the world, and it is institutionalized in the way in which they do business. It typically involves bribery. In fact, there are special words for bribery. In Latin America it is called *la mordita*, which literally means "bite"; in the Arab countries, it is called *baksheesh*, which can be translated as "rake-off"; and in the Russian Federation it is called *blat*, which means "under the table." The moral implications are irrelevant in these countries. To customs officials and other bureaucrats, a bribe is often regarded as a way to supplement an income that is typically low. Sociological factors also can contribute to corruption. Public officials are more likely to do favors for their relatives in countries where family ties are strong.

The main criticism of corruption is that it inhibits economic growth. It prevents competition. Contracts will be awarded on the basis of factors other than cost and efficiency. When contracts are awarded on the basis of favoritism, what typically happens is that taxpayers end up with a project of inferior quality that will require upkeep and repair.[8] Corruption can also contribute to a decline in government tax revenue if it contributes to tax evasion, improper tax exemptions, or weak tax administration. Corruption can be associated with low government revenues, thus preventing spending on schools and social goods. Corruption can also erode public confidence in the effectiveness of the role of government in the political, legal, and economic systems of a country.

Table 10-7 presents a corruption perception index for eighty-five countries ranked from least corrupt to most corrupt. Denmark ranks as the least corrupt of all of the countries, with a perfect score of 10.0. The United States ranked 17 and the Russian Federation 76. Those countries that are rated among the most corrupt

TABLE 10-7
Corruption Perception Index (CPI) from Least to Most Corrupt

Country Rank	Country	CPI Score
1	Denmark	10.0
2	Finland	9.6
3	Sweden	9.5
6	Canada	9.2
7	Singapore	9.1
15	Germany	7.9
17	United States	7.5
21	France	6.7
25	Japan	5.8
39	Italy	4.6
46	Brazil	4.0
52	China	3.5
55	Mexico	3.3
59	Argentina	3.0
66	India	2.9
71	Pakistan	2.7
76	Russian Federation	2.4
77	Venezuela	2.3
79	Colombia	2.2
80	Nigeria	1.9
84	Paraguay	1.5
85	Cameroon	1.4

Source: Transparency International, *1998 Corruption Perception Index* (Berlin: September 1998).

in the world are located in either Latin America, Africa, or Asia. Of the bottom fifteen in the corruption index, five countries are located in Latin America, five are located in Africa, three in Asia, and two in the transition countries of the Russian Federation and Latvia.

Political Instability

Sociocultural factors affecting social and political stability can also provide obstacles to economic development. Such instability is a world-wide problem, examples of which include the internal warfare between African tribal groups, the rivalry between Moslem Pakistan and Hindu India, and the animosity between Kurds and Turks. Religious fundamentalists—who feel that traditional values are being replaced by materialistic Western values—are active in Algeria and Iran, while in Colombia Marxist guerrillas seek to overthrow the Colombian government.

Capital Flows

It was pointed out in an earlier chapter that capital flows generally move from developed countries to other developed regions of the world. As Table 10-8 indicates, the

TABLE 10-8   *Financial Flows to the Less Developed Countries, 1997*

Country	Net Private Capita Flows ($ millions)	Foreign Direct Investment ($ millions)	Portfolio Investment Bonds ($ millions)	Equity ($ millions)
Bangladesh	92	15	0	0
China	50,100	40,180	4,668	5,264
Ethiopia	−205	5	0	0
Guatemala	5	−77	−33	0
Haiti	4	4	0	0
Honduras	65	75	−13	0
India	6,404	2,587	−457	4,398
Kenya	−104	13	0	43
Malawi	−3	−1	0	0
Nigeria	706	1,391	0	5
Pakistan	1,936	690	150	700
Philippines	4,600	1,408	2,319	1,333
Rwanda	1	1	0	0
Senegal	34	45	0	0
Sudan	0	0	0	0
Tanzania	143	150	0	0
Uganda	114	121	−80	0
Viet Nam	2,061	1,500	0	390

Source: The World Bank, *1998 World Bank Indicators* (Washington, D.C.: The World Bank, 1998), 334–37.

capital that is a basic requisite for economic development does not flow from rich countries to poor countries unless there is a chance for monetary gain. There has been a considerable amount of foreign direct investment in China because of its financial potential, but Rwanda and the Sudan, two countries that have experienced internal conflicts, have been virtually ignored. India is regarded as having less economic potential than China, and is considered to be more politically unstable. In addition, although Nigeria is the largest country in Africa and is rich in resources, it has not attracted much capital because it is considered to be corrupt and is politically unstable. However, Kenya has had a capital outflow, as has Malawi, and although Viet Nam is a poor and communist country, it is considered to be relatively stable and to have development potential.

Population Trends

In 1798 the English clergyman Thomas Malthus published his book *An Essay in the Principles of Population.* His world outlook was pessimistic; it suggested that population grows faster than the food supply. Based on scattered empirical evidence, including the colonizing of North America, Malthus calculated that population tended to double every twenty-five years in a geometric progression, whereas food supplies tended to increase in an arithmetic progression. An example is shown in Table 10-9.

His proposition was based on two assumptions: Technological change could not increase food supply faster than population, and population growth would not be limited by fewer births, only by more deaths. Although both assumptions have proved to be wrong, there is an element of truth in his predictions. It took more than 4,000 years of recorded history for China to have its first 500 million people, but only a little more than three decades to increase the population to one billion. Regardless of a country's size, natural resources, or level of development, countries with large populations and high birth rates face increasing problems. At current rates of population increase, the population of developed countries will double in 432 years and the population of less developed countries will double in 36 years.

Population Growth and an Ever-Increasing Labor Force.   In 1965 there were 1.3 billion workers in the world. Twenty-one percent of this labor force lived in high-income countries, 27 percent in middle-income countries, and 52 percent in low-income countries.[9] Twenty-five percent of the world's labor force lived in sub-Saharan Africa and South Asia, the two poorest regions in the world. By 1995 the world labor force had almost doubled, but the percentage of the labor force living

TABLE 10-9   *Malthusian Progressions for Population and Food Supply*

Year	0	25	50	75	100	125	150	175	200
Population size	1	2	4	8	16	32	64	128	256
Food supply	1	2	3	4	5	6	7	8	9

in the high income countries had decreased from 21 percent in 1965 to 15 percent in 1995. Conversely, the percentage of the labor force living in the low-income countries increased from 52 percent in 1965 to 58 percent in 1995. By 2025, the world labor force is projected to be 3.7 billion, of which 61 percent will be in the low-income countries and 11 percent in the high-income countries. The greatest gains will be in sub-Saharan Africa and South Asia. Table 10-10 presents average annual growth rate projections in percent for selected countries for 1995–2025.

Urbanization.   Urbanization and congestion are population-related problems. Often peasants are driven off the land into the cities by poverty or land takeovers by rich landowners or foreigners. Overcrowding can lead to increased population, unemployment, stress, and a demand for human services that can be greater than what the urban area can provide. Overcrowding can lead to an increase in health costs, not only from communicable disease, but also from heart disease, cancer, and other ailments caused by a stress-related breakdown in the body's immunity. Urbanization problems are particularly acute in less developed countries because they lack the financial resources to provide the necessary services to cope with

TABLE 10-10

Projected Population and Increase in Labor Force Participation, 1995–2025 (average annual percentage growth rate)

High-income countries	
Canada	0.65
France	−0.07
Germany	−0.31
United States	0.44
Japan	−0.41
Latin America	
Argentina	1.25
Brazil	2.90
Mexico	1.83
Peru	2.16
East Asia	
China	0.41
Korea	0.55
Malaysia	2.01
Thailand	2.66
South Asia	
Bangladesh	2.75
India	1.60
Africa	
Egypt	2.35
Ivory Coast	3.91
Kenya	3.45
Nigeria	3.19
Zaire	3.54

Source: The World Bank, *World Development Report, 1995* (New York: Oxford University Press, 1995), 144–146.

their problems. By the end of the century, at least 22 cities in the world will have a population of more than 10 million; 60 will have more than 5 million.

Food Shortages.   Although famines on a large scale are a thing of the past, food shortages are common, and millions of children go to bed hungry. Both a rural population and a rising tide of urban consumption compete for a limited agricultural output. In most less developed countries the need to satisfy a demand for food has prevented the allocation of resources to economic development. As a result, the inability to industrialize reduces the potential to earn money from exports to pay for the import of food products. In the main, further growth of the land frontier is constrained in many countries. In Africa, for example, the expansion of farmland is limited by the Sahara Desert, rivers, jungles, and mountains and also by diseases that destroy livestock and farm products. Insecticides used to try to control the diseases have undesirable effects on the environment.

In October 1998 demographers at the United Nations reduced their estimates of the world population in the year 2050 to 8.9 billion, a reduction from a prior estimate of 10 billion. But the world is still demographically divided into countries that have stabilized their population with low birth rates and death rates. In the less developed countries the problem remains serious. It is estimated that 2.8 billion people will be added to the world's population over the next 50 years. Ethiopia, one of the poorest countries in the world, is expected to increase its population from 58 million in 1999 to 169 million by 2050. These countries are barely able to keep up with the demands of their rapidly growing populations, from educating the young to creating enough jobs.

Although food production in the less developed countries has been increasing, it has just kept pace with the population growth in some countries and has failed to do so in others, including thirty African countries. In Nigeria, the largest country in Africa, the average annual rate of agricultural production declined from 1970 to 1980. The output of food in China and India has exceeded population growth, but only by a narrow margin.

Moreover, in the less developed countries, increases in agricultural acreage have been relatively small. In the main, further growth of the land frontier is constrained in many countries. In India the number of rural households and people trying to earn a living in agriculture has increased at a rate far in excess of cultivated land.

Infrastructure

Capital can be classified in two ways—social overhead capital and physical capital. The former includes the structures and equipment required for shelter, public health, and education. The latter consists of plants and equipment used in industry and agriculture. Poor countries are deficient in both forms of capital because savings and incomes are low. They cannot afford the medical services and education facilities necessary to improve the quality of the labor force. In Bangladesh, for example, there is one physician for every 5,220 persons; in the United States there is one physician for 470 persons. In Malawi, only 4 percent of people of secondary school age are in school and only 1 percent of those in the college age group are in some form of higher education. In Japan the corresponding statistics are 97 percent and 20 percent. Only 2 percent of the relevant age group attends college in China; however, this is a legacy of the Cultural Revolution, when universities were closed down.

Infrastructure, or social overhead capital, is a descriptive economic concept that refers to the existence of highways, railways, airports, sewage facilities, housing, schools, and other social amenities that indicate the development or lack of development of an area or region. Once an infrastructure is in place, it encourages both economic and social development. Developed countries have developed infrastructures; less developed countries generally do not. This creates a problem for economic development because industry will not normally locate plants in areas where there is a poor infrastructure. In particular, mass consumption products require the existence of skilled labor, sewage disposal facilities, transportation and communication facilities, and other amenities for their marketing.

Education.   Educational facilities are a key component in the infrastructure of any area or region. Education itself is directly related to the quality of life and constitutes a form of human capital. Literacy, or rather the lack of it, is not as directly related to a country's population as it is to the country's stage of economic development. There is a positive correlation between a lower standard of living and a higher rate of illiteracy. It has been estimated that one-third of the world is illiterate. Most of this illiteracy is concentrated in countries with high birth rates, large populations, and the least to spend on education. A lack of educational opportunities maintains the distinction between the haves and have-nots in society and perpetuates class differences. It also reduces the base of educated labor on which the economic development of the country depends.

Roads.   A requisite for the economic and social development of a country is an adequate system of roads. Few countries can depend exclusively on other forms of transportation. Air transportation is too expensive for most products, and railroads are limited to specific routes between main access points. Poor countries do not usually have the resources to maintain an adequate road system. Physiography also works against the development of an adequate highway system. Most of the less developed countries are located in geographic areas of the world with barriers to transportation. For example, the Sierra Madre and Andes mountains have inhibited the east–west development of Mexico, Bolivia, and Peru. Transportation is also hard to develop in countries dominated by tropical jungles, because vegetation overtakes roads in only a short time.

Other Facilities.   Dams, bridges, sewage disposal, and other facilities are a vital part of a region's infrastructure but are usually inadequate in the less developed countries. Dams control flooding and provide the water supply and electric power necessary for economic and social development. Bridges create more efficient transportation by linking areas that are separated by bodies of water. Inadequate sanitary facilities can result in the spread of communicable diseases such as cholera and typhoid fever. Garbage and waste materials dumped in city streets attract rats and other animals, which increase the possibility of epidemics. Communication facilities must be adequate to handle the needs of a region. The cost and efficiency of service must be considered. Government-owned telephone and postal services are notoriously inefficient in less developed countries.

Low Savings Rate

As mentioned, there is an extreme imbalance in the distribution of income in less developed countries, exacerbated in part by the existence of a large component of unskilled labor. The vast majority of workers do not earn enough to do any saving; moreover, a minority of households get most of the income. In Mexico, for example, in 1995 the top 10 percent of income earners received 39.2 percent of national income; in Brazil in 1995 the top 10 percent received 47.9 percent of national income. This group should provide much of the saving necessary for capital formation. However, savings are usually invested out of the country or in real estate, where there is a quick and high rate of return. Political instability provides a good reason to invest one's income in, say, Swiss bonds, which will be safe from possible expropriation by a new government.

Savings are a requisite for capital formation, for without it investment for capital formation cannot take place. Inadequate amounts of capital and the inability to increase the capital are obstacles to economic development. It can be said that less developed countries are caught in a vicious circle. Because savings are small, investment is low and the capital stock is small, and the real gross national product is small. Nations that save little grow slowly and are locked into a cycle of poverty.

Limited Range of Exports

Less developed countries usually depend on the export of agricultural products, fuels, minerals, or metals such as copper. Many depend on the export of a single product for the bulk of national income. Nigeria depends on the export of oil for around 96 percent of its total export earnings. Thus the drop in the world market price of oil has created problems for the Nigerian economy. When oil prices were high during the early 1970s, Nigeria benefited. It ran a surplus in its balance of payments, and it could use foreign earnings to improve living standards. Government spending increased to improve the infrastructure of the Nigerian economy. However, during the early 1980s, the world demand for oil declined, and oil prices fell from a peak of $35 a barrel in 1980 to $15 by the end of the decade. Revenues from oil exports declined, Nigeria had a deficit in its balance of payments, and it now has the problem of a large foreign debt incurred when oil prices were high and earnings were good.

Countries that depend on exports of agricultural products and minerals are usually at a disadvantage in trade with the developed countries. The terms of trade, the real quantity of exports required to pay for a given amount of real imports, favor the developed countries. Brazilian coffee and Mexican oil are much more subject to shifts in world prices than are American computers and Japanese cars. When prices decline for coffee or oil, Brazil and Mexico will have to give up more income to import computers and cars. Conversely, the United States and Japan will have to give up less income to acquire coffee and oil. There is an inelastic demand for many products exported by the less developed countries. When prices for a product fall, there is no offsetting increase in revenue resulting from a more than proportionate increase in demand.

Foreign Debt

About forty of the world's poorest countries are classified by the World Bank as having an unsustainably high foreign debt burden. This means that the value of their total debts is more than 220 percent of their export earnings. Compounding the problem is the fact that in many poor countries, export earnings fluctuate wildly because raw material prices are subject to greater changes than prices of manufactured goods. For many countries, foreign debt has set back economic development. Moreover, the world financial system has been disrupted by the prospect of widespread default on the foreign debts of the developing world. Many debtor countries are unable to borrow in the international financial markets on normal credit terms. Table 10-11 presents the debt ratios for selected countries. As the table indicates, the foreign debt of some countries is as much as ten times export earnings.

Physiography

The physiography of a country can have an impact on its economic and social development for better or worse. Flat, fertile soil, supported by water and suitable climate, provides the basis for agriculture. Dense forests provide a renewable resource—wood—and also furnish a refuge and habitat for wildlife as well as a root base that prevents soil erosion. Fast-running rivers and streams offer a potential for hydroelectric development. Water is vital to the support of life and forms a primary source of transportation. Given the state of world technology, deserts, once a barrier to economic development, are now less formidable. In many of the less developed countries, a combination of physical forces has had an adverse effect on economic and social development.

Soil.   Because humans must eat to survive and because nearly all of our food is either directly or indirectly a product of the soil, agriculture is probably the most important activity on earth. A shortage of productive land is one of the major problems facing the world and its rapidly growing population. Although this problem

TABLE 10-11   *External Debt of Selected Less Developed Countries, 1997*

Country	As a Percent of GNP	As a Percent of Exports
Bangladesh	30	166
Cambodia	54	191
Cameroon	106	399
Congo	260	342
Ethiopia	149	1,093
Haiti	20	297
Honduras	92	200
India	22	152
Kenya	64	177
Malawi	76	294
Mozambique	411	1,344
Nicaragua	322	763
Nigeria	114	240
Pakistan	39	206
Rwanda	47	682
Sudan	260	1,964
Tanzania	114	499
Uganda	32	294
Viet Nam	123	322
Zambia	181	369
Zimbabwe	67	154

Source: The World Bank, *1998 World Development Indicators* (Washington, D.C.: The World Bank, 1998), 242–244.

hardly exists in the United States, it is endemic in most of the less developed countries. The ratio of arable lands to people is basic to agricultural productivity and consumption rates. As the maximum productivity per unit of agricultural land is achieved, the per capita amount of food available must decrease as the population continues to increase. Maintenance of soil fertility, vital to productivity, is a growing problem as soils are becoming more and more exhausted throughout the world.

Less than 5 percent of the total land area of Latin America and Africa has the combination of climate and physiographic conditions necessary for agricultural production. The mountainous nature of Bolivia and Peru makes cultivation of most of the land impossible. In most of Latin America, climatic variations run to the extremes of either too much or too little rain; the Amazon basin of Brazil, for example, receives too much rainfall, resulting in the rapid leaching of nutrients from the soil. The tropical lands of Africa have sufficient moisture and are very fertile, but the presence of human and botanical tropical diseases results in low agricultural productivity. The remaining lands, which occupy an enormous expanse, are semidesert or desert and can produce little without irrigation.

Mountains.   While mountains provide a basis for tourism and winter sports, they are a barrier to economic development. Mountainous terrain makes farming difficult, if not impossible, makes mining expensive and hazardous, and inhibits the construction of transportation facilities. The forests that cover many mountain slopes are a valuable resource, but harvesting is difficult. Transportation is hard to develop in countries such as Guatemala, Bolivia, and Peru, which are dominated by mountain ranges. In Asia, the Himalaya range makes a large land area inaccessible and unavailable for development. In China, economic development of the whole country is difficult because much of the land area is isolated from the main population centers by insurmountable mountains.

THE TWENTY-FIRST CENTURY

One thing is for certain, the world of the twenty-first century will be totally different from the world of the twentieth century. Knowledge rather than natural resources will be the required need for economic and human development. New communications technologies are shrinking distances and eroding borders and time. But it is entirely possible that the information revolution will bypass the poorest countries of the world, making them worse off than they were in the twentieth century when at least some of the countries had raw materials to export. There are slums and villages without telephones, electricity, and running water, much less fax machines and computers. Few people go on to college or even finish secondary schools, so they lack the knowledge to be assimilated into an ever more complicated world.

At the beginning of the twentieth century, most of the less developed countries of the world were colonies of some European power. All but one of the African countries of today were colonial possessions of five European countries—England, France, Germany, Belgium, and Portugal. Bangladesh, India, and Pakistan were part of the British empire. The present countries of Laos, Cambodia, and Viet Nam were French colonial possessions. From a political, economic, and social standpoint everything was in place. Administration was provided by the colonizing government. The legal systems of the colonial possessions were based on the legal systems of the ruling countries—common law for those countries that were a part of the British empire, and code law for the former colonies of France, Germany, Belgium, and Portugal. The civil service and educational systems imposed by the colonial powers have largely remained intact.

Dependencia Theory

The dependencia theory is offered as a reason why many countries, but particularly the former colonies, have underformed during most of the twentieth century. It covers a wide range of interpretations. Some theorists argue that Latin America, Africa, and parts of Asia have not performed well because the development countries formed alliances with the elites of these countries to inhibit economic and social development that could undermine the position of the elites. They are unlikely to act against their own self-interest to give the poor more power. Dependencia interests place most of the blame for low economic growth in Latin America and Africa on foreign investment that exploits natural and human resources and on multinational corporations that promote the interest of the few at the expense of the many.

Progress in the Twenty-First Century

http://

The U.S. Census Bureau provides a variety of international statistics and data at www.census .gov/ipc/www.

In May 1996 the Development Assistance Committee of the OECD published a policy paper called "Shaping the Future." The paper called for a global partnership to pursue a development strategy that would focus on six main goals:

1. To reduce by one-half the proportion of the world population who lives in extreme poverty by the year 2015. International comparisons of extreme poverty are based on a common international poverty line of $1 a day. Some 600 million of the extremely poor live in China and India. Inadequate incomes and consumption levels are not only undesirable in themselves, but also can lead to problems such as crime and violence.
2. To achieve universal primary education in all countries by 2015. Through education, people acquire knowledge, skills, and shared values. Through schooling, individual and societal ideas, aspirations, and values change. Universal primary education is the beginning. It is the entry point for further education, and it begins the expansion of personal horizons and potential.
3. To demonstrate progress toward gender equality and the empowerment of women by eliminating gender disparities in primary and secondary education by 2015. Fewer girls go to school than boys, and they are more likely to end up poorer and more illiterate than men when they become adults. Moreover, the lack of marketable skills by women has a deleterious effect on economic development. Human capital is being wasted.
4. To reduce by two-thirds the mortality rates for infants and children under 5 and by three-fourths the mortality rates for mothers by 2015. Beyond its obvious relevance as a measure of health conditions, child mortality is one of the best indicators of overall socioeconomic development in a community. The reduction of maternal mortality rates is designed to improve the social status of women and to ensure gender equity in health care.
5. To provide access to reproductive health services for all individuals of appropriate age no later than 2015. This area encompasses many health needs and behaviors, cultural and religious attitudes, and supply-side behavior. The use of contraception and lower fertility reduce the chances of dying during pregnancy and childbirth. A well functioning referral system for emergency obstetric complications is also desirable.
6. To implement national strategies for sustainable economic development by the year 2005 to ensure that the current loss of environmental resources is reversed globally by the year 2015. Economic and social change has placed

increasing pressure on the world's environmental resources. Much of the world's biological diversity is in the developing nations and it is estimated to be disappearing at 50 to 100 times natural rates. Wetlands and forests are being lost at a rate of 0.3 to 1.0 percent a year.

Poverty Reduction Goals

Is it possible to reduce by one-half the number of people who live in poverty by 2015? Almost half of the world's poor live in two countries, China and India, and twelve countries account for 80 percent of the world's poor. It is argued that income poverty is a function of economic growth and the extent to which people participate in this growth. Increase the growth rate; decrease the poverty. Growth is also contingent on income distribution. A highly unequal distribution of income, which is typical of the Latin American countries and some of the African countries, will make it harder to reduce poverty. Reducing income inequality, which is easier said than done, will increase the number of people who will benefit from the same average rate of growth. Conversely, higher inequality will increase the rate of growth needed to yield the same.

Table 10-12 presents income inequality for the twelve countries that account for around 80 percent of the world's poor. Income inequality is measured by the Gini coefficient. The higher the coefficient, the greater the income inequality; the lower the coefficient, the lower the income inequality. A coefficient of 50 and above would indicate a high degree of income inequality. However, India has a low Gini coefficient, and an income distribution that is far more equal than most coun-

TABLE 10-12 *Comparisons of Income Inequality for the Twelve Countries That Account for 80 Percent of World Poverty (% share of income)*

Country	Gini Index	Bottom 10%	Bottom 20%	Upper 20%	Upper 10%
Brazil	60.1	0.8	2.5	64.2	47.9
China	41.5	2.2	5.5	47.5	30.9
Ethiopia	—	—	—	—	—
India	29.7	4.1	9.2	39.3	28.3
Indonesia	34.2	3.6	8.4	43.1	28.3
Kenya	57.5	1.2	3.4	62.1	47.7
Mexico	50.3	1.6	4.1	55.3	39.2
Nepal	36.7	3.2	7.6	44.8	29.8
Nigeria	45.0	1.3	4.0	49.4	31.4
Pakistan	31.2	3.4	8.4	39.7	25.2
Peru	44.9	1.9	4.9	50.4	34.3
Philippines	42.9	1.9	4.9	50.4	34.3
Sweden	25.0	3.7	9.6	34.5	20.1
United States	40.1	1.5	4.8	45.2	28.5

Source: The World Bank, *1998 World Development Indicators* (Washington, D.C.: The World Bank, 1998), 5, 68–71.

tries, although 50 percent of its population lives in poverty. China has had one of the highest growth rates in the world, yet over 200 million of its people live in poverty. These twelve countries are so different culturally that it is hard to imagine that any standard growth policy will have the same effect.

SUMMARY

The world has changed rapidly during the latter part of the twentieth century. Revolutions in communication have created a new global economy. In most less developed countries, however, the use of the new technologies, although growing, is still limited. Low incomes, inadequate human capital, and weak regulatory environments slow their use. Sociocultural differences also pose a barrier, because people throughout the world tend to trust only what they know and feel at home with. The average high-income country has over 100 times more computers per capita than the average low-income country, and that gap is not going to be narrowed at any time in the foreseeable future. Indeed, in the great majority of low-income countries, the problem at hand is a lack of supply of educational facilities, infrastructure ranging from communications to hospitals, and favorable trade balances to earn income. The odds are probably stacked against the chance that the majority of the world's population will be increasing their living standards by much, at least in the short run.

QUESTIONS FOR DISCUSSION

1. What is the difference between economic growth and economic development?
2. Even though population is declining in the less developed countries, it still remains a problem. Discuss.
3. What impact does corruption have on economic development?
4. What is the dependencia theory of economic development? Apply it to Africa.
5. What are some of the sociocultural factors that block economic development?
6. The twenty-first century will pose a new set of challenges to the less developed countries. Discuss.

RECOMMENDED READINGS

Brown, Lester. *Beyond Malthus: Nineteen Dimensions of the Population Challenge*. Washington, D.C.: Worldwatch, 1998.

DeRose, Laurie, Ellen Messer, and Sara Mellman. *Who's Hungry? And How Do We Know?* New York: United Nations University Press, 1998.

Landes, David S. *The Wealth and Poverty of Nations*. New York: Norton, 1998.

OECD. *The World 2020: Toward a New Global Age*. Paris: Organization for Economic Cooperation and Development, 1998.

Tanzi, Vita, and Hamid Davoodi. *Roads to Nowhere: How Corruption in Public Investment Hurts Growth*. Economic Issues No. 12. Washington, D.C.: International Monetary Fund, 1998.

United Nations Development Program. *Human Development Report, 1998*. New York: Oxford University Press, 1998.

World Bank. *World Development Report, 1998/99*. Washington, D.C.: The World Bank, 1998.

ENDNOTES

1. Bruce Harrick and Charles F. Kindleberger, *Economic Development*, 4th ed. (New York: McGraw-Hill, 1983), 21–23.
2. The United Nations classifies countries on the basis of developed and less developed. The United States, Europe, Japan, Canada, and Australia would be developed.
3. The World Bank, *1998 World Bank Atlas* (Washington, D.C.: The World Bank, 1998), 38.
4. Many women die in childbirth or of malnutrition.
5. Sixty-four countries are included at the high HDI level.
6. Sixty-five countries are included in the medium level of development.
7. Haiti is the only country in the Western hemisphere to be represented.
8. The World Bank, *World Development Report, 1995* (Washington, D.C.: The World Bank, 1974), 9.
9. The World Bank, *World Development Report, 1998* (Washington, D.C.: The World Bank, 1997), 84–88.

CHAPTER 11
China

China, or the People's Republic of China, remains the last great bastion of communism in the world. Contrary to the former Soviet Union, China, although run by the Communist Party, has managed to survive and do well because its leaders are more pragmatists than ideologues. China has become a mixed economy of private enterprise and state-owned enterprises. Much of resource allocation in the country is done through the market mechanism, and stock exchanges exist to raise capital. Moreover, China's rate of economic growth has been among the highest in the world since the 1970s. Its standard of living has increased to the point where the World Bank no longer includes it among the poor countries of the world, but ranks it among the low-income countries (Table 11-1). The United Nations' human development index ranks China among countries with a medium level of human development, well above that of other Asian countries such as India and Pakistan.

Moreover, China is becoming one of the leading trading powers of the world. Hong Kong became a part of China in 1997, giving China a major seaport and financial center. Hong Kong and China along with Taiwan, which is considered by China to be another Chinese province, constitute what is called the Chinese Economic Area, bound together by a common history, language, and culture. In 1997 the combined foreign trade of China and Hong Kong added up to $650 billion, more than any other country in the world with the exception of the United States,

TABLE 11-1   *Economic and Social Data for China, 1997*

Population (million)	1,227.2
Land area, thousands of square kilometers	9,326.0
Average annual population growth rate, 1991–1997 (%)	1.1
Real GDP ($ billions)	4,382.5
World rank out of 123 countries	2nd
Real per capita GDP	3,570
World rank out of 123 countries	65
Average annual growth in GDP (%)	
1980–1990	10.2
1990–1998	11.9
World Trade ($ billions)	
Export	171.7
Imports	154.1
Poverty rate (% earning less than $1 a day)	22.0
Human development index out of 174 countries	106
Life expectancy at birth (years)	69.2
World rank out of 174 countries	76
Adult literacy rate (%)	81.5
Gender related index rank out of 174 countries	93
Share of earned income (%)	
Male	61.9
Female	38.1
Gini coefficient of income inequality	41.5
U.S. coefficient	40.1

Source: The World Bank, *World Development Report, 1998/99* (New York: Oxford University Press, 1998), 191, 195, 211, 219; The World Bank, *1998 World Bank Atlas* (New York: World Bank Publications, 1998), 25–33; United Nations Development Program, *Human Development Report, 1998* (New York: Oxford University Press, 1998), 129, 133.

Germany, and Japan. When Taiwan's trade figure is added to the total of foreign trade, the combined amount is around $800 billion, making the Chinese Economic Area the third most important trading area in the world.[1] Foreign direct investment in China amounted to $40.1 billion and portfolio investment in China amounted to $50.1 billion in 1996, contributed to in part by Chinese living in the United States and Singapore.[2]

However, China is far from free from economic and social problems. One problem is an ever-increasing population. Even though the birth rate has declined, the population is still increasing in rural areas. China is one of the eight countries of the world that account for most of world poverty. Corruption is endemic in China, with the sons and daughters of the nomenklatura elite enjoying positions of privilege. Although a successor to Deng has been chosen, there is still an element of political instability in the system. Chinese foreign trade practices have left the country open to criticism from the United States and Europe. The banking and financial systems need to be improved, and the majority of state-owned enterprises remain inefficient and unprofitable. There is also the question of whether

http://

See the World Factbook for background information on China at www.odci.gov/cia/publications/factbook/index.html.

or not China will be able to sustain its high economic growth rate into the first part of the twenty-first century.

HISTORY OF CHINA

To understand contemporary China, it is necessary to look at its history. China is an old country. In the tenth century, it was the world's leading economy in terms of per capita. Europe was still in the Dark Ages when China developed a civil service system based on competitive examinations. It developed gunpowder, yet never learned to make modern guns. It had a road system and its merchants traded through East Asia. It developed an efficient system of public finance. It outperformed Europe in levels of technology, the intensity with which it used its natural resources, and its capacity for administering a large empire. Between 1500 and 1800 Europe gradually overtook China in real income technology and scientific capacity. China had been adversely affected by the Mongol conquest and by internal dynastic rivalries.

In 1820 China had the highest level of real GDP in the world. Its GDP was $199,212 billion compared to $21,831 billion for Japan, $34,829 for England, and $12,412 for the United States.[3] Its population was 381 million. But the twentieth century proved to be the undoing of China. Its political system had become fragile and China was invaded twice by British and French armies, with the resultant loss of territory.[4] For all practical purposes China became an economic enclave of England and France. It served as a market for British and French goods and provided raw materials for England and France. China was ruled by a succession of weak leaders. The culminating blow to China came in 1900 with the Boxer Rebellion, which prompted military intervention by an international army consisting of troops from the United States, England, Germany, France, and Japan.[5] The result was a Chinese defeat and the division of a part of its territories into economic enclaves controlled by the Americans, British, French, Germans, and Japanese.[6]

Chaos dominated China during the first half of the twentieth century. In 1911 the Manchu dynasty was overthrown by a revolution. This was followed by a prolonged civil war that destroyed much of China and encouraged the Japanese to invade China in 1937. Japan had already had territorial designs on China, seizing Formosa (now Taiwan) from the Chinese in 1895. After the defeat of the Japanese in 1945, two rival factions fought for dominance of the country. One faction, which had American support, was the Kuomintang, which was created by Chiang Kai-shek in 1928. He established a republican form of government and his armies controlled much of the western part of China when the Japanese invaded China in 1937. The second faction was the Chinese Communist Party, which was created in 1921 and dominated much of the rural areas of China. A civil war between the two factions broke out in 1946. The Communists eventually won in 1949.

Over a little more than one hundred years, China had lost two wars with Japan and was invaded three times by England and France and once by Russia and the United States. Its rulers were corrupt and incompetent and were eventually replaced. Its warlords were no better. China went backward, while the rest of the world went forward. Its real per capita GDP declined and its share of world GDP fell from one-third to one-twentieth. Its real per capita income fell from parity to a quarter of the world average. When the communists took over in 1949, the economy had nowhere to go but up. The first thing they did was to expel foreign companies, including Coca-Cola, and expunge foreign influence.

DEVELOPMENT OF THE ECONOMIC SYSTEM

When the communists formally announced the creation of the Chinese People's Republic on October 1, 1949, they were able to begin consolidating power and developing a new type of economic system. The masses were illiterate and had to be trained and educated to fit into an industrial base that was to be the fountainhead for the development of the communist economic system. There was a fundamental change in property rights, with landlords and capitalists being targeted for expropriations. There was an increase in investment, particularly in heavy industry. There was an increase in expenditures on military preparedness. The administrative mechanism of government was established and a common currency came into use.[7] Foreign trade became a state monopoly whose goal was economic self-sufficiency.

The Period of Consolidation, 1949–1952

Certainly the task of developing a new economic order was not easy. Years of fighting and inflation had debilitated the economy. Widespread corruption had been rampant under the Nationalist government.

During this period, Chinese industry was also placed under the control of the government. In 1949, the communist government took over those state organizations it identified as bureaucratic capital. During 1951 and 1952, the government took over all foreign-owned businesses. In 1952 and 1953, private enterprises were placed under government control.

The First Five-Year Plan, 1953–1957

The First Five-Year Plan marked the second stage in the economic development of the People's Republic of China. To implement the plan, the Chinese relied heavily on Russian expertise. Soviet technicians were imported to develop the plan and to run the factories. Agreements were reached providing for Soviet aid in building or expanding electric power plants and supplying agricultural, mining, and chemical equipment. Soviet financial aid took the form of low-interest loans. The Soviets also contracted for the construction of factories producing a wide variety of products, including chemicals, synthetic fibers and plastics, liquid fuel, and machine tools. The Soviets also built modern iron and steel complexes, nonferrous metallurgical plants, refineries, and power stations and trained Chinese technicians to operate them. Sets of blueprints and related materials giving directions for plant layouts were also provided.

The land reforms of 1949 to 1952 were followed by a series of organizational reforms beginning with the simplest form of social enterprise, the mutual aid team, and progressing through successive stages of producer cooperatives to complete collectivization of the farms in 1957. At that time the peasants lost all title to the land. This same organizational pattern was followed for craftspersons and small retailers. By 1957, practically all industrial enterprises were state owned or collectives.

The Great Leap Forward, 1958–1960

In 1958 the Chinese departed from the pattern of economic development set by the First Five-Year Plan and moved to a new approach that relied on the idealistic fervor of the masses of workers and peasants to drive the economy ahead much more quickly. This approach was called the *Great Leap Forward*. It is an example of idealistic extremism that substituted zeal for the material incentives developed under the First Five-Year Plan. China's enormous population was regarded as an economic asset, not a liability—the more people, the more hands to build communism. Emphasis was placed on indigenous methods of production and the development of labor-intensive investment projects. To put the basic objective of the Great Leap Forward simply, the population was to be harnessed to increase production and make China a world power.

Agriculture. In agriculture economic policy involved the formation of communes. The communes marked the final stage in the transition of agriculture away from private enterprise, which had existed during the first years of communist rule. Under communal organization, all vestiges of private property were eliminated. The peasants were deprived not only of the private plots, livestock, and implements that had been left to them through previous collectivization, but also of their homes. The purpose was to turn the peasants into mobile workers ready for any task in any area to which they might be assigned.

Industry. In industry economic policy emphasized the use of labor to create thousands of tiny industrial units throughout the country. Again, the communists planned to capitalize on the presence of a large labor surplus to accomplish rapid industrialization, particularly in rural areas. During that part of the year when the rural population was underemployed, labor could be employed for useful output. Small, indigenous industrial plants were created to harness the energies of the labor force. These plants included handicraft workshops, iron and steel foundries, fertilizer plants, oil extraction, machine shops, cement manufacture, coal and iron ore mining, and food processing. The capital used to build the small plants came from the local communes and from taxes on state enterprises. Labor, however, was the key factor in the development of local industry.

Top priority was given to the iron and steel industry. Lack of technology and equipment was replaced by mass fervor. This has been called facetiously "the steel mill in every backyard" policy. Some 80 million people were involved in an attempt to create a do-it-yourself steel industry. Two million backyard furnaces were developed throughout China. Many millions of Chinese worked day and night turning out steel, while millions of others labored extracting iron ore and coal. The result was the development of labor-intensive, small-scale steel production with a low capital-to-output ratio. Although the output of iron and steel was increased by the backyard furnace method, much of it was of poor and often unusable quality, reflecting the absence of quality control standards and necessary technical expertise. Production in other areas suffered as well because more than one-tenth of the population was diverted from other pursuits into the production of steel.

Failure of the Great Leap Forward.   The Great Leap Forward was not a success. Although industrial and agricultural output rose sharply in 1958, much of the gain was spurious. The output was often of such poor quality that most of it had to be scrapped. Production costs were high, reflecting an indiscriminate development of small plants in almost all industries. There was also a disregard for cost considerations at the level of the local plant because the most important success indicator was the degree to which the local cadre (leaders) could fulfill or overfill physical quotas. Output was maximized at the expense of quality and cost, and inputs of labor and raw materials could have been more effectively employed elsewhere. A shortage of fuel and raw materials caused by the waste involved in the backyard furnace method of production and a lack of adequate transportation facilities were responsible for the demise of many plants.

Sino-Russian Relations.   The Great Leap Forward also caused a rift in the relationship between the Chinese and the Soviet advisers and technicians that had been sent to help them. In essence, the Soviet blueprints for making China a self-sufficient world power were set aside in favor of a development program that made little economic sense. The Chinese persisted in ignoring the advice of their Soviet technicians despite the fact that the USSR intimated that support would be withdrawn unless the Great Leap Forward was discontinued. In 1960 the Soviet technicians were withdrawn from China. With them went the equipment, financial aid, and blueprints that had played a paramount role in the development of the Chinese economy during the First Five-Year Plan. This departure en masse of the technicians had a negative effect on China, which could not replace their expertise.

The Proletarian Cultural Revolution, 1966–1969

The Third Five-Year Plan, which began in 1965, was eclipsed by a political aberration of the first magnitude called the *Proletarian Cultural Revolution*. This was an attempt by Mao Tse-tung to mold Chinese society into his prescribed pattern. It placed primacy on ideological cant over scientific expertise and reverted to the

Great Leap Forward period in its attempt to replace material incentives with political ideology and to denigrate any emphasis on technical excellence.[8] It aimed at annihilating, throughout China and particularly in the universities, any tendency toward a moderate or revisionist viewpoint concerning the role of communism in world affairs. Intransigence toward the Western countries in general and the United States in particular was to be maintained until Western influence was eliminated from Asia. The Soviets did not escape the general opprobrium that the Chinese engendered toward the West, because Mao was furious with them for drawing back from war and subversion with the West in the interest of coexistence.

The rationale of the Cultural Revolution was political as well as economic. It involved Mao's attempt to develop a new socialist morality that would place public interest above individualism. He believed that Stalin had permitted the development of a new class structure in the form of a state bureaucracy that differed little from a capitalist class structure. Soviet claims of egalitarianism ignored the special privileges for this small bureaucratic and technical elite. Moreover, Mao believed that the Soviet Union and other socialist countries had moved away from the utopian idea of an egalitarian society by introducing material incentives and bonuses, which tended to differentiate among workers. An ethical revolution was needed, for people had to be changed to create a new order of society.

The Cultural Revolution represented a step backward in terms of economic growth. The average annual rate of growth of gross national product from 1966 to 1968 was -2.5 percent, reflecting a general decline in industrial output of around 15 to 20 percent in 1967. More important, the Cultural Revolution encouraged an ideological polarization within the regime and weakened consensus on the nation's fundamental values and priorities. The regime faced the task of rebuilding a stable institutional structure and working out a new pattern of relationships among various groups.

The Post–Cultural Revolution Period, 1970–1976

The end of the Cultural Revolution ushered in another stage of Chinese economic development. For one thing, central economic planning in the form of a Fourth Five-Year Plan was reintroduced. Both the Second and Third Five-Year Plans were largely shunted aside by sudden shifts in Chinese ideological policies—the former by the Great Leap Forward and the latter by the Cultural Revolution.

However, there were additional political interruptions during this period. The leaders began jockeying for power as it became evident that both Chairman Mao and Premier Chou En-lai were in failing health. Radical elements in the Communist Party wanted to continue the Cultural Revolution. Denouncing material incentives, orderly economic planning, and reliance on foreign technology, they brought disorder into production by opposing rules and regulations. Toward the end of 1975 and the beginning of 1976, the radicals increased their attacks on government bureaucrats and party leaders who were in favor of economic modernization. Serious riots occurred in some of the largest Chinese cities.

The year 1976 was a momentous one for China. Premier Chou died in February, and Chairman Mao died in September. With the death of the two major political leaders, a struggle for succession developed between those who wanted to maintain a rigid ideological status quo, with collective behavior and control and a closed door to the outside world, and those who wanted to modernize the economy and increase the rate of economic growth. The latter faction won out, and Deng Xiaoping was elected party leader.[9]

In December 1978 the Central Committee of the Communist Party convened in Beijing (Peking). The session declared that if China were to develop successfully, it must turn from class struggle to modernization and completely restructure its economy. *The Four Modernizations Program*, originally started by Premier Chou in 1975, was incorporated into a Ten-Year Plan that called for increases in grain output, steel production, and capital construction through the purchase of foreign plants and technology. The program emphasized the development of four major economic sectors—agriculture, industry, science, and technology—and national defense. The centerpiece of the program was to be the creation of the massive Baoshan steel complex, which would turn out 6.7 million tons of steel a year with the most advanced technology imported from Japan, West Germany, and the United States. Baoshan was an expensive failure, however, caused in part by China's inability to assimilate foreign technology and in part by an unrealistic emphasis on the role of heavy industry in developing the Chinese economy. A period of retrenchment and reappraisal of Chinese economic goals set in.

The 1980s

The early 1980s marked a liberalization of the Chinese economy as the ambitious goals of the Four Modernizations Program were scaled down and the government turned its attention to more immediate objectives, such as improving productivity and increasing output. It introduced more competition into the economy, not only by permitting private businesses to exist, but also by turning over small, unprofitable state-owned enterprises to private collectives. In 1984 a number of reforms were introduced to improve the structure of the Chinese economy. There was a separation of government from state enterprise functions. The purpose was to give state enterprises more autonomy over their operations. Prices were restructured away from uniform prices set by the state and toward a floating price system for some products and free prices for others. In enterprises, differences in wages among various trades and jobs were widened to apply fully the principle of awarding the diligent and punishing the indolent.

These and other measures promoted rapid economic growth during the 1980s, but they also created some problems. The gap in living standards between the richer coastal areas and the poorer areas of the interior grew wider. The rate of inflation increased to around 30 percent, and in 1988 the government initiated a series of austerity measures, which included cutbacks in investment projects, reimposition of price controls on industrial projects, and a cessation of further experiments with market reforms.[10] It also tightened credit ceilings for domestic banks and raised interest rates on bank loans. Unemployment increased, and consumer living standards declined. Worker unrest increased as thousands of factories were closed or operated below capacity. The decline in revenues contributed to an increase in the deficit in the Chinese state budget for 1988 and 1989. The government also increased its state control over the economy by giving more power over industrial enterprises to the State Planning Commission.

Table 11-2 presents the performance of the Chinese economy in the 1980s as measured by the average annual increase in real industrial output and retail prices. Foreign trade and investment from abroad during the 1980s made an important contribution to Chinese economic development, and by the end of the decade its foreign trade had almost tripled.

THE COMMUNIST PARTY

The Communist Party is the official political party of China, and its leaders function as the ruling class. A self-selected group beholden to no one, they oversee government and industry. The party delegates much of the running of the country to a government bureaucracy organized separately but subordinate to it. It exercises its control over government by a system of parallel rule. A party committee keeps watch within every institution of government at every level. This results in an enormous duplication of work. The bureaucracy is closely controlled. The main instrument of the party's power over the bureaucracy is the nomenklatura system, which specifies the thousands of official posts and public offices that can be filled only by personnel whom the party has selected and approved.

A new power elite has also developed in China, where family ties have always mattered. As the nation has prospered, so have the children of the revolutionaries who founded the Communist Party. Members of these families lead lives of privilege, attend the best schools, and make the right contacts. Political rule and eco-

TABLE 11-2   *Performance of the Chinese Economy in the 1980s (%)*

	Real GNP	Real Gross Industrial Output	Retail Prices
1980	7.9	9.3	6.0
1981	4.4	4.3	2.4
1982	8.8	7.8	1.9
1983	10.4	11.2	1.5
1984	14.7	16.3	2.8
1985	12.8	21.4	8.8
1986	8.1	11.7	6.0
1987	10.9	17.7	7.3
1988	11.3	20.8	18.6
1989	4.4	8.5	17.8

Source: Michael W. Bell, Hoe Ee Khor, and Kalpana Kochhar, *China at the Threshold of a Market Economy*, Occasional Paper 107 (Washington, D.C.: International Monetary Fund, November 1993), 66.

nomic rule overlap, with the latter involving increased control of the Chinese economy by an oligarchy of powerful families. They are becoming similar to the Chinese family clans that dominate business in much of East Asia. To maintain their power and privilege, members of the new family elites also hold high party, government, and military positions. In the so-called classless society of the past, one leader, Mao, reigned supreme; almost everybody else lived in relative equality, which usually meant poverty. But times have changed, and the communists are no longer shooting landlords; they have become landlords themselves.

Deng Xiaoping, who was responsible for the economic reforms that took place in China during the 1980s and early 1990s, died in early 1997 and was replaced by Jiang Zemen, who became president of China, and Zhu Rongji, former mayor of Shanghai, who became premier.[11] The big question that had to be answered after the death of Deng was whether the leaders would follow the same pragmatic path of economic development. A second question was whether the country would fragment along economic lines, with the rich coastal regions going their own way and eventually discarding communist rule. But the new leaders appear committed to continue the economic reforms started by Deng. Emphasis has been placed on efficiency, as millions of workers have been laid off from overstaffed state enterprises. It is likely that the Communist Party will remain in power for some time to come because it controls the apparatus of government and the army.

Comparing China to the former Soviet Union highlights some differences. China was not involved in an arms race with the United States, so it did not have to expend as much of its resources. Despite the fact that the Soviet Union helped the Chinese to adopt the Soviet model for economic development, there was little love lost between the countries, because Russia had occupied Manchuria. China has become an important world trading nation; the Soviet Union had little exposure to international trade and lagged far behind other nations in technology. China committed itself to a series of economic reforms during the 1980s that brought about an improvement in the performance of the economy. The reforms in the Soviet Union were too little too late.

THE ECONOMIC SYSTEM

http://

An expansive site with links to many sites about the economics, politics, and culture of China is at http://freenet .buffalo.edu/ ~cb863/china .html#Chinanews.

The Chinese economy can be called a "mixed" economy in that both economic planning and free markets are used to allocate resources. There is a mixture of private, collective, and state enterprises. Large inflows of foreign and Chinese overseas capital have contributed to the diversification of property forms outside of the state-owned sector. Tens of millions of Chinese either own their own businesses outright or work for private enterprises. Changes in the ownership structure of agriculture have occurred, where households now have extensive rights of use to their share of land plots, including the right to transfer the use. The spread of consumerism has been facilitated by the information revolution, which has made the Chinese desirous of acquiring what they see as the American way of life as represented by McDonalds and Coca-Cola.[12]

Economic Planning

Economic planning is a fundamental part of the Chinese economy. It gives the state, as represented by the Communist Party, control over resource allocation. The Chinese have developed nine five-year plans, the latest of which is the Ninth Five-Year Plan (1996–2000). There is also a ten-year development plan for the 1990s that aimed to develop new energy sources and agriculture. The objective of the current five-year plan is increased investments in state-owned enterprises in energy and transportation. Investments in the nonenergy industrial sector are to be scaled back because of excess capacity. Increased investment is concentrated in the coastal growth areas of China, particularly the Shanghai and Guangdong areas. The Ninth Five-Year Plan also places priority on the development of more efficient distribution channels for meat, poultry, and other agricultural products. It also aims at balancing the state budget by the year 2000.

Formulation of Economic Plans.   The State Planning Commission has overall responsibility for economic planning, including the drafting of the five-year plans and the annual operating plan. An economic commission reviews the fulfillment of the annual economic plans and institutes economic reforms. Both are responsible to the State Council, which is the executive branch of the government. It, in turn, is responsible to the National People's Congress, the highest elected organ of the Communist Party.

The five-year and annual operating plans can be broken down into sectoral plans that indicate what and how much individual enterprises should produce. In agriculture, specific goals are set for consumption within the agricultural sector and for distribution to other sectors. In transportation, the plan covers the construction of facilities, with particular emphasis on the development of the railroad system. Then there is a plan that covers capital formation for individual economic sectors and is concerned with resource allocation. A labor plan covers the allocation of labor inputs to the various sectors of the economy. Plans for foreign trade, social and cultural development, and regional development are also used. The foreign trade plan covers export and import commodity targets and the use of foreign exchange. Finally a set of financial plans controls government income and expenditures. The objectives are to regulate resource allocation between consumption and investment and the flow of credit from the banking system.

Implementation the Plans.   The State Council, through its various ministries, is responsible for implementing the economic plans. There are forty ministries, each dealing with the different segments of the economy. These ministries also operate at the intermediate levels of Chinese government. The central government prepares its economic plans through the administrative units at the different levels. Directions pass downward through the various administrative levels to the factories and enterprises.

Public Finance

China spends more of its budget than does the U.S. government. In China many goods and services that would be financed by private enterprises in the United States are financed to a considerable degree by the Chinese state budget. It is also linked to economic planning. The national economic plan sets forth the level and distribution of economic resources. The state budget is part of the financial plan. It is through the state budget that taxes are collected and redistributed. The state budget is the prime vehicle for allocating resources among various ends. It is a control mechanism because it provides a considerable proportion of investment funds for the state-owned enterprises. Tables 11-3 and 11-4 provide the revenues and expenditures of the Chinese state budget for 1997.

Recent reforms have reduced the role of the state budget in the Chinese economy. Larger tax powers have devolved down to regional governments, particularly local governments that share revenues with regional governments. There has also been a growing use of extra budgetary funds. These are off-budget funds, which are of two different types, five social funds and other off-budget funds that are earmarked for specific expenditure purposes, including infrastructure.[13] Thus, it is hard to measure the size and impact of government operations. The Chinese fiscal system is expected to change as a result of comprehensive social security reforms that involve creating nationwide pension funds by the year 2000.

There has also been a significant change in the tax structure in the Chinese state budget. Table 11-5 presents its breakdown by taxes for 1986 and 1996. Of particular importance is the increased reliance on the use of the value added tax (VAT). It is now the most important tax in China. Taxes on income and profits have declined in importance.

TABLE 11-3

Chinese State Budget Revenues, 1997 (billions of yuan)*

Total revenue	873.9
Tax revenue	800.6
Taxes on income and profit	86.5
Collectives	16.0
State enterprises	70.5
Taxes on goods and services	534.0
Excises	65.6
Value added tax	333.1
Business turnover tax	135.3
Customs duties	34.0
Other taxes	146.2
Nontax revenue	73.3

* In 1997 the exchange rate was approximately 8.3 yuan = $1.00.

Source: International Monetary Fund, *People's Republic of China—Recent Economic Developments* (Washington, D.C.: IMF, September 1997), 73.

Total expenditures and net lending	990.9
Current expenditures	841.2
Administrative	114.7
Defense	80.6
Culture, education, health	193.5
Economic services	72.4
Agriculture	59.2
Other	13.2
Social welfare relief	17.0
Subsidies	84.6
Daily living expenses	50.5
Operating losses of state enterprises	34.1
Interest payments	60.0
Other	218.4
Capital expenditures	149.7
Capital construction	90.9
Development of state enterprises	58.8

TABLE 11-4
State Budget Expenditures and Net Lending by Functions, 1997 (billions of yuan)*

* *In 1997 the exchange rate was approximately 8.3 yuan $1.00.*

Source: International Monetary Fund, *People's Republic of China—Recent Economic Developments* (Washington, D.C.: IMF, September 1997), 74.

	1986	1996
Total taxes	100.0	100.0
Taxes on income and profits	38.4	21.5
Enterprise profit tax	36.4	13.4
On state-owned enterprises	—	11.3
Personal income tax	—	2.8
Agricultural income tax	2.0	5.3
Consumption taxes	46.8	66.8
VAT	10.3	42.8
Excises	24.3	8.9
Business taxes	11.6	15.1
Other	0.6	0.0
Customs duties	6.8	4.4
Other taxes	8.1	7.3

TABLE 11-5
Changes in the Tax Structure of the Chinese State Budget, 1986–1996 (% of total tax revenue)

Source: International Monetary Fund, *People's Republic of China—Recent Economic Developments* (Washington, D.C.: IMF, September 1997), 75.

Banking

The banking system in the People's Republic of China represents a financial control mechanism for carrying out economic planning. All state enterprises and cooperatives have accounts with the central bank, and control can be exercised because most transactions are in terms of money through bank transfers. Purchases and sales of goods by each enterprise can be matched against authorized payments and receipts. Government control over income and expenditures is also expedited through the credit and cash plans of the banking system.

The People's Bank of China.   The People's Bank of China (PBC) was formed in 1959 as the central bank of the country. It is under the jurisdiction of the Staff Office for Finance and Trade and is responsible for the supervision of financial transactions that correspond to the physical production plans. All state enterprises have accounts in branch banks under its direct jurisdiction. In this way, the People's Bank can exercise control because all expenditures and transfers made by the enterprises come under its scrutiny.

As the central bank of China, the People's Bank has the following responsibilities:

1. Issuing Chinese currency.
2. Financing credit to state enterprises. Funds to support credit expansion are obtained from the national budget, from retained profits, and from customer deposits.
3. Supervising expenditures of state enterprises to see that they conform to national planning objectives.
4. Developing the credit plan and the cash plan, which are financial counterparts of the physical economic plans.
5. Monitoring the performance of state enterprises.

The credit plan is concerned with the amount of short- and medium-term credit that is to be provided to state enterprises and agricultural communes by the People's Bank. Funds can be allocated only for purposes that conform to the national plan. The cash plan consists of a set of cash inflows and cash outflows essentially in the form of a balance sheet. Cash inflows include retail sales receipts, savings deposit receipts, repayment of agricultural loans, deposits of communes, and public utility receipts. Cash outflows consist of wage payments by state enterprises and communes, government purchases of industrial and agricultural products, government administrative expenses, transfer payments by the state to individuals, management expenditures of state enterprises, new loans to agriculture, and withdrawals of savings deposits.

The credit and cash plans are coordinated with the physical production plans to provide financing for expenditures required by the production plans. This means that the People's Bank can supervise the operations of state enterprises to enforce conformance to production plans because purchase and sales of goods can be matched against authorized payments and receipts.

Cash Plan.   The Chinese economy is largely cash-based. Cash remains the only payment instrument for the household and consumer sectors, and it is the preferred medium of exchange for most of the industrial enterprise sector. Thus, the currency management practices of the People's Bank of China have not changed much since before the reforms period. The cash plan continues to function as a central planning instrument in determining the supply of currency. The annual cash plan is prepared by the PBC based on estimates of growth, inflation, fixed asset investment, cash requirements in the agricultural sector, and growth in the consumption fund, which covers wages, salaries, and pensions paid by state enterprises. The State Council approves the cash plan, with inputs from various ministries and the State Planning Commission. These procedures tend to introduce an inflationary bias to the plan.

Other Financial Institutions.   A two-tiered banking system was created in China in 1994 when the People's Bank of China became a central bank responsible for monetary policy and four specialized state-owned banks were established to handle commercial lending operations. The four specialized banks are the Agricultural Bank of China, the Bank of China, which is responsible for financing both domestic and foreign trade, the Industrial and Commercial Bank of China, and the People's Construction Bank of China. The Agricultural Bank, for example, provides agricultural loans. It also controls the allocation of rural savings to rural credit cooperatives that provide credit to individual cooperatives and to individual undertakings involving private plots of land. Each specialized bank is under the jurisdiction of a government ministry.

In addition to the four state-owned specialized banks, there are state-owned national or regional universal or comprehensive banks and three major development banks. The regional development banks, responsible for loans to both state and private enterprises, are located in the fastest-growing regions of China. Then there is a network of rural and urban credit cooperatives. The rural credit cooperatives are under the jurisdiction of the Agricultural Bank of China and collect deposits from and extend credit to rural households and enterprises. The urban cooperatives provide the same functions in urban areas. There are foreign and joint-venture banks in China, and a large network of financial intermediaries that are also affiliated with the four specialized state-owned banks. The structure of the Chinese financial system is presented in Table 11-6. The banking system is under the jurisdiction of the State Council.

Weaknesses of the Chinese Banking System.   The four state banks that are directly under the control of the People's Bank of China control around 80 percent of the financial assets in the country. They have to support the some 100,000 state-owned enterprises that are the backbone of the socialist economy. Most of the loans are never paid back because many state enterprises lose money. Meanwhile, the most profitable part of the economic sector, private enterprises and cooperatives, find it difficult to obtain loans. Many private enterprises must rely on personal loans to get started and then can expand only with retained earnings. Instead of operating on the basis of commercial banking principles and rejecting customers who are a poor credit risk, the state banks simply do what the government tells them to do. Local governments, which own 80 percent of state enterprises, pressure banks for favorable treatment.

TABLE 11-6   *Structure of the Chinese Financial System*

Central bank
  People's Bank of China
Specialized banks
  Industrial and Commercial Bank of China
  Agricultural Bank of China
  Bank of China (domestic and foreign)
  People's Construction Bank of China
Nationwide commercial banks
  China Merchants Bank
  Bank of Communications
  China International Trust and Investment Bank
  Fujean Industrial Bank
Development banks
  China Investment Bank
  Ouangdong Development Bank
  Shenzhen Development Bank
Cooperative banks
  Rural Credit Cooperatives (53,000)
  Urban Credit Cooperatives (5,100)
Other
  Finance Companies and Financial Leasing Companies
  Trust and Investment Companies
  China Minsheng Bank (privately owned by nonstate enterprises)
  Foreign and Joint-Venture Banks (foreign currency operations)
  Savings Banks

Source: International Monetary Fund, *People's Republic of China—Recent Economic Developments* (Washington, D.C.: IMF, September 1997), 12.

Securities Markets.   Two stock exchanges were opened in Shanghai and Shenzhen in 1994.[14] Both Chinese citizens and foreigners are allowed to buy and sell stock in Chinese companies. State-owned enterprises can form joint-stock companies and sell stock. The emergence of joint-stock companies and equity markets has represented a major change in the ideological framework of Chinese reforms. They are no longer considered at odds with the institutional framework of a socialist economy because stock ownership is seen as being compatible with public ownership of enterprise. The addition of the Hong Kong stock market in 1997 provided China with one of the largest stock markets in Asia and a link to the European and American equity markets.[15] However, the Hong Kong market has added an element of instability into the Chinese financial markets as a result of the East Asian financial crisis.

Organization of Industry

Chinese industry can be divided into five categories: state-owned enterprises, collective enterprises, joint-ventures, foreign-owned enterprises, and individual companies. The share of state-owned enterprises in industrial output has been steadily declining, while the share of cooperatives and private enterprises has been steadily increasing. In 1978 the share of state-owned enterprises in Chinese industrial output was 78 percent; by 1995 about 43 percent of the industrial output came from state-owned enterprises.[16] The private sector has increased its share of industrial output from 22 percent in 1978 to 57 percent in 1995.

State-Owned Enterprises.   State-owned enterprises may employ from several hundred to many thousands of workers. Most of them own clinics or hospitals, dining halls, apartments, nurseries, kindergartens, libraries, and theaters. They function as largely autonomous communities. The Communist Party provides political leadership. The party secretary and the manager jointly control the enterprise, but do not report to each other. The economic plan determines production. The performance of most state-owned enterprises has generally been poor. Waste and inefficiency are problems. Many enterprises lose money because they carry surplus workers who likely would be unemployed.[17] Although some state-owned enterprises are efficient, the ones that are not have to be subsidized out of the state budget or out of provincial and local budgets. But reforms are designed to create efficiency by giving more autonomy to these enterprises. They are free to form joint-stock companies, issue stock, and merge with each other.

Collectives.   Collective enterprises account for about 38 percent of China's gross value of industrial output.[18] Although they are supposed to be collectively owned, they operate largely in a market-based economy. A group of citizens can take the initiative in establishing a collectively owned enterprise. The means of production are neither private property nor public property, but the property of the collective. They are typically under the jurisdiction of lower-level governments, such as a county or city. The collective has the exclusive right to own, control, and handle its means of production and products. It keeps its own accounts and is responsible for its profits and losses. The higher authorities of a collective are typically county or city leaders. Collectives are equally owned by every member of a particular group.

Private Enterprise.   The existence of private enterprise in China is justified on the grounds that it serves an economic purpose in certain sectors of the Chinese economy where state control is not feasible. The great majority of private enterprises are in retail stores and restaurants (Table 11-7). There are also a number of private manufacturers in China in such areas as clothing and textiles. Private enterprise has become more important since it was officially tolerated back in 1978, especially in cities such as Beijing and Shanghai and in the special enterprise zones (SEZ) in the coastal regions of China.[19] Its major problem is a general shortage of finance capital because the state banks favor the state-owned enterprises. It depends on the generation of earnings to finance internal development. Nevertheless, its importance in the Chinese economy has increased.

TABLE 11-7   *Share of Retail Sales in China by Various Types of Enterprises (%)*

Enterprises	1991	1992	1993	1994	1995	1996
State commercial	40.2	41.3	37.5	31.9	29.8	27.5
Collective outlets	30.0	27.9	22.0	20.8	19.3	19.0
Individual outlets[1]	19.6	20.3	24.2	28.4	30.3	31.3
Joint ownership[2]	0.5	0.7	0.3	0.4	0.4	0.4
Others[3]	9.7	9.8	16.0	18.5	20.2	21.8

[1] *Firms with less than seven employees.*
[2] *Domestic enterprises only.*
[3] *Consists of retail sales by farmers to nonagricultural residents, individual outlets with more than seven employees, shareholder enterprises, and joint ventures.*

Source: International Monetary Fund, *People's Republic of China—Recent Economic Development* (Washington, D.C.: IMF, September 1997), 52.

Joint Ventures.   The Chinese government has made an active effort to promote foreign investment. One approach that has been used since 1980 involves joint ventures between Chinese state enterprises and Western firms. The foreign firm brings money, technology, and marketing expertise; the government unit, state enterprise, or collective provides land, labor, and a market. An example of a joint venture is an agreement between the Fedders Company, maker of air conditioners, and a Chinese municipality to produce air conditioners to be sold in China.[20] Licensing and franchising agreements have been reached with foreign firms. One example is Coca-Cola, which has the right to produce and sell the drink in China. Coca-Cola provides the syrup and the authorized use of its trademark, and the drink is bottled for sale in China.[21]

Foreign-Owned Enterprise.   As China has expanded, the number of foreign-owned enterprises has increased. Some of them are a carryover from Hong Kong, when it became a part of China. Examples would be banks and securities firms. Typically, there is going to be joint ownership with a government unit, because the Chinese government places restrictions on the extent of foreign ownership. There are also laws that govern the employment of local Chinese. The sales aspect is often a critical success factor for foreign-owned enterprises trying to sell their products in China. Some form of payment or "kickback" is typically the requisite for success. Most foreign-owned enterprises operate as subsidiaries of larger foreign corporations.

Organization of Agriculture

Agriculture is the most important sector in the Chinese economy, accounting for around one-third of the Chinese GNP and two-thirds of the labor force. It has gone through a number of phases since the communists came to power in 1949. Producers' cooperatives created in 1955 were incorporated into collective farms in

1956. Land was no longer privately owned; it was collective property, with the peasants allowed to own farm animals and small plots of land. In 1958 communes replaced the collective farms. A commune was a multipurpose unit that was supposed to perform administrative as well as economic functions. All vestiges of private property were removed, the peasants ate in mess halls, and the distribution of food was based in part on the needs of individuals and in part on work performed. The communes remained the highest level of collective organization in China until the end of the 1970s.

A series of agricultural reforms was initiated in the 1980s. Recollectivization of farmland and reform in production planning were designed to encourage production incentives. The self-responsibility system (*baochan dasho*) was introduced. Although still owned by the state, land was divided into small plots and contracted out to be farmed privately. Each farm family was given the necessary inputs, including land, cattle, farm machinery, and equipment. The only obligation of a farmer besides paying rent and a small agricultural tax was to deliver a fixed amount of produce, which was sold to the state at a fixed price. Any amount produced in excess of the fixed amount belonged to the farm family to consume, to sell to the state at a higher price, or to sell in the free market.

Agricultural reforms continued during the 1980s. In 1988 purchase prices for grain production under state contract were raised. The dual-track pricing system was changed by reducing the share of grain produced under state contracts and increasing free-market transactions. Compulsory contract procurement quotas for grains and cotton were replaced by contract purchases. In 1988 the government raised the price it paid for contract grain and instituted price differences based on grain quality. Peasants were given permission to purchase and transfer land-lease rights, a system designed to permit more efficient, larger-scale operations. The government also strengthened the land-leasing period for rural land from fifteen to thirty years to provide greater incentives for farmers to adopt land-use measures. Finally, the government increased investment in fertilizer and pesticide production, transportation, and distribution networks, and agricultural infrastructure projects such as irrigation.

Until 1979 the Chinese government followed a policy of food self-sufficiency, particularly in the production of grain, irrespective of the difference in regional comparative advantages. It also kept producer prices of agricultural goods at levels far below what they would have been if market factors had been used to provide consumers with low-cost food. Consumer prices, too, were administratively set. Producers' sales quotas were fixed. State purchase prices and state selling prices bore little relationship to each other. Prices were irrelevant to distribution, since farm products were allocated in a planned way through the administrative process. Finally, prices did not affect consumer behavior because supplies of most goods were rationed by state economic planning.

The trend toward liberalization of the state procurement and pricing systems led to a situation where by 1995, about 79 percent of all agricultural purchases took place at market-determined prices, 4 percent were subject to state-guided prices, where maximum and minimum prices were set, and the remaining 17 percent

TABLE 11-8   *Proportion of Agricultural Output and Retail Sales Sold at Fixed, Guided, and Market Prices (%)*

Year	Agricultural Output			Retail Sales		
	Fixed	Guided	Market	Fixed	Guided	Market
1978	92.6	1.8	5.6	97.0	0.0	3.0
1979	88.4	4.9	6.7	—	—	—
1980	82.3	9.5	8.2	—	—	—
1981	79.1	11.5	8.4	—	—	—
1982	78.3	11.5	10.2	—	—	—
1983	76.1	13.4	10.5	—	—	—
1984	67.5	14.4	18.1	—	—	—
1985	37.0	23.0	40.0	47.0	19.0	34.0
1986	35.3	21.0	43.7	35.0	25.0	40.0
1987	29.4	16.8	53.8	33.7	28.0	38.3
1988	24.0	19.0	57.0	28.9	21.8	49.3
1989	35.3	24.3	40.4	31.3	23.2	45.5
1990	25.0	23.4	51.6	29.7	17.2	53.1
1991	22.2	20.0	57.8	20.9	10.3	68.8
1992	17.0	15.0	68.0	10.0	10.0	80.0
1993	10.0	2.0	88.0	5.0	1.0	94.0
1994	16.6	4.1	79.3	7.2	2.4	90.4
1995	17.0	4.4	78.6	8.8	2.4	88.8

Source: International Monetary Fund, *People's Republic of China—Recent Economic Developments* (Washington, D.C.: IMF, September 1997), 58.

were sold at state-determined prices (Table 11-8). Price and procurement reforms had an impact on the Chinese agricultural and rural economy in several ways. Production and productivity of grain crops and livestock products showed a substantial increase, and rural incomes, savings, and investment also increased. Regional comparative advantages have been exploited more fully, and interregional markets have developed. On the other hand, rising farm productivity has left millions of rural workers out of work. Farm incomes tend to lag well behind urban incomes.

However, agriculture has lagged behind other sectors in China. It is constrained by its limited cultivable area and insufficient water in northern China. Only 10 percent of the land area of China is cropland compared to 21 percent in the United States and 35 percent in Germany.[22] Agricultural productivity per worker in China is low, reflecting too much reliance on labor. In the period 1994–1996 agricultural value added per hectare amounted to $193 in China compared to $6,961 in Korea and $12,445 in Japan.[23] Concern over agriculture is reflected in the priorities of the Ninth Five-Year Plan. The plan aims to achieve greater self-sufficiency in grain; to make better use of technology and to speed up the development of agroprocessing industries; and to raise the standard of living for farmers. The plan will also emphasize soil conservation.

Foreign Trade and Investment

China is one of the leading trading nations of the world. In 1997 it ranked 10th in the world in total value of trade.[24] It also ranks among the five most important exporters to the United States.[25] Foreign direct investment inflows increase by $140 billion during 1993–1997, nearly half of the inflows into developing countries. The broadening and deepening of economic reforms have helped enhance China's attractiveness to foreign investors. The bulk of foreign investment in China has originated in Hong Kong, one of the money centers of East Asia. Other major investors are Japan, Taiwan, and the United States, each accounting for around 10 percent of the investment inflows. An attraction is the tax incentives offered in the SEZs. Two-thirds of foreign direct investment has been concentrated in the eastern and southern coastal regions of China.

In foreign trade, there is reliance on market mechanisms to determine the price of most exports and imports. Some imports are handled through import licensing, which is used to implement the economic plan and to protect certain sectors of the economy. Foreign trade corporations, which are under the jurisdiction of provincial governments, handle the bulk of trade. Foreign Exchange is handled in several ways. First, there is a swap market covering foreign exchange earnings retained by foreign trade corporations and other exporters. In the swap market, holders of foreign exchange can sell any excess to enterprises offering the best price. Second, actual purchase of foreign exchange outside of the swap market is usually limited to foreign funded enterprises (FFEs). Subject to the approval of the Ministry of Foreign Trade and Economic Cooperation, FFEs can use foreign exchange for operating needs.

PERFORMANCE OF THE CHINESE ECONOMY

China's economic reforms have succeeded in transforming the Chinese economy. Before the reforms, all important economic decisions were made by bureaucrats at the state planning commission and ministries who were insulated from the direct consequences of their actions. Today, economic decisions in China are made by a broad and diverse number of economic agents, who respond to market prices and who are accountable for the economic consequences of their actions. Despite the existence of the communist party and of economic planning, China is in most respects a market economy. Moreover, it made the transition from a state-directed to a market economy without experiencing the transitional market contraction that Russia and other countries have faced. Human resources have adapted readily to the needs of a market economy. Table 11-9 presents the performance of the Chinese economy in the 1990s.

But this development hardly means the disappearance of government from the Chinese economy. It is very much involved at all levels. Governments from the villages to the national level own and operate factories. The national government is committed to an economic plan that stresses industrial development. Governments at all levels interfere with the allocation of bank credit. Corruption

http://

Current information and reports on China are available at www.state .gov/www/ current/debate/ china.html.

TABLE 11-9
Performance of the Chinese Economy in the 1990s (annual percent change in real GDP)

Average 1980–1989	9.5
1990	3.8
1991	9.2
1992	14.2
1993	13.5
1994	12.6
1995	10.5
1996	9.6
1997	8.8
1998[1]	9.0
1999[1]	8.3

[1] *Estimates by* The Economist

Source: International Monetary Fund, *World Economic Outlook*, October 1998 (Washington, D.C.: IMF, 1998), p. 179.

is a problem in China; in a corruption index compiled by Transparency International, China ranked 52 out of 85 ranked countries. Despite the existence of a body of commercial law, enforcement of intellectual property rights remains weak and is a bone of contention between the United States and China. Both the banking and public finance systems need to be improved. Many activities continue to escape taxation.

Strengths

In 1997 China ranked seventh in the world in the size of its money GNP and second in the world in the size of its real GDP. It is ranked as a lower-middle income country rather than a poor country. In terms of quality of life, it is ranked in the middle level of human development. Table 11-10 presents real GNP and real per capita GNP for China and selected countries for 1997. Certainly, China cannot be considered a developed country along the lines of the United States and France, but few countries can match its economic performance during the latter part of the twentieth century. It ranked first among countries during the period 1965–1996 in the average annual growth of value added in services and ranked third in the world in average annual growth of GNP per capita during the same period. Table 11-11 compares growth indicators for selected countries between 1965 and 1996. It ranked 10th in the world in the value of foreign trade.

Weaknesses

Despite its high rate of economic growth and vast improvement in living standards, China has serious problems. The first involves its infrastructure, which has to be upgraded. Toppling bridges, roads, dams, and buildings can be attributed to corruption and favoritism in the Chinese government. Economic growth and urbani-

TABLE 11-10   *Rankings of China and Selected Countries in Real GNP and Real per Capita GNP, 1997*

	Real GNP ($ billions)	Rank[1]	Real per Capita GNP ($)	Rank[2]
United States	7,690.1	1	28,740	2
China	4,382.5	2	3,570	65
Japan	2,950.7	3	23,400	6
Germany	1,748.3	4	21,300	13
India	1,587.0	5	16,500	92
France	1,280.9	6	21,860	11
United Kingdom	1,208.9	7	20,520	14
Italy	1,152.1	8	20,060	16
Brazil	1,019.9	9	6,240	47
Indonesia	690.7	10	3,450	67

[1] *Rank out of 123 countries.*
[2] *Singapore ranks first with a real per capita income of $29,000.*

Source: The World Bank, *World Development Report, 1998/99* (Washington, D.C.: Oxford University Press, 1998), 190–91.

TABLE 11-11   *Growth Indicators for Selected Countries, 1965–1996 (% average annual growth)*

Country	GNP	Per Capita GNP	Agriculture	Industry	Services	Exports
Argentina	1.2	−0.3	1.3	1.0	2.4	4.8
Brazil	4.6	2.4	3.5	4.6	5.4	1.7
China	8.5	6.7	4.3	11.0	11.1	11.1
France	2.7	2.1	1.9	0.9	2.7	2.0
India	4.5	2.3	2.8	5.4	5.5	6.1
Indonesia*	6.7	4.6	3.9	9.1	7.5	5.6
Japan	4.5	3.6	−0.1	4.6	4.8	7.7
Korea*	8.9	7.3	2.0	13.8	9.0	16.1
Mexico	4.1	1.5	2.3	4.6	4.3	7.9
Pakistan	5.9	2.7	4.0	6.8	6.3	6.4
Russian Federation	3.3	1.7	—	—	—	—
United Kingdom	2.1	1.9	—	—	—	—
United States	2.4	1.4	4.0	1.7	2.5	5.5

* *The data do not include the East Asian currency crisis, which had an adverse effect on the economies of Korea and Indonesia. Japan, too, was adversely affected. These countries experienced low to negative growth rates.*

Source: The World Bank, *1998 World Bank Indicators* (Washington, D.C.: The World Bank, 1998), 24–26.

zation since the 1980s have led to a deterioration of the environment. The concentration of air and water pollutants is among the highest in the world. Most of the state-owned enterprises are inefficient, lose money, and operate at excess capacity. There are also problems with the state banking system. The big four state banks have had to be recapitalized at $33 billion. Then there is the future of the Communist Party. Until now economic growth has papered over its problems, including corruption and poverty. When international poverty standards are used, 57.8 percent of its population live on less than $2 a day.

SUMMARY

Beginning in late 1978, the leaders of China have tried to move the economy from an inefficient Soviet-style centrally planned economy to a more market-oriented economy, but still within the framework of Communist Party control. They have permitted the creation of a wide variety of small-scale enterprises in services and light manufacturing and have opened the economy to increased foreign trade and investment. The result has been a quadrupling of the Chinese GDP since 1978. At that time, China was among the world's poorest countries, with 80 percent of the population living on incomes of less than $1 a day. Today China is no longer classified as a poor country. The level of consumption has more than doubled, less than 10 percent of the population is illiterate, and the poverty rate has declined by more than one-half since 1978.

QUESTIONS FOR DISCUSSION

1.   In your opinion, will it be possible for China to maintain its high growth rate into the twenty-first century?
2.   What are some of the problems confronting the Chinese economy as it enters the twenty-first century?
3.   Discuss some of the problems that the Communist Party will have to face in the future.
4.   China can be considered one of the success stories of the twentieth century. Discuss.
5.   What are some of the problems that affect the political relationship between the United States and China?

RECOMMENDED READINGS

Economy, Elizabeth. "Painting China Green." *Foreign Affairs*, Vol. 78, No. 2 (March–April 1999): 14–19.

Hu, Zuliu, and Melvin S. Klein. *Why Is China Growing So Fast?* Economic Series No. 8. Washington, D.C.: International Monetary Fund, 1997.

Huang, Quanyu, Joseph Leonard, and Chen Tong. *Business Decisionmaking in China.* New York: International Business Press, 1998.

International Monetary Fund. *People's Republic of China—Recent Economic Developments.* Washington, D.C.: IMF, September 1997.

Jefferson, Gary, and Inderjit Singh. *Enterprise Reform in China: Ownership, Transition, and Performance.* New York: Oxford University Press, 1998.

Lardy, Nicholas R. *China's Unfinished Economic Revolution*. Washington, D.C.: The Brookings Institution, 1998.

Maddison, Angus. *Chinese Economic Performance in the Long Run*. Paris: Organisation for Economic Cooperation and Development, 1997.

World Bank. *China 2020: Development Challenges in the New Century*. Washington, D.C.: The World Bank, 1997.

NOTES

1.   Taiwan is not recognized as a country by the United States and other countries because China considers Taiwan as one of its provinces and other countries do not want to offend China by extending diplomatic recognition to Taiwan.

2.   It is estimated that overseas Chinese have contributed $2 trillion in investments in China.

3.   Angus Maddison, *Monitoring the World Economy, 1820–1992* (Paris: OECD Development Center Studies, 1997) 184, 191.

4.   The first war, called the Opium War, lasted from 1840 to 1842. The British exported opium to China in exchange for tea. Opium was England's most important export in terms of income. When China banned the use of opium, the British seized Hong Kong, bombarded Chinese seaports, and received from the Chinese an indemnity of $27 million for destroying opium. The second war, from 1858 to 1860, occurred when the British and French decided to expand their commercial interest in China. They occupied Peking and destroyed the royal palace, and again the Chinese had to compensate the invaders for the cost of the invasion.

5.   This was actually started by the Chinese. The Boxers, a group opposed to anything foreign, burned churches and killed foreign missionaries. They attacked and burned foreign embassies in Peking and murdered several diplomats. The Empress declared war on the foreign powers.

6.   The Americans were in China largely as a result of the "open door" policy advanced by Secretary of State John Hay. It meant that if other countries were given privileges in China, so should we.

7.   For years, there was no common currency in China. Each warlord would print his own currency.

8.   The Proletarian Cultural Revolution effectively set Chinese economic development back by at least ten years.

9.   The "gang of four," including Mao's wife, wanted to continue the Cultural Revolution. In a showcase trial in 1978, they were found guilty and imprisoned.

10.   Barry Naughton, "Inflation: Patterns, Causes, and Cures," in *China's Economic Dilemmas in the 1990s: The Problems of Reforms, Modernization, and Interdependence*, Vol. 1, Joint Economic Committee, Congress of the United States (Washington, D.C.: U.S. Government Printing Office, 1991), 135–44.

11.   Jiang was not expected to last long in power during the power struggle that occurred after the death of Deng Xiaoping, but he remains in office as president and Communist Party secretary. Prime Minister Zhu Rongji is the second most powerful man in China.

12.   There are now more cars in Beijing than there are bicycles. Chinese consumers have more money than they ever had before. Ordinary citizens have gained considerable personal freedom—the ability to choose their line of work and to live where they want, how they get information, and how they spend money.

13.   The five funds are for pensions, unemployment, medical, injury, and maternity. The unemployment fund is mainly employer financed and contributions range from 0.6 percent to 1 percent of wage costs.

14.   Prior to World War II, Shanghai was the financial center of Asia.

15.   The Hang Seng index of Asian securities is one of the more important indexes in the world.

16.   Harry G. Broadman, *Meeting the Challenge of Chinese Enterprise Reform* (Washington, D.C.: The World Bank, 1995), 12.

17.   Zhu Rongji, the premier of China, has cracked down on inefficient state enterprises. Some three million workers lost their jobs in 1998.

18.   Broadman, *Meeting the Challenge*, 12.

19.   Special enterprise zones are designed to attract foreign capital to China. They are specifically limited to areas created to import modern technology. Foreign investors are offered a wide variety of inducements such as preferential tax rates and less bureaucratic interference.

20.   Even though air conditioners can cost as much as six month's wages, they are considered a status symbol in China.

21.   Its Shanghai plant was nationalized by the Chinese in 1949. It was reopened in the 1970s. McDonalds operates in China under a franchise agreement. It has encouraged Chinese competition in fast foods. Chinese fast food shops sell Peking duck and rice.

22.   The World Bank, *World Development Report, 1998/99* (Washington, D.C.: The World Bank, 1998), 204–5.

23.   A hectare is 2.4 acres.

24.   *World Development Report, 1998/99*, 218–19.

25.   In 1998 China's exports to the United States amounted to $71 billion, while Chinese imports from the United States amounted to $14 billion. China ranked fourth behind Japan, Canada, and Mexico.

CHAPTER 12
India

India was once called "the jewel in the crown" when it was a part of the British Empire.[1] It was England's largest and most important colonial possession, the great outpost of British civilization. The products of England's best families and schools served in the British army and civil service in India. It was romanticized by British authors such as Rudyard Kipling, who wrote *The Jungle Book* and *Kim* and the poem "The White Man's Burden," the first lines of which are as follows:

Take up the white man's burden,
send forth the best ye breed,
go bind your sons in exile,
to serve your captive's need.[2]

Although British rule in India ended in 1947, its institutions, including the tea break, still remain intact.

India has the second largest population in the world (Table 12-1). It is expected to reach one billion people by the end of 1999. Combined, China and India have more than 40 percent of the world's population. India was created as an independent country in 1947, and the People's Republic of China was created in 1949. Both have been occupied by foreign powers. India was occupied at one time or another by the British, French, and Portuguese, while China was controlled var-

TABLE 12-1   *Economic and Social Data for India, 1997*

Population (millions)	961.2
Land area, thousands of square kilometers	2,973.2
Average annual population growth rate, 1991–1997 (%)	1.8
Real GDP ($ billions)	1,587.0
World rank out of 133 countries	5th
Real per capita GDP ($)	1,650
Rank out of 123 countries	95th
Average annual growth in GDP (%)	
1980–1990	5.8
1990–1998	5.9
World trade ($ billions)	
Exports	42.7
Imports	54.5
Poverty rate, less than $1 a day (%)	52.5
Human development index out of 174 countries	139
Life expectancy at birth (years)	61.6
World rank out of 174 countries	130
Adult literacy rate (%)	52.0
Gender related index out of 174 countries	128
Share of income (%)	
Male	74.6
Female	25.4
Gini coefficient of income inequality	29.7
U.S. coefficient	40.1

Source: The World Bank, *World Development Report, 1998/99* (New York: Oxford University Press, 1998), 191–95, 211, 219; The World Bank, *1998 World Bank Atlas* (New York: World Bank Publications, 1998), 25–33. United Nations Development Program, *Human Development Report, 1998* (New York: Oxford University Press, 1998), 129–33.

http://

For background on India, including economic information, visit the World Factbook at www.odci.gov/cia/ publications/ factbook/in.html.

iously by the Americans, British, Germans, Russians, and Japanese. China's economic development was predicated along the lines of the standard Leninist model, which emphasized the creation of heavy industry, and it is run by the Communist Party. India also followed a state-directed approach to economic development, but it has maintained democratic institutions.

However, China and India are far more dissimilar than they are similar. China has a much more homogeneous population and a generally common language, while India has a very heterogeneous population and a number of languages and religions, both of which create political instability.[3] China has no such problem. India risks becoming fragmented into a number of parts.[4] This is far less likely in China. The Chinese economy has outperformed the Indian economy. There is far less illiteracy and poverty in China than in India. China is now classified as a lower middle income country, while India is still classified as a poor country. China and India became independent nations at about the same time, but as Tables 12-2 and 12-3 indicate, regardless of the criteria used, China has done better.

Year	China	India
1950	614	597
1955	818	665
1960	878	735
1965	945	785
1970	1,092	878
1975	1,250	900
1978	1,352	972
1979	1,420	900
1980	1,462	938
1981	1,494	978
1982	1,582	994
1983	1,697	1,045
1984	1,886	1,062
1985	2,084	1,096
1986	2,700	1,127
1987	2,369	1,158
1988	2,586	1,246
1989	2,649	1,296
1990	2,700	1,316
1991	3,832	1,360
1992	3,098	1,348

TABLE 12-2

GDP per Capita for China and India, 1950–1992 (Real 1990 $)

Source: Angus Maddison, *Monitoring the World Economy, 1820–1992* (Paris: OECD, 1997), 204–5.

A HISTORY OF INDIA

The British influence on India, which lasted for some two hundred years, cannot be minimized. First, India's legal system is based on the British-based common law, which dates back to the Norman Conquest of England in 1066. Precedents in common law countries, including India, provide the stability necessary for people and businesses to plan future actions. Second, the English language is used extensively in India. Third, India's educational system is patterned after the British educational system, even the elite public schools, which are models of Eton and Harrow. The great majority of Indian students who study abroad attend universities in England and the United States. Their culture is oriented toward the West. India's political system is also a product of British rule. It is a democracy, with free elections and the active participation of major political parties.

England and Mercantilism

Mercantilism was a trade theory that formed the foundation of economic thought from about 1500 to 1800. According to mercantilist theory, countries should export more than they import, and if successful, would receive the value of their trade

TABLE 12-3
GDP Indices for China and India, 1950–1992 (1913 = 100)

Year	China	India
1950	111.5	128.4
1955	165.4	156.5
1960	194.6	191.1
1965	224.6	228.2
1970	297.0	284.5
1975	380.6	327.5
1978	429.6	378.0
1979	457.2	358.1
1980	476.6	381.8
1981	493.4	406.8
1982	530.1	422.1
1983	577.0	453.5
1984	649.8	470.2
1985	727.7	495.9
1986	779.9	520.0
1987	853.2	544.5
1988	946.7	598.1
1989	984.8	633.7
1990	1,017.2	668.7
1991	1,082.4	703.5
1992	1,201.5	711.9

Source: Angus Maddison, *Monitoring the World Economy, 1820–1992* (Paris: OECD, 1997), 158–59.

surpluses in the form of gold from the country or countries that ran deficits. To export more than they imported, governments established monopolies over their countries' trade. Colonial possessions were used to support this trade objective. First, the colonies supplied many commodities that the mother country would otherwise have to purchase from another country, thus having to expend gold. Second, the colonial powers sought to run trade surpluses with their colonies as a way to obtain revenue. They did this not only by monopolizing colonial trade but also by preventing the colonies from engaging in manufacturing. Thus the colonies had to export less highly valued raw materials and import more highly valued manufacturing products.

Countries that embraced mercantilist policies were Portugal, Spain, England, France, and the Netherlands. All were sea powers. The Portuguese were the first to develop contact with India, establishing possession in the western part of the country in 1511.[5] The Portuguese were followed into India by the Dutch East India Company, which established control over ports in the southern part of the country around 1600. However, the two major protagonists in India, as in North America, were the British and the French. The British established possession at Bombay and the French at Calcutta in the early part of the seventeenth century. The two countries controlled most of India's foreign trade for one hundred fifty years through chartered monopolies. In England, the British East India Company was chartered by Queen Elizabeth and became a joint-stock company. It controlled trade with India until it was dissolved in 1833. The French had an equivalent company,[6] which had a monopoly of trade between France and India.

British Ascendancy in India

The French controlled much more territory in India than did the British, but they lost India, like Canada, to the British primarily because England had become the leading maritime power in Europe. France was engaged in wars in Europe and did not have resources to pour into Canada and India. British control over India was also made easier by the breakup of the Mogul Empire into a number of different principalities with no central control. It was easy for the British to divide and conquer, and by 1750 they were de facto rulers of much of the country. In successive wars, the British conquered the rest of India, and it became part of the British Empire. The concept of empire was confined to the establishment of law, the foundation of an administrative system, the dispensing of justice, and the creation of a tax system. India served as a market for British manufactured products and sent cotton and other raw materials to England.

Independence of India, 1947

The movement for Indian independence from England dates back to the nineteenth century. Certain reforms made by the British to provide India with more autonomy did not go far enough, and various separatist groups formed in India around the end of the nineteenth century. It was not until after the end of World War I that the British became willing to give India some voice in its government, but the British maintained executive control. After the end of World War II it was only a matter of time before India would receive its independence. A campaign of civil disobedience to British authority, which had begun with Mohandas Gandhi and others during the 1920s, was initiated against England after the end of the war. In 1947 the British relinquished control of India. Eventually, India became two countries based on religion, Hindu India and Muslim Pakistan.

THE ECONOMIC AND POLITICAL DEVELOPMENT OF INDIA

India was the center of British imperial rule in Asia, so when it achieved its independence in 1947, certain economic and political institutions were a carryover from British rule. The cities of Bombay, Calcutta, and Madras were the business and financial centers of India and were also the centers of politics and government administration. The infrastructure consisted of good railroads, trunk roads, and a modern communications system plus a centralized administrative system. The medium of the English language provided the means for the political and cultural unification of the country. Education facilities were in place. In the cities, educa-

http://

Links to women's issues in India can be found at www.census.gov/ipc/www/publist.html#WID.

tion in high schools, colleges, and universities had expanded rapidly since the founding of universities in the cities of Bombay, Calcutta, and Madras in 1857. An engineering school was also established in 1886.

However, there was also a downside to freedom and independence, for a number of problems still remained. When India drafted its constitution in 1950, 80 percent of the wealth of the country was held by 2 percent of the population. The great majority of Indians lived in rural areas, and most were poor and illiterate. They lived and worked on small farms, using antiquated farm implements that hadn't changed in centuries. The infrastructure in the rural areas was poor. Medical facilities were inadequate, so there was a high rate of infant mortality. Even so, the high birth rate in the rural areas contributed to the ever-increasing rate of population growth. The lot of women was particularly bad. More were likely to be illiterate than men, and they had few rights.[7]

Government

The government established by the Constitution of 1950 follows a federal pattern, with specific powers divided between state governments and the central government. India consists of twenty-four states, each with its own language and culture. The Indian Constitution is based on the British Magna Carta and on the French and American Constitutions. The ideals of liberty, equality, and fraternity are taken from the French Constitution, while the notion of a secular state and a federal republic of states is taken from the American Constitution. The legislature in India is just like the British system, with the prime minister as the head of the government and the source of executive power. There is a Parliament headed by a president who presides over a bicameral legislature. There are also a Cabinet and a Supreme Court, which is the highest judicial body in India.

Executive Power.   The executive power of government in India technically is held by the president in New Delhi, the capital of India, and by state governors. These ceremonial heads of state have the power to assent to bills passed by the legislature and brought to them for consideration, and they also have the right to return to the legislature bills they feel should be reconsidered. The president and the governors also summon the legislatures into session, and they address the legislatures on problems facing their respective governments. But they have no real executive strength. That is held by the prime minister of India and the heads of the cabinets of the national and state governments. The prime minister has authority until such time as he or she recommends to the president that Parliament be dissolved and new elections be held.

Legislative Power.   Legislative power in the central government and in the state governments follows the British form of government. The Indian Parliament is made up of two houses that are similar to the British House of Commons and House of Lords. The lower house, the Lok Sabha (House of the People), is made up of 520 members, and the upper house, the Rajya Sabha (Council of States), of no more than 250 members. The upper house is by no means as important as the lower house for purposes of legislation. Like the British House of Lords, it is not subject to dissolution and functions as a continuous body. It serves as a repository for a large number of India's elder statesmen. Members of the lower house are elected by direct vote; members of the upper house are elected by state legislatures.

Judicial Power.   The Indian judicial system is somewhat similar to that of the United States. The Supreme Court is the highest court in India. It is headed by a chief justice, who is joined by no more than seven associates. Judges of the Supreme Court are appointed by the president after consultation with such of the judges of the state supreme courts and the high courts as the president deems necessary. The Supreme Court is the final interpreter of the Constitution and is the final court of civil appeals. At the state level, there are high courts that hold full legal powers within their particular states, with the exception of those cases where the Supreme Court has jurisdiction. The governor in each state, in consultation with the high court, appoints district judges within the state.

Bureaucracy.   India inherited from England an efficient administrative system. The old Indian civil service was a model to the world because it selected intelligent persons who were expected to be competent.[8] They were also expected to assume responsibility for administration over any level of operation in government. Indian civil service personnel moved in their careers from a subordinate office in a district up to district and divisional administration in the states, then up to positions of responsibility at the central government level. For many years, civil service positions were held only by the British, except for minor positions at the local level, which were held by Indians. This began to change after World War I, when more Indians began to enjoy positions of authority. After independence from England, a new Indian civil service simply followed an established administrative framework.

ECONOMIC DEVELOPMENT AFTER INDEPENDENCE

After India became an independent nation, the leaders of the country beginning with Jawaharlal Nehru were faced with a number of problems. The first was to create a new economic order that would lessen India's dependent relationship with England, where it had continued to send raw materials in return for manufactured goods. The Indian economy was underdeveloped, with resulting low standards of living for the great majority of the population. Eight percent of the people were illiterate. The riots and destruction that accompanied the partition of India and Pakistan were costly in lives and in property damage and had brought the country to an economic standstill.[9] So something had to be done to develop a new economic order. The result was the development of a state-directed economy based on economic planning.

Economic Planning

Contrary to what some people may think, India is not a communist country even though it had close ties with the former Soviet Union. It preferred to call itself a democratic socialist country and to emphasize the welfare state. There were both a public sector and a private sector. Many Indian industries were state-owned. There was reliance on broad-scale economic and social planning. Economic planning was more similar to the French indicative form of planning than to the Soviet imperative type of economic planning, and like France, India is a capitalist country with a considerable amount of state ownership of industry.[10] Control over credit allocation gave the planners control over the direction of planning objectives. India relied on five-year plans.[11] A planning commission was responsible for developing plan objectives. As in the Soviet model, reliance was placed on input-output tables to determine the consistency of the plan.[12]

The First Five-Year Plan (1951–1956).   Under this plan, priority was given to increasing agricultural production, rehabilitating the railroad system, and starting river valley developments to increase irrigation and the supply of electric power. Some attention was given to the revitalization of rural Indian life through a community development program. The development of industries such as cement, paper, chemicals, and light engineering was emphasized. Government monetary policy was aimed at maintaining price stability. Financial support for the development of agriculture and industry came from both the government and private sectors of the economy and from foreign aid, mostly provided by the United States.

The Second Five-Year Plan (1956–1961).   The government announced in 1956 that its objective was to create a mixed economy in which government enterprise would carry out activities essential to the state. Private enterprise would carry out the rest. However, a greater emphasis was placed on the public sector than on the private sector. The Second Five-Year Plan was more ambitious than the first, giving much greater emphasis to improving transportation and communications and the development of electric power. Another goal was to increase the production of iron and steel through the construction of new steel mills, with technical assistance provided by West Germany and the Soviet Union.

The Third Five-Year Plan (1961–1966).   The major objective of this plan was to increase the production of food grains, cotton, oil seeds, jute, and sugar cane. A second objective was to increase the generation of electric power. A third objective was to increase the production of such industrial products as steel, aluminum, cement, and pig iron. Target goals were set. For example, food grains were to be increased from 75 million tons in 1961 to 105 million tons in 1966, and the output of cotton was to increase from 5.4 million bales in 1961 to 7.2 million bales in 1966.[13] Finished steel was to be increased from 2.6 million tons in 1961 to 6.9 million tons in 1966. In the social welfare area, an objective was to introduce health care into the rural areas of India, along with the improvement of education facilities.

The Fourth Five-Year Plan (1966–1971).   The third plan met with some reversals. Even though agricultural harvests showed some improvement, India's population continued to grow at a rate of more than 2 percent a year, well above plan estimates.[14] There were also wars with China and Pakistan. Industrial construction proceeded at a lower rate than called for in the plan. The Fourth Five-Year Plan and the annual plans stressed agriculture because India had experienced a broad-scale famine for the first time in twenty years. Emphasis was placed on the output of such industrial products as fertilizer and equipment meant for agricultural use. Efforts were to be intensified to complete factories in the process of construction and to improve export potential.

The objective of the four five-year plans was to convert a poor, primarily agricultural and traditional economy to a richer, dynamic, industrial, and modern nation—and to do so in a generation or two. Growth was to expand employment, reduce the unevenness in the distribution of income and wealth, and provide more equality of opportunity. Public investment was supposed to increase total investment, which would increase growth and employment. Public enterprises would replace some private enterprises and would replace profit with social gains. Changes in people's activities and in their motivation and attitudes were assumed to be logical derivatives of planning programs, but as in the Soviet Union, it didn't work out that way.[15]

In 1967 the government decided to end the fourth plan because India's development record did not match what had been expected in the plans even though much outside assistance had been received. The United States had provided development loans and grants to the extent of $6.5 billion over the period 1951–1969, most of which was in agricultural commodities. The World Bank was also a major participant in providing loans to India during the four plans to the extent of $2 billion. The Soviet Union also was associated with the Indian growth effort, providing loans and technical assistance. Altogether, some $13 billion was poured into India between 1951 and 1967, but the end result was average growth rates well below expectations.[16] India's food deficit also exceeded expectations, and its dependence on foreign assistance, particularly the provision of food grains, had increased.

Nationalization of Industry

A major wave of nationalization occurred in India after India's national elections of 1971. Jawaharlal Nehru, leader of the Congress Party of India, envisioned the creation of a socialist economy, which he held to be compatible with a democratic society.[17] He rejected capitalism along with its underlying principles of private property, private profit, and income inequality. He recognized that class conflict was inherent in society, but he did not agree with the Marxist view that violence should be used to overthrow capitalism. Instead, he wanted to achieve a transition through democratic means to a mixed economy where economic planning would allocate resources. As Nehru and the Congress Party became the dominant political leader and party in India, nationalization of industry became the instrument of state control over the Indian economy.

The government had nationalized life insurance companies in 1956 and the major commercial banks in 1969, with the stated objective of creating a socialist society.[18] In 1971 the government nationalized general insurance companies, but more important was the nationalization of the coal industry. In October 1971 some two hundred coal mines and coking ovens were taken over by the state; in May 1972 the coal mines were nationalized. The rationale for nationalization of the coal industry was to integrate its output to the production of iron and steel, which was also put under state control, as was copper. The cotton textile industry, India's oldest and largest industry, contributing some one-fifth of the country's national income, was also nationalized. The industry had experienced serious financial problems during the 1960s, and many factories had closed by the end of the decade. In agriculture, the wholesale wheat trade was nationalized with the objective of socializing the distribution of grain.

The Government Dominance in Industry.   By 1975 the Indian government was dominant in key sectors of the economy. As Table 12-4 indicates, it had a 95 percent or larger share in many industries. In terms of employment in 1977, 70 percent of all Indian workers were employed in the public sector, while 30 percent were employed in the private sector. In only three areas—agriculture, manufacturing, and wholesale/retail trade—did private employment exceed public employment. Public employment in the coal industry amounted to 97 percent of its labor force; it was 100 percent in insurance, 75 percent in banking, 90 percent in construction, and 95 percent in the public utilities. In terms of gross domestic

TABLE 12-4
Industries in Which the Indian Government Accounted for 95% or More of Production

Manufacturing
  Paper
  Chemicals and chemical products
  Drugs and pharmaceuticals
  Petroleum products
  Electrical equipment and machinery
  Basic and nonferrous metals
  Transportation equipment
  Fertilizers
Minerals
  Fuels
  Metallic minerals
  Nonmetallic minerals
Other Areas
  Banking and insurance
  Transportation and communications
  Commercial energy

Source: Baldev Raj Nayar, *India's Mixed Economy* (Bombay, India: Popular Prakashan, 1989), 378.

capital formation during the 1970s, the public sector share ranged from a high of 52 percent in 1976 to a low of 41 percent in 1970. However, the bulk of gross domestic savings for the private sector averaged 80 percent of total saving for the period 1950–1980.

The major wave of nationalization took place during 1969–1973. It had a generally deleterious effect on the economy.[19] Inflation and food shortages caused industrial unrest. Business was alienated by nationalization and the restrictions placed on the private sector. The rich and middle-class peasants turned against the government because it had nationalized the wheat trade. Strikes occurred in the public sector and were put down by the police and the Indian army. A state of emergency was declared by Prime Minister Indira Gandhi in June 1975.[20] Making an effort to appeal to every disaffected group in India, she stated that the government had no intent of continuing its nationalization policies. Nevertheless, the government nationalized the oil industry by acquiring Esso and Shell, thus gaining control over 95 percent of the industry in India.[21]

India in the 1980s

The process of nationalization was finished by 1975. State control over key sectors of the Indian economy, particularly heavy industry and banking and insurance, had been established. Prime Minister Gandhi and her Congress Party were voted out of office in 1976, but the reason was political, not economic. When she returned to power in 1980, her ideological approach had changed. The country experienced a balance of payments crisis that demonstrated that it could not finance its energy needs without increasing its exports.[22] Foreign trade had been largely ignored during the process of economic development, and foreign investment in India had been made unwelcome. Its production apparatus had been denied technological modernization through a restrictive policy on the import of technology. Thus, it had to provide a more outward bias to its largely inward-based economy.

Nevertheless, no real change in the structure of the Indian economy occurred. In terms of investment, the public sector was favored over the private sector. Moreover, the economic infrastructure, which was a monopoly of the public sector, had reached a state of crisis. The Sixth Five-Year Plan (1980–1985) emphasized the development of energy, improvement of transportation facilities, and irrigation and flood control. What change did occur was a relaxation on investment by the private sector in certain areas of industry. Although still under bureaucratic control and monitoring, the private sector was allowed to increase its investments in core industries, such as chemicals, drugs, ceramics, and cement. The government also opened to the private sector areas of industrial activity, such as oil exploration and power development, that were previously closed to it.[23]

After Mrs. Gandhi's assassination in 1984, her son, succeeding her as prime minister,[24] continued the policies implemented by his mother and the Congress Party in the early 1980s. These involved a relaxation of controls placed on private enterprise in the area of investment and the setting of performance-based standards. However, not much changed and government control over the economy continued. At the same time there was a pronounced shift in Chinese economic strategy that began in 1978 and continued during the 1980s. This strategy involved a greater reliance on market-driven forces, with more freedom for private enterprise to function. Moreover, India had fallen out of favor with the West, but particularly with the United States, while China gained in favor and attracted the foreign investments that India needed for its economic development.

Why, then, did India's economy not perform well between 1950 and 1990? Efficiency and growth were stultified for three main reasons:[25]

1. Industry and trade were controlled by an all-powerful state bureaucracy that regulated market entry and import competition. It penalized unauthorized expansion of capacity; it required licenses to perform many types of business activity; and it controlled most aspects of investment and production.

2. While other countries were expanding their foreign trade, Indian development policy was doing just the opposite. It did not use the exchange rate mechanism to promote exports, and it protected home markets through the use of high tariffs and import quotas. Countries with a much smaller industrial base than India's exported far more manufactured goods and eventually passed India in the size of their manufacturing sectors. India's share of world exports fell from 2.1 percent in 1950 to 0.4 percent in 1980.

3. A large public sector reduced overall efficiency and productivity. The central government controlled 244 enterprises, most of them overstaffed for political reasons. Few budget constraints, and few incentives to make these enterprises profitable, contributed to a fiscal and foreign exchange crisis in the 1980s that forced India into near bankruptcy and required loan assistance from the International Monetary Fund (IMF).

Since 1951 India's industrial development has been, and still is, promoted within a planning framework. While government-controlled monopolies were responsible for supplying inputs to the infrastructure and heavy industry, the activities of the private sector were controlled by the government through the use of industrial and import licensing. In accordance with national priorities as set forth in the economic plan, the government issued industrial licenses for installing equipment in different production units. The import licensing system was used to control the allocation of foreign exchange to different sectors of the economy. The importer had to present to the relevant government authority an industrial license for the good produced and, based on the category of the good to be imported, was issued an import license.

Operating within a highly regulated economic environment the Indian private sector often obtained its supply of essential inputs from the public sector, either directly from state-owned enterprises or indirectly, as in the case of imported inputs from foreign trade organizations. For reasons that are now well established, the supply of these inputs was not fully responsive to demand conditions. Administered pricing and lack of economic incentives to managers and workers hindered

http://

Population projections for India can be seen at www.census.gov/ipc/www/idbsum.html.

the appropriate responses of state-owned enterprises to market signals. In addition, restrictive trade policies in the guise of protecting infant industries and economizing on foreign exchange involved the imposition of quantitative restrictions on imported inputs. Shortages in government-regulated inputs occurred at the same time that high rates of capacity underutilization in manufacturing industries occurred.

India in the 1990s

The world changed dramatically during the early 1990s, leaving India more of a backwater country. Two major developments occurred, the most important of which was the collapse of communism. The Soviet Union, which had maintained close economic and political ties with India for more than thirty years, was no more. A number of new countries, including the Russian Federation, were created out of it and wanted foreign aid from various international lending sources to implement their conversion to market economies. Many claimants were in line for limited loanable funds. A second development was the collapse of India's international credit rating. Borrowing from public or private sources was impossible without first making an effort to reform the Indian economy. Tax reforms were needed and restrictions on foreign trade had to be loosened.

http://

Information on India's economic and trade policies is available at www.state.gov/ www/issues/ economic/ trade_reports/ south_asia97/ india97.html.

Tax Reforms.   Tax reforms have been an integral part of economic reforms in India. The overall objectives of the reforms were to stimulate economic growth by encouraging savings and investment through tax incentives. Marginal tax rates had been around 50 percent for both corporate and personal income taxes. Excise taxes could reach as high as 125 percent, and import duties averaged 80 percent. Corporate tax rates were reduced to 35 percent. A capital gains tax of 20 percent was introduced. The personal income tax rate was reduced to 30 percent. Efforts have also been made to improve tax administration and to reduce tax evasion. A vast array of tax incentives are in place to promote exports and foreign capital inflows. Excise taxes have been reduced on most manufactured goods. Maximum tariff rates were reduced from 400 percent in 1991 to 40 percent in April 1997.

Foreign Trade.   India pursued an import-substitution policy since independence in 1947, which was based on the notion of attaining self-reliance. It sought to encourage agricultural development and to develop home industry. Restrictions were placed on foreign direct investment in India. The import licensing system was used as a mechanism to control the allocation of foreign exchange to different sectors of the economy. The importer had to present to the relevant government authority an industrial license for the good produced, and based on the category of the good to be imported, was issued an import license. Exchange controls and import licenses, although used to some extent, have been liberalized, and foreign direct investment in India has been encouraged. Investment policy includes approval for majority foreign equity participation of up to 100 percent in certain priority industries, in particular technology. In certain industries free repatriation of profits is permitted.

Banking.   Commercial banks are the most important financial intermediaries in India. Prior to 1969 all banks, with the exception of the Central Bank of India and its seven branch banks, were privately owned. Under the Nationalization Act of 1969, the fourteen largest private sector banks were nationalized, and a further six were nationalized in 1980. The commercial banking system is dominated by the public sector banks. While private sector banks and foreign banks were allowed to operate alongside the public banks, their operations were strictly regulated. How-

ever, in 1993 new private and foreign banks were allowed to enter the banking market. Nevertheless, the public sector banks account for 84 percent of commercial bank assets in India. Their financial performance has been very poor and their profitability low. All of the most important nationalized banks have received capital injections from the government to enable them to compensate for bad loans.

A program of far-reaching financial sector reform was introduced in India during the 1990s to enhance the productivity and efficiency of the banking and financial systems. The vast majority of state controls over interest rates have been removed and more stringent regulatory standards over lending have been introduced. However, there is still considerable state regulation. Banks are required to lend a minimum of 40 percent to agriculture, small-scale industry, and the export sector. Before the reforms, these loans were made at below market rates of inter-

est, with the difference being paid by the Indian government. Although these subsidies have been eliminated by the reforms, the overall priority sectors remain the same.

AN EVALUATION OF THE INDIAN ECONOMY

It was said that the hybrid system of Indian capitalism and socialism failed because it combined the worst of both systems, failing to deliver either economic growth or social welfare. It constrained the growth of the private sector by allowing it to expand only with government permission. Government control was omnipresent. Foreign trade was controlled by import quotas and high tariffs, access to foreign exchange was limited, controls were placed on land use and on trade in farm products, and heavy industry was owned by the public sector. The Indian bureaucracy increased in size and became increasingly more corrupt. During the 1980s, the government began to push for higher economic growth by increasing its borrowing from abroad. The end result was little gain in economic growth but an increase in the foreign debt to double what it was in 1980.[26]

India's economic plans failed to promote high rates of economic growth and an increase in per capita income. A goal was to double per capita income between 1950 and 1975, but it failed. Meanwhile, its performance was surpassed by every other country in East Asia. Table 12-5 compares the performance of India, Pakistan, Indonesia, and South Korea for 1950–1992. Pakistan, too, had achieved its

TABLE 12-5   *A Comparison of Real per Capita GDP by Years for Selected Asian Countries, 1950–1992 (1990 $)*

Year	India	Pakistan	Indonesia	South Korea
1950	597	650	874	876
1955	665	644	1,016	1,197
1960	735	661	1,131	1,302
1965	785	795	1,096	1,578
1970	878	995	1,239	2,208
1975	900	992	1,531	3,131
1978	972	1,071	1,753	4,124
1979	900	1,078	1,783	4,350
1980	938	1,155	1,870	4,103
1981	978	1,210	1,957	4,318
1982	994	1,250	1,876	4,553
1983	1,045	1,294	1,938	4,991
1984	1,062	1,320	2,028	5,431
1985	1,096	1,376	2,034	5,777
1986	1,127	1,408	2,116	6,426
1987	1,158	1,453	2,181	7,107
1988	1,246	1,516	2,265	7,829
1989	1,296	1,542	2,394	8,294
1990	1,316	1,595	2,525	8,977
1991	1,360	1,650	2,639	9,645
1992	1,048	1,642	2,749	10,010

Source: Angus Maddison, *Monitoring the World Economy, 1820–1992* (Paris: OECD, 1997), 204–5.

independence from England. Indonesia, which was a Dutch possession, also became an independent country. South Korea's real per capita GDP increased tenfold during the period, while India's real per capita GDP has not even doubled. Pakistan, which broke away from India in 1947, has done somewhat better.

It has been argued that India has done far better than it did when it was a part of the British Empire.[27] This is true. Living standards have improved, and people are living longer. But other countries that were formerly colonies of England have done better. An example is Malaysia. From 1965 to 1996, the average annual growth rate for Malaysia was 4.1 percent compared to 2.3 percent for India. Taiwan, a colonial possession of Japan, increased its real per capita GDP between 1950 and 1992 from $922 in 1950 to $11,590 in 1992. In 1997, fifty years after independence, 52.5 percent of the people in India live on less than $1 a day and 48 percent are illiterate.

The real per capita GNP of India in 1990 was $350; in 1997 it was $370. China had a real per capita GNP of $370 in 1990; in 1997 its real per capita GNP was $860. When real per capita GNP is measured in terms of international purchasing power parity, India's real per capita GDP amounted to $1,660 compared to $3,070 for China. Table 12-6 shows the ranking of India on the United Nation's Human Development Index. In 1997 India ranked 139th out of 174 countries, showing little

TABLE 12-6   *Human Development Index for India, 1997*

Human development index, rank out of 174 countries	139
Gender development index, rank out of 174 countries	128
Prevalence of child malnutrition, percent of children under 5	66
Adult illiteracy rate, people 15 and above (%)	
Male	35
Female	62
Population below international poverty line of less than $1 a day (%)	52.5
Population below $2 a day (%)	88.8
Children not reaching grade 5 (%)	38
Gender empowerment index, rank out of 102 countries*	95

* *This index refers to women's participation in the economic and political life of a country.*

Sources: United Nations Development Program, *Human Development Report, 1998* (New York: Oxford University Press, 1998), 130, 133, 135, 145; The World Bank, *World Development Report, 1998/99* (New York: Oxford University Press, 1998), 192, 193, 194.

change since the index was first developed. It ranks in the bottom fourth of the countries. The literacy and poverty rates have not improved.

SUMMARY

India based its economic development after it achieved its independence in 1947 on a series of economic plans. It became a state-directed economy with a mixture of state and private enterprises. The state was heavily involved in every phase of economic activity. The 1990s brought about a series of economic reforms designed to promote efficiency, liberalize foreign trade, and encourage foreign investment. Nevertheless, the state is still heavily involved in the economy, and there has been little effort to privatize state-owned industries. Corruption and political instability are problems that the country has to confront, along with high rates of poverty and illiteracy. Although the birth rate declined in the 1990s, the population of India is expected to double in the twenty-first century.

QUESTIONS FOR DISCUSSION

1.   Compare China and India in terms of their level of economic development. Why has China outperformed India?
2.   Discuss the economic and social problems that continue to retard economic development in India.
3.   What legacy did British rule leave India? Was it on balance good or bad?
4.   What were some of the reasons for the generally poor performance of the Indian economy during 1950–1990?
5.   How was economic development in India similar to that in the Soviet Union?

6. The Indian government pursued an import substitution approach to economic development after its independence. What did this approach involve and why was it unsuccessful?

NOTES

1. India represented the largest market for British exports in the nineteenth century and was the leading source of raw materials.

2. The poem was written by Kipling in 1899. The British felt that they had an obligation to export their culture throughout their empire.

3. Ninety-nine different languages and dialects are spoken in India. Although Hinduism is the dominant religion in India, there are a number of others.

4. Separatist movements exist in India, and include Sikh separatists, Kashmiri separatists, and Tamil separatists.

5. They remained there until India declared its independence in 1947.

6. In the latter part of the 1800s, the British East India Company began to sell opium grown in India to China. It was the company's and England's leading export.

7. Even today, women are killed in rural India because they commit adultery or their dowry is not large enough.

8. The British civil service has had far more prestige than the United States civil service. People from the British aristocracy went into civil service, particularly the army.

9. During the first three days of Indian independence 750,000 people were killed in riots between Hindus and Moslems.

10. French indicative planning involves a set of directives that are used to guide the private sector as well as the public sector of the economy.

11. An annual plan was also published for each year by the state planning commission. It was released at the beginning of each fiscal year, which for India was July.

12. Economic planning in the Soviet Union consisted of physical input–output planning and financial planning. Input–output planning meant that the economy was divided up into a number of branches, each of which was assigned inputs and outputs. These branches were presented on a grid showing how much each economic sector bought and sold from other sectors.

13. Wilfred Malenbaum, *Modern India's Economy* (Columbus, Ohio: Merrill, 1971), 91–102.

14. The projected growth was 1.3 percent a year.

15. Malenbaum, *Modern India's Economy*, 62–63.

16. Ibid., 57.

17. Nehru had studied in England and observed the class divisiveness that existed in the country. He was influenced by the teachings of Beatrice and Sidney Webb, leaders of the Fabian Socialist movement who advocated a democratic approach to socialism.

18. Baldev Raj Nayar, *India's Mixed Economy* (Bombay, India: Popular Prakashan, 1989), 297.

19. Ibid., 330–31.

20. Indira Gandhi was the daughter of Prime Minister Nehru.

21. The government also ran the Coca-Cola corporation out of India because it refused to give the government its formula for the soft drink.

22.   OPEC increased the price of oil, and oil imports as a percentage of export exchange earnings increased from 30 percent in 1978 to 90 percent by 1980.

23.   It is necessary to point out that state-owned banks owned equity shares in the major private firms. For example, banks owned 40 percent of the largest private firm in India and 42.5 percent of the common stock of the second largest firm. In some firms bank ownership was more than 50 percent.

24.   This means that since independence in 1947 India was ruled for most of the time by a family dynasty beginning with Nehru, continuing with his daughter, and then continuing with her son, who might still be prime minister of India today had he not been assassinated while campaigning for reelection.

25.   The World Bank, *World Development Report, 1995* (New York: Oxford University Press, 1995), 200.

26.   Jagdish Bhagwati, *India in Transition* (Oxford: Clarendon Press, 1993), 23.

27.   Bhagwati, *India in Transition*, 46–67.

CHAPTER 13

Latin America: Argentina, Brazil, and Mexico

There are twenty-six countries in Latin America. These countries account for one-half of the land area of North and South America.[1] Most of them share a number of economic, political, and social characteristics. First, with the exception of Brazil and a few other countries, all are former colonies of Spain.[2] Second, except for Brazil, Spanish is their common language. Third, Catholicism is their common religion. Fourth, political instability and corruption have been characteristic of Latin America, and military dictators have been in power throughout much of the twentieth century. Democratic governments, for the most part, have been unstable. Fifth, economic development has been very uneven during the twentieth century, and Latin American countries have lagged well behind East Asian countries in their rate of economic growth. Finally, during the 1990s the countries have followed the wave of privatization that occurred throughout the world, and they are privatizing their state-owned industries.

Latin America is a direct product of the mercantilism that prevailed in the Western European countries and their overseas dependencies for three hundred years.[3] Mercantilism was a theory of government that posed the following question: What is the right policy for a government to pursue to increase its national wealth and power? The answer involved a strong central government and the acquisition of colonies to provide wealth for the home country, hopefully gold and silver,[4] and to buy its goods in return. Trade was regulated and trading rights were

289

given to companies to develop foreign markets. The British East India Company and the Dutch East Indies Company are examples.

Spain was the model for all mercantilist countries. Its explorers and soldiers in Mexico and South America opened up a great supply of gold and silver. The import of gold and silver enabled the Spanish kings to spend for military operations. Spain became the most powerful country in Europe during the sixteenth and seventeenth centuries, and the world's leading seapower. Trade with the colonies was tightly regulated; for example, imports of wine were prohibited to protect home producers. To ensure proper control, trade was required to pass through designated seaports. The colonies were ruled by viceroys sent from Spain, and the whole administration was run by people sent from Spain. Typically, positions in the colonies were granted by the king in return for monetary contributions. In return, viceroys and others exploited the colonies.

Spain had a far greater cultural impact on its colonies than either England or Holland. First, Spanish became the common language; this was not true in the British and Dutch possessions. Second, the Roman Catholic religion became the religion of the Spanish colonies; this was not true of the British and Dutch colonies either. In Latin America, conquest and religion went hand in hand. As the soldiers conquered, the Jesuit priests converted. The cross and the sword operated simultaneously. Finally, racial miscegenation occurred under Spanish rule. The Spaniards intermarried freely with the native Indian population, creating a new social class called mestizos. In the British and Dutch empires, miscegenation, particularly through marriage, was almost nonexistent.

Canada and the United States, particularly the latter, were also products of mercantilism. The British and the French fought for the possession of both countries. They wanted the same thing Spain wanted—to export finished foods to the colonies and to receive raw materials from them. British trade with the American colonies was tightly regulated from London. Trade between England and the American colonies had to be carried on British ships. British goods had to be bought by the colonies and were taxed. The colonies were ruled by governors sent over from England. Eventually the British ousted the French from Canada and it became a colonial possession of England. Thus, both North America and South America became the colonial possessions of England, France, Holland, Portugal, and Spain. Eventually most of the colonies achieved their independence through revolution.

When the twentieth century began, the five most important countries in North America and South America were Canada, the United States, Mexico, Brazil, and Argentina. The United States and Canada were colonies of England; Mexico and Argentina were colonies of Spain; and Brazil was a colony of Portugal. Different cultures were imposed on these countries. The British found a land lightly populated and encouraged settlement; the Spanish found a land densely settled and intermarried. The British migrated by the thousands to the eastern and central parts of the United States; Spain discouraged the emigration of Spanish families to the New World, thus depriving its colonies of needed skills. The Spanish Inquisition pursued heresy in its colonies. This may have been good for religious purity, but bad for knowledge.

TABLE 13-1 *Comparisons of GDP per Capita for the United States, Canada, Argentina, Brazil, and Mexico, 1900–1994 (1990 $)*

Year	Canada	United States	Argentina	Brazil	Mexico
1900	2,758	4,096	2,756	704	1,157
1910	3,564	4,648	3,822	795	1,380
1915	4,011	4,870	3,244	826	1,435
1920	3,878	5,559	3,473	937	—
1925	4,112	6,290	3,919	980	1,616
1930	4,558	6,220	4,080	1,061	1,371
1935	3,743	5,473	3,950	1,164	1,406
1940	5,086	7,018	4,161	1,302	1,556
1945	6,758	11,722	4,356	1,352	1,808
1950	7,047	9,573	4,987	1,673	2,085
1955	7,445	10,948	5,237	1,923	2,416
1960	8,459	11,193	5,559	2,335	2,781
1965	10,173	13,316	6,371	2,461	3,265
1970	11,758	14,854	7,302	3,067	3,659
1975	14,158	16,060	8,132	4,230	4,408
1980	16,280	18,270	8,245	5,246	5,004
1985	17,954	20,050	6,912	4,902	5,141
1990	19,599	21,866	6,581	4,812	4,997
1992	18,159	21,558	7,616	4,637	5,112
1993	18,300	21,972	7,985	4,739	5,045
1994	18,350	22,569	8,373	4,862	5,098

Source: Angus Maddison, *Monitoring the World Economy, 1820–1992* (Paris: Organization for Economic Cooperation and Development, 1997), 201, 202, 203, 204.

Table 13-1 presents a comparison of the five countries as measured by real per capita GDP during the twentieth century. Canada at the beginning of the century was still a part of the British Empire. In 1900 Canada and Argentina had the same real per capita GDP. Both countries are located in temperate climates and have large land areas. Both countries had about the same incomes from 1900 to 1935. From 1940 Canada began to pull away from Argentina. Brazil's greatest gain was during the 1970s, which encouraged it to increase its foreign debt by borrowing from abroad. Mexico's problem was similar to Brazil's. Its prosperity during the 1970s was based on an increase in oil revenues, as oil prices rose throughout the world. Mexico borrowed from abroad, pledging increasing oil revenues as collateral. But oil prices decreased during the 1980s, adversely affecting the Mexican economy.

THE ECONOMY OF LATIN AMERICA

The 1980s were years that the Latin American countries would like to forget. The economic gains made during the 1960s were largely canceled out by the poor performance of the 1980s. Inflation was rampant in many of the countries. During the good times of the 1970s when world prices were high for such products as coffee and petroleum, Mexico, Brazil, and other Latin American countries borrowed heavily in the world capital markets, pledging future revenue from coffee and petroleum for debt repayment. However, world market prices for these and other products plummeted during the 1980s, leaving the Latin American countries with a debt they could not repay. The rate of economic growth for most of the Latin American countries was negative during the 1980s, and unemployment and social unrest increased.

Inflation

In addition to stagnant economic growth, inflation was a problem during the 1980s for the Latin American economies. Argentina, once the dominant economic power in Latin America, is a case in point. It experienced inflation running at a rate of 1,000 percent a year or higher, until the economy collapsed and a new currency unit was introduced. The political pendulum swung between government conservatives and reformers, with the result that much of the national wealth was exported abroad. Political instability was exacerbated by Argentina's loss of the Falkland Islands war with Great Britain.

Foreign Trade.   For most of the twentieth century the economies of Latin America have been dependent on the exportation of natural resources. In Mexico and Venezuela the natural resource was oil. Most of the revenue from its sale to other countries was used to finance government expenditures. Chile depended on exports of copper and nitrates to support its economy, and Bolivia depended on the production and export of tin. Other countries that were not endowed with mineral resources depended on the production of agricultural products to support their economies. Brazil became the world's largest producer of coffee, and Argentina, given its land area and climate, became one of the world's largest exporters of beef, wheat, and other products.

But the terms of trade were usually against these countries. When world prices of oil were high, Mexico and Venezuela prospered; when they were low, Mexico and Venezuela suffered. When world coffee prices were high, the economies of Brazil and Colombia were the beneficiaries; when world coffee prices declined, the economies of the two countries declined and social unrest occurred. Bolivia benefited when world prices for tin were high, but Bolivia was a high-cost producer of tin and other countries replaced it. Chile was one of the world's largest producers of copper and nitrates, but world demand declined for these products during the 1930s, and the Chilean economy was devastated.

Population

Although the birth rates in most of the Latin American countries have declined dramatically since the 1970s, they still are high and create major problems. First, the rate of economic growth has to continue to expand to provide more jobs for an ever-increasing labor force. Second, the infrastructure of the major Latin American cities is not adequate to support urban migration. In most large cities, the water supply and educational and health facilities are becoming more inadequate as urbanization continues. Urbanization also places a burden on both national and municipal governments' social welfare expenditures. In Mexico, for example, over 65 percent of municipal government revenues comes from transfers from the budget of the Mexican government. Third, an ever-increasing population compounds the problem of unemployment and underemployment in both urban and rural areas.

Foreign Debt

Foreign debt became the number-one problem for most of the Latin American countries during the 1980s and threatened their economic and political stability. The foundation of the problem was laid during the 1970s when Latin American governments, including those of Brazil and Mexico, buoyed by optimistic forecasts for the prices of their commodity exports, borrowed heavily from foreign banks, usually at floating interest rates. The total Latin American debt to foreign banks increased from $115 billion in 1978 to $280 billion by 1984. The optimistic forecasts on commodity prices proved wrong, and the burden of the foreign debt increased as exports declined. In August 1982 Mexico declared its inability to service its debt, and in November 1982 Brazil found itself in the same position. Costa Rica declared a moratorium on its debt payment.

By 1986 Brazil's foreign debt was one-third of its GNP and three times larger than its exports. In Mexico, foreign debt was larger than its GNP. As export values fell in world trade, the Latin American countries had to reduce social welfare expenditures for the poor to meet interest payments on the foreign debt. However, interest arrears had increased from $100 million in 1980 to $8.1 billion in 1987 and $10.6 billion by 1989. Meanwhile, social unrest increased in Latin America. Several international plans were developed to help the Latin American debt problems. The Baker Plan of 1985 involved the use of International Monetary Fund (IMF) loans to foster economic growth. IMF credit increased from $3.0 billion in 1982 to $18.2 billion in 1987. The countries had to make structural changes in their economies; Argentina, for example, changed its whole monetary system. In 1989 the Brady Plan was designed to ease the debt burden of the Latin American countries by direct debt reduction and stretching out the remainder over a longer time.

Political Instability

Income inequality, poverty, and corruption create an excellent prescription for political instability, which has been a characteristic of Latin American life during the twentieth century. Just about every country has been involved in revolutions, wars, and border disputes. In Venezuela, there were two military coups in 1992 and 1993, where attempts were made to overthrow the government. Fighting occurred

http://

For information on population issues in Latin America, visit www.undp .org/popin.

http://

Additional information on politics of Latin American countries can be found at www .tradeport.org/ts/ countries.

for several days and several hundred people were killed. In 1993 President Carlos Andres Perez was impeached for corruption and misuse of funds, and General Hugo Chavez, who led the army in one failed coup, was jailed for two years and was also accused of taking bribes. Chavez then became president of Venezuela in 1998. Peru, which has been one of the more unstable countries in the world, had to contend with the Sendero Luminoso (Shining Path), a radical Marxist group, in a civil war that lasted for years. El Salvador, Guatemala, and Mexico have had to deal with opposition groups that are protesting the enormous dichotomy between rich and poor and the corruption that primarily benefits the rich.

Income Inequality

Income inequality is greater in Latin America than in other areas of the world. As Table 13-2 indicates, income distribution is skewed toward the top 10 percent of the population. Incomes received by the top 10 percent are 50 times greater than incomes received by the bottom 10 percent. In the United States it is 19 times, and in Sweden it is 5.5 times. In Chile, for example, the top 10 percent of the population received 46.1 percent of income while the bottom 80 percent of the population received 39 percent. In Brazil the top 10 percent of the population received 47.9 percent of income while the bottom 80 percent received 35.8 percent of income. The Gini coefficient, which measures the extent of income inequality, is high in Latin America. The Gini coefficient for Brazil is 60.1 compared to a Gini coefficient of 25.0 for Sweden. The United States, which has the most unequal income

TABLE 13-2   *Income Inequality in Latin America, 1997 (% share of income)*

Country	Gini Coefficient	Lowest 10	Lowest 20	Highest 20	Highest 10
Brazil	60.1	0.8	2.5	64.2	47.9
Chile	56.5	1.4	3.5	61.0	46.1
Colombia	57.2	1.0	3.1	61.5	46.9
Guatemala	59.6	0.6	2.1	63.0	46.6
Mexico	50.3	1.6	4.1	55.3	39.2
Nicaragua	50.3	1.6	4.2	55.2	39.8
Panama	56.8	0.5	2.0	60.1	42.5
Paraguay	59.1	0.7	2.3	62.4	46.6
Peru	44.9	1.9	4.9	50.4	34.3
Venezuela	46.8	1.5	4.3	51.8	35.6
Sweden	25.0	3.7	9.6	34.5	20.1
Canada	31.5	2.8	7.5	39.3	23.8
United States	40.1	1.5	5.8	45.2	28.5

Gini coefficient: 0 = perfect income equality; 1 = perfect income inequality.

Source: The World Bank, *World Development Report, 1998/99* (New York: Oxford University Press, 1998), 198–99.

distribution of the developed countries, has a Gini coefficient of 40.1, well below the coefficients for any Latin American country.

Income inequality has had a deleterious effect on Latin America in several ways. First, the wealthy have invested little of their monies in their countries, instead preferring to invest in the United States and Europe. Fortunes are often made in real estate speculation, which does not create wealth. Second, the import substitution policy that Argentina, Mexico, and other Latin American countries used to achieve economic development primarily benefited the rich. By contrast, the export-oriented development strategy, followed by the East Asian countries, put them on a far higher growth path. Third, investment in human resources has been greater in East Asia than in Latin America because the demand for educated workers is greater. A stronger demand for educated workers elicits a greater supply, thus reducing income inequality.

Poverty

Although the extent of poverty is less in Latin America than in Africa and Southeast Asia, it still exists and creates social unrest. One thing that has exacerbated the problem of poverty is outmigration of people from the rural areas to the cities in search of employment opportunities. This has created slums like the favelas of Rio de Janiero, where many people do not have access to sanitation facilities or drinking water. Table 13-3 presents the extent of poverty in Latin America. In Chile, which is one of the richer nations of Latin America, 38.5 percent of the population live on less than $2 a day. One of the poorest countries in Latin America is Guatemala, where 77 percent of the population lives on less than $2 a day.

TABLE 13-3   *Poverty in Latin America, 1998*

Country	People Living on Less Than $1 a Day (%)	People Living on Less Than $2 a Day (%)
Brazil	23.6	43.5
Chile	15.0	38.5
Colombia	7.4	21.7
Costa Rica	18.9	43.8
Ecuador	30.4	65.8
Honduras	46.9	75.7
Mexico	14.9	40.0
Nicaragua	43.8	74.5
Panama	25.6	46.2
Peru	28.4	66.5
Venezuela	11.8	32.2

Source: The World Bank, *World Development Report, 1998/99* (New York: Oxford University Press, 1998), 196–97.

Corruption

History has shown that corruption is endemic to Latin America, dating back to the time of the conquistadores. More recently, during the 1990s the presidents of Brazil, Ecuador, and Venezuela resigned following charges of corruption. The scandals led to rioting and street demonstrations in the capitals of all three countries. It is almost an article of faith that any Latin American politician worth his, and sometimes her, salt will amass at least a small fortune before leaving office. Corruption has resulted in a waste of resources and has had an adverse effect on economic development.

Table 13-4 presents an index of corruption for 21 countries. Out of 85 countries ranked, a majority of the Latin American countries were ranked in the bottom half or bottom third. The table ranks the countries from 1 through 85, with the least corrupt being number 1, and with a number of countries tying for a particular position. The United States, which prides itself on being the world's moral watchdog, ranked 17th.

Militarism

The question can be posed: What does Latin America produce? The answer is generals and more generals. The military has generally dominated the political life

TABLE 13-4
International 1998 Corruption Index for Countries

Country	Country Rank	Score
Denmark	1	10.0
Finland	2	9.6
Sweden	3	9.5
Canada	6	9.2
Singapore	7	9.1
United Kingdom	11	8.7
Germany	15	7.9
United States	17	7.5
Japan	25	5.8
Italy	39	4.6
Peru	41	4.5
Brazil	46	4.0
Mexico	55	3.3
Argentina	59	3.0
Guatemala	59	3.0
India	66	2.9
Ecuador	77	2.3
Venezuela	77	2.3
Colombia	79	2.2
Honduras	83	1.7
Paraguay	84	1.5

Source: *Transparency International* (Berlin, Germany, September 22, 1998).

of Latin America for two hundred years. During the twentieth century, one or more generals has ruled every Latin American country. Elected governments have been overthrown by the military, but in some cases military rule has been better than civil rule. In Mexico the Mexican Revolution of 1910 was fought by rival political factions, each led by a general. Argentina has been dominated by the military during most of the century, sometimes with disastrous results. Human rights are usually a casualty of military rule, as witnessed by events in Chile after the Allende government was ousted during the 1970s and thousands of people suspected of having ties with Allende were shot.

Often democracy has proved to be no better than military rule. Latin America has little history of democratic institutions. Three hundred years of Spanish and Portuguese rule did not exactly equip Latin America for democratic rule. Books that expressed any opposition to the status quo were banned from Latin America. Authoritarian rule was the norm in Latin America, and it continued to be so after the Spaniards left. During the twentieth century corruption and mismanagement have been all too evident among elected leaders. In Mexico the same political party has dominated Mexican politics for seventy years, and there has been little military involvement in the political process. In Argentina the military intervened on several occasions to prevent civil war. Sometimes, it has been with the tacit agreement of the United States. Mexico, Chile, and Nicaragua are examples.

ARGENTINA

In several ways Argentina is similar to the United States. It is located in a temperate climate. It was colonized by immigrants from Europe, most of whom came from Italy and Spain, but others came from England and France. In terms of land area it is the eighth largest country in the world. It is as large as Western Europe. Its population of 36 million is small compared to the land area. (See Table 13-5 for economic and social data.) Like the United States during most of its history, Argentina was primarily an agrarian economy dependent on the export of cattle and grain. Agricultural products still account for an important part of total exports. Politically, Argentina has patterned itself after the United States in that it always has been a democracy. Unfortunately for Argentina, it has often been honored in the breach rather than the observance. Additionally, Argentina was never a colonial possession of Spain.[5]

Argentina has never lived up to its economic potential, given its geographic, cultural, and climatic advantages. It began the twentieth century with the highest real per capita GDP of all of the Latin American countries. Its real per capita GDP was larger than Japanese or Russian real per capita GDP and on a par with Germany's. It was at a much higher level of economic development than either Brazil or Mexico. By 1913 it had become the second largest beef and grain exporting nation in the world. Its economy was also helped by World War I because it was able to sell its products to the Allied nations. In 1930 its real per capita GDP was twice that of Japan's and almost three times that of the Soviet Union. In 1950 its real per capita GDP was still twice that of Japan's. No other Asian nation was close.

http://

Economic, political, and social data and information on Argentina can be found through www.un .org, www.imf.org, and www.state .gov/www/issues/ economic/index .html#Topics.

TABLE 13-5

Economic and Social Data for Argentina, 1997

Population (millions)	35.7
Land area (thousands of kilometers)	2,737.0
Average annual population growth, 1990–1997 (%)	1.3
Real GDP (% billions)	355.0
World rank out of 123 countries	19
Real per capita GDP	9,950
World rank out of 123 countries	30
Average annual growth in GDP (%)	
1980–1990	−0.3
1990–1998	4.5
World trade ($ billions)	
Exports	27.0
Imports	27.9
Poverty rate (% earning less than $1 a day)	—
Human development index out of 174 countries	36
Life expectancy at birth	72.6
World rank out of 174 countries	44
Adult literacy rate (%)	96.2
Gender related index rank out of 174 countries	48
Share of earned income (%)	
Male	77.9
Female	22.1
Gini coefficient	—
U.S. coefficient	40.1

Sources: The World Bank, *World Development Report, 1998/99* (New York: Oxford University Press, 1998), 191, 195, 211, 219; The World Bank, *1999 World Bank Atlas* (Washington, D.C.: World Bank Publications, in press), 29–42; United Nations Development Program, *Human Development Report, 1998*, (New York: Oxford University Press), 129–30.

Political Instability

A major factor contributing to the below-average performance of the Argentine economy is political instability. During much of the century, Argentina has been controlled by a land-based oligarchy that has manipulated the political system for its own advantage. The government was almost overthrown in 1919 when riots that caused the deaths of hundreds of people were put down by the Argentine army. Social unrest occurred during the 1930s because the Depression had an adverse impact on the Argentine economy, which was based on the export of beef and grain. In 1930 President Irigoyen was overthrown by the military, supported by the landed oligarchy. Authoritarian rule prevailed during the 1930s and 1940s where the army controlled the elections. During the 1930s Argentina also adopted an import-substitution policy to develop home industry.

The Peron Years, 1945–1955.   Juan Peron is overshadowed by his wife Eva, or Evita, who upstaged him and became immortalized in the stage and movie versions of *Evita*. Between the two of them, they almost destroyed the Argentine economy. Peron and a succession of other generals ruled Argentina from 1932 to 1973. He nationalized foreign industries, diverted resources for agriculture into pay increases for the workers, and played on class hatreds between the unions and the landed oligarchy. He succeeded in ruining agriculture and was overthrown by the military in 1955. Free elections were eventually held, but a winner who was favorable to Peron was ousted by the military. In 1973 with the economy in disarray, Peron returned from exile, became president, died in office, and was succeeded by his second wife Isabel. Argentina was in crisis, and the military returned to power. A succession of generals ruled from 1976 to 1982, when the military decided to divert attention from the economic and political problems at home by invading the Falkland Islands (or Malvinas Islands to the Argentines) and promptly got whipped by the British.[6]

The 1980s.   The 1980s were an unmitigated disaster for the Argentine economy. Real per capita GDP, which was $8,245 in 1980, had declined to $6,581 by 1990. South Korea's real per capita GDP was half of Argentina's in 1980; by 1990 it was higher, as was Taiwan's. In Latin America Chile would close the per capita income gap of some $3,000 in 1980 and would eventually go ahead of Argentina.[7] Three major problems confronted Argentina in the 1980s: economic stagnation, inflation, and a large foreign debt that was a result of rising world oil prices. The average growth rate in Argentina during the 1980s was −2.2 percent. The consumer price index increased from 163 percent in 1993 to 3,079 percent in 1989. The Argentine currency unit, the astral, increased from an exchange rate of 2.6 astrals to $1.00 in 1982 to 8,753 astrals to $1.00 in 1988, and by 1990 the Argentine foreign debt amounted to 88 percent of its GNP.[8] The Argentine government collapsed, and in a special election in 1989, Carlos Menem was elected president and is still in office.

The 1990s.   A number of reforms were introduced by the Menem government. The astral was replaced by the peso and pegged to the American dollar to stabilize its exchange rate ($1 = 1 peso). The Menem government committed itself to a program of economic stabilization, privatization, encouragement of foreign investment, reduction of tariffs, and export promotion. Argentina, along with Brazil, Paraguay, and Uruguay, formed a customs union called MERCOSUR (Mercado Commun del Sur) in 1991 that reduced trade barriers among the four countries, and is much like NAFTA. Between 1991 and 1994 the Menem government privatized 90 percent of the state-owned industries, and between 1989 and 1992 it abolished all price controls. These and other reforms increased the Argentina growth rate during the early 1990s. Table 13-6 presents the growth rate of the Argentine economy during the 1990s as measured by annual changes in real GDP. Table 13-7 presents additional figures on the domestic economy. Foreign direct investment in Argentina increased on an average of $3 billion a year during 1992–1995.

An economic crisis developed in Argentina during the latter part of 1998 and the first part of 1999. The main cause was economic problems in Brazil occasioned

TABLE 13-6
Real Increase in GDP for
Argentina in the 1990s (%)

1990	−1.3
1991	10.5
1992	10.3
1993	6.3
1994	8.5
1995	−5.8
1996	4.8
1997	8.6
1998	4.3
1999	−0.2*

* *Estimate.*

Source: International Monetary Fund, *World Economic Outlook, October 1998*
(Washington, D.C.: IMF, 1998), 180.

TABLE 13-7   *Argentina's Domestic Economy*

	1997	1998*	1999*
Income, production, and employment			
Nominal GDP ($ billions)	310	330	343
Population (millions)	35	35.5	36
Change GDP (%)	8.0	5.0	4.0
GDP per capita ($)	8,900	9,300	9,500
Labor force (thousands)	13,800	14,000	14,200
Unemployment (%)	14.9	13.5	13.0
Money and prices			
Domestic savings (% of GDP)	21.0	21.0	22.0
Investment (% of GDP)	23.0	24.0	25.0
Consumer prices (% increase)	0.3	0.5	1.0
Average exchange rate (peso/US$)	1.0	1.0	1.0

* *Data for 1998 and 1999 are revised embassy projections.*

Source: *USDOC Survey of Current Businesses*, GOA, Ministry of Economics, Washington D.C., 1998.

by financial crises in East Asia and Russia. The Brazilian growth rate declined to
0.2 percent in 1998 and a projected −4.8 percent in 1999; about 35 percent of
Argentina's exports go to Brazil. In early 1999 President Menem proposed that
Argentina drop its peso, which is on a one-to-one parity with the U.S. dollar, and
replace it with the U.S. dollar. That would mean that Argentine salaries, car payments, store purchases, and other financial transactions would be denominated in
dollars. In the short run, this is possible but not probable. It is also possible, but
not probable that other Latin American countries may want to do the same thing.

BRAZIL

Brazil is the largest country in Latin America in terms of land area and population. Its land area of 8.5 million kilometers is three times that of Argentina and a little less than the size of the United States. Its nominal GNP of $773.4 billion in 1997 ranks it first among the Latin American countries and eighth in the world in 1997 (Table 13-8). When its GNP is converted into comparable world standards by using purchasing power parity, its real GNP amounted to a little more than $1 trillion, which ranked it ninth in the world, not far behind France, Italy, and the United Kingdom. Brazil is richly endowed with both mineral resources and agricultural resources. It is the world's largest exporter of coffee. Like all Latin American countries, it possesses three common characteristics. The first is extreme inequality in the distribution of income, wealth, and economic opportunity. The second is the difficulty in building democratic institutions, and the third is that it has never lived up to its economic potential.

Population (millions)	163.4
Land area (thousands of square kilometers)	8,456.5
Average annual population growth, 1990–1997 (%)	1.4
Real GDP (billions)	1,019.9
World rank out of 123 countries	9
Real per capita GPD ($)	6,240
World rank out of 123 countries	47
Average annual growth in GDP (%)	
1980–1990	2.8
1990–1998	3.1
World trade ($ billions)	
Exports	52,641
Imports	63,293
Poverty rate (% earning less than $1 a day)	23.6
Human development index out of 174 countries	62
Life expectancy at birth (years)	66.6
World rank out of 174 countries	107
Adult literacy rate (%)	83.3
Gender related index rank out of 174 countries	56
Share of earned income (%)	
Male	70.7
Female	29.3
Gini coefficient of income inequality	60.1
U.S. coefficient	40.1

TABLE 13-8
Economic and Social Data for Brazil, 1997

Sources: The World Bank, *World Development Report, 1998/99* (New York: Oxford University Press, 1998), 191, 195, 211, 219; The World Bank, *1999 World Atlas* (Washington, D.C.: World Bank Publications, in press), 24, 32; United Nations Development Program, *Human Development Report, 1998* (New York: Oxford University Press, 1998), 128–32.

History of Brazil

Brazil was the only Western hemisphere possession of the Portuguese empire, which also included possessions in Africa and Asia. They were considered much more important than Brazil, and most of the wealth came from them. Unlike Spain, Portugal did not maintain strict control over its Latin American possession, because it did not yield much wealth. Brazil was primarily colonized by slaves and Portuguese Jews, who were run out of Portugal by the Inquisition. When sugar became an important export around 1750, Portuguese interest in its colony began to pick up, some semblance of rule was established from Lisbon, and an economic system based on mercantilism was established. Viceroys were sent from Lisbon to rule Brazil and the Jesuits established Catholicism. The Portuguese intermarried with the natives, just as the Spaniards did in their colonies.

Brazil achieved its independence from Portugal about the same time that Mexico and other Latin American countries achieved their independence from Spain, in the mid-1800s. It retained most of the institutions of Portugal, including its language, law, and religion. It even had a king during much of the nineteenth century. Dom Pedro I ruled from 1822 to 1831, and Dom Pedro II ruled from 1830 to 1889. Brazil distinguished itself during the nineteenth century by fighting wars with Argentina, Paraguay, and Uruguay. However, slavery was abolished and Brazil became a leading exporter of coffee. Its economy made little gain during the nineteenth century. Its real per capita GDP in 1820 was $670 and by 1900 it had increased to only $704. Both Argentina and Mexico had higher real per capita GDPs than Brazil in 1900. A democratic form of government was established in Brazil in 1889, which provided for the direct election of a period of four years and was patterned along the lines of the U.S. government.

The history of Brazil in the twentieth century is similar to that of other Latin American countries. The military has dominated. The most important leader of Brazil was General Getulio Vargas, who was the dictator of Brazil for nineteen years. During this period, he reoriented the Brazilian economy away from reliance on the export of agricultural products to reliance on an import substitution policy that stressed the development of industry and the export of industrial goods. Other leaders who followed Vargas continued his policies. Between 1965 and 1980, the Brazilian economy was one of the fastest growing in the world, with an average annual growth rate of 9.4 percent. Real per capita GDP, which was $1,673 in 1950, increased to $5,276 in 1980. With few exceptions, the military ruled the Brazilian economy from 1930 to 1985, but provided more stability than their Argentine counterpart.

The 1980s represented hard times for Brazil, just as they had for other Latin American countries. It had borrowed heavily from abroad during the 1970s when times were good, but the Arab oil embargo of 1973 had an adverse impact on the Brazilian economy. It doubled the price Brazil had to pay for oil imports from $6.2 billion in 1973 to $12.6 billion in 1979. The Arabs increased the price of oil a second time and there were dramatic increases in world market interest rates. The Brazilian foreign debt, which was $12.5 billion in 1973, increased to $92 billion by 1980. During the 1980s Brazil had severe economic problems. The average annual increase in consumer prices during the decade was 400 percent. The terms of trade for Brazilian exports during the decade were negative, and real wages declined by an average of three percent. The Brazilian currency, the cruzeiro, was devalued during the 1980s, which aided Brazilian exports, but the current account was negative for most of the years. (The real is now the currency in Brazil.)

Brazil in the 1990s

During the 1990s Brazil has followed the same economic path as Argentina and Mexico. It jettisoned much of the state intervention in the economy by privatizing banks and state-owned industries. It developed a free economy open to the world market and foreign investment and reduced tariff barriers. The Brazilian economy was adversely affected during the 1990s by the Mexican currency crisis of December 1994, and the financial crises in East Asia in 1997 and Russia in 1998, which had a negative impact on Brazil's foreign reserves. The deficit in its balance of payments resulted in a $41.5 billion loan from the IMF to help bolster the economy. Table 13-9 presents the growth rate of the Brazilian economy during the 1990s as measured by annual changes in real per capita GDP, and Table 13-10 provides additional economic data. The performance of the economy in 1998 and 1999 is much poorer than for the rest of Latin America as a whole.

Brazil has a number of problems as it enters the twenty-first century. One is corruption. It ranked 46 out of 85 countries in Transparency International's corruption index. As a recent example, in April 1999 an official of the Brazilian central bank allegedly made money on the devaluation of the Brazilian real by using insider information to send $1.6 million abroad before the devaluation.[9]

Another of Brazil's problems is poverty. Its distribution of income and wealth is among the most unequal of all countries in the world. Although the government has raised taxes on wealth and increased expenditures for education and other

http://

Economic data for Brazil is available at www .worldbank.org/ data/countrydata/ countrydata.html.

1980–1989 (average)	2.8
1990	−3.7
1991	1.0
1992	−0.5
1993	4.9
1994	5.9
1995	4.2
1996	4.2
1997	2.8
1998	0.2
1999	−4.8*

TABLE 13-9
The Performance of the Brazilian Economy in the 1990s as Measured by Changes in Real GDP (%)

* *Estimate.*

Source: International Monetary Fund, *World Economic Outlook, October, 1998* (Washington, D.C.: IMF, 1998), 180.

TABLE 13-10   *Brazil's Domestic Economy*

	1997	*1998*[1]	*1999*[1]
Nominal GDP ($ billions)	803.0	806.1	809.0
GDP real growth rate (%)	3.0	2.0	3.0
GDP per capita ($)	5,022	4,950	4,940
Federal government nominal Spending (% of GDP)[2]	27.8	30.8	35.3
Annual inflation (%)[3]	4.3	6.0	5.0
Unemployment rate (%)[4]	5.7	8.0	8.0
Foreign exchange Reserves ($ billions)	52.1	68.0	65.0
Average exchange rate (for $1)	1.077	1.160	1.250
Foreign debt ($ billions)	193.7	220.0	240.0
Debt service/exports (%)	27.2	27.6	26.8
U.S. economic/military assistance ($ millions)[5]	12.0	13.0	14.2

[1] *1998 = estimate; 1999 = projection.*
[2] *Ministry of Finance forecast.*
[3] *Inflation as measured by the National Consumer Price Index (INPC) produced by the Brazilian Institute of Geography and Statistics (IBGE).*
[4] *Open unemployment as percent of economically active workforce.*
[5] *No military assistance; USAID figures only.*

Source: USDOC Survey of Current Business, GOA, Ministry of Economics, 1998.

social services that benefit the poor, it remains to be seen how successful their efforts will be.

The challenges of global trade also face Brazil. A wide fluctuation in the competitiveness of Brazil's manufacturing exports occurred during the 1980s and first half of the 1990s and contributed to a significant loss in market shares, particularly in developed countries. The competitiveness of Brazilian exports has to improve. The lack of qualified workers to produce high-value-added manufactured goods is a major problem because of a low educational level of much of the population.[10]

MEXICO

History of Mexico

Mexico was conquered by Hernan Cortez in 1519, and the presence of gold and silver made it Spain's most important colonial possession. Mexico was the most important part of Spanish mercantilist policy because it provided the gold and silver that enabled Spain to become the dominant military power in Europe during the seventeenth century. Catholicism was introduced into Mexico by the Jesuits, who also spread their influence into the southwestern part of the United States. Those who came from Spain to Mexico did so to get rich, not to work. That was left to the natives, who were put to work mining for gold and silver. Wealth opened many doors, and bribery of officials sent by Spain to administer laws became the accepted way of getting things done.

Mexico achieved independence from Spain in 1821 and inherited a legacy that continues to this day. Bribery was the way to get things done, and the wealthy, rather than the meek, inherited the earth. Authoritarian rule continued under various generals, ranging from Santa Anna, who lost half the land of Mexico to the United States, to Porfirio Diaz, who ruled Mexico for thirty-four years and who gave half of the wealth of Mexico to the United States.[11] Free elections, which were rare, were always rigged in favor of the government. In 1910 the Mexican Revolution occurred, an event that defines the Mexico of today. It was fought over who was to control Mexico, the Catholic Church and foreign business interests. It eventually led to the creation of a political system that still exists now.[12]

In some ways Mexico changed during the twentieth century; in others it did not. It has achieved the status of an upper-middle income country. Its nominal and real per capita incomes are among the highest in Latin America and are on a par with those of countries such as Hungary and Poland. It is industrialized. It is the leading foreign trade country in Latin America. It also has a number of the problems that are endemic to Latin America. Corruption is pervasive at all levels of society, there is extreme inequality in the distribution of income and wealth in Mexico, and poverty is widespread. Even though elections are relatively free from election fraud, the same political party, the PRI, has remained in office for most of the twentieth century.

http://

Statistics on Mexico can be found at www.inegi.gob .mx/homeing/ estadistica/ estadistica.html.

Economic Development Strategy

Mexico began to pursue economic development during the early 1950s through a policy of import substitution. The intent was to make Mexico less dependent on foreign imports, particularly those from the United States. It relied heavily on state intervention in the economy. Exchange controls, import quotas, and other exchange restrictions designed to limit imports were used by the Mexican government to promote the development of home industries by making imports more expensive. In 1962 a decree was passed that required foreign automobile plants operating in Mexico to go beyond simple auto assembly to car manufacturing in Mexico or leave the market. The import-substitution strategy compelled Mexican consumers to pay higher prices for imported goods or buy domestic products. In effect, consumers were forced to subsidize the development of Mexican industry through the substitution of domestic products for foreign products.

The government intervened in the economy in other ways. It passed regulations that restricted foreign firms to minority stock ownership positions. In 1982 the government nationalized the banking industry. In addition, it owned the oil industry, most of the public utility industry, and subsidized government enterprises that were in direct competition with private enterprises in the same industry, such as steel production. It exercised control over credit allocation through Nacional Financiera, a government-owned bank. Its function was and is to promote industrial development by allocating credit to industries that are a part of the government's program for economic development. Its main source of revenue has been from the government budget and interest on loans. By the 1980s the extent of government intervention in the economy was greater in Mexico than in any other Latin American country.

Oil and the 1980s.   Oil was discovered in the state of Tamaulipas in the latter part of the nineteenth century and has dominated the economy of Mexico ever since.[13] It has been a blessing and a curse to Mexico. Wide swings in world oil prices have brought the country boom and bust. On more than one occasion, the United States has intervened militarily and behind the scenes to protect American oil interest in Mexico. In 1938 the government nationalized British and American oil properties and created a state-owned oil company, Petroleos Mexicanos (PEMEX), which is supported out of the national budget. It is also a source of corruption, where workers have had to pay to get jobs and directors have accepted payments from suppliers of oil equipment.

During the 1970s world oil prices skyrocketed because of the Arab oil embargo. Mexico and Nigeria, two of the world's most important oil-exporting countries, benefited enormously. Oil revenues flowed into Mexico and were spent on social welfare programs. Assuming that there would be no tomorrow, Mexico borrowed heavily from abroad, using future oil revenues as a pledge to repay the loans. However, the price of oil, which had been as high as $35 a barrel in the 1970s, declined at the time world interest rates were rising. In 1982 an international debt crisis occurred when Mexico declared it could not meet interest payments on its debt. Mexico requested a rescheduling of its debts and a moratorium on repayment principal. The International Monetary Fund (IMF) agreed to provide a loan package only if foreign banks agreed to allow Mexico to reschedule its debt. This was called the Baker Plan. A later plan, called the Brady Plan, allowed for the writing off of part of the debt by Mexico.

The 1980s has been called the "lost decade" for Mexico and other Latin American countries. In Mexico the peso was devalued against the dollar so many times that it was almost worthless. The growth rates for Argentina and Mexico were negative. Mexico and the other Latin American countries reversed their economic development strategies based on import substitution. They lowered tariff barriers, sought free trade agreements with their neighbors, privatized their industries, and positioned their economies to compete internationally. Restrictions against foreign investment were dropped. Emphasis has been placed on lessening dependence on the export of one or a few products and increasing industrial exports. Subsidies to industries have been reduced or eliminated outright and governments, including Mexico's, have relied on restrictive monetary and fiscal policies to reduce inflation.

Mexico in the 1990s

The prelude to the 1990s began in 1988 when Carlos Salinas de Gortari was elected president of Mexico. He inherited a number of economic and social problems that had to be resolved. Economic deterioration had led to growing political radicalism. Economic growth had been stagnant throughout the decade, and the peso had declined against the dollar to the point where $1 equaled 2,461 pesos. The massive foreign debt of Mexico had to be reduced. To promote more efficiency in the Mexican economy the previous administration of Miguel de la Madrid privatized a number of state enterprises. It had inherited more than 1,000 state enterprises when it took office in 1983 and, by 1988, had sold to private investors 112 of them, mainly in cement, soft drinks, hotels, and petrochemicals. The de Gortari government continued the process of privatization, and by early 1992 Mexico had merged, liquidated, or sold 822 out of the 1,155 state enterprises and had completed the sale of 9 state-owned banks as well as steel mills and mines.

A second thing the de Gortari government did was to relax laws prohibiting or restraining foreign direct investment in Mexico. There were long-standing restrictions on investments in Mexico, dating back to the period following the Mexican Revolution of 1910. The purpose of these restrictions was to prevent American dominance in the Mexican economy. As a result of its restrictions on foreign investment, Mexico had the lowest foreign investment rate of any major Latin American country. Most restrictions on foreign investment were eliminated or relaxed by the government to attract foreign capital. Many areas of economic activity that were formerly off-limits to foreign investors were freed for investment, and the government no longer required a controlling interest in the equity of foreign subsidiaries.

The Exchange Rate Crisis, December 1994.   In December 1994 Mexico experienced a currency crisis of the first order that led to the devaluation of the peso and the near collapse of the Mexican economy. An uprising in Chiapas, a state in southern Mexico, over the subject of land distribution to the poor shook investor confidence in Mexico. Probably a more important cause of the crisis was that Mexico had a massive debt in its current account. Between 1987 and 1993 while exports rose by roughly one-half, imports increased by 100 percent. In 1993 Mexican exports amounted to roughly $50 billion, while Mexican imports amounted to $65 billion. This resulted in a loss of foreign financial reserves by the Mexican government. Finally, interest rates around the world, but particularly in Mexico, were rising, making it a less attractive place for investment.

The problem got worse in 1994. By December foreign reserves held by the government had dropped from $26 billion to $7 billion. The peso, which had been pegged to the dollar at a rate of 3.4 pesos to $1, was let loose to float against the dollar. The purpose was to stimulate Mexican exports by making them cheaper in world markets. This would help reduce the deficit in the current account. By the end of December, the peso had dropped in value to an exchange rate of 5.8 to $1. The impact of the currency devaluation on the Mexican economy and on the rest of Latin America was enormous. It shook investors' confidence in not only Mexico but also the rest of Latin America. The so-called "Tequila effect" spread to Argentina and Brazil, adversely affecting their stock markets and foreign direct investments.

To shore up confidence in the Mexican economy, the Clinton Administration provided a $40 billion assistance package to guarantee the sale of Mexican government dollar-denominated Treasury bonds to foreign investors. Mexican financial flows depend on capital from abroad, particularly the United States. Low Mexican savings rates create a trap. When Mexico's economy grows at a rate of 4.5 percent or more—levels considered necessary to alleviate poverty—it imports more goods and builds up a deficit in its current account that only capital inflows can finance. But inflows of foreign capital are based on foreign confidence in the stability in the exchange rate of the peso and short-term interest rates. The U.S. bailout required Mexico to raise short-term interest rates to attract foreign capital and to pledge oil revenue as collateral for the loan.

The Presidential Election of 1994.   Carlos Salinas de Gotari was replaced by Ernesto Zedillo, who became president. However, the election illustrated the main problem with Mexican politics: the same party, the PRI, won. Zedillo was not the first choice of the PRI. The first choice, Luis Donaldo Colosio, was assassinated in March 1994. Later, another politician was assassinated: Jose Francisco Masseau, secretary general of the PRI, was shot in Mexico City.[14] Later elections have proved to be somewhat more honest than the 1994 election. Opposition parties won governors' elections in six states, and the opposition won the mayor's race of Mexico City. National elections will be held in 2000, and the PRI will handpick its candidate to succeed Zedillo, who has not been touched by scandal. If the PRI wins, as is likely, it means the same party will have been in power since 1929.

The Performance of the Mexican Economy in the 1990s

Outside of 1995 the Mexican economy has performed well (Table 13-11). Privatizing inefficient state industries and relaxing rules limiting foreign investments has been an important factor in stimulating economic development. NAFTA has also been a key factor. In 1998 Mexico exported more than $80 billion of goods to the United States. It has a favorable trade balance with the United States. Membership in NAFTA also has increased its trade with other Latin American countries. There has also been an increase in investment from the United States in Mexico, largely because of NAFTA. Although there are still problems with rebel groups wanting economic and political reforms, the government of Ernesto Zedillo has maintained political stability and, in comparison with previous administrations, has appeared to be relatively honest. Table 13-12 presents growth rates for the Mexican economy in the 1990s, and Table 13-13 provides additional economic and social data.

Nevertheless, there are severe economic and social problems that are not easy to resolve. There is an enormous income disparity between rich and poor. Forty percent of Mexico's population, or 38 million people, live on less than $2 a day, probably an underestimation of the true extent of poverty. The highest 10 percent of income recipients have more than the bottom 60 percent. Wealth disparity is probably greater than income disparity. This situation creates a social and eco-

TABLE 13-11 *Mexico's Domestic Economy*

	1995	1996	1997	1998*	1999*
Gross domestic product ($ billions)	287	335	378	387	409
GDP growth (%)	−6.2	5.2	7.0	4.7	3.7
GDP per capita (current $)	2,741	3,312	3,591	4,135	4,625
Government spending (% GDP)	23	23	24	23	23
Inflation, Dec.–Dec. (%)	52.0	27.7	17.0	13.0	10.9
Unemployment (%)	6.3	5.5	3.7	3.5	3.4
Foreign exchange reserves, end period ($ billions)	15.3	19.1	28.1	31.5	35.0
Average exchange rate (for $1)	6.4	7.6	8.2	9.0	9.8
Debt service ratio (interest payments/exports)	17	15	13	15	12

* *Projected figures.*

Source: Bank of Mexico, *Annual Report, The Mexican Economy* (1996).
At the time of this report, there were no government projections available for 1998. Some of the information was available from private organizations.

		TABLE 13-12
1980–1989 (average)	2.3	*The Performance of the*
1990	5.1	*Mexican Economy in the*
1991	4.2	*1990s as Measured by*
1992	3.6	*Changes in Real GDP*
1993	2.0	
1994	4.4	
1995	−6.2	
1996	5.2	
1997	7.0	
1998	4.5*	
1999	5.0*	

* *Estimates.*

Source: International Monetary Fund, *World Economic Outlook, October 1998* (Washington, D.C.: IMF, 1998), 180.

nomic gulf that is unlikely to disappear. Also, social class, as is true in other Latin American countries, is based on color. The purebloods who can trace their heritage back to Spain are called criollos and are at the top of the social pyramid. Then there are the Mestizos, or mixed-bloods, who were a product of intermarriage between the Spanish and Indians, who occupy the middle, and finally there are the Indians, who are at the bottom levels of Mexican society.

TABLE 13-13   *Economic and Social Data for Mexico, 1997*

Population (millions)	94.3
Land area (thousands of square kilometers)	1,909.0
Average annual population growth, 1990–1997 (%)	1.8
Real GDP ($ billions)	770.3
World rank out of 123 countries	10
Real per capita GDP ($)	8,120
World rank out of 123 countries	35
Average annual growth in GDP (%)	
1980–1990	1.1
1990–1998	1.8
World trade ($ billions)	
Exports	95,199
Imports	97,630
Poverty rate (% earning less than $1 a day)	14.9
Human development index out of 174 countries	49
Life expectancy at birth (years)	72.1
World rank out of 174 countries	51
Adult literacy rate (%)	89.6
Gender related index rank out of 174 countries	49
Share of earned income (%)	
Male	74.3
Female	25.7
Gini coefficient of income inequality	50.3
U.S. coefficient	40.1

Sources: The World Bank, *World Development Report, 1998/99* (New York: Oxford University Press, 1998), 191, 195, 211, 219; The World Bank, *1999 World Bank Atlas* (Washington: World Bank Publications, 1999), 24, 32; United Nations Development Program, *Human Development Report, 1998* (New York: Oxford University Press, 1998), 128–32.

SUMMARY

Latin America has not yet lived up to its potential. The twentieth century was characterized by political instability, growing income inequality, and corruption. Militarism has circumvented the democratic process in Argentina and many other Latin American countries, but democracy hasn't done much better, as witnessed by corrupt elections in Mexico. Argentina, Brazil, and Mexico are the three most important countries in Latin America. It has been said that Argentina was the only country that began the twentieth century as a first world country and ended up as a Third World country. Although this statement is incorrect, Argentina has underperformed and has been left behind by countries that did not even exist at the beginning of the century. Monetary devaluations by Argentina and other Latin American countries have created inflation, lowered the real wages of the working class, and fostered political instability.

QUESTIONS FOR DISCUSSION

1. The Latin American countries based their economic development strategies in the 1950s and 1960s on a policy of import substitution. Discuss this policy.
2. What are some of the factors that are responsible for extreme income inequality in Latin America?
3. Argentina, of all the Latin American countries, had the greatest potential to develop an economy that would be on a par with that of the most developed countries today. What went wrong?
4. Compare the economies of Argentina and Brazil.
5. What impact did the 1980s have on the Mexican economy?
6. In what ways has Mexico changed in the 1990s? In what ways has it not changed?

RECOMMENDED READINGS

Edwards, Sebastian, and Moisés Naím. *Mexico 1994: An Anatomy of an Emerging Market Crash*. Washington, D.C.: The Brookings Institution, 1998.

Harrison, Lawrence E. *The Pan-American Dream*. New York: Basic Books, 1998.

Inter-American Development Bank. *Economic and Social Progress in Latin America, 1998*. Baltimore: Johns Hopkins University Press, 1998.

Lustig, Nora. *Coping with Austerity: Poverty and Inequality in Latin America*. Washington, D.C.: The Brookings Institution, 1995.

_____. *Mexico: The Remaking of an Economy*, 2nd ed. Washington, D.C.: The Brookings Institution, 1998.

OECD Economic Surveys. *Mexico*. Paris: Organisation for Economic Cooperation and Development, 1998.

Thorp, Rosemary. *Progress, Poverty and Exclusion: An Economic History of Latin America in the 20th Century*. Baltimore: Johns Hopkins University Press, 1998.

World Bank. *Argentina: Recent Economic Developments, 1998*. Washington, D.C.: The World Bank, 1998.

_____. *Brazil: Recent Economic Development, 1998*. Washington, D.C.: The World Bank, 1998.

NOTES

1. The Caribbean countries are also included in this number. New countries have been added in the Caribbean region including Belize (former British Honduras), Trinidad-Tobago, Jamaica, Grenada, Antigua and Barbuda, Dominica, and others, so that there may actually be more than twenty-six.
2. Brazil was a colony of Portugal and Portuguese is the common language. Suriname was once Dutch Guinea. Belize was once a British possession, as was Jamaica. Independence from Spain was accomplished by revolutions similar to the American Revolution.
3. There were a number of mercantilist writers. Thomas Mun is considered to be the leading English mercantilist writer; in France, it was Jean Bodin.

4.   The British, Dutch, and French were not as lucky. The British tried to find gold and silver in the American colonies; instead they found tobacco.

5.   Argentina was sparsely populated and had no gold or silver, so it was of no use to Spain. It had no markets for Spanish goods and nothing worthwhile to ship to Spain.

6.   The generals had the misfortune to run up against Margaret Thatcher, who immediately sent the military to the Falklands some 6,000 miles from England. When asked what she would do if the British failed to retake the islands, she said: "The possibility does not exist." She was right.

7.   Chile and Argentina are very similar. They were both colonized by immigrants from Europe. More Germans settled in Chile than in Argentina. Chile was endowed with more mineral resources, including copper, so it attracted American capital. In 1997 Chile had the highest real per capita GDP of all of the Latin American countries, and it is considered to be the best run country in Latin America.

8.   Inter-American Development Bank, *Economic and Social Progress in Latin America, 1992* (Baltimore: Johns Hopkins University Press, 1992), 25.

9.   *The Economist*, May 1, 1999, p. 35.

10.   In 1995 only 45 percent of Brazilians who were of the age to be in secondary schools were actually enrolled.

11.   The Treaty of Guadalupe Hidalgo, which ended the Mexican American war of 1847, gave the United States Texas, New Mexico, and the southern part of California. Diaz granted oil and other mineral concessions to American business interests, including Standard Oil, that took the wealth out of Mexico and gave little in return except to Diaz.

12.   The Catholic Church owned 70 percent of the wealth of Mexico. The revolutionaries led by Villa, Zapata, and Obregon won the revolution. The Constitution of 1917 gave Mexico ownership of mineral resources, American and British oil interests were nationalized, and a state-owned oil company called PEMEX was created. The power of the Catholic Church was broken. A political party called the National Revolutionary Party (PRN) was established, which later became the Institutional Revolutionary Party (PRI). Regardless of the name change, the same party has ruled Mexico since 1929.

13.   The state of Tamaulipas is in northeast Mexico. Its major seaport is Tampico. British and American oil interests were quick to get their hands on oil rights, and oil companies, including Standard Oil, Sinclair, Gulf, and Royal Dutch Shell, were given concessions to drill for oil. By 1910 Mexico was the leading producer of oil. The oil companies bribed government officials to get even more property rights and paid Mexican bandits to protect their properties. Billions in oil revenues flowed out of the country to pay British and American investors; the Mexican people got very little.

14.   Carlos Salinas de Gortari is accused of stealing millions of dollars while he was in office. His brother Raul is also accused of stealing millions of dollars and of having Masseau shot even though they were brother-in-laws.

CHAPTER 14

Africa: Nigeria and South Africa

Africa is the poorest continent in the world. Of the 61 low-income countries of the world (those classified as having a per capita GNP of $785 or less) 27 are in Africa.[1] Of the 44 countries of the world classified by the United Nations as having a low level of human development, 32 are in Africa. The bottom 15 countries are also African countries.[2] The life expectancy of men and women in most of the African countries is the lowest in the world. The adult literacy rate is less than 50 percent; the adult literacy rate for women is as low as 9.2 percent in Burkino-Faso and 6.7 percent in Niger. Eighteen of the African countries had a negative GNP per capita growth rate from 1980 to 1997. Finally, population growth rate is the fastest in Africa than in any other area of the world, which has had an adverse effect on economic development and the environment.

Africa is a continent with approximately 750 million people. It can be divided into two separate land areas with a totally distinct culture and population—Northern Africa, which is sparsely populated, and sub-Saharan Africa, which has most of Africa's population. Northern Africa includes such countries as Algeria, Morocco, Tunisia, Libya, and Egypt, which are predominantly Moslem. Sub-Saharan Africa includes the great majority of African countries. The Northern African countries would be classified as lower-middle-income countries and are located on the Mediterranean Sea, a factor that has fostered economic development. The sub-Saharan

http://

For economic and demographic information about Africa, visit http://infoserv2.ita.doc .gov/afweb.nsf.

countries have not been favored by either climate or geographical location, which has had an adverse effect on their economic development.[3] Heat and humidity have had a deleterious consequence: they have encouraged the proliferation of life forms hostile to humans.

CHARACTERISTICS OF AFRICAN COUNTRIES

The map of most of the colonial world was drawn by Europeans. It covered all of North America, South America, Africa, Australia, and much of Asia. Thus, all former colonies have much in common. All countries that were formerly a part of the British empire had English as their common language and their legal system is based on English common law, regardless of whether the country is Nigeria, India, Belize, or the United States.[4] All countries that were formally a part of the Belgian, Dutch, French, German, Spanish, and Portuguese empires adopted the legal system of these countries, which is code law, usually the Napoleonic code.[5] They have also adopted the language of the country that ruled them.[6] All colonies, regardless of the country to which they belonged, existed for the same reason—to supply their owners with raw materials and to serve as a market for manufactured goods.

Colonialism

Africa was the last continent to be colonized by the Europeans, even though the British, Dutch, and Portuguese had trading posts at the Cape of Good Hope as early as the 1500s. Africa was known as the Dark Continent. Very little was known about it and it possessed nothing of interest to Europeans.[7] The colonization of Africa took place during two separate periods. The first occurred around the first part of the nineteenth century, when the British and the French took possession of Northern Africa. The British added Egypt as a colony, and the French acquired Algeria, Morocco, and Tunisia. These colonies were located on the Mediterranean Sea and were of strategic importance to England and France. The opening of the Suez Canal in 1869 made Egypt the crossroads of the British empire. Owning Egypt enabled England to acquire the Sudan. Algeria and Morocco provided the troops necessary to govern France's empire.

The second wave of colonization of Africa began in the 1880s. Prior to 1878, the colonies owned by the European countries were mostly located along the sea coasts of Africa. South Africa had been settled by the British and the Dutch, where the British established the states of Natal and the Crown Colonies, and the Dutch (Boers) established the Orange Free State and the Transvaal. But imperialist rivalries among the European nations began when it appeared that Africa had something of value to offer. The Belgians discovered copper in the Congo, which became the largest copper-producing area in the world, and the British discovered diamonds and gold in southern Africa. Cecil Rhodes, who controlled the diamond interests, began to expand into other parts of south Africa and claimed them for England.[8]

The success of the Belgians and the British provoked the interests of other European countries, and the race began to grab up the rest of Africa. By this time, the British had taken most of the valuable lands in South Africa. To avoid possible wars over territory, the European countries agreed at the Berlin Conference of 1885 to divide up Africa. Five countries shared in this division. England kept what it already had, plus Nigeria, other parts of southern Africa, and the Sudan. France was given the rights to West Africa and recognition to its rights in Tunisia. Germany, which had been a country for only fifteen years, was given parts of East Africa, including the area that is now the country of Tanzania and parts of southwest Africa. Belgium got what it already had, and Portugal got what was left, including the areas that are now Angola and Mozambique.

Consequences of European Rule in Africa

There is a distinct similarity today between the problems in Yugoslavia and those in Africa. The Treaty of Versailles, which ended World War I, created Yugoslavia out of disparate parts of the Austro-Hungarian empire. Assuming that all Slavs are alike, Yugoslavia became an amalgam of Catholic Slavs, Greek Orthodox Slavs, and Moslem Slavs, all of whom harbored resentment against each other, going back for 600 years. Similarly, in Africa the European powers paid no attention to territories or societies. Tribes that had hated each other for centuries found themselves lumped together in the same colonies. When these colonies became countries, the rivalries were still there. In Burundi and Rwanda, Hutus and Tutsis have taken turns trying to exterminate each other.

The undoubted benefits brought by western medicine and sanitation had the effect of increasing the population and stressing the limited supply of land, which in some cases had already been taken up by Europeans. Landless Africans went to work for wages on European farms or in cities, thus further breaking down the traditional tribal society. In the cities they were treated as racial inferiors by the Europeans, prohibited from using the same facilities and given little in the way of housing. The economies of the colonies were run exclusively for the benefit of Europeans. The entire export and import business was in the hands of Europeans and Asians, as were the facilities for credit. Everything produced by African labor was sold at a low price; everything bought by the Africans was expensive.

European penetration quickly undermined the basis on which African society had been organized. The land in most African territories had been held in common by the whole tribe, and although the chief was responsible for its allocation, he did not own it himself. It was therefore improper for him to have granted any rights to the Europeans, which had the effect of separating the lands from his people. However, the Europeans made use of the chiefs for their own purposes, by using them to maintain law and order among the Africans and by using them to collect taxes. The chiefs were paid salaries or allowed to keep a share of the taxes. Thus, a feudal society was created by the Europeans instead of the communal society that had once existed.

Each colonial country imposed its educational system on the Africans. For a long time, primary education was the responsibility of the missionaries and public education was neglected. Education as a rule involved the conversion of the natives to Christianity, which made the process of Westernization easier. Secondary education was made available for a select few, and graduates were allowed to attend universities in England, France, and the other European countries. Colleges were created in Africa, but their curricula were based on European patterns and had little relevance to Africa. Graduates were allowed to hold minor colonial offices or work as professionals. The French did a much better job of assimilating Africans into their culture than did the British or Belgians. As in India, the Africans were shut off from social contact with their British masters.

POSTCOLONIAL AFRICA

The postcolonial Africans had no experience with self-government, and leadership often involved being connected with the right tribe. As in the days of the tribal chiefs, strong-man rule developed. This led to corruption on a grand scale. Bureaucracies expanded to provide jobs for the supporters of the leader, who usually was a military officer. Most foreign aid has ended up in the hands of the rulers. An example was Mobuto Sese Seko, who ruled Zaire for thirty years before he was thrown out.[9] His fortune, which was deposited in Swiss Banks, was said to total billions of dollars.[10] When Zaire achieved its independence from Belgium in 1960, it had 88,000 miles of usable roads; by 1985 this was down to 12,000 miles.[11] What happened to Zaire has been replicated time and again in Africa.[12]

Poverty

Africa is by far the poorest continent in the world. It has 14 percent of the world's population and less than 3 percent of its GDP. Sub-Saharan Africa, which houses almost 90 percent of Africa's population, had a combined GDP of $309 billion in 1997, which is less than the GDP of Canada, a country of 30 million, and a little larger than the GDP of Belgium, a country of 10 million. Mozambique, the poorest country in the world, had a per capita income of $140 in 1997, followed by Niger with a per capita income of $210. Nigeria, the largest country in Africa with a population of 118 million, had a total GDP of $33 billion in 1997 which is less than half of that of Chile, which has a population of 15 million. No country in Africa would qualify as a developed country. Libya, which has the highest per capita income of all African countries, produces oil but has a population of only 5 million.

Human Development

Human development covers a number of economic and social areas ranging from adult literacy to the existence of sanitation facilities. In the poor countries the level of human development is low. The infrastructure is poor. There are few roads, hospitals, and educational facilities. The great majority of children do not finish secondary school. Some do graduate and go on to college, but in some countries that is the exception rather than the rule. Fewer women go to school than men, more women are illiterate, and more women live in poverty than men. In terms of what is called gender empowerment, few women hold positions of authority in poor countries, but particularly in the African countries. The poorer the country, the lower the rate of longevity. Although women live longer than men in most countries, in the poorest African countries women may not outlive men. In some African countries, both women and men may live on the average 45 years.

Tables 14-1 and 14-2 present the extent of poverty and the low level of human development in Africa. Table 14-1 presents the percentage of the population living below the international poverty line for selected African countries. It is necessary to point out that there was no data available for Ethiopia, Mozambique, and other of the poorest countries in Africa. Table 14-2 presents the human development index (HDI) of the African countries. The United Nations classified 174 countries into three categories of human development. The first category includes 64 countries with a high level of human development. Libya is the only African

TABLE 14-1   *Population below the International Poverty Line for Selected African Countries, 1998 (%)*

Country	Population below $1 a day (%)	Population below $2 a day (%)
Côte d'Ivoire	17.7	54.8
Egypt	7.6	51.9
Guinea-Bissau	88.2	96.7
Kenya	50.2	78.1
Lesotho	48.8	74.1
Madagascar	72.3	93.2
Nigeria	31.1	59.9
Rwanda	45.7	88.7
Senegal	54.0	79.6
South Africa	23.7	50.2
Tanzania	10.5	45.5
Tunisia	3.9	22.7
Uganda	69.3	92.2
Zambia	84.6	98.1
Zimbabwe	41.0	68.2

Source: The World Bank, *World Development Report, 1998–99* (Washington, D.C.: The World Bank, 1998), 196–97.

TABLE 14-2 *Human Development Index (HDI) for Selected African Countries, 1998*

Country	Rank (out of 174 Countries)	Life Expectancy (years)	Adult Literacy (%)	HDI
Medium Level				
Algeria	82	68.1	61.6	0.746
Tunisia	83	68.7	66.7	0.748
South Africa	89	64.1	81.8	0.717
Botswana	97	51.7	69.8	0.678
Namibia	107	55.8	76.0	0.644
Egypt	112	64.8	51.4	0.612
Zimbabwe	130	48.9	85.1	0.507
Low Level				
Cameroon	132	55.3	63.4	0.481
Kenya	137	53.8	78.1	0.463
Nigeria	142	51.4	57.1	0.391
Benin	145	54.4	37.0	0.378
Zambia	146	42.7	78.2	0.378
Tanzania	150	50.6	67.8	0.358
Angola	156	47.4	42.0	0.344
Sudan	157	52.2	46.1	0.343
Senegal	158	50.3	33.1	0.342
Uganda	160	40.5	61.8	0.340
Ethiopia	169	48.7	35.5	0.252
Mali	171	47.0	31.0	0.236
Burkina Faso	172	46.3	19.2	0.219
Niger	173	47.5	13.6	0.207
Sierra Leone	174	34.7	31.4	0.185

Source: United National Development Report, *Human Development Report, 1998* (New York: Oxford University Press, 1998), 129–30.

country represented. Sixty-six countries are classified as having a medium level of human development. Ten are African countries. The bottom 64 countries are classified as having a low level of human development. Thirty-five are African countries, including the bottom 15.

A low rate of economic growth has not helped alleviate the problem of poverty. In some countries, the growth rate has been negative. From 1965 to 1996, the average annual per capita growth rate for Nigeria was 0.1 percent, and for Niger it was −2.8 percent. Table 14-3 presents real per capita GDP for selected African countries with 1980 as the base period. Some of the countries, particularly Botswana, have done well; most have not. Nigeria has been one of the worst performers of all of the African countries. Its per capita income was $780 in 1980; in 1997 it was $260. The countries of North Africa showed a gain from 1980 to 1997; the sub-Saharan countries did not.

TABLE 14-3   *Performance of Selected African Countries, 1980–1997 (per capita GDP)*

Countries	1980	1988	1989	1990	1992	1994	1996	1997
North Africa	1,357	1,532	1,466	1,430	1,350	1,336	1,459	1,505
Algeria	2,080	2,790	2,590	2,400	1,980	1,660	1,520	1,490
Egypt	520	870	830	810	790	880	1,080	1,180
Morocco	990	950	980	1,030	1,090	1,060	1,290	1,250
Sub-Saharan Africa	639	536	537	522	520	485	503	503
Angola	—	740	570	410	300	200	280	340
Botswana	1,030	1,670	2,080	2,500	2,950	3,200	3,250	3,260
Cameroon	680	1,130	1,080	970	940	640	650	650
Ethiopia	—	180	170	160	110	110	110	110
Kenya	450	410	400	380	330	260	320	330
Madagasia	560	260	230	240	230	240	250	250
Namibia	—	1,610	1,790	1,900	2,090	2,120	2,220	1,823
Niger	440	340	340	340	290	210	200	200
Nigeria	710	270	270	270	280	230	260	260
South Africa	2,500	2,640	2,810	2,860	3,210	3,430	3,510	3,400
Zambia	630	320	410	440	370	340	350	380
Zimbabwe	950	870	900	920	740	650	710	750

Source: The World Bank, *African Development Indicators, 1998–99* (Washington, D.C.: 1999), 35.

Income Inequality

Some of the African countries have among the most unequal income distributions in the world. In this respect, they are similar to Latin American countries. In Kenya, the richest 10 percent of the population received 47.7 percent of total income compared to 1.2 percent for the bottom 10 percent of the population—a ratio of 40 to 1. The richest 20 percent received 62.1 percent of total income compared to 3.4 percent for the bottom 20 percent. In South Africa, the richest 10 percent of the population received 47.3 percent of income compared to 1.4 percent for the bottom 10 percent—a ratio of 33 to 1. In other countries, the distribution of income is more equal. This is particularly true of the North African countries. In Algeria, the richest 10 percent of the population received 26.8 percent of income, while the poorest 10 percent received 7.8 percent of income—a ratio of less than 4 to 1. Table 14-4 presents income distribution for selected African countries.

Population Dynamics

Africa's population is growing faster than the population of other continents. This will continue to be a burden for most African countries in terms of resource allocation. Most resources have to be used for consumption. Incomes are low, so human and physical capital is less developed. Population growth affects both the demand for and the supply of savings. Household savings are reduced by the high

TABLE 14-4 *Income Distribution for Selected African Countries, 1998 (share of income held by population groups)*

Country	Poorest 10%	Poorest 20%	Richest 20%	Richest 10%
Northern Africa				
Algeria	2.8	7.0	42.6	26.8
Egypt	3.9	8.9	41.1	26.7
Morocco	2.8	6.6	46.3	30.5
Tunisia	2.3	5.9	46.3	30.7
Sub-Saharan Africa				
Guinea	0.9	3.0	50.2	31.7
Guinea-Bissau	0.5	2.1	58.8	42.3
Kenya	1.2	3.4	62.1	47.7
Lesotho	0.9	2.8	60.1	43.4
Niger	3.0	7.5	44.5	29.3
Nigeria	1.3	4.0	49.3	31.3
Senegal	1.4	3.5	58.6	42.8
Sierra Leone	0.5	1.1	64.4	43.6
South Africa	1.4	3.3	63.3	47.3
Tanzania	2.9	6.9	45.4	30.2
Uganda	3.0	6.8	48.1	33.4
Zambia	1.5	3.9	50.4	31.3
Zimbabwe	1.8	4.0	62.3	46.9

Source: The World Bank, *African Development Indicators, 1998–99* (Washington, D.C.: The World Bank, 1998/99), 327.

http://

The U.S. Census Bureau provides an international database on demographics, including population, at www .census.gov/ipc/ www/idbnew.html.

dependency burdens associated with rapid population growth. At any level of per capita income, greater numbers of dependents cause consumption to rise, so savings per capita will fall. Governments can, within limits, use fiscal and monetary policies to change a country's rate of savings, irrespective of demographic conditions. However, the effectiveness of fiscal and monetary policies is predicated on the existence of a well-developed system of public finance and banking that most African countries do not have.

Table 14-5 presents population dynamics for selected African countries. It includes birth rates, death rates, and projected population increases from the year 2000. Even though birth rates have fallen in these countries, they are well above the two-child replacement level, thus causing the population to swell. The mortality rate will also decrease. This means more entrants into the labor force, compounding problems of education. More school-age children will require more spending on education. In an age of rapid technological development, these countries will have to improve their schools both quantitatively and qualitatively, and that is difficult to do because of limited resources. To improve education, they will have either to generate more national savings or reduce spending in other areas.

Population growth has put pressure on the infrastructure of the African countries. There is mass migration from the rural areas to the cities. The end result is that Cairo, Lagos, and other African cities are becoming among the largest in the

TABLE 14-5   *Population Dynamics for Selected African Countries, 1998*

Country	Population (millions)	Birth Rate (per 1000)	Death Rate (per 1000)	Projected Increase (millions)
Northern Africa				
Algeria	29	26	5	31
Egypt	60	25	8	58
Morocco	27	25	7	25
Sub-Saharan Africa				
Angola	12	48	19	37
Benin	6	42	13	13
Burkina Faso	10	45	18	31
Cameroon	14	40	11	29
Chad	7	42	17	15
Congo*	47	45	14	156
Ethiopia	60	40	13	216
Ghana	18	36	10	33
Guinea	7	43	18	17
Kenya	20	34	9	42
Malawi	10	46	20	24
Niger	10	51	18	33
Nigeria	118	41	13	280
Senegal	9	40	14	18
South Africa	41	27	8	32
Sudan	28	34	12	48
Uganda	20	49	19	50
Zambia	9	43	18	15

formerly Zaire.

Source: The World Bank, *1998 World Development Indicators* (Washington, D.C.: The World Bank, 1998), 46–48.

world. Population pressure leads to poverty and disease. In Nigeria, 36 percent of children under 5 are underweight. In Madagascar, 72 percent of the children do not reach the fifth grade. In Benin, 80 percent of the population is without drinking water and 82 percent is without health facilities. In Ethiopia, 54 percent of the population has no access to health services. The adult illiteracy rate is 65 percent, and 88 percent of the population is without sanitation.

Political and Social Instability

Political and social instability are common problems in the majority of African countries and inhibit their economic development. In 1994 Rwanda was wracked by a civil war that resulted in tribal genocide. A civil war occurred in Zaire that resulted in the ouster of the longtime dictator General Mobutu. Nigeria has been run by military leaders who have postponed free elections, jailed political opponents, and hanged critics of the government. A civil war without end continues in the Sudan, and in Algeria the internecine struggle between Islamic fundamentalists and the government is a serious threat to the stability of Northern Africa. Terrorism has also occurred in Egypt where Islamic fundamentalists hope to topple the rule of Egyptian President Hosni Muburak. Genuine political democracy exists in only a handful of African countries.

A number of factors have contributed to the political and social instability of Africa. Poverty is obviously a very important factor, and uncontrolled population growth another. Corruption is also a major factor. As Table 14-6 indicates, Africa ranks with Asia and Latin America when it comes to corruption. Politicians and bureaucrats line their pockets at the expense of the public. As often as not, large amounts of foreign food, cash, and equipment aid never reach their intended destination. Political and social instability has had an adverse effect on attracting foreign investment in Africa. In the United States, the Export-Import Bank will not make or underwrite loans to many African countries. The credit rating of more African countries is so low that it is next to impossible for them to raise the capital in the international financial markets that is needed to finance the construction of schools, highways, hospitals, and transportation facilities.

TABLE 14-6
Corruption Perception Index for Selected Countries, 1998*

Country	Rank	CPI
Denmark	1	10.0
United States	17	7.5
Botswana	23	6.1
Namibia	29	5.3
South Africa	32	5.2
Italy	39	4.6
Zimbabwe	43	4.2
Malawi	45	4.1
Morocco	50	3.7
China	52	3.5
Zambia	52	3.5
Ghana	54	3.3
Mexico	55	3.3
Senegal	56	3.3
Egypt	66	2.9
India	67	2.9
Uganda	73	2.6
Kenya	74	2.5
Russia	76	2.4
Nigeria	81	1.9
Tanzania	82	1.9
Cameroon	85	1.4

* African countries in Italics.

Source: Transparency International, "1998 Corruption Perceptions Index" press release, Berlin. http://www.transparency.deldocuments/press releases.

Table 14-6 ranks the African countries on the basis of a Corruption Perception Index published by Transparency International. Only 85 countries of the more than 200 countries in the world are ranked, and these are typically the largest and most important countries. Botswana, a small African country of 1.2 million, ranked 22 ahead of Japan and Italy. Namibia ranked 29, also ahead of Italy. Nigeria, Tanzania, and Cameroon ranked among the bottom five countries.

Foreign Trade and Investment

The composition of foreign trade is a factor that has worked against the economic development of most of the African countries. Their exports, based on raw materials, have included such products as oil, cotton, and copper, while their imports have included manufactured goods. Nigeria offers an excellent example. In 1997, ninety-seven percent of its revenues from foreign trade came from oil exports, while manufactured products accounted for 80 percent of its imports. Food represents 90 percent of Malawi's exports, while manufactured goods represent 73 percent of Malawi's imports. The price of oil and agricultural products usually fluctuates far more in international markets than do the prices of manufactured goods. The end result is that the terms of trade have been unfavorable to most African countries, which has had an unfavorable impact on their balance of payments and repayment of their foreign debt.

In 1997 foreign direct investment in Africa amounted to $5 billion, which is less than the amount of U.S. direct investment in Chile, a country whose population is one-fiftieth of that of Africa's. Africa is unattractive to foreign investors for several interrelated reasons. First, many of the African countries are politically unstable, so there is political risk involved in investing in Africa. Second, their credit ratings are poor. The United States and other countries may not want to invest in countries where the risk of debt default is considerable. Third, to attract foreign investment, African countries are going to have to offer high rates of return, thus discriminating against home industries. One-third of foreign direct investment in Africa is in Nigeria where the attraction is oil.

AIDS

AIDS is the number one economic and social problem in Africa. It is already responsible for over half of the deaths by infectious disease not only in Africa, but elsewhere in the world. More people suffer from AIDS in Africa than in the rest of the world combined, resulting in the lowering of life expectancy in such countries as Nigeria, South Africa, and Zimbabwe. In these and other countries in Africa and Asia, until prevention programs become more effective, life expectancy will fall, the number of orphans will increase, poverty will worsen, and health care resources will come under increased financial strain. The circumstances under which AIDS occurs are different from in the developed countries, which will make its eradication more difficult. As Table 14-7 indicates, in some of the African countries one-fourth of the adult population is infected by AIDS.

http://

Information on AIDS issues around the world can be found at www.who.org.

TABLE 14-7 *AIDS in Selected African Countries, 1997*

Country	People Currently Infected	Percent of Population 15 to 49
Botswana	190,000	25.1
Burkina Faso	370,000	7.2
Cameroon	320,000	4.9
Congo	950,000	4.4
Ethiopia	2,600,000	9.3
Kenya	1,600,000	11.6
Malawi	710,000	14.9
Mozambique	1,200,000	14.2
Nigeria	2,300,000	4.1
Rwanda	370,000	12.8
South Africa	2,900,000	12.9
Tanzania	1,400,000	9.4
Zimbabwe	1,500,000	25.8

Source: The World Bank, *1999 World Development Indicators* (Washington, D.C.: The World Bank, 1999), 106–8.

THE DEVELOPMENT OF NIGERIA

Nigeria became a part of the British empire in 1860 and was recognized by other European powers as a British enclave. British colonial rule proved to be a mixed blessing for Nigeria. Its main direct contributions were the building of railroads and port facilities, the introduction of the legal system of common law, and the development of an administrative framework to rule the colony. Administrative measures were also used to encourage and regulate the production of cotton and other crops for export. Trade and banking were run by companies chartered in England. Barclay's Bank ran the banking system, and the Royal Niger Company was responsible for the development of crops for export. Rules, attitudes, and monopolistic practices by the British colonial administration excluded Nigerians from any participation in administration and commerce. It was not until after the end of World War II that Nigerians were able to participate in the economy and in government. (See Table 14-8 for social and economic data.)

Nigeria is a federation consisting of the federal government, thirty-six state governments, a federal capital territory, and some 589 local government councils. There is enormous ethnic diversity in Nigeria: more than 250 groups with different languages and customs. Active tribal rivalries compound the problem of government, with the leaders coming from the largest and most dominant tribe. The areas of greatest population density are either the cities, which do not have an adequate infrastructure, or areas that are remote from transportation facilities. Given the high birth rate and a declining death rate, the population is young. A young population tends to have an adverse effect on the size and productivity of the labor force and also creates problems in terms of education.

Population (millions)	117.9
Average annual population growth, 1980–1997 (%)	2.9
Land area (thousands of square kilometers)	910.8
Real GDP ($ billions)	103.5
World rank out of 123 countries	45
Real per capita GDP ($)	880
World rank out of 123 countries	114
Average annual real growth rates in GDP (%)	
1980–1990	−0.2
1990–1997	0.7
National poverty rate (%)	43
Human development rank out of 174 countries	142
Life expectancy at birth (years)	51.4
Rank out of 174 countries	151
Life expectancy for males at birth	49.8
Rank out of 174 countries	150
Life expectancy for females at birth	53.0
Adult literacy rate (%)	57.1
Gender Related Index out of 174 countries	142
Share of earned income (%)	
Males	70
Females	30
Gini coefficient of income inequality	45.0

TABLE 14-8
Economic and Social Data for Nigeria, 1997

Source: The World Bank, *World Development Report, 1998–99* (Washington, D.C.: Oxford University Press, 1998), 190, 191, 192, 193; The World Bank, *1999 World Bank Atlas* (Washington, D.C.: The World Bank, 1999), 24–25, 42–43; United Nations Development Program *Human Development Report, 1998* (New York: Oxford University Press, 1998), 130–32.

Oil

Oil and the Nigerian economy are almost synonymous. In 1997, ninety-seven percent of Nigeria's revenue from foreign trade came from oil exports, which accounted for 44 percent of the Nigerian GNP. The price of oil in the world market has determined the success or failure of the Nigerian economy. In the late 1970s when oil prices were high, the Nigerian economy was the wealthiest in Africa. It fueled the prosperity of Nigeria from 1965 to 1980, and Nigeria, like other oil-producing nations, borrowed heavily from abroad, pledging revenue from oil exports as collateral. The worldwide oil glut of the 1980s had a disastrous impact on the Nigerian economy. Earnings from exports of Nigerian oil declined from a high of $26 billion in 1980 to a low of $6.2 billion in 1988. The Nigerian economy has never recovered from its loss of oil revenue. The Nigerian GNP has declined from $76 billion in 1976 to $33 billion in 1997. Growth in the non-oil sector of the Nigerian economy has barely kept up with population growth. Table 14-9 presents the impact of oil exports on the Nigerian economy.

TABLE 14-9   *Nigerian Oil Exports, 1991–1997 (Index, 1985 = 100)*

Year	Export Value Index	Export Unit Value	Terms of Trade
1991	95.3	75.6	50.6
1992	98.4	73.1	47.9
1993	90.2	65.0	44.4
1994	76.1	58.8	39.4
1995	84.9	62.1	39.6
1996	126.1	76.7	51.5
1997	118.3	72.5	53.5

Source: International Monetary Fund, *Nigeria Selected Issues and Statistical Appendix* (Washington, D.C.: IMF, 1998), 126.

The Role of the Government

The Nigerian government has played an active role in the development of the economy. Like the Latin American countries, it has relied on a policy of import substitution to develop home industries. This policy has been implemented in three ways. First, Nigerian industries, including textiles, motor vehicles, furniture, glass products, and consumer appliances are heavily protected by tariffs. Successive tariffs have been increased, producing a sharp decline in the rate of increase of such goods. Second, these and other manufacturing industries have been favored by tax policies including accelerated depreciation and special relief from taxes for a period of three to five years depending on the amount of local capital invested. Third, many businesses are reserved for Nigerians. This restricts the amount of foreign involvement in local industries.

The Nigerian government has also relied on economic planning to facilitate the process of economic and social development through the creation of national goals and priorities.[13] Financing for projects that have planning priorities comes from the federal budget and from credit provided by the banking system. Some projects have been financed by various international lending agencies, including the International Monetary Fund. There is also a Petroleum Special Trust Fund that was created in 1995 as an extension of the capital budget. Any gain from excess oil revenue is set aside to rehabilitate decaying social infrastructure and services nationwide. The initial funds to finance these development funds came from a tripling in the retail price of gasoline in 1994. Projects that have to do with the improvement of the oil infrastructure, such as the construction of pipelines and refineries, are the responsibility of the state-owned Nigerian National Petroleum Corporation.

Political Instability

Nigeria is not exactly a role model for democracy. Corruption and political instability are related, and Nigeria scores high in both categories. It has been ruled by

http://

More information on Nigeria can be found through the United Nations site at www.un.org/Depts/eca/stats/index.htm.

generals for most of the time since it gained its formal independence from England in 1960, except for brief rules by civilian governments. The usual excuse
made for military rule has been that Nigeria is not ready for democracy, so the generals would have to rule until they thought the people were ready. A proposed
handover of the government to civilian rule was delayed until the summer of 1992
because of ethnic and religious unrest and property rights. Nigeria was ruled for a
number of years by General Sani Abacha, who was not known for his admiration
for democratic institutions. He jailed dissidents and achieved international notori-
ety for hanging some of them, including a respected Nigerian writer. His death
paved the way for relatively free elections in 1998.

An Evaluation of the Nigerian Economy

In spite of its rich resource endowment, Nigeria remains one of the poorest countries in the world, with a 1997 per capita income of $260. Only thirteen countries
in the world had a lower per capita income. In recent years growth in the non-oil
sector of the economy has barely kept pace with population growth, which is
around 2.9 percent per year. Policy reversals, widespread fuel shortages, frequent
interruptions in the supplies of power and water, and fertilizer shortages have
depressed private investment and lessened non-oil output growth. There are also
uncertainties regarding the ongoing transition to civil rule. On the plus side, world
prices for oil are increasing and should help the Nigerian economy. Nigeria has also
implemented prudent financial policies that have led to stabilization of the economy. Inflation has declined and real interest rates have turned positive.

Private Enterprise.   Economic activity in most sectors of the Nigerian economy
is primarily the function of private enterprise. To some extent, British colonial rule
facilitated the development of a local entrepreneurial class in Nigeria. The British
financed the development of railroads and port facilities. They abolished the trading monopolies of coastal tribal kingdoms, internal tolls, and the arbitrary interference of African tribal rulers with the free conduct of commerce. The British pound
was introduced as the common medium of exchange. The increase in world
demand for export crops in the early years of the twentieth century encouraged
British firms to advance credit for the production of cash crops. This credit in turn
facilitated the sale of imported goods. The expansion of export production and the
increase in the money supply in the form of produce advances increased local
opportunities in retailing and in handicraft and food production for the domestic
market. The initial expansion of British colonial rule encouraged competition in
the distributive trades.

   To develop new export crops, traders and farmers adapted existing social institutions to regulate land ownership or use, mobilize savings and credit facilities, and
recruit labor to clear, weed, plant, and harvest crops. The successful creation of
export production by Nigerian traders and planters contrasted with the failure of
British government and foreign company plantations. Thus, in Nigeria, colonialism

enabled Africans to develop agricultural production and generally stimulated the domestic production of other goods.

British ownership and operation were limited primarily to railroad investments, banking, and mineral resources. A dual economy developed, with the Nigerians controlling farm production, trading, and small business enterprises. Nevertheless, the British controlled the economy, and Nigerian private enterprise was not allowed to compete with British commercial interests. British investments in railways led them to prevent the development of any form of local transportation system that might provide competition.

The economic orientation of British colonial rule changed after World War II from maintaining the dual colonial economy to increasing the extent of Nigerian participation in all sectors. This goal was to be accomplished through government financial support of private enterprise, which the Nigerians themselves would run but the British would control. However, increasing nationalism sharply increased the Nigerian desire for more participation and control in the development of the economy. Control by Nigerians over private enterprises increased. This participation was limited primarily to the trade and services sectors of the economy. Very few Nigerians possessed the expertise or the capital to own and manage a modern production enterprise. Publicly owned Nigerian corporations began a growing number of enterprises intended to be run as profitable business ventures. At the time of Nigerian independence in 1960, state capitalism existed side by side with private capitalism. Political abuses of public corporations made them largely unsuccessful, and Nigeria relied increasingly on foreign-owned enterprises to develop a modern economy.

Postcolonial Development. The private sector of Nigerian economy increased in importance during the period following independence. Gross private fixed investment increased from less than half of the total fixed investment in 1960 to 65 percent by 1975. Most of this increase took the form of foreign direct investment. The reliance on private investment in general and foreign direct investment in particular has encouraged foreign and private domestic investment by offering financial incentives to invest in those sectors that contribute most to economic development.

Results of Private Enterprise. Nigerian entrepreneurs have established a large variety of very small enterprises. Such undertakings are easy to start, even by men and women with little education, training, or business experience, and barriers to entry are negligible. The technical knowledge is simple, and many have acquired it as workers or apprentices in other small firms or through experience with large firms or in government. Capital requirements are usually minimal, and individual entrepreneurs can often operate with virtually no capital of their own, relying instead on advances from their suppliers. Requirements for skilled labor are usually negligible, and there is an abundance of semiskilled and unskilled labor. What all of this means is that there are a very large number of small enterprises in Nigeria producing and distributing in local markets. However, it is difficult for any of these enterprises to acquire the capital and technological know-how to make the transition to large-scale operations.

Corruption.   Corruption is a fact of life in Nigeria and assumes many forms. There is the standard low-level bribe, called *dash* or *chai,* which is payment for services rendered or anticipated. This payment may take the form of a package of razor blades, a case of scotch, or a digital watch. Higher-level bribes include payment of money or a very expensive gift. Then there is political corruption, including bribery, inflated results, fake voter rolls, reversal of election results, and underage voters. State-owned corporations are often run by political hacks rather than trained civil servants. Public projects are often not completed because politicians and contractors have appropriated the funds. The tax system of the country is so inefficient that much of the revenue potential is not realized because tax evasion is widespread and tax officials are often corrupt.

SOUTH AFRICA

South Africa is regarded as the country with the greatest economic development potential of all of the African countries, particularly since it has become a democracy.[14] It has the most advanced, broadly based, and productive economy in Africa. It possesses a modern infrastructure supporting the distribution of goods to major urban centers, it has well-developed financial, legal, communications, and transport sectors, and its stock exchange ranks among the top fifteen in the world in the value of transactions.[15] Its average per capita income of $3,210 in 1997 ranks it as an upper-middle-income country, along with such countries as Brazil and Mexico.[16] Although mining is of some importance to the South African economy, manufacturing accounts for around half of the value of its exports.

However, there are economic and social problems. South Africa has one of the most unequal distributions of income in the world. The bottom 20 percent of its population receive 3.3 percent of income, while the top 20 percent receive 63.3 percent of income. Using the international poverty standards, 50.2 percent of its population live on less than $2 a day.[17] The whites and blacks, for all practical purposes, are divided into two separate worlds, with the whites having by far the greater amount of income and wealth, even though they account for only 12 percent of the population, and the blacks, who account for 88 percent of the population, receiving far less of the income and wealth.[18] Moreover, the population growth averaged 2 percent a year during 1990–1997, while the average annual real growth rate in GNP during the same period decreased by -0.2 percent. (See Table 14-10 for social and economic data.)

Gold and diamonds became to South Africa what oil became to Mexico and Nigeria. During the first fifty years of the twentieth century, the South African economy was based on the mining of these products for export. As was also true of oil in Mexico, income from these mines left South Africa for England and helped to finance the maintenance of the British empire. Gold and diamonds accounted for 90 percent or more of South African exports from 1911 to 1961. But during the 1960s, economic prosperity, which was based on gold and diamond exports, began to end. An economic downturn occurred as the world prices for gold and diamonds

http://

Additional information on South Africa can be found at the following sites: www.state.gov/ www/regions /background_info_ countries.html and www.mac.doc.gov/ tcc/country.htm.

TABLE 14-10
Economic and Social Data for South Africa, 1997

Population (millions)	40.6
Annual average population growth, 1980–1997 (%)	3.0
Land area (thousands of square kilometers)	1,221.0
Real GDP ($ billions)	286.9
World rank out of 123 countries	20
Real per capita GDP	7,490
World rank out of 123 countries	37
Average annual real growth rates in GDP (%)	
1980–1990	−1.2
1990–1997	1.7
National poverty rate (%)	50.2
Human development rank out of 174 countries	89
Life expectancy at birth (years)	64.1
Rank out of 174 countries	118
Life expectancy for males	61.2
Rank out of 174 countries	119
Life expectancy for females	67.2
Rank out of 174 countries	110
Adult literacy rate out of 174 countries	74
Share of earned income (%)	
Males	69.1
Females	30.9

Sources: The World Bank, *World Development Report, 1998–99* (Washington, D.C.: Oxford University Press, 1998), 190, 191, 192, 193; The World Bank, *1999 World Bank Atlas* (Washington, D.C.: The World Bank, 1999), 24–25, 42–43; United Nations Development Program, *Human Development Report, 1998* (New York: Oxford University Press, 1998), 130–32.

began to fall. New sources of gold were discovered in other parts of the world, and platinum became more valuable. Cheaper industrial substitutes for diamonds were also found.

Democracy

After South Africa gained its independence in 1966, a political and social policy of apartheid was practiced. Whites and blacks were strictly segregated. Only whites were allowed to hold public office. The best jobs were reserved for whites, and schools were also segregated. The blacks were concentrated in ghettos, which had very few social amenities. As a result, a civil war broke out between whites and blacks, with terrorism used on both sides. Eventually, the United States and other countries placed an embargo on South Africa by refusing to buy its exports and by putting pressure on multinational corporations in South Africa to work to end apartheid. It was inevitable that the white minority could no longer continue to rule. As a result of the external pressures, the South African government extended voting rights to all of its citizens in 1994. Nobel Peace Prize winner Nelson Mandela was elected president in May 1994 in the country's first multinational elections.

At one time South Africa was expected to become the South Korea of the future, but South Korea was hit by the East Asian currency crisis of 1997 and its economy was damaged, and South Africa has a number of problems with which it has to contend. Many of its industries have been protected by tariffs and are uncompetitive by world standards. Moreover, labor productivity is lower in South Africa than it is in comparable countries such as Mexico. But there are also other problems as well. Will Thabo Mbeke have the stature to hold the country together as Nelson Mandela did? Will the current political arrangement, which allows shared power among several political parties, end up like many African countries where there is only one political party? There is also the potential for tribal warfare among the Zulus and other tribes.[19] Political instability does not foster foreign direct investment in any country.

THE FUTURE OF AFRICA

Africa is the world's poorest continent. While the rest of the world has grown more prosperous, Africa has not. Moreover, as Table 14-11 indicates, the real per capita incomes of some of the African countries have not increased since 1950. Ethiopia is an example. Income differences among countries have widened since 1950. For example, real per capita GDP in Kenya in 1950 was $609 and in South Africa $2,251. For South Korea and Taiwan, the respective values were $876 and $922. In 1992 the real per capita GDP for Kenya was $1,055 and for South Africa $3,451, while the real per capita GDP for South Korea was $10,010 and for Taiwan $11,590.[20] It can be argued that climate and cultural factors have worked in favor of South Korea and Taiwan to promote their economic development, while other climate and cultural factors have worked against the development of the African countries.[21]

At the beginning of the twentieth century, the presence of natural resources was a factor promoting economic development. Countries that had natural resources had something of value to export. The multinational corporations of that time period were resource based. They went to wherever the resources were located. The mass production manufacturing companies that developed during the early part of the twentieth century also depended on resources. The Goodyear Tire Company established rubber plantations in Brazil and Malaysia. Manufacturing firms also needed cheap labor, so they built assembly plants abroad. Education was no particular requisite for success. Unskilled workers could be used for work on banana plantations, while semi-skilled workers could work on the Ford assembly line and make $5 a day.

Today, knowledge is everything, and knowledge depends on education. Poor countries, particularly those in Africa, differ from rich countries because they have not only less capital but also less knowledge. Knowledge is costly to create and

http://

For more information and links, go to www.state.gov/ www/regions/ africa/index.html and www.state .gov/www/regions _missions.html.

TABLE 14-11   *Levels of GDP per Capita for Six African Countries, 1950–1992 (1990 $)**

Year	Ethiopia	Ghana	Kenya	Nigeria	Tanzania	Zaire
1950	277	1,193	609	547	427	636
1955	295	1,162	690	636	478	812
1960	302	1,232	717	645	498	808
1965	370	1,255	737	777	537	729
1970	393	1,275	894	944	615	711
1975	396	1,125	920	1,153	668	704
1980	401	1,041	1,031	1,193	657	538
1981	399	1,015	1,013	1,129	629	533
1982	394	917	1,032	1,101	617	514
1983	403	847	998	982	595	504
1984	384	888	977	905	592	516
1985	342	900	981	965	573	501
1986	358	914	1,013	971	574	516
1987	379	926	1,036	943	585	514
1988	374	946	1,060	1,011	592	502
1989	367	963	1,071	1,059	595	484
1990	350	966	1,079	1,178	599	458
1991	336	983	1,065	1,140	604	407
1992	300	1,007	1,055	1,152	601	353

* *Zaire used to be the Belgian Congo. Now it is the Democratic Republic of the Congo. Ethiopia was an independent country in 1950 and still is. Kenya and Nigeria were a part of the British Empire. Tanzania was a part of the German Empire until 1918; then it became a British protectorate. Ghana was a part of the British Empire.*

Source: Angus Maddison, *Monitoring the World Economy, 1820–1992* (Paris: Organization for Economic Cooperation and Development, 1997), 192.

that is why most of it is created in the rich countries. Poor countries differ from rich countries in that they have far fewer institutions to impart knowledge and far fewer people attend these institutions. The knowledge gap between the rich and poor countries widened during the 1990s and will continue to widen in the future. International institutions such as the World Bank and the International Monetary Fund can do only so much. One way in which to attract technology is through foreign trade and investment, but Africa has received little foreign investment because of corruption, political instability, a weak infrastructure, a poor legal system, low growth rates, and high fiscal deficits.

SUMMARY

Africa appears to continue to be in a state of crisis that has existed during the 1990s. Although there are some noteworthy exceptions—Botswana, Mauritania, Tunisia, and a few other countries—the majority of African countries are in chaos. Nigeria, Kenya, Sudan, and the Democratic Republic of the Congo have 30 percent of Africa's population but are among the poorest countries in the world. Nigeria has been ruled by generals during most of the time it has been independent. It is also one of the most corrupt countries in the world. Kenya is no better. Its president is one of the most corrupt in the world and democracy does not work. The Sudan is engaged in an ongoing civil war between rival political factions, and the Democratic Republic of the Congo, formerly Zaire, is not democratic but is ruled by a dictator.

QUESTIONS FOR DISCUSSION

1.   Discuss some of the factors that have held back the economic development of Africa.
2.   What was the impact of British colonialism on the development of Nigeria and South Africa?
3.   What are some of the problems that confront the future development of South Africa?
4.   Why has democracy failed to take hold in most African countries?
5.   Discuss the influence of oil on the Nigerian economy.
6.   Twenty years ago such East Asian countries as South Korea, Malaysia, and Thailand were behind Nigeria and other African countries in terms of per capita income and GNP. Now they are well ahead. Why has this happened?
7.   Compare the South African economy to the economies of Mexico and Brazil.
8.   In your opinion, will the economies of the African countries improve in the future?

RECOMMENDED READINGS

International Monetary Fund. *Nigeria: Selected Issues and Statistical Appendix*. Washington, D.C.: IMF, 1998.

Lancaster, Carol. *Aid to Africa: So Much to Do, So Little Done*. Chicago: University of Chicago Press, 1998.

Landes, David S. *The Wealth and Poverty of Nations*. New York: Norton, 1998.

United Nations Development Program. *Human Development Report, 1998*. New York: Oxford University Press, 1998.

The World Bank. *African Development Indicators, 1998–99*. Washington, D.C.: The World Bank, 1999.

The World Bank. *World Development Report, 1998–99*. Washington, D.C.: Oxford University Press, 1998.

The World Bank. *1999 World Bank Atlas*. Washington, D.C.: The World Bank, 1999.

NOTES

1.   The World Bank, *1999 World Bank Atlas* (Washington, D.C.: The World Bank, 1999), 42–44.

2.   United Nations Development Program, *Human Development Report 1999* (New York: Oxford University Press, 1998), 130.

3.   David S. Landes, *The Wealth and Poverty of Nations* (New York: Norton, 1998), 130.

4.   Common law dates back to 1151 C.E. It is based on legal precedent.

5.   Code law dates back before Roman law. It is statutory law. The Napoleonic code was introduced by Napoleon in 1804, and is the law in France, Spain, Portugal, Italy, and Latin America. The Germanic code was introduced in Germany in 1896 and is the law in Germany, Austria, Poland, the Czech Republic, Turkey, and Japan.

6.   People in Senegal and other former French possessions still speak French.

7.   The slave and ivory trades were the two exceptions. Slaves were a valuable commodity, and so was ivory.

8.   Cecil Rhodes was to England in the nineteenth century what John D. Rockefeller was to the United States. Rhodes became the richest man in England, while Rockefeller was the richest man in America. Rhodes made his money in diamonds; Rockefeller made his in oil. Rhodes was knighted by Queen Victoria; Rockefeller ran afoul of the U.S. antitrust laws.

9.   Zaire was formerly the Belgian Congo. Now, it is the Democratic Republic of the Congo.

10.   Much of this money came from the United States, which regarded him as a friend.

11.   David S. Landes, *The Wealth and Poverty of Nations*, 510.

12.   Idi Amin, Dictator of Uganda, is one of many examples.

13.   Economic planning of the inductive type is used in Nigeria. This gives the government considerable control over resource allocation in that it decides national priorities through the plan. There have been five development plans since 1960, but their implementation has been interrupted from time to time by military coups.

14.   It is the only African country to be listed by the U.S. Department of Commerce as one of the big emerging markets of the future. Argentina, Brazil, and Mexico are also listed.

15.   The World Bank, *1999 World Bank Indicators* (Washington, D.C.: the World Bank, 1999), 206–10.

16.   Its per capita income of $3,210 placed it in the upper-middle income range from a per capita income of $3,126 to $9,655. Out of the 26 countries in that category, five are African countries—Botswana, Gabon, Mauritius, Libya, and South Africa.

17.   The World Bank, *World Development Report, 1998/99* (Washington, D.C.: Oxford University Press, 1998), pp. 197, 199.

18.   The ratio between the average white income and the average black income is 9 to 1.

19.   The Zulus were once regarded as the most powerful tribe in South Africa. They fought the Boers and British in various wars and destroyed a British army at Isandliwana in 1879.

20.   Angus Maddison, *Monitoring the World Economy, 1820–1992* (Paris: Organization for Economic Cooperation and Development, 1997), 204–05, 206.

21.   David S. Landes, *The Wealth and Poverty of Nations*, Africa, pp. 499–507; South Korea, pp. 377, 436–38, 475–77; Taiwan, pp. 377, 437, 438, 475; climate, temperate v. tropical, pp. 5–16.

PART V

Toward a New World Order

CHAPTER 15

World Economic Integration

The countries of the world are forming into regional trading groups based on a communality of interests. In 1999 there were an estimated thirty-two groups in existence. They range in importance from the European Union (EU), which has grouped together fifteen European countries to create an entity that can be called the United States of Europe, to the Caribbean Community (CARICOM), which is a free-trade area consisting of a number of small countries in the Caribbean whose combined population is not much larger than that of Denmark.[1] In between, there are such groups as the North American Free Trade Agreement (NAFTA), which combines the United States, Canada, and Mexico into a free-trade area with a total population and GNP the size of the European Union, and the South American customs union (MERCOSUR), which combines Argentina, Brazil, Paraguay, and Uruguay into one trading group.[2]

http://

Look up statistics and other information on CARICOM at www .caricom.org.

TYPES OF ECONOMIC INTEGRATION

Economic integration in a broad sense is the expansion of financial and trade ties among nations. Some of the great empires of the past, such as the British Empire, the Spanish Empire, and the Roman Empire, pursued economic integration as a method of economic development and to benefit from trade and a specialization of skills. Since World War II, economic integration has been pursued by small groups of countries desiring to expand their national markets, increase their economic and political power, and achieve the economic gains that result from greater intergroup trade. There are five levels of economic integration. At each level the countries involved must give up more economic and political control to the overall group than at the previous level.

1. The first level of economic integration is called a *free-trade area*. In a free-trade area tariffs on trade among member nations are eliminated. A member country of a free-trade area benefits by producing goods and services in which it has a comparative advantage. Conversely, it imports goods and services in areas in which it has a comparative disadvantage.

2. The second level of economic integration is known as a *customs union*. This level is characterized not only by the elimination of tariffs among member countries, but also by the creation of a common external tariff toward non-member nations. The common external tariff is designed to eliminate import biases. If external tariffs differ among member countries, then outside countries will export to the country with the lowest tariff barriers to sell to the whole group. Therefore, the lowest tariff member of the group benefits. A common external tariff eliminates this problem.

3. The third level of economic integration involves the creation of a *common market*. It has the same tariff policy as a customs union and also allows for the freedom of movement for the factors of production, such as labor and capital, among member countries. Some members of the European Union were once a part of the European Common Market. There is a common trade policy toward other countries.

4. The fourth level of economic integration is an *economic union*. This level is characterized by the harmonization of economic policies beyond those of a common market. Specifically, an economic union seeks to unify monetary and fiscal policies among member countries. A common currency or permanently fixed exchange rate is a feature of an economic union. The European Union has adopted the euro as the common currency for its member countries. Also, the national governments of the countries participating in an economic union must forego control over most of their national economic policies to the group. There is the harmonization of standards of weights and measurement, a common tax system, the free flow of individuals from one country to another without passport requirements, and the free flow of capital.

5. The fifth level of economic integration involves the creation of a *political union*. In a political union all economic and political policies are united under a single governing body. Countries that form a political union tend to lose their national identities and become a part of a single country. An example of a political union is the former Soviet Union, which united various disparate groups, some of which it had conquered, into one state. When the Soviet Union collapsed, the constituent republics became independent countries.

THE EUROPEAN UNION

To understand why the European Union was created, it is necessary to look at the history of Europe during the twentieth century. Two major wars were fought in Europe during this century. Both caused immense damage to the European economy. World War I was fought in northern France, Russia, northern Italy, and the Balkans. An estimated 20 million people were killed and property damage amounted to billions of dollars. Germany was forced to pay reparations to the victorious Allied countries, which bankrupted it and eventually led to the creation of the dictatorship under the control of Adolf Hitler. When the Germans invaded Poland on September 1, 1939, World War I began and lasted until 1945. More than 50 million people were killed, property damage was much greater than in World War I, and Europe was in a state of collapse.

http://

Policies, data, news, and links can be found at http://europa.eu .int.

The Genesis of the European Union

After the end of World War II the idea of a European Union was first conceived. It was hoped that this would promote peace between France and Germany, two countries that had been involved in three major wars in less than a century. The idea involved the creation of a common market that would create an economic and political force that could compete with the Soviet Union and the United States. The United States supported the idea of a common market from the beginning, and through Marshall Plan aid, provided some $200 billion for the reconstruction of Europe. In 1952 the European Coal and Steel Community, a cooperative venture between France, The Federal Republic of Germany, Italy, Belgium, the Netherlands, and Luxembourg was organized.[3] Its purpose was to remove tariff barriers on coal, iron, and steel among the countries.

The Treaty of Rome (1957).   The Treaty of Rome formally established the European Community, which became the forerunner of the European Union. It created a plan to eliminate tariffs among the six members, to create a common external tariff, and to harmonize economic policies such as exchange rates and controls, immigration among member countries, and agricultural support programs. With the Treaty of Rome, a formal common market was established.[4] Eventually, the European Community was expanded to include other European nations to form the European Union. Denmark and the United Kingdom joined in 1973, Greece in 1981, and Spain and Portugal in 1986. After all the necessary institutional arrangements had been made, Austria, Finland, and Sweden joined in 1995, leaving Norway and Switzerland the only major European countries that have not joined. Table 15-1 presents the population, GNP, and real per capita income of the European Union countries.

TABLE 15-1   *Population and Income for the European Union, 1997*

Country	Population (thousands)	Real GNP ($ millions)	Real GNP per Capita (international PPP[1])
Austria	8,072	177.5	22,010
Belgium	10,190	227.3	23,090
Denmark	5,284	120.0	23,450
Finland	5,140	97.6	19,660
France	58,607	1,280.3	22,210
Germany	82,071	1,748.3	21,170
Greece	10,522	137.5	12,540
Ireland	3,661	60.7	17,420
Italy	57,523	1,152.1	20,170
Luxembourg[2]	422	—	—
Netherlands	15,607	332.8	21,130
Portugal	9,945	137.6	14,180
Spain	39,323	617.6	15,690
Sweden	8,849	168.4	19,010
United Kingdom	59,009	1,208.9	20,710
Total	374,225	7,466.6	

[1] *Purchasing power parity with the U.S. dollar as the denominator or frame of reference.*
[2] *Luxembourg is too small to be counted.*

Source: The World Bank, *1999 World Bank Atlas* (Washington, D.C.: The World Bank, 1999), 24, 25, 42, 43.

The European Monetary System

In 1979 a move toward an eventual monetary integration of the European Community was made through the creation of the European Monetary System (EMS), which was designed to coordinate the monetary policies of the member nations. It did two things:

1. It created the exchange rate mechanism (ERM), which was designed to limit fluctuations among the EC currencies. For example, the franc could increase or decrease sharply in value against the mark. This worked to the disadvantage or advantage of the parties affected by the fluctuations of the currencies. Thus, most of the EMS members chose to participate in the ERM. They pledged to maintain fixed exchange rates among their currencies within a limit of ±2.25 percent.[5] It was the responsibility of the central banks of the member countries to keep their currencies within the range of ±2.25 percent. If German interest rates rose, then the interest rates of other countries had to rise; if German interest rates fell, the interest rates of the other countries also had to fall.[6]

2. It created the European Currency Unit (ECU). Its value was determined by a weighted "basket" of the currencies of the EC members based on the importance of their currencies in the world market. The German mark accounted for

32 percent of the value of the ECU, the French franc accounted for 20.4 percent, and the British pound accounted for 11 percent.[7] The ECU was a unit of account. It was important in international financial circles and had a value. It was used as a denomination for Eurobonds, traveler's checks, bank deposits, and loans. It also constituted bank reserves and could be moved from one bank to another. In 1992, the Maastricht Agreement created the ECU as a real currency designed eventually to replace the marks, francs, pounds, and pesos used by member nations. Eventually it became the euro.

Prelude to Maastricht

The period from 1979 to 1993 witnessed the expansion of the European Community beyond its original concept of a common market, where trade barriers would be lowered, toward a political and economic union. Greece was admitted to the EC in 1981 and Spain and Portugal were admitted in 1986. During this period, the European Commission, one of the governing bodies of the European Community, issued the White Paper on Completing the Internal Market. Its objective was to remove all trade barriers among member countries and to promote the free movement of people, services, goods, and capital among countries. The Single European Act, confirming these objectives, was ratified in 1986 and set the goal for the creation of a single European market by December 31, 1992. Various trade barriers were removed, most passport controls were eliminated, and technical standards, which varied from country to country, were made uniform.

The Maastricht Treaty (1991).   In December 1991 leaders of the 12 EC member countries met in Maastricht, the Netherlands, to discuss the future of the EC. An agreement was worked out that would change the future of Europe. It was agreed that a common currency was required to cement a closer economic union similar to that of the United States. The advantage of a single currency would be the elimination of the exchange rate problems when the different currencies were exchanged for each other. This would benefit banking, business, and tourism. This new currency would go into effect on January 1, 1999. The treaty also laid down the framework of a future European government, with a common foreign and defense policy, a common parliament, and a common citizenship with the right to live, work, vote, and run for office anywhere within the EC. The treaty was ratified and became effective on November 1, 1993.

European Monetary Union (EMU).   The European Monetary Union is one part of the European Union. There are two major parts to the EMU which are as follows:

1. A new central bank called the European Central Bank (ECB) has replaced the central banks of the fifteen member countries and will be based in Frankfurt, Germany. It has replaced the former German central bank (Deutsche Bundesbank), which pretty much dictated monetary policies, not only for Germany but also for Western Europe. The central banks of the EU member nations

http://

The text and provisions of the Maastricht Treaty can be found at http://europa.eu .int/en/record/ mt/top.html.

http://

Visit the European Central Bank web site at http:// www.ecb.int.

have lost their former autonomy and would come under the jurisdiction of the ECB. It is very similar to the U.S. monetary system in that the Federal Reserve is based in Washington and there are twelve Federal Reserve Banks located in major economic areas throughout the United States. The ECB coordinates monetary policy for the member nations.

2. A new currency unit called the euro would eventually replace the currencies of the member countries as the single currency. The euro can be compared to the dollar in that it will be the standard medium of exchange. On January 1, 1999, irrevocably fixed exchange and a common monetary policy were set for the EMU countries. National currencies will exist, but with fixed exchange rates. By January 2002 at the latest, the French franc, the mark, and other currencies of the member nations will no longer exist, and the euro will be the common currency.

The Maastricht Treaty set up several financial criteria for membership into the European Union:

1. Budget deficits had to be below 3 percent of GDP.
2. The public ratio of debt to GDP had to be below 60 percent.
3. The inflation rate had to be no higher than 1.5 percentage points above the average of the three lowest-inflation countries in the union.
4. Long-term interest rates, as a measure of inflationary expectations, could not exceed by more than 2 percentage points those of the three best performing countries.
5. Candidates could not experience a devaluation in their currencies for at least two years. Austria, Finland, and Sweden were admitted as members to the EU in 1995, bringing the total to fifteen members. Norway was also expected, but Norwegian voters voted against membership on two separate occasions. In 1997 the Treaty of Amsterdam was concluded. The Treaty pledged that EU members would promote higher levels of employment, increase gender equality, achieve greater environmental protection, and strengthen consumer and social policies. Other measures included creating freer movement of persons in the EU and more effective ways of combating international crime.

As January 1, 1999, approached, four countries decided not to change their currencies into the euro. They were the United Kingdom, Denmark, Sweden, and Greece. Greece was unable to satisfy the Maastricht requirements for membership. With regard to Sweden's position on the EMU, the Swedish government proposed that Sweden not join the monetary union because there was no public support to do so. Whether the Swedes will eventually join the EMU will depend on a referendum.[8] The British decision is based in part on the history of the pound sterling. A nation's past inevitably influences its attitude toward the present and future. The British national currency has an unbroken history going back more than 900 years. It was the first European nation to have a single national currency in post-Roman times. Thus, there is a reluctance to give up a currency so entrenched in British history to accept the euro.[9]

Political Union

The political system of the European Union will become very much like that of the United States. It consists of the Council of the European Union, the European Commission, the European Parliament, and the European Court of Justice. There are now fifteen members. Austria, Sweden, and Finland became members in 1995, while Norway and Switzerland have opted out. Other countries, such as Poland, Hungary, and Slovenia, have applied for membership in the EU, but their admission is unlikely in the immediate future. The functions of each component of the EU political system are as follows:

1. *The European Council of Ministers.* It is based in Brussels and consists of fifteen members who are selected by their home governments for a term of five years. Normally, a country's foreign minister represents his or her own country. The Council presidency rotates among the members every six months. The Council is the premier decision-making body of the EU, but, unlike the United States where each state regardless of size has two senators, decision-making in the EU is weighted toward those countries with the largest economies. In Council decisions, France, Germany, Italy, and the United Kingdom have ten votes each, while Luxembourg, the country with the smallest economy, has two votes. Approval on proposals requires a unanimous or qualified vote depending on the importance of the proposal.

2. *The European Commission.* Based in Brussels, it consists of twenty members selected to serve for five years. The larger countries get two members; the smaller countries get one. It has several major functions:
   a. It proposes legislation to be considered by the Council.
   b. It implements all EU treaties including the Treaty of Rome.
   c. It has extensive legislative powers in implementing various internal agreements, such as the completion of the Common Agricultural Policy (CAP).

3. *The European Parliament.* It is based in Strasbourg, France, and has 626 members who are directly elected by their respective countries based on population size. Germany, the largest country, has 99 members, while the United Kingdom, France, and Italy have 87 each.[10] Members are elected for five-year terms. It is a consultative rather than a legislative body. It debates legislation proposed by the Commission and forwarded to it by the Council. It can propose amendments to that legislation, but they are not binding to the Commission or the Council.

4. *The European Court of Justice.* It is based in Luxembourg and is comprised of one judge from each country. Like the Supreme Court of the United States, the Court of Justice is the supreme appeals court for EU law. It is also somewhat similar to the Supreme Court in that member nations' courts as well as other states' courts can refer their cases to it.

5. *National governments.* The legislatures of each of the fifteen member nations implement approved proposals as their laws. They will collect taxes and commit revenues for state functions such as education and road building. The value-added tax, which is a tax levied on the value created at each stage of the

http://

Information on the institutions within the EU can be found at http://europa.eu.int/index-en.htm.

production process, is the single most important tax used by the European countries.

The Euro

On January 1, 1999, the euro became the official currency unit for eleven members of the European Union, thus providing the world with three major currencies—the dollar, the euro, and the yen. The old currencies of these countries are no longer traded in international exchange markets around the world. European stocks and bonds are quoted in euros, and the euro is increasingly used for bank transactions, business deals, and public finances. It also will be used for noncash transactions until the year 2000, when it will formally replace the old coins and notes of each of the eleven nations. Until that time, conversion rates of each currency into the euro has been set by the European Commission. For example, one euro = 1.95583 German marks, 6.5595 French francs, and 1,936.27 Italian lira. The United Kingdom, Denmark, and Sweden opted out of accepting the euro because of public anxiety that dropping their national currencies would mean giving up too much independence. Greece did not meet the eligibility requirements.

The basic rationale for the euro was that it would eliminate the problem of currency conversion when transactions had to be made in different currencies. Tourists visiting Europe would have to exchange dollars for pounds when they were in England, pounds into marks if they visited Germany, and marks into lira if they visited Italy. These and other European currencies would fluctuate against the dollar and against each other daily. There was a cost in converting from one currency to another and also a transactions risk. Contractual relationships between buyer and seller usually involve payment at some time in the future. An exporter in Germany would contract with an importer in France for payment in 90 days. By the time of payment, if the franc fell in value against the mark, the French importer would lose; if the mark fell in value against the franc, the German exporter would lose. By using the same currency unit, the euro, neither would lose.

It remains to be seen whether or not the euro and indeed the European Union will be successful. Supporters of the euro contend that a single currency will save Europeans $25 to $30 billion annually by eliminating exchange rate risks and the costs of exchanging different currencies. With the euro, foreign investors will have easier access to investment opportunities across a broad territory. And those investments will be priced in a single currency that is expected to be more stable than a number of different currencies. It represents the culmination of an effort that began after the end of World War II to promote peace by uniting the European economies. Finally, there are those analysts who predict that the euro will present the first serious challenge to the dollar since the dollar dethroned the British pound as the world's leading currency.

There are also critics of the euro who contend that it will not solve Europe's problems, which are a high unemployment rate and numerous rules and regulations that tend to stultify entrepreneurship. The euro has dropped 10.4 percent against the dollar since it was introduced on January 1, 1999. There is concern over the economic soundness of the European Union, in part attributable to the conflict in Kosovo. The euro is also supposed to facilitate a flow of investment from one European nation to another, but some nations may benefit while others may not. Finland, with an unemployment rate of 15 percent, should presumably benefit, but will not because it is expensive to hire Finnish labor. Under Finnish law, if a salary is $1,000 a month, an employer pays a tax payment of $900 to the Finnish government. Firing someone is very difficult, no matter the cause.

The Importance of the European Union to the United States

The European Union is a major foreign trade rival of the United States. It forms the world's largest trading bloc, accounting for 30 percent of the value of world foreign trade. Table 15-2 provides a comparison of the monetary value of foreign trade to the European Union and its most important rival, NAFTA. The European

TABLE 15-2   *Foreign Trade of the European Union Countries and of NAFTA Members, 1997 ($ millions)*

	Merchandise Exports	Merchandise Imports	Service Exports	Service Imports
European Union				
Austria	57,684	62,638	26,669	24,942
Belgium*	165,725	151,973	34,855	31,866
Denmark	48,793	44,427	15,146	14,990
Finland	40,933	30,991	7,168	8,377
France	282,944	266,165	81,144	63,651
Germany	510,570	434,861	79,904	119,507
Greece	10,788	25,191	9,287	4,650
Ireland	53,258	39,192	6,159	15,069
Italy	238,161	204,098	72,310	70,429
Netherlands	184,295	162,155	49,774	45,197
Portugal	23,510	34,338	7,593	6,387
Spain	101,228	118,478	43,902	24,675
Sweden	81,057	62,854	17,848	19,559
United Kingdom	278,784	305,074	87,239	72,032
Total	2,077,730	1,942,435	538,998	521,331
NAFTA				
Canada	211,966	195,039	30,018	36,361
Mexico	109,890	111,847	11,140	12,616
United States	637,505	894,995	256,163	166,194
Total	959,361	1,201,881	297,321	215,171

Belgium includes Luxembourg.

Source: The World Bank, *1999 World Bank Indicators* (Washington, D.C.: The World Bank, 1999), 204, 205, 206, 209, 210, 212, 213, 214, 216, 217, 218.

TABLE 15-3

U.S. Foreign Trade with the EU and EU Foreign Trade with the U.S., 1998 ($ millions)

Country	U.S. Exports	U.S. Imports
Austria	2,506	2,558
Belgium-Luxembourg	14,524	8,796
Denmark	1,874	2,382
Finland	1,915	2,595
France	17,728	24,077
Germany	26,642	49,824
Greece	1,355	467
Ireland	5,653	8,385
Italy	9,027	21,013
Netherlands	19,004	7,591
Portugal	888	1,266
Spain	5,465	4,784
Sweden	3,819	7,837
United Kingdom	39,070	34,793
Total	149,470	176,368

Source: U.S. Department of Commerce, International Trade Administration, Foreign Trade Highlights 1998, *http://www.ita.doc.gov.icgilotea*, Tables 6, 7.

Union is an important outlet for American goods and services, and an important supplier of the same to the United States. In terms of foreign investment, 40 percent of U.S. foreign direct investment is in the European Union countries, and over half of foreign direct investment in the United States comes from the European countries. Table 15-3 compares U.S. merchandise trade with the European Union and European Union trade with the United States for 1998. Table 15-4 compares U.S. direct investment in the European Union and European Union direct investment in the United States.

The United States, and for that matter Canada and Mexico, is bound to Europe by culture and history. The great majority of immigrants who came to this country during the latter part of the nineteenth century and the early part of the twentieth century came from Europe, and ties still remain. The Protestant and Catholic religions were exported from Europe to the United States. Democratic institutions exist in Europe and in the United States. Living standards in the United States and Europe are comparable, so there is a mass market for consumer goods that has promoted increased investment in Europe by U.S. business firms, and conversely by European business firms in the United States. As the European Union expands to take in more countries, its importance to the United States will increase.

For all practical purposes the world can be divided up into three major economic areas: the euro area, which consists of the eleven countries that have adopted the euro as their common currency, the United States, and Japan. The three most important currencies of the world are the euro, the dollar, and the yen. The combined population of the three areas is around 700 million, or about 12 percent of the world's population, and their combined share of GDP is around 43 per-

TABLE 15-4   *U.S. Direct Investment in the EU and EU Direct Investment in the U.S., 1997* (*$ millions*)

Countries	U.S. Direct Investment	EU Direct Investment in U.S.
Austria	2,621	1,831
Belgium	17,403	6,771
Denmark	2,576	3,025
Finland	1,338	3,089
France	34,615	47,089
Germany	43,931	69,701
Greece	638	—
Ireland	14,476	10,514
Italy	17,749	3,318
Luxembourg	9,796	6,218
Netherlands	64,648	84,862
Portugal	1,498	—
Spain	11,642	2,643
Sweden	7,299	13,147
United Kingdom	138,765	129,551
	368,995	381,759
World direct investment by US	860,723	World direct investment in U.S. 681,651

Source: U.S. Department of Commerce, Bureau of Economic Analysis, U.S. Direct Investment Position Abroad on a Historical Cost Basis and Foreign Direct Investment in the United States on a Historical Cost Basis, *http://www.bea.doc.gov/bea.doc.gov/bea/di/diapos.97*, June 1998.

TABLE 15-5   *A Comparison of the Euro Area with the United States and Japan, 1998*

	Euro Area	United States	Japan
Population (millions)	292.0	270.0	127.0
Share of world GPP	15.0	20.0	7.7
Government receipts (% of GDP)	46.7	35.9	33.0
Exports (% of GDP)	13.6	8.5	10.0
Imports (% of GDP)	12.0	11.1	8.1
Real GDP growth	3.0	3.3	−2.5
Inflation	0.9	1.5	0.8
Unemployment rate	10.8	4.4	4.4
Gross debt (as a % of GDP)	73.8	59.3	115.6
Current account balance (% of GDP)	1.1	−1.7	2.3

Source: European Central Bank, *Monthly Bulletin, January 1999* (Frankfurt am Main, Germany: European Central Bank, 1999), 12.

cent. As Table 15-5 indicates, the three areas account for around one-third of the foreign trade of the world. Assuming that the United Kingdom, Denmark, and Sweden adopt the euro and Greece meets the eligibility requirements, the euro area and the European Union will be the same. Currently, what you have is a

United Europe, the United States, and Japan accounting for the bulk of economic activity in the world.

THE NORTH AMERICAN FREE TRADE AGREEMENT (NAFTA)

Another important example of regional economic integration is the North American Free Trade Agreement (NAFTA), but it is totally different from the European Union. It is not an economic union or a political union as is the European Union. It has no common monetary unit, no common central bank, no common judicial system, and no common political system. It is simply a free trade area where the United States, Canada, and Mexico have agreed to remove trade and other barriers to international trade among themselves. It represented an extension of the Canada–U.S. Free Trade Agreement, which was signed in 1988 and entered into effect in 1989. NAFTA was negotiated among the United States, Canada, and Mexico in 1992, ratified in 1993, and came into effect on January 1, 1994. It is an area that accounts for around 6 percent of the world's population and around 28 percent of its GNP.

NAFTA was and remains controversial in the United States. It passed Congress by a small margin after weeks of acrimonious debate.[11] It also had some opposition from Mexicans on the grounds that it represented a prime example of American imperialism. Many Americans felt that the United States had little to gain by admitting Mexico into NAFTA. After all, it was argued it was a Third World country with a standard of living much lower than ours or Canada's. The arguments for NAFTA were that it would create jobs that were higher paying than those that were lost to Mexico, and tariffs would be lower and more manufactured goods could be sold to Mexico.

The importance of Canada and Mexico to the United States cannot be minimized. In terms of the total value of merchandise trade, Canada ranks as the most important trading partner of the United States, and Mexico ranked third in 1998. The United States does more trade with Canada and Mexico than with the entire European Union, and this will continue in the future. The United States has more direct investment in the European Union than it does in Canada and Mexico. Table 15-6 presents the population, real GNP, and real per capita GNP for the

http://

The NAFTA home page is at www .iep.doc.gov/ nafta/nafta2.htm.

TABLE 15-6   *Population, Real GNP, and Real per Capita GNP for NAFTA Members, 1998*

	Population (thousands)	Real GNP ($ millions)	Real per Capita GNP (%)
United States	267.6	7,690.1	28,740
Canada	30.3	661.6	21,860
Mexico	94.3	770.3	8,120
Total	392.2	9,122.0	

Source: The World Bank, *1999 World Bank Atlas* (Washington, D.C.: The World Bank, 1999), 24, 25, 42, 43.

Country	Exports	Imports	Total	TABLE 15-7
Canada	156,308	177,844	334,152	*U.S. Trade with Canada and Mexico, 1998 ($ millions)*
Mexico	79,016	94,709	173,725	
Total	235,324	272,553	507,877	

Source: http://www.ita.doc.gov/cgi.bin/otea, Tables 6, 7.

TABLE 15-8   *U.S. Direct Investment in Canada and Mexico and Canadian and Mexican Direct Investment in the U.S., 1997 ($ millions)*

Country	U.S. Direct Investment	Foreign Direct Investment in the U.S.
Canada	99,859	64,022
Mexico	25,395	1,723
	125,254	65,745

Source: U.S. Department of Commerce, Bureau of Economic Analysis, U.S. Direct Investment Abroad and Foreign Direct Investment in the U.S. on an Historical Cost Basis, http://www.bea.doc.gov/bea/di/fdi.web

NAFTA countries. Table 15-7 presents the value of merchandise trade with Canada and Mexico for 1998. The total value of exports and imports exceeds the value of U.S. exports and imports with the EU. Table 15-8 presents the value of U.S. direct investments in Canada and Mexico and the value of Canadian and Mexican investments in the United States.

Provisions of NAFTA

There are several provisions to NAFTA ranging from the elimination of tariffs and other barriers to the free flow of goods and services between the three countries to cooperation on environmental problems. These provisions are:

Market Access
1. Within fifteen years after its implementation in 1994, all tariffs will be eliminated on North American products traded between Canada, Mexico, and the United States.
2. Within five years of its implementation, 65 percent of all U.S. exports of industrial goods to Mexico will enter tariff-free.
3. Mexico, once the treaty was implemented, would immediately eliminate tariffs on nearly 50 percent of all industrial goods imported from the United States.
4. Government procurement was to be opened up over ten years, with firms of the three countries able to bid on government contracts.
5. Tariffs are to be removed on car imports over a period of ten years. Mexico's import quota on cars is also to be lifted during the same period.

6.   Most tariffs between the United States and Mexico on agricultural products
     were eliminated immediately after implementation of the agreement in 1994.

Investment
1.   NAFTA gives U.S. companies the right to establish firms in Mexico and
     Canada or to acquire existing firms.
2.   Investors have the right to repatriate profits and capital; the right to fair com-
     pensation in the event of expropriation;[12] and the right to international arbi-
     tration in disputes between investors and government that involve monetary
     damage.
3.   NAFTA broadens investments to cover such areas as banking, real estate, legal
     services, consulting, publishing, and tourism.
4.   Certain types of investments are restricted. Mexico prohibits foreign invest-
     ment in petroleum and railroads;[13] Canada prohibits investment in its cultural
     media; and the United States excludes investments in aviation transport, mar-
     itime, and telecommunication.

Intellectual Property Rights
1.   NAFTA requires each country to enforce the rights of authors, artists, and
     inventors against infringement and piracy.
2.   It ensures protection for North American producers of computer programs,
     sound recordings, motion pictures, encrypted satellite signals, and other cre-
     ations.
3.   It locks in the availability of patent protection for most technologies in Mex-
     ico, allowing U.S. firms to patent a broad range of inventions in Mexico.

Environment.   Environmentalist groups in the United States were opposed to
NAFTA on the grounds that the Mexican government had done very little about
controlling environmental problems. Major cities such as Mexico City, Guadala-
jara, and Monterey have serious air pollution problems.[14] However, the main cause
of environmental concern was the U.S.–Mexico border where maquiladora plants
were operating from Matamoros to Tijuana.[15] These plans import unfinished
goods or component parts from the United States, further process these goods or
parts, and re-export them to the United States. The goods produced by
maquiladoras enjoy preferential customs and tax treatments by both countries'
governments. The plants by themselves create pollution, but they attract thousands of workers to such border cities as Matamoros, Juarez, and Tijuana, creating
air and water pollution. To address this concern, the U.S. and Mexican governments created the Border Environmental Plan, which covers air, water, hazardous
materials, and ground pollution. Its objectives are:

1.   To strengthen existing environmental laws
2.   To build waste water treatment systems
3.   To create joint air pollution monitoring programs
4.   To increase cooperative planning, training, and education

Production for U.S. Workers

1. NAFTA provides a transition period of up to fifteen years to eliminate U.S. tariffs on the most labor-sensitive U.S. products, such as household glassware, footwear, and some fruits and vegetables.
2. It provides safeguards that permit a temporary hike in U.S. tariff rates to pre-NAFTA levels to protect U.S. workers and farmers from being injured or threatened with injury by increased imports from Mexico.
3. It provides tough rules of origin to guarantee that the benefits of NAFTA tariff reductions go only to products made in North America.
4. It holds the three countries liable for penalties for nonenforcement of child, minimum wage, and health and safety laws.

Other Treaty Provisions

1. Any country can leave the treaty with six months' notice.
2. It allows for the inclusion of any additional country. Chile was to be invited to join in 1996, but there was little support for its membership.[16]

Results of NAFTA

The early years of NAFTA were affected by the Mexican currency crisis of December 1994. Mexico's trade deficit increased in 1993 and 1990 to the point where it was losing its foreign financial reserves. In December 1994, at a time when foreign exchange reserves held by the government had dropped from $26 billion to $7 billion, the peso, which had been tied to the dollar at an exchange rate of approximately 3.4 pesos to the dollar, was devalued by about 35 percent against the dollar. To shore up confidence in the Mexican financial system, the Clinton administration provided a $40 billion assistance package to guarantee the sale of Mexican government dollar-denominated Treasury bonds to foreign investors. The devaluation of the Mexican peso increased Mexican exports to the United States and Canada because they were cheaper than before. Conversely, U.S. and Canadian exports to Mexico declined because they became more expensive.[17]

In general, criticisms of NAFTA have become rather subdued in the United States. The American economy has performed well, the unemployment rate has fallen to its lowest level in twenty-five years, and the stock market is up, transforming many Americans into paper millionaires. Moreover, U.S. exports to Mexico were up by 11 percent in 1997; conversely, Mexican exports to the United States increased by 10 percent in the same year. In 1997 as well U.S. exports to Canada were up 3 percent and U.S. imports from Canada increased by 4 percent. Some U.S. jobs were lost to Mexico, but jobs were also created as a result of an increase in exports to Mexico and Canada. Typically, the jobs created by increased trade with Mexico are in the higher paying, higher value-added industries, such as communications, and the jobs lost to Mexico have been in the lower-paying, low-value-added industries.[18]

TABLE 15-9   *Population and Income for MERCOSUR Countries, 1997*

Country	Population (thousands)	Real GNP ($)	Real GNP per Capita (international PPP)
Argentina	35,677	355.0	9,950
Bolivia	7,767	22.4	2,810
Brazil	163,689	1,019.9	6,240
Chile	14,622	176.6	12,240
Paraguay	5,085	19.7	3,870
Uruguay	3,266	27.3	8,460
Total	230,106	$1,620.9	

Source: The World Bank, *1999 World Bank Atlas* (Washington, D.C.: The World Bank, 1999), 24, 25, 42, 43.

MERCOSUR

http://

Visit the MERCOSUR home page at www .mercosur.org.

On March 26, 1991, the Asuncion Treaty was signed by four South American countries, Argentina, Brazil, Paraguay, and Uruguay, to create a customs union called the Mercado Comun del Sur (MERCOSUR). The treaty linked four contiguous countries, two of which are Argentina and Brazil, the largest and most important countries in South America, and the other two, Paraguay and Uruguay, are among the smallest and least important countries in South America. These countries have been at war with each other or with someone else during part of their history. Two other countries, Bolivia and Chile, have applied for membership and are supposed to be admitted in 2000. The customs union will create another regional market that will encompass 65 percent of the population of South America, close to 70 percent of its land area, and 65 percent of its GDP. Table 15-9 presents the population, real GNP, and real per capita GNP for the MERCOSUR countries.

Reasons for MERCOSUR

The performance of the Latin American countries was poor during the 1980s. Inflation was high, economic growth rates were low, foreign debts increased, and currency instability was common. Argentina had a negative growth rate during the 1980s. Its currency problems were so bad that the peso was replaced by a new currency called the astral. Brazil had borrowed heavily in the world capital markets, pledging future revenues from the sale of coffee as debt repayment. However, like oil prices, the world price of coffee fell during the 1980s. Uruguay had its internal problems with urban terrorists called the Tupumaros who had a nasty habit of kidnapping, and sometimes executing, American businessmen.[19] Paraguay was ruled by a military dictatorship and had one of the lowest living standards in South America.

Table 15-10 presents the value of U.S. trade with the MERCOSUR countries for 1998. The total value of trade between the United States and MERCOSUR is less than half of the value of its trade with Mexico. Brazil is the most important

Country	Exports	Imports
Argentina	5,585	2,252
Bolivia	403	224
Brazil	15,157	10,123
Chile	3,985	2,453
Paraguay	786	34
Uruguay	591	256
Total	26,507	15,342

TABLE 15-10
U.S. Trade with MERCOSUR, 1998 ($ millions)

Source: U.S. Department of Commerce, International Trade Administration, United States Foreign Trade Highlights, March 1999, http://www.ita.doc.gov./cgi.bin/otea.

Argentina	9,766
Brazil	35,727
Chile	7,767
Total	53,260
South America	67,112
Central America	48,881
Caribbean[2]	56,489
Total	172,482

TABLE 15-11
U.S. Direct Investment in MERCOSUR, 1997 ($ millions)[1]

[1] *No data for Bolivia, Paraguay, and Uruguay*
[2] *Of the total, $33,092 is invested in Bermuda to build hotels and condominiums to attract the Yankee dollar.*

trading partner for the United States. Table 15-11 presents U.S. direct investment in the MERCOSUR countries. Brazil and Argentina constitute two-thirds of U.S. direct investment in South America. Total U.S. direct investment in all of Latin America mounted to $172.4 million in 1997. Conversely, Latin American direct investment in the United States amounted to $35.7 billion in 1997. This imbalance goes back to the beginning of the twentieth century when the Latin American countries were the most important area for U.S. direct investments. Countries that attracted American investments were those that were rich in natural resources. Mexico and Venezuela became particularly important to U.S. investors because they possessed oil.

APEC

The Asian Pacific Economic Cooperation (APEC) is the largest trade group in the world. It consists of 40 percent of the world's population, over half of the world's real GNP, and accounts for over half of the world's foreign trade. As Table 15-12 indicates, it is a very diverse group, ranging from China, the largest country in the world, to Brunei, which has a population of 308,000. Using real GNP as

http://

Information on APEC can be seen at www.apec.org.

TABLE 15-12   *Population, Real per Capita GNP, and Real GDP for APEC Countries, 1997*

Country	Population (thousands)	Real per Capita GNP ($)	Real GDP ($ millions)
Australia	18,532	19,510	373.2
Brunei[1]	308	—	—
Canada	30,287	21,750	661.6
Chile	14,622	12,240	176.6
China	1,227,117	3,570	4,382.5
Hong Kong	6,502	24,350	—
Indonesia	200,390	3,390	690.7
Japan	126,091	24,400	2,950.7
Korea	45,991	13,430	621.1
Malaysia	21,667	3,340	229.3
Mexico	94,349	8,110	770.3
New Zealand	3,761	15,780	60.9
Papua New Guinea	4,501	—	—
Philippines	73,527	3,670	269.2
Singapore	3,104	29,230	89.6
Chinese Taipei[2]	—	—	—
Thailand	60,602	6,490	399.3
United States	267,336	29,080	7,690.1
Total		2,298,687	19,365.1

[1] *Brunei is an oil-rich country ruled by a sultanate.*
[2] *Taipei is the capital of Taiwan, which is not recognized as a country.*

Source: The World Bank, *1999 World Bank Atlas* (Washington, D.C.: The World Bank, 1999), 24–25, 42–43.

a measurement of the size of an economy, it has the three largest economies in the world—the United States, China, and Japan. Unlike the European Union, APEC covers an enormous amount of territory and distance. Geographically, Australia, Canada, China, and the United States are all much larger in size than the European Union. In terms of distance the EU is much more compact than APEC. Australia and Japan are more than halfway around the world from Canada and the United States.

So why then is APEC important enough for the United States to join? As is shown in Table 15-13 the total value of U.S. foreign trade with China, Japan, Singapore, and Taiwan is larger than its trade with the EU and Canada and Mexico. Also, until the Asian currency crisis, South Korea, Malaysia, Thailand, and Indonesia had much higher growth rates than most countries, and China has maintained one of the highest growth rates of any country in the world. However, the East Asian currency crisis has had an adverse impact on the economies of South Korea, Malaysia, Thailand, and Indonesia. Japan, before it developed serious economic problems, had outperformed the other major industrial countries. The Chinese Economic Area consisting of China, Hong Kong, and Taiwan has become an important trading bloc on its own.

	Exports	Imports
Australia	14,226	5,382
Chile	3,985	2,453
China	14,258	71,156
Hong Kong	12,928	10,538
Japan	57,888	121,982
Malaysia	8,953	19,001
Philippines	6,736	11,949
Singapore	15,674	18,357
South Korea	16,528	23,937
Taiwan	18,157	33,123
Thailand	5,233	13,434
Total	174,566	331,312
Canada	156,308	174,844
Mexico	79,010	94,709
Total	409,884	600,865

TABLE 15-13
U.S. Foreign Trade with the APEC Countries, 1998 ($ millions)

Source: U.S. Department of Commerce, International Trade Administration, United States Foreign Trade Highlights 1998, http://www.ita.doc.gov .icqi.lotea, Tables 6, 7.

Purpose of APEC

APEC was formed in 1998 as an informal group of twelve countries, with the purpose of creating economic cooperation in the East Asian countries. The first formal meeting of APEC was held in Seattle, Washington, in November 1993 and was attended by President Clinton. The countries attending the meeting agreed to a broad vision of free trade and investment to be defined within a year. A second meeting was held in Bogor, Indonesia, in 1994 where the countries agreed to a policy of free trade and investment by the year 2020. A subsequent meeting in Osaka, Japan, endorsed an action agenda that would provide a blueprint for the implementation of free trade. At Subic, Philippines, in 1996 individual member countries published short- and medium-term plans that contained time frames for the elimination of trade and investment barriers by 2020. The 1997 APEC meeting in Vancouver, Canada, resulted in the liberalization of trade in key economic sectors, including chemicals, forest products, automobiles, food, and aircraft.

EUROPE-LATIN AMERICA FREE TRADE ZONE

European Union and Latin American leaders met on June 29, 1999 to attempt to forge an economic alliance to counterbalance the political and economic dominance of the United States. It would merge the 15 countries of the European Union with the 33 nations of Latin America and the Caribbean into a free-trade zone. In November 1999 representatives from Europe and Latin America will meet to set a goal of creating the zone by 2001. Europe is the most important trading partner and investor in Latin America. Culturally, there is a closer link between Europe and Latin America than between the United States and Latin America. The historical link with Spain is evidenced by the fact that Spain accounts for one-third of European direct investment in Latin America.

CRITICISM OF REGIONAL TRADING BLOCS

Regional trading blocs have proliferated like dandelions. IN addition to the EU, NAFTA, MERCOSUR, and APEC, others include:

1. The Central American Common Market (CACM). CACM consists of the Central American countries of Costa Rica, El Salvador, Guatemala, Honduras, and Nicaragua, with a combined population of 32 million. It is a free-trade area.
2. The Central European Free Trade Area (CEFTA). CEFTA consists of the countries of the Czech Republic, Hungary, Poland, Slovak Republic, and Slovenia, with a combined population of 66 million. With the exception of Slovenia, the other countries were formerly a part of the Council for Mutual Economic Assistance (CMEA) dominated by the former Soviet Union.[20] Free trade is to be phased in by the year 2000.
3. Southern Africa Development Community (SADC). SADC consists of twelve southern African countries, including South Africa, with a population of 145 million. Its objective is to eliminate tariff barriers in the region.
4. Common Market for Eastern and Southern Africa (COMESA). COMESA consists of twenty countries in Eastern and Southern Africa, with a population of 275 million. It began as a preferential trade area in 1981. Its goal is the creation of a common market by 2000 and eventually an economic union.
5. Australia-New Zealand Closer Economic Relations (ANZCERTA). ANZCERTA includes two countries with a combined population of 21 million and a GDP of $425 billion. Its purpose is to eliminate tariff and non-tariff barriers, including subsidies and government procurement policies, on all trade between the two countries.

Regional trading blocs are criticized on the basis of their exclusivity. It is probably good for those countries who belong because it combines their interests toward achieving a common goal. However, by liberalizing trade only with their neighbors, countries are by definition discriminating against those not lucky enough to be asked to join the bloc. Some goods will be imported from other members of the free-trade area at the expense of producers elsewhere; and members will begin to specialize in areas where they lack comparative advantage. Slow progress has also bedeviled regional trade integration. Despite much talk about expanding NAFTA to include every country in North America and South America by early in the twenty-first century, the membership in NAFTA remains stuck at three and will stay there for the foreseeable future. NAFTA also has complicated rules of origin requirements by stipulating how much of a car needs to be made in Mexico to qualify as NAFTA admissible.

http://

See the SADC site at www.sadc.int.

http://

See the COMESA home page at www.comesa.int.

There are also arguments for regional trading blocs. The first argument is economic. Regions can achieve additional gains from the free flow of trade and investment among the member countries beyond those normally attainable through trade. They can specialize in the production of goods and services that they can produce most efficiently. Foreign direct investment can stimulate economic growth. In the case of NAFTA investments in the three countries have increased since its inception in 1994. In that year U.S. direct investment in Canada was $72.8 billion; in 1997 it was $99.8 billion, a gain of 40 percent, while U.S. direct investment in Mexico increased from $16.4 billion in 1994 to $25.4 billion in 1997, a gain of 55 percent. Conversely, Canadian investment in the United States increased from $43.2 billion in 1994 to $64 billion in 1997, a gain of 48 percent, while Mexican direct investment in the U.S. increased from $1.1 billion in 1994 to $1.7 billion in 1997, a gain of 55 percent. (See Table 15.8.)

The second argument for regional trading blocs is political. A main argument for the creation of the European Union is that old enemies would be brought together as trading partners. Within seventy years, France and Germany fought three major wars on French soil, with Germany as the invader. Italy and Austria have also been enemies and have gone to war over territorial claims. Political relationships between the United States and Mexico have been anything but smooth, and MERCOSUR brings together two old enemies, Argentina and Paraguay. Thus, by linking neighboring economies and making them more dependent on each other, incentives are created for political cooperation among the countries. In turn, the potential for violence between the countries is reduced.

SUMMARY

The world has merged into regional trading blocs, the most important of which are the European Union, NAFTA, and APEC. The EU is more than just a trading bloc. Its goal is to achieve the complete economic and political integration of Western Europe, with a common currency called the euro. It will rival the United States and Japan as a world economic and political superpower. Other regional trading blocs are not nearly as ambitious in their scope. NAFTA involves the integration of the United States, Canada, and Mexico into a free-trade area. There is no common currency, no common political system, and no common central bank. MERCOSUR is a customs union created by Argentina, Brazil, Uruguay, and Paraguay. It is to be expanded to include Chile and Bolivia. APEC is the largest trading bloc in the world and includes the United States, China, and Japan among its members. Its purpose is to lower tariffs and other trade barriers.

QUESTIONS FOR DISCUSSION

1. Discuss the differences between the European Union and NAFTA.
2. Discuss the economic and political arrangements of the European Union.
3. What is the euro? Why is it important?

4. In your opinion, has NAFTA helped or hindered the United States? Should Mexico have been admitted?

5. How does MERCOSUR differ from NAFTA?

6. Are regional trading blocs good or bad? Discuss.

RECOMMENDED READINGS

Bannister, Rebecca R. *The NAFTA Success Story: More Than Just Trade.* Washington, D.C.: Progressive Policy Institute, 1997.

Bergsten, E. Fred. "America and Europe: The Class of the Titans." *Foreign Affairs* Vol. 78, No. 2 (March/April 1999): 20–34.

Drucker, Peter F. "The Global Economy and the Nation State." *Foreign Affairs* Vol 76, No. 5 (September/October 1997): 159–71.

Frankel, Jeffrey. *Regional Trading Blocs.* Washington, D.C.: Institute for International Economics, 1997.

Heifbauer, Gary Clyde, and Jeffrey J. Schott. *Western Hemisphere Economic Integration.* Washington, D.C.: Institute for International Economics, 1994.

NOTES

1. CARICOM is a common market consisting of Antigua and Barbuda, Bahamas, Barbados, Belize, Dominica, Grenada, Guyana, Jamaica, Monserrat, St. Kitts-Neves, St. Lucia, St. Vincent and the Grenadines, Surinan, and Trinidad-Tobago, with a combined population of around five million.

2. Mercado comun del Sur. Bolivia and Chile became members in 2000.

3. There were two separate Germanies then—West Germany, called the Federal Republic of Germany, and East Germany, called the German Democratic Republic.

4. The Treaty of Paris in 1951 and the Treaty of Rome in 1957 form the constitutional foundation of the European Union. The Treaty of Paris created the European Coal and Steel Community.

5. In September 1992 the United Kingdom and Italy pulled out of the ERM. In August 1993 the 2.25 fluctuation band was widened to 15 percent.

6. The Deutsche Bundesbank was the most powerful central bank in Europe and the mark was the strongest currency.

7. The ECU was used for accounting purposes within the EU and international financial markets. It exchanged with the U.S. dollar at a rate that varied. On December 16, 1998, the rate was $1 = 1.18$ ECUs.

8. The same is also true of Denmark. It remains to be seen whether Norway and Switzerland will join.

9. The British pound was the center of the Gold Standard (1821–1931). All countries of the world had their currencies linked to the pound.

10. This is true of the U.S. House of Representatives.

11. It was an issue in the 1992 presidential election. Ross Perot capitalized on it to get around 19 million votes as a third-party candidate.

12.   In 1938 the Mexican government expropriated the British and American oil companies operating in Mexico.

13.   The petroleum industry was once owned by the Americans and British. The railroads were once owned by the Americans.

14.   Monterey is the industrial center of Mexico. Increased population has contributed to pollution in the major Mexican cities.

15.   Maquiladora plants, or "screwdriver plants," as they are called, are assembly plants. They have had little supervision from Mexican authorities.

16.   Given Chile's distance from NAFTA, it made little sense. Chile is a member of MERCOSUR and APEC.

17.   In 1998 Mexico had a favorable trade balance with Canada and the United States.

18.   Textile plants and parts assembly plants have moved to Mexico.

19.   Apparently, the Tupumaros were sophisticated enough to distinguish Americans from other foreigners. One way to tell Americans was by the shoes they wore.

20.   CMEA used barter as a medium of exchange. There was no price competition among the countries and no reason to be efficient.

CHAPTER 16

The Twenty-First Century

At the beginning of the twentieth century, people inherited a world in which household electricity was a luxury, an automobile was an object of curiosity, and recreation represented a trip to the local band concert or vaudeville show. People did not live very long because diseases, such as malaria, pneumonia, and typhoid fever killed them. As the century progressed, people witnessed an unparalleled progression of advances. The movies became a common form of recreation. Mass production of the automobile made it affordable for the masses and stimulated the development of highways that ended community isolation. It took scarcely thirty years from the Wright brothers' first airplane flight at Kitty Hawk, North Carolina, to the launching of commercial aviation. Electric power became available for everyone. Relief from diseases arrived with the development of a number of wonder drugs that increased the length of life of people.[1]

Changes in technology, transportation, and communications have created a world where anything can be made anywhere on the face of the earth and sold everywhere else in the world. Education has become far more important than it was at the beginning or even the middle of the twentieth century because technology has increased the need for skilled workers. National boundaries are no longer as important because we have entered an era of globalization. A facet of globalization is an increased level of integration of production across national boundaries. Large multinationals have become more powerful than most nations.[2] Most of the world's population live in either rich countries or poor countries. The population has become older and more affluent in the rich countries, while it is expanding in the poor countries. Income inequality between rich and poor nations has increased.

So, what will the world of the twenty-first century be like? Will capitalism remain the triumphant economic ideology of the world? Can Europe hold together the world's largest regional trading bloc bolstered by a common currency, or will old political rivalries cause it to fall apart?[3] Does the future hold any hope for the poverty-stricken countries of the world? All of these questions are economic in nature, and their answers depend on the prospect of general peace in the century, which is predicated on the elimination of the nuclear arms threat that has held most of the world in thrall since the middle of the twentieth century. As witnessed by what has happened in Kosovo, ethnic rivalries still remain a destabilizing force throughout the world. The global financial crisis that began in Thailand and spread to other Asian countries is far from over.

The remainder of this chapter discusses some of the issues that will confront the twenty-first century. Population is certainly an important issue, as is the environment. There are those who feel that the time will come that the limits of the earth's natural resources and environmental degradation will slow growth in food production.[4] Also, is it a given that capitalism and democracy will be the dominant economic and political systems of the twenty-first century? Will it be true, as Francis Fukuyama contended, that the human race now has one common destiny, a destiny that began with the French Revolution and its ideals of liberty and equality and ended with the victory of the democratic state?[5] But as history teaches us, nothing remains constant in the world.[6]

POPULATION

http://

Check the World Population Profile at www.census .gov/ipc/www/ wp98.html.

In 1900 the population of the world was around 1.6 billion, one-third of whom lived in China and India. In October 1999 the world population is expected to reach 6 billion, one-third of whom live in China and India. In 1900 the population of India was 235.7 million. At the time of its independence in 1947 its population was 344.4 million, an increase of a little more than 100 million. In 1999 the population of India reached 1 billion, an increase of 665 million since 1947. Life expectancy in India for both sexes increased from 24 years in 1900 to 62 years in 1999. In 1900 births per 100 population in India were 4.6; in 1992 births per 100 population in India had decreased to 3. In the first 50 years of the twentieth century, India's population increased by 12 million a year. Even though birth rates and death rates have declined in India during the century, death rates have declined more than birth rates.

Table 16-1 compares the population growth of China, India, and Nigeria in the twentieth century. India and Nigeria were possessions of the British Empire, so they have somewhat similar backgrounds. Also presented is a comparison of real

Statistics on population growth:

1. Population increased during most of this century. It took all of human history to reach a world population of one billion in 1804. It took 123 years to reach two billion in 1927, 33 years to reach three billion in 1960, 14 years to reach four billion in 1974, 13 years to reach five billion in 1987, and 12 years to reach six billion by October 1999.

2. Although the growth rate has started to slow, world population still increases by 78 million a year. That is like adding 1.5 million people, or a city the size of Philadelphia, every week.

3. All of these people consume more resources, with the United States being the greatest consumer. In 1900, only a few thousand barrels of oil were consumed each day worldwide. Today, people use 72 million barrels a day. The use of metals has risen from 20 million tons a year to 1.2 billion tons a year.

4. People have never been healthier or wealthier, but the gap between rich nations and poor nations has widened. Half of all Americans are overweight, yet elsewhere 13,000 young children per day die of malnutrition and related illnesses.

5. Ozone depletion, global warming, overfishing, and falling water tables are a direct result of population and prosperity.

TABLE 16-1   *Population Growth and Real per Capita GDP Growth for China, India, and Nigeria*

	China		India		Nigeria	
	Population (millions)	*Real GDP ($)*	*Population (millions)*	*Real GDP ($)*	*Population (millions)*	*Real GDP ($)*
1900	400	523	235	531	16	—
1910	423	—	243	688	—	—
1920	472	—	253	629	—	—
1930	489	—	279	655	—	—
1940	519	—	318	650	—	—
1950	547	614	359	597	36	547
1955	609	818	393	665	40	646
1960	667	878	434	735	44	645
1965	715	945	485	785	48	777
1970	818	1,092	541	878	53	944
1975	916	1,250	607	900	59	1,153
1980	981	1,462	679	938	67	1,193
1985	1,015	2,084	755	1,096	76	965
1990	1,119	2,700	848	1,316	86	1,059
1995	1,200	2,920	929	1,400	111	750
2000*	1,280	3,524	1,003	1,660	124	880

*Estimate.

Source: Angus Maddison, *Monitoring the World Economy, 1820–1992* (Paris: Organization for Economic Cooperation and Development, 1997), 114, 115, 116, 204, 205, 206; World Bank, *1997 World Bank Atlas* (Washington, D.C.: World Bank, 1997), 16, 17, 36, 37.

per capita GDP for the three countries. Real GDP data are missing for China from 1910 to 1950 because the country was in a state of chaos. Warlords were running the country during much of the period, and China was at war with Japan from 1937 to 1945. The population of China was 381 million in 1820, 400 million in 1900, 547 million in 1950, and an estimated 1.3 billion in 2000. India's population increased by 60 million from 1820 to 1900, 125 million from 1900 to 1950, and 650 million from 1950 to 2000. Nigeria's population increased from 16 million in 1900 to 36 million in 1950. Its real per capita GDP reached its highest point in 1980 when world oil prices were high. In 1995 real per capita GDP was more than $300 less than it was in 1980, but the population had increased by 44 million.

Knowing the size, growth rate, and age distribution of a country's population is important for evaluating the welfare of the country's people, assessing the productive capacity of its economy, and estimating the quantity of goods and services that will be needed to meet its future needs. Table 16-2 presents birth rates and death rates for selected countries for two time periods, 1980 and 1997, and projected population by the year 2030. Birth rates and death rates for these countries were higher in 1980 than they were in 1997. The important point to make is that birth rates are not falling fast enough in the poor countries, and they are not increasing fast enough in the rich countries. In India, for example, both birth rates and death rates have fallen, yet the population is expected to increase by more than 400 million by 2030.

In general the unproductive segments of a country are persons younger than 15 and older than 64. In the poor countries the population is getting younger,

TABLE 16-2 *Birth Rates and Death Rates and Population Projections for Selected Countries (per 100 persons and millions of people)*

Country	Birth Rates		Death Rates		Population 1999	Population 2030
	1980	1997	1980	1997		
Bangladesh	44	28	18	10	123	189
China	18	17	6	8	1,227	1,486
Ethiopia	48	46	22	20	60	115
India	34	27	13	9	962	1,384
Nigeria	50	40	18	12	118	241
Pakistan	47	36	15	8	128	244
France	15	12	10	9	59	61
Germany	11	10	12	10	82	76
Italy	11	9	10	10	58	51
Russian Federation	16	9	11	14	147	132
United Kingdom	13	12	12	11	59	60
United States	16	15	9	8	268	313

Sources: The World Bank, *1999 World Development Indicators* (Washington, D.C.: The World Bank, 1999), 46–48; the World Bank, *1999 World Bank Atlas* (Washington, D.C.: The World Bank, 1999), 24, 25.

TABLE 16-3   *Labor Force Structure in Selected Countries, 1997 (millions)*

Country	Total Population	Total Population 15–64 in Labor Force	Total Population Not in Labor Force
Bangladesh	124	63	61
China	1,227	736	491
Ethiopia	60	26	34
India	962	423	539
Nigeria	118	47	71
Pakistan	128	48	80
France	59	26	33
Germany	82	41	41
Italy	58	25	33
Russian Federation	147	78	69
United Kingdom	59	30	29
United States	268	136	132

Sources: The World Bank, *1999 World Development Indicators* (Washington, D.C.: The World Bank, 1999), 50, 51; The World Bank, *1999 World Bank Atlas* (Washington, D.C.: The World Bank, 1999), 24, 25.

which increases the need for more expenditures on education. In the rich countries the population is getting older, which increases the need for expenditures on health care and pensions. Table 16-3 presents the population between the ages of 15 and 64 for selected countries. This segment is considered to be the productive segment that supports the rest of the population. In Bangladesh, for example, almost half of the population is not in the age group 15–64. The life expectancy at birth is 56.9 years, and the birth rate in 1997 was almost three times that of the death rate, so many more people are in the under 15 group than the 65 and over group. It would be exactly the opposite in Germany.[7]

Population and the Environment

Almost 45 percent of the world's population live in countries that have a low level of human development. The ratio of births to deaths is approximately 3 to 1.[8] If this ratio remains constant, many countries will double their population in 30 years. An ever-increasing population can also have an impact on the world's capacity to continue to feed it. Altogether, some 1 billion of the world's population are malnourished. Ninety-four percent of children under age 5 are malnourished in Malawi, 56 percent in Bangladesh, and 37 percent in India.[9] Environmental damage almost always hits those living in poverty the hardest. The majority of those who die each year from air and water pollution are poor people living in poor countries. Even though poor people carry the burden of environmental damage, it is the rich who pollute more and who generate more waste. But the poor put pressure on natural resources as they struggle to survive.

http://

Visit the UN Environment Programme at www.unep.org for information on global environmental issues or the World Bank site at www.worldbank.org.

Water Pollution.   Although considerable advances have been made in reducing water pollution, more than 1.3 billion people lack access to safe water and 2.5 billion people lack access to basic sanitation. Excrement ends up in ponds, streams and ditches, and open ground. Most of the waste waters of the lower-income countries and poor countries is discharged directly into streams, open drains, rivers, lakes, and coastal waters without treatment. In India there are major cities, towns, and thousands of villages along the banks of the Ganges River. Even though the river is sacred to millions of Hindus who believe that immersion or drinking it waters will lead to salvation, it is one of the most polluted rivers in the world. The 400 million people who live along the banks of the Ganges deposit nearly all their sewage into it. Industrial waste is added to this by the hundreds of factories along the river banks. To the human and factory effluents are added the runoffs from more than 6 million tons of chemical fertilizers.[10]

Table 16-4 presents the percentage of people from various geographic areas of the world without access to safe drinking water and without access to basic sanitation. These areas are not just limited to poor countries. The Latin American countries range from Argentina and Chile, the two richest countries in Latin America, to Haiti and Nicaragua, the two poorest.

Air Pollution.   Air pollution from industrial emissions, car exhaust, and indoor pollution kills more than 2.7 million people each year. Although air pollution is seen as predominantly a problem of the developed countries, most of the pollution-related deaths occur in the less developed countries. The great majority of these deaths are from indoor pollution. Poor people must burn dung, wood, and crop residues indoors for their heating and cooking, especially in Africa. These fuels are much more polluting than modern alternatives such as kerosene and electricity. Burning them fills huts with smoke, carrying hundreds of toxic substances and causing deaths mainly from respiratory damage, heart and lung disease, and cancer. In Latin America, where a large proportion of the poorest people live in city slums, nearly two-thirds of the deaths from causes related to indoor pollution are in urban areas.[11]

TABLE 16-4   *Lack of Access to Safe Water and Basic Sanitation*

Region	People without Access to Safe Water (%)	People without Access to Basic Sanitation (%)
Sub-Saharan Africa	48	55
South-East Asia and the Pacific	35	45
Latin America and the Caribbean	23	29
East Asia	32	73
South Asia	18	64
Developing countries	29	58
Least developed countries	43	64

Source: United Nations Development Program, *Human Development Report, 1998* (New York: Oxford University Press, 1998), 68.

TABLE 16-5   *Deaths from Air Pollution by World Regions, 1996 (thousands)*

| Regions or Country | Deaths from Indoor Pollution | | Deaths from Outdoor Pollution |
	Rural	Urban	Urban
India	496	93	84
Sub-Saharan Africa	490	32	—
China	320	53	70
Other Asian countries	363	40	40
Latin America/Caribbean	180	113	113
	1,849	331	307

Source: United Nations Development Program, *Human Development Report, 1998* (New York: Oxford University Press, 1998), 70.

Table 16-5 presents the number of deaths in 1991 from indoor pollution and outdoor pollution in the developing and least developed countries of the world. Some of the world's largest cities are located in the least developed countries. The result is more air pollution and more deaths. Rapid industrialization in some countries also increases air pollution. Lead, which is still used in gasoline in many parts of the world, continues to be a hazard to human health, permanently impairing children's development.

Deforestation.   Another casualty of an ever-increasing population is the loss of forests and, with them, the loss of a diverse species of life forms. One of the worst offenders is Brazil. As its population has increased, so has its expansion into rural areas, with the end result that much of the rain forests of the Amazon have been destroyed. The average annual rate of deforestation in Brazil between 1990 and 1995 was 25,544 square kilometers, the highest for any country in the world. In Brazil and other countries, poor people are encouraged to clear forests and build settlements, only to find later that the soil is not good for agriculture. That leads to further deforestation, soil erosion, and flooding. There is a loss of biodiversity, which is an important factor in safeguarding the world's food supply. Table 16-6 presents the extent of deforestation for selected countries. Some of the major offenders are Latin American countries.

Global Warming.   The greenhouse effect is held to be the major cause of global warming. Carbon dioxide from the burning of fossil fuels such as oil, coal, and gasoline—all concomitants of higher living standards—accumulate in the atmosphere. These and other gases act like the glass in a greenhouse that lets in light but traps heat, causing the warming of the world. This disrupts a wide range of human and natural activities. A hotter climate could trigger an increase in floods, droughts, hurricanes, and heat waves.[12] These would disrupt crop harvests, inundate heavily populated low-lying coastal areas, and upset human settlement patterns. There would also be an increase in the number of infectious diseases such as malaria, yellow fever, and viral encephalitis.

TABLE 16-6
Average Annual Deforestation for Selected Countries, 1990–1995 (km²)

Angola	2,370
Bolivia	5,814
Brazil	25,544
Cameroon	1,638
Indonesia	10,844
Malaysia	4,002
Mexico	5,080
Nigeria	1,214
Philippines	2,624
Sudan	3,526
Tanzania	3,226
Venezuela	5,034
Zambia	2,644

Source: The World Bank, *1999 World Development Indicators* (Washington, D.C.: The World Bank, 1999), 122–24.

TABLE 16-7
A Comparison of per Capita Carbon Dioxide Emissions for Selected Countries, 1995 (metric tons)[1]

Country	Per Capita Metric Tons
Austria	16.0
Belgium	10.2
Canada	14.7
China	2.7
France	9.0
Germany	10.2
India	1.0
Italy	6.6
Japan	9.0
Norway	16.6
Russian Federation[2]	12.3
Singapore	21.3
United Kingdom	9.3
United States	20.8

[1] *Average for low-income countries including China and India, 1.4 per capita metric tons; average for high-income countries, 12.5 metric tons.*
[2] *The Russian Federation is a lower-middle income country. Little attention was given to pollution when the Soviet Union and Eastern Europe were communist.*

Source: The World Bank, *1998 World Development Indicators* (Washington, D.C.: The World Bank, 1998), 146, 147, 148.

Table 16-7 presents per capita carbon dioxide emissions for various countries for 1995. The United States, European Union, and Japan account for 13 percent of the world's population but produce 42 percent of global carbon dioxide emission. The rich countries account for 40 times as much global carbon dioxide emissions as do the poor countries. The United States, which has more cars than any other country, is one of the worst offenders. The average American produces 21 metric tons of carbon dioxide, more than twice as much as the average German or Japanese, even though their countries are much smaller and have a far greater population density. Singapore, which has one of the highest living standards in the world, is the leader when it comes to emission of carbon dioxide, but its land area is smaller than that of most American counties.

Depletion of the Ozone Layer.   The depletion of the ozone layer is a global problem. The ozone layer is one of the factors that has allowed life to thrive on earth by protecting living organisms by using up ultraviolet and other high-energy forms of radiation through a cycle of chemical reactions. When it is weakened, as it has been by the emission of freon gasses into the atmosphere, ultraviolet radiation interacts with genetic material, damaging it and increasing the incidence of various forms of skin cancer. It also would affect food supplies. More than two-thirds of crop species are damaged by ultraviolet light, which also can penetrate the sea, killing plankton that are vital to the marine food chain. The depletion of the ozone layer is a direct byproduct of higher living standards in the rich countries, in particular the United States.

Pesticides.   Pesticides create health problems in both rich countries and poor countries. Throughout the world various types of insects have made life miserable for farmers. In the United States the boll weevil destroyed the cotton economy of the South, and grasshoppers periodically would destroy corn and other farm products in the Great Plains states.[13] The development of pesticides was supposed to be a boon for farmers all over the world by killing the insects that ravished their crops, but it proved to be a double-edged sword. The grasshoppers and potato bugs of the world were destroyed but, in the process, the soil was polluted. Rain washed the pesticides into rivers and lakes, polluting the drinking water and killing the marine life.[14]

Uneven Effect of Environmental Pollution.   It can be said that the developed countries of the world do most of the polluting, but the damage done by it hits the poor countries the hardest. It is the wealthy countries of the world that contribute the most to global warming and generate the most waste. Yet, the overwhelming majority of those who die each year from air and waste pollution are poor people. There is a self-reenforcing spiral downward. Yesterday's resource despoilage causes today's poverty. As a result of increasing poverty and the absence of alternatives, poor people put increasing pressure on the natural resource base to survive. In the poor countries pressure on the environment intensifies every day as the world population continues to grow. By 2050 the population of Africa is projected to be three times greater than that of Europe's.[15]

   If the world population continues to grow as projected, it will put increased pressure on the world's food supply. At some point the limits of the earth's natural systems, the cumulative effects of environmental degradation on cropland productivity, and the shrinking backlog of yield-raising technology will slow the growth in food production. For example, there is a limit to the number of fish that oceans and inland waters can produce. As population has grown, and, along with it, the demand for fish that limit is being reached. Countries that are already densely populated risk losing cropland at a rate that exceeds the rise in land productivity, initiating a long-term decline in food production. The world's rangelands, a source of animal proteins, are also under pressure.

INCOME INEQUALITY AND ECONOMIC DEVELOPMENT

http://

Look up the UN's World Economic Situation and Prospects for the coming year at www.un.org/esa/ analysis/ddpa.htm.

In 1997 thirty-five percent of the world's population lived in the low-income or poorest countries in the world with a per capita GNP of $785 or less. Conversely, 16 percent of the world's population lived in the high income or rich countries with a per capita GNP of 9,565 or more. But that doesn't tell the complete story. Not only in the United States, but elsewhere, the rich of the world are getting richer, and the poor of the world are getting poorer. In 1960 the 20 percent of the world's population who lived in the rich countries had 30 times the income of the poorest 20 percent of the people. By 1980 the ratio between the richest 20 percent and poorest 20 percent had increased to 45 to 1, and by 1995 the ratio between the richest 20 percent and poorest 20 percent was 82 to 1. It is estimated that the world's 225 richest people have a combined wealth of over $1 trillion, equal to the annual income of the poorest 47 percent of the world's population.[16] Table 16-8 presents the ratios from 1960 to 1995.

Table 16-9 presents income disparities between the rich countries of the world and the poor countries of the world for 1997. The ratio between the average per capita incomes of the rich countries and the poor countries was 72 to 1; in 1989 it was 55 to 1. Per capita income growth from 1980 to 1997 showed little change for Sub-Saharan Africa and South Asia.[17] Nigeria's per capita GNP in 1989 was $250; in 1997 it was $280. India's per capita GNP in 1989 was $350; in 1997 it was $370.

Table 16-10 presents the extent of world poverty based on international standards. Different countries have different standards for measuring poverty, making comparisons between countries difficult. International poverty standards as used by the World Bank attempt to hold the real measure of poverty constant between

TABLE 16-8

Global Income Disparities between the Richest 20% and Poorest 20% of the Population

	Ratio of Richest to Poorest
1960	30 to 1
1970	32 to 1
1980	45 to 1
1989	59 to 1
1995	82 to 1

Source: United Nations Development Program, *Human Development Reports, 1992, 1998.* (New York: Oxford University Press, 1992, 1998), 36 (1992), 29 (1998).

TABLE 16-9   *GNP and GNP per Capita Based on Income for the World Countries, 1997*

	Number of Countries	GNP ($ millions)	Population (millions)	GNP per Capita (%)
Low ($785 or less)	61	712,452	2,036	350
Lower middle ($786–3,125)	59*	2,802,834	2,283	1,230
Upper middle ($3,125–9,655)	36	2,608,335	574	4,540
High ($9,656 or more)	54	24,001,123	927	25,890
World	210	30,124,744	5,820	5,180

Includes China, which had a per capita GNP of $860 in 1997.

Source: The World Bank, *1999 World Bank Atlas* (Washington, D.C.: World Bank, 1999), 38.

TABLE 16-10   *People Living on Less than $1 a Day (%)*

Country	Population (millions)	Percent below $1 a Day	Number (millions)
Bangladesh (est.)[1]	124	50	62
Brazil	164	33	54
China	1,227	22	270
Ethiopia (est.)[1]	60	70	42
Guatemala	11	55	6
India	962	47	420
Kenya	29	50	15
Madagascar	14	72	10
Mexico	94	15	14
Nepal	22	50	11
Nigeria	118	30	35
Pakistan	128	26	33
Peru (est.)[2]	24		13
Philippines	74	27	20
South Africa	41	24	10
Uganda	20	69	14
Zimbabwe	11	41	4
			1,033

[1] *Bangladesh is among the poorest countries in the world. The estimate, made by the author, may be too conservative. Ethiopia is the poorest country in the world.*
[2] *National poverty line.*

Sources: The World Bank, *1999 World Development Indicators* (Washington, D.C.: The World Bank, 1999), 66–68.

countries. The standard of $1 a day is measured in international prices and adjusted to local currencies by using purchasing power parity (PPP). The PPP is updated periodically to reflect changes in the cost of living in each country. Consumption is usually used as the indicator for deciding who is poor. In the table below the percentage of the population living on less than $1 a day is presented for countries with populations of 10 million or more. Several countries which are not considered to be among the poor countries are listed. A number of countries were left out because there were no data.[18] The total of 1 billion people represents 16 percent of the world's population.

Solutions

In 1996 the Development Assistance Committee of the OECD published a position paper titled "Shaping the 21st Century." It set six major goals for the first part of the twenty-first century:

1. Reduce by half the proportion of people in extreme poverty by 2015.
2. Achieve universal primary education in all countries by 2015.
3. Demonstrate progress toward gender equality and the empowerment of women by eliminating gender disparities in primary and secondary education by 2005.
4. Reduce by two-thirds the mortality rates for infants and children under five and by three-fourths the mortality rates for mothers by 2015.
5. Provide access to reproductive health service for all individuals of appropriate age no later than 2015.
6. Implement national strategies for sustainable development by 2005 to ensure that the current loss of environmental resources is reversed nationally and globally by 2015.

Implementing these goals will be easier said than done. For one thing, it calls for individual countries to take the initiative to achieve these goals, but the solutions will cost money which most of these countries do not have. More development assistance from the wealthy nations has to be forthcoming. Economic growth, although essential, is by no means sufficient to eliminate poverty or to bring about lasting economic and social development. True development entails the expansion of social services and of a basic infrastructure, in particular schools, hospitals, and transportation. It has to be built on good government, which is lacking in many countries. All of these requisites for development are necessary to attract private investment and to build a successful economy.

POLITICAL AND FINANCIAL INSTABILITY

The 1990s will not be known as a particularly peaceful decade. When the Cold War ended, the era of struggle was supposed to end, and with it a period of peace and prosperity was to begin. The Soviet Union disintegrated and the Warsaw Pact was dissolved. History was at an end, and liberal democracy combined with free markets were to become the only model a state would follow and would prevail everywhere.[19] To some extent it has worked out that way. Countries throughout the world have privatized most of their state-owned industries and have reduced trade barriers to promote a more open trade among countries. Economic reform would bring about political reform. Free trade, open markets, and capital flows would democratize virtually every country in the world, and democracies are not supposed to fight each other.[20]

However, at least for the present this brave new world has not come to fruition.[21] *accomplishment* Political instability has increased and terrorism has become an overt threat to the peace of the world. More countries now have the capability to develop nuclear weapons. There are still quite a few dictators running around, and democracy has yet to become a household word in many countries. The Japanese economy is still trying to work its way out of a recession. Four major financial crises have destabilized the financial world. The Mexican financial crisis had an adverse impact on the Latin American economies. The most serious financial crisis of the decade hit the East Asian countries in 1997, and the economies of Thailand, Malaysia, Indonesia, and South Korea went into an economic meltdown.

Political Instability

It was assumed that since the Cold War between the United States and the Soviet Union was over, hostilities throughout the world would cease. But that has not happened. If anything, the world has become more unstable. The dispute in Kosovo is a prime example. It involves ethnic and religious rivalries that date back for many centuries. It also involves a dispute over territorial claims. Military intervention on the part of the NATO alliance may have resolved the problem temporarily, but the problem will still be there long after the peacekeeping forces have been withdrawn. Serbian ethnic cleansing probably will strengthen the position of the Kosovo Liberation Army (KLA), which may well prepare for a guerrilla war to create an independent Kosovo and a larger Albania.

India and Pakistan.   India and Pakistan were once a part of the British empire, but that did not bind them into a common entity. For some 150 years the British army was able to keep control over a wide variety of disparate groups, but once India became an independent country in 1947, it did not take long for these groups to have a go at it. During the first three days of independence, Hindus and Moslems engaged in riots that resulted in the loss of many lives and the destruction of property. Eventually, two countries were created—Pakistan, which is predominantly Moslem, and India, which is predominantly Hindu. Millions of people had to leave their ancestral homes and migrate to one or the other of the independent countries. They lost most of their possessions, including factories and business establishments.

But religion is not the only problem between India and Pakistan. The two countries have been involved in territorial disputes that resulted in military conflict. In May 1998 India engaged in a series of nuclear tests, and it proclaimed itself a nuclear weapons state. Fifteen days later, Pakistan followed suit by conducting a series of nuclear tests and declaring that it, too, had nuclear weapons. In May of 1999 the Indian army was engaged in a fight with Kashmir separatists who India claimed had the support of the government of Pakistan. To some extent, Kashmir,

http://

Visit the Treasury Department's site on foreign asset control at www .treas.gov/ofac.

a province in northern India, is like Kosovo. Both India and Pakistan claim it. India wants it as a buffer against China, and Pakistan claims it because it was supposed to be given to it under the treaty that created an independent India and Pakistan.

China and the United States.   Although hardly in the same league as India and Pakistan, U.S.-Chinese relationships took a turn for the worse when the United States blew up the Chinese embassy in Belgrade and the Chinese stole U.S. military secrets. U.S.-Chinese relations have been remarkably one-sided in favor of the United States ever since the administration of Theodore Roosevelt proclaimed its Open Door policy, which opened up trade for the United States in China. As a result of this policy, China was exposed to the glories of American capitalism, as represented by Coca-Cola, and American religions, as represented by thousands of missionaries who spread the gospel to uncomprehending Chinese masses. Of the two, the latter did more good because they provided mission schools and hospitals.[22] When China became a communist country in 1949, it eliminated any form of capitalism and religion from its premises. After Mao, capitalism and Coca-Cola are back—after Deng Xiao Ping said "to get rich is glorious"—but religion is not.

The Middle East.   Despite his defeat in the Gulf War, Saddam Hussein is still in power in Iraq and remains a threat to stability in the area. Iraq is supposed to possess nuclear, chemical, and biological weapons of mass destruction that can destabilize the world. Then, there are Islamic fundamentalists who are hell-bent on returning the Islamic countries to the thirteenth century. A civil war exists in Algeria between the fundamentalists and the Algerian government. The potential for political instability exists in the Russian Federation and other parts of the former Soviet Union. Afghanistan, though unimportant in the world, is ruled by religious fundamentalists, who, among other things, do not believe women should be educated. Then, there is always the possibility of an outright war between Israel and its Arab neighbors.

Terrorism.   Terrorists in one form or another have always been around. In the nineteenth century, they were called anarchists and they threw bombs at people they did not like. They espoused a philosophy that any form of government or institution whatsoever was bad and that everyone should be free to do whatsoever he or she pleased. They were a force with which to be reckoned. An anarchist assassinated President William McKinley of the United States. Another anarchist assassinated Alexander the Czar of Russia, and a Serbian anarchist, Gavrito Princip, assassinated Franz Ferdinand, the Arch Duke of Austria, and started World War I. But anarchism as a political concept went out of style long ago and has been replaced by a far more deadly form of terrorism.

    In 1998 terrorists destroyed the American embassies in Kenya and Tanzania, killing more than 500 people, most of whom were citizens of the two countries.[23] There was no attempt to discriminate on the basis of nationalities. Unlike the anarchists of the last century who were overt in their assassinations, modern terrorists remain hidden. They can strike at any time as witnessed by the destruction of the Pan America passenger plane over Lockerbie, Scotland. Weapons of mass destruction are available anywhere in the world. The terrorists of today are likely to harbor ethnic grievances, harder to distinguish from others outside the law, and may be the computer hacker next door.[24] Terrorism has become a reality that countries will have to deal with.

Financial Instability

There have been four major financial crises during the 1990s, in Mexico, Brazil, East Asia, and the Russian Federation, that have created an element of financial instability in the world. The Mexican currency crisis of 1994 was the first of these crises. It occurred in 1994 and was caused by a number of factors, including an overvalued peso that was pegged to the U.S. dollar. Long-term interest rates increased in the United States as a result of the monetary policy of the Federal Reserve, which aimed at preventing inflation. As interest rates rose in the United States, foreign capital invested in Mexico and elsewhere poured into the United States, increasing the value of the dollar in world markets and also the value of the Mexican peso. Mexican imports increased, Mexican exports decreased, currency reserves left the country, and the peso collapsed. Recovery was aided by a bailout package put together by the United States.

The Tequila Effect.   The collapse of the Mexican peso caused severe financial headaches throughout Latin America, and international investors fled from financial markets throughout Latin America, not just Mexico. This so-called "tequila effect" reflected what many investors saw as only the first domino to fall in a long series of failures to come. The flight of capital from many Latin American countries was a cost they had to pay for previous financial mismanagement and political instability.

The Collapse of the Southeast Asian Currency Market.   Southeast Asia and Korea were a part of what was once called "the Asian miracle." All, with the exception of Thailand, were a part of the British, Dutch, and Japanese empires. For years, their growth rates were well above the world average. They outperformed the Latin American countries, which had relied on an import substitution approach to economic development by relying on policies to promote exports and relied on government intervention in key sectors of their economies. They made heavy investments in education and their labor force was among the best educated in the world. Their economies, unlike those of Latin America, were open to foreign trade and investment and, through reliance on economic planning, made capital investments in their infrastructure. Even when the Japanese economy developed serious problems during the first half of the 1990s, Southeast Asia and Korea continued to perform well.

However, in 1997 and 1998 the currencies of four Asian countries, Korea, Indonesia, Malaysia, and Thailand, collapsed with disastrous consequences to their economies. Fundamental problems were responsible for the collapse:

http://

Both the IMF and World Bank are valuable sources of international financial information at www.imf.org and www.worldbank.org.

To fix a price at certain level.

1. Most of the countries kept their currencies pegged to the dollar. This policy worked when the dollar was weak because their exports would sell cheaply in the world markets. But the dollar strengthened relative to other currencies in the world markets, and Asian exports became less competitive pricewise.
2. There was rampant corruption at the top levels of government. Corruption is by no means limited to Latin America and Africa; it exists in Asia as well. Unsecured loans were made by government officials to friends who speculated in real estate.
3. The financial and banking systems were weak and unregulated. There was no equivalent of the U.S. Securities and Exchange Commission or the Federal Reserve System.
4. Increased competition from China was also a factor. Chinese labor costs were lower than in the East Asian countries, and Chinese exports increased.

Much of the prosperity in Korea and the other countries was not based on rising productivity, but on speculation in real estate and stocks. As their economies weakened, businesses could not pay their debts, and banks were saddled with bad loans. Investors, including international currency speculators, lost confidence in their countries and began selling their currencies, driving their values and the stock markets downward.

The Russian Financial Crisis of 1998.   The Russian financial crisis of August 1998 has had a deleterious impact on the economy and may cause its eventual collapse. Over the last five months of 1998, consumer prices rose by more than 75 percent and the ruble depreciated by more than 70 percent against the U.S. dollar.[25] In 1998 real GDP fell by around 5 percent and foreign direct investment decreased from $6.2 billion in 1997 to $1.2 billion in 1998. The financial crisis was created by several problems. The first was the instability of the Russian government. Foreign investors viewed Boris Yeltsin as a weak leader and were concerned about a swing back to communism in the national elections. There were problems in the enterprise and banking sectors of the economy, as loans were mismanaged and corruption was endemic. The Asian financial crisis decreased investor confidence in Russia. Interest rates rose, which increased the cost of financing the national debt.

The Brazilian Financial Crisis of 1998.   Brazil was adversely affected by the Russian financial crisis of 1998 when international investors reassessed the risk of their exposure to emerging markets. To stem this capital outflow, the Brazilian government increased interest rates by around 43 percent during the latter part of 1998.[26] These increases had an adverse effect on consumer and business loans. The deficit in Brazil's balance of payments with other countries increased as did the national debt. The Brazilian currency unit, the real, declined in value in international trade, further exacerbating the balance of payments problem. The end result was that in early 1999 the International Monetary Fund implemented an international rescue operation that led to a commitment of $41.5 billion to Brazil to resolve its balance of payments problems.

Remedies for Fiscal Crises.   In a world where money flows relatively freely across national borders, financial crises may come to rival death and taxes in their inevitability. While the stock, bond, and currency markets around the world have recovered from the panic sales that devastated Russia, Brazil, and East Asia, the after effects are still being felt in these countries and elsewhere. Production is down, growth rates are projected to be negative in Brazil for 1999, and thousands of persons have witnessed a rapid decline in their living standards.[27] It could be only a matter of time before some new financial crisis erupts and threatens to destabilize the world economy. A major problem is that the financial sectors of most economies are so small that they can easily be destabilized by a major inflow or outflow of capital. In Thailand, an inflow of capital, most of it speculative, increased borrowing to speculate in Thai real estate, increased the value of the currency unit, the baht, increased the value of stock and bonds, and raised interest rates. The end result was a collapse of the Thai economy.[28]

Regional Currency Zones.   An important reason for the creation of the European Monetary Union (EMU) was that by creating a common currency, the euro, exchange rate fluctuations between countries would be eliminated, thus reducing the opportunity for speculation and the cost of exchange rate conversion. Although the euro is currently used by only eleven countries and has not proved itself one way or the other, it is possible that in the future every European country from Spain to Romania will use it as a medium of exchange. It can be argued that a currency zone should be created in the Western hemisphere.[29] It would include every country from Canada to Argentina. It would be called the American Monetary Union (AMU) and the dollar would become the common currency unit. It would eliminate the financial crises that occurred in Brazil and Mexico.

There are a number of problems that would be involved in the creation of an AMU. First, the United States would dominate it much more than Germany dominates the EMU. The GNP of the United States is three times larger than all of the other countries in North America and South America. Political and economic relations between the United States and Latin America were not all that great during the twentieth century. Yankee imperialism has been a rallying point for Latin American politicians for decades. There is no particular continuity in Latin America as there is in Europe. The countries that are in the EMU have a high standard of living and are close to each other geographically. Argentina and Canada are at opposite ends of the Western hemisphere. GNP per capita would range from a high of $29,080 for the United States to a low of $380 for Haiti and $410 for Nicaragua.

A PREVIEW OF THE TWENTY-FIRST CENTURY

One World, Ready or Not is the title of a book written by William Greider.[30] It is a portent of what is supposed to happen in the twenty-first century, which will be dominated by the United States to the extent that England dominated the nineteenth century. The U.S. dominance is based on technology in which it has a large lead over the rest of the world and on the existence of a set of institutions designed to maintain the lead—a university system that churns out scientists, a market-based financial system that provides venture capital to improve technologies, and a fluid labor market. These work well because the operation of each is complemented by the operation of the others, and they can survive only in a world of high capital mobility and cutthroat competition. The world will evolve into a winner-take-all society with the winner being the United States.

Thomas L. Friedman, in his book *The Lexus and the Olive Tree*, contends that globalization is inevitable and irreversible; the forward march of technology makes it so.[31] Lower communication costs, expanding free markets, and digital technology have shrunk the world. Countries will respond to globalization in several ways, and how they respond will determine their success or failure. To succeed, they will have to attract international investment. To do this, they need the prerequisites for a free market, with regulation of financial markets abuses, shareholder rights, and an end of "crony" capitalism. Capital is no longer contained within borders; billions of dollars can be moved with a click of a key. In an age of instantaneous communications, companies can and do outsource production to poor countries where labor costs are lower, thus creating what is called a "global web."[32]

But before te deums are sung proclaiming the reign of the United States as the leader of the twenty-first century, a caveat is in order. It was only a few years ago that many experts were proclaiming the twenty-first century as the Japanese century. In 1992 Lester Thurow, one of the most respected economists in America, confidently predicted that Europe would dominate the twenty-first century because of its superior type of capitalism.[33] It can be argued that economic growth in the United States during the 1990s has not been particularly spectacular; it is just that other countries have done worse. The current sense that the United States is on top of the world is based on an exaggeration of the implications of a few good years here and a few bad years elsewhere. It will certainly begin the twenty-first century with a headstart over Europe and Japan, both of which have major problems.

In 1992 *Time* published a special issue called *Beyond the Year 2000*.[34] In one of the articles, "How The World Will Look in Fifty Years," predictions were made that Japan would weaken, Europe would triumph, and the United States would swallow some bitter cures. Its batting average at the end of the century was one out of three. Japan has weakened. It posed the question that was relevant at the time the article was written,"Is the United States in an irreversible decline as the world's premier economic power?" At that time it appeared to be so, but it is no longer true. However, there is no guarantee that this will continue to be true in the twenty-first century.

SUMMARY

The 1990s were one of the most important decades of the twentieth century. Communism, one of the major political ideologies of the century, collapsed, and the Soviet Union, one of the two world powers during the Cold War, fragmented into a number of different countries. The vaunted Japanese economy developed serious problems that have yet to be resolved. The European Union is now a reality and the euro has become, along with the dollar and the yen, one of the world's important currencies. The United States is projected to dominate the twenty-first century. The new frontier is the global economy, and America dominates the world of the Internet. On the reverse side of the coin, the divide between rich countries and poor countries is growing wider, and more than a billion persons live in poverty. There were four financial crises during the decade. Ethnic and religious rivalries continue to exist and have the potential to create tensions.

QUESTIONS FOR DISCUSSION

1.   The world has experienced some dramatic changes during the 1990s. Discuss some of the changes that have occurred and the impact they have had on the world.
2.   The United States is expected to continue its dominance as the world's leading economic power through the twenty-first century. Discuss the reasons why.
3.   In what ways has the technological revolution of the latter part of the twentieth century changed the world?
4.   What are some of the causes of political instability in the world?
5.   What are some of the problems confronting the poor countries of the world? How can these problems be resolved?

RECOMMENDED READINGS

Bazan, Barry, and Gerald Segal. *Anticipating the Future: Twenty Millenia of Human Progress*. London: Simon and Schuster, 1998.

Bosworth, Barry, and Gary Burtless, eds. *Aging Societies*. Washington, D.C.: The Brookings Institution Press, 1998.

Freidman, Thomas L. *The Lexus and the Olive Tree*. New York: Farrar, Straus, and Giroux, 1999.

Greider, William. *One World, Ready or Not*. New York: Simon and Schuster, 1997.

Haase, Richard, and Robert Litan, "Globalization and Its Disconnects." *Foreign Affairs* Vol. 77, No. 3 (May/June 1998): 2–6.

Landes, David L. *The Wealth and Poverty of Nations*. New York: Norton, 1998.

Longman, Philip J. "How Global Aging Will Challenge the World's Economic Well-Being." *U.S. News and World Report* March 1, 1999: 30–35.

United Nations Development Program. *Human Development Report, 1998*. New York: Oxford University Press, 1998.

World Bank, *Global Economic Prospects and the Developing Countries*. New York: The World Bank, 1999.

NOTES

1.   Polio was a dreaded disease. If it didn't kill you, it could cripple you for life. President Franklin D. Roosevelt contracted polio when he was an adult and was confined to a wheelchair during his terms in office. The Salk vaccine was the cure for polio.

2.   In 1998 General Motors was the largest multinational in the world with total sales of $161 billion. Only 25 out of 215 countries had a larger GNP.

3.   The conflict between India and Pakistan over the Kashmir is serious because both countries detest each other and have nuclear weapons.

4.   Lester R. Brown and Hal Kane, *Full House* (New York: Norton, 1994).

5.   Francis Fukuyama, *The End of History and the Last Man* (New York: Basic Books, 1991).

6.   Romans living during the time of Augustus Caesar when Rome was at its zenith were probably as sure that the Roman Empire would live forever.

7.   Germany's death rate exceeds its birth rate. The number of workers in the German labor force is decreasing, while the number of Germans of retirement age is increasing. The number of Germans of retirement age exceeds the number of Germans 14 and younger.

8.   The World Bank, *1999 World Development Indicators* (Washington, D.C.: The World Bank, 1999), 46.

9.   United Nations Development Program, *Human Development Report, 1998* (New York: Oxford University Press, 1998), 147.

10.   The Ganges also serves as the final resting place for thousands of Hindus whose cremated ashes or half-burned corpses are put into the river for spiritual rebirth. The crocodiles that used to serve as garbage collectors of refuse thrown in the river have largely disappeared, victims of civilization.

11.   Although measures have been taken to reduce air and water pollution, Mexico City remains one of the most polluted cities in the world. One-third of its population live in slums, without drinking water and sanitation facilities. Young children and old people are most likely to be adversely affected by air pollution from the exhaust fumes of millions of cars.

12.   June 1999 provided some of the hottest weather recorded in the Northeastern United States.

13.   The Great Plains states are North Dakota, South Dakota, Nebraska, Kansas, and Oklahoma.

14.   It is estimated that as many as 50 million Americans may be drinking water polluted by pesticides.

15.   *Human Development Report, 1998* 66.

16.   Ibid., 30.

17.   The World Bank, *1990 World Bank Atlas*, 10; *1999 World Bank Atlas*, 38.

18.   Examples are the Russian Federation and the Ukraine. Using national poverty standards for the Russian Federation, some 50 million Russians are below the poverty line, and for the Ukraine, some 25 million Ukrainians live below the poverty line.

19.   Fukuyama, *End of History*. According to Fukuyama, the end of history will be a sad time. In his view the struggle for recognition, the willingness to risk one's life for a purely abstract goal, the ideological struggle that called for daring, courage, and imagination are what make the world interesting.

20.   Since leaders are voted in by the people in a democracy, it is assumed that they will always opt for peace.

21.   In Aldous Huxley's novel *Brave New World*, the population of countries is divided into two classes—the leaders and the masses. The masses are kept in check by sex and soma. Soma is a drug that keeps the masses placid and obedient. In a play on

Rousseau's concept of the "noble savage," an Indian is found on a reservation in the United States who has not been corrupted and is brought to the new environment. He is so appalled, he commits suicide.

22.   For the most part, the capitalists were ensconced in the most elite areas of Shanghai, Peking, and other Chinese cities, protected by guards, provided with private golf courses unencumbered by Chinese except as caddies, and with private clubs. The missionaries were not so fortunate and some were killed. But they did teach English, and many students were able to come and study in the United States.

23.   Apparently, the Kenyans have learned American ways. Within hours after the American embassy was destroyed, American lawyers arrived in Nairobi to encourage families of those killed to sue the U.S. government on the grounds of negligence. Since all embassies and the grounds they are on belong to their governments, Kenyans can sue in the United States. If successful, the plaintiffs could win more money than the GNP of Kenya. As one Kenyan said, "why settle for $500 in Kenya when we could become millionaires in America."

24.   Rajiv Gandhi, former prime minister, was assassinated by a Tamilese separatist who blew up him and herself with a bomb. An American intelligence official was quoted as saying that with $1 billion and 20 computer hackers he could shut down America. If he could, so could terrorists.

25.   International Monetary Fund, *World Economic Outlook* (Washington, D.C.: IMF, May 1999), 31.

26.   Ibid., 29.

27.   In South Korea, Thailand, Malaysia, and Indonesia, it was the middle and upper middle classes that were hurt the most. These are the ones who speculated in real estate and the stock market, using borrowed money. When the stock market collapsed and real estate values fell, they lost everything. One result was the political upheaval in Indonesia, where the dictator Suharto was deposed. He and his family had accumulated $35 billion illegally.

28.   There is a parallel between the Thai economy and the collapse of the U.S. economy in 1929. In both countries, prosperity was based on stock market and real estate speculation.

29.   Zanny Minton Beddoes, "The Rise of Currency Blocs," *Foreign Affairs* Vol. 78, No. 4 (July/August 1999): 8–13.

30.   William Greider, *One World, Ready or Not* (New York: Simon and Schuster, 1997).

31.   Thomas L. Friedman, *The Lexus and the Olive Tree* (New York: Farrar, Straus, and Giroux, 1999). The Lexus automobile represents the modern world. The olive tree represents tradition.

32.   Robert B. Reich, *The Work of Nations* (New York: Alfred A. Knopf, 1991), 110–18. The threads of the global web are computers, fax machines, satellites, high-resolution monitors, and modems—all of them linking designers, engineers, and other skilled workers worldwide.

33.   Lester Thurow, *Head to Head: The Coming Economic Battle among Japan, Europe, and America* (New York: Morrow, 1992).

34.   *Time, Beyond the Year 2000*, Fall 1992.

Index